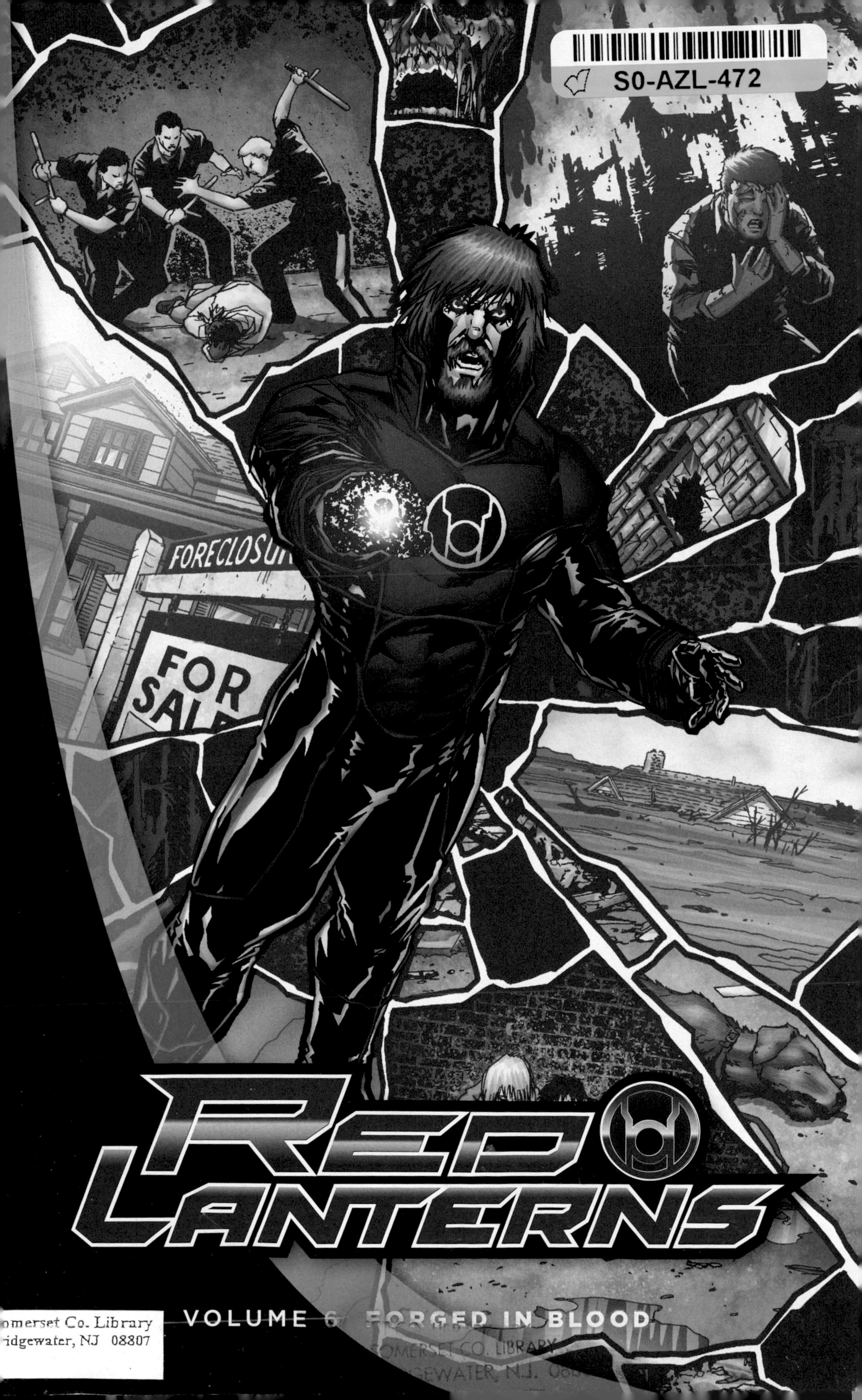
FORECLOSU
FOR
SAL

RED LANTERNS

VOLUME 6: FORGED IN BLOOD

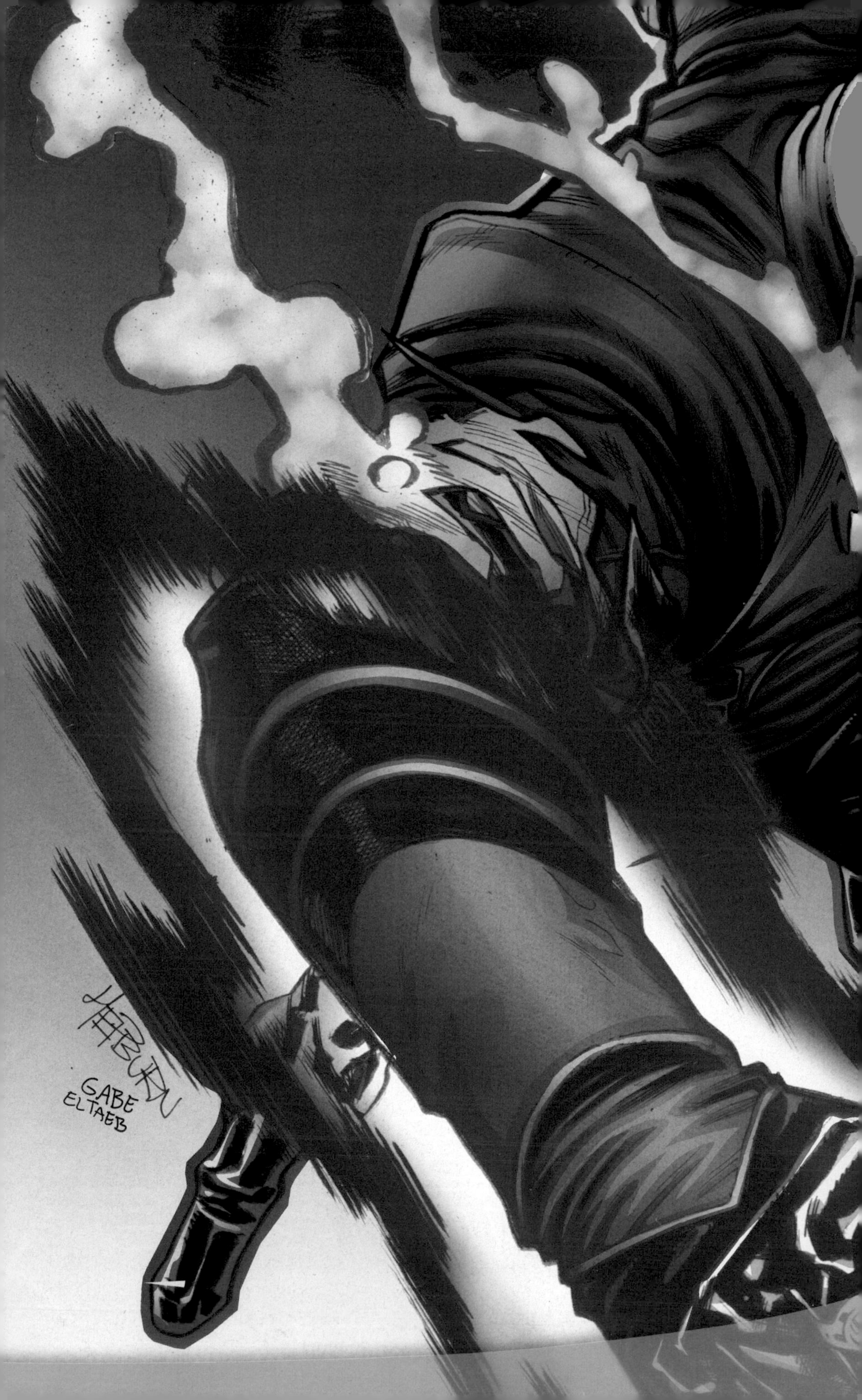
GABE
ELTAEB

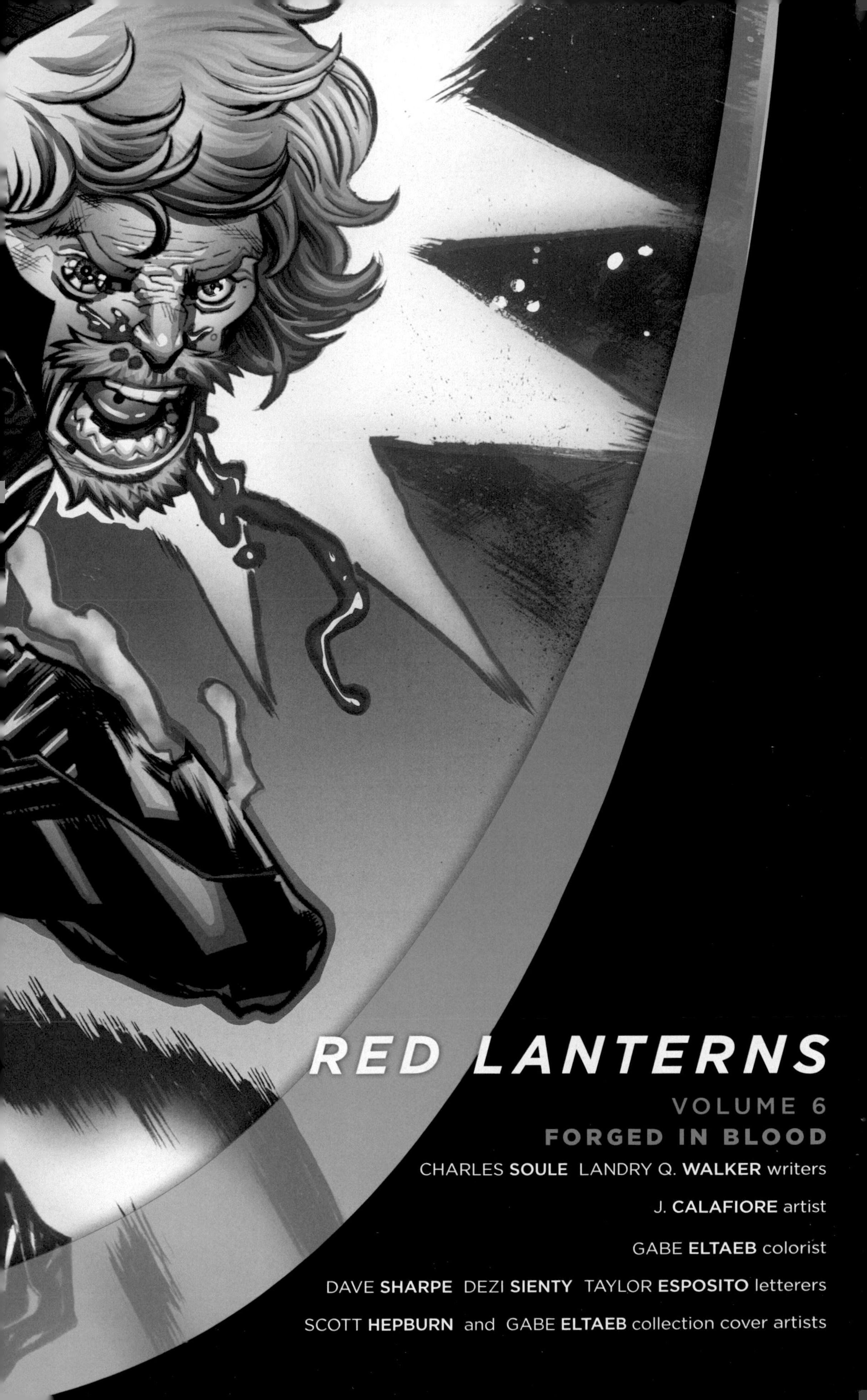

RED LANTERNS

VOLUME 6
FORGED IN BLOOD

CHARLES **SOULE** LANDRY Q. **WALKER** writers

J. **CALAFIORE** artist

GABE **ELTAEB** colorist

DAVE **SHARPE** DEZI **SIENTY** TAYLOR **ESPOSITO** letterers

SCOTT **HEPBURN** and GABE **ELTAEB** collection cover artists

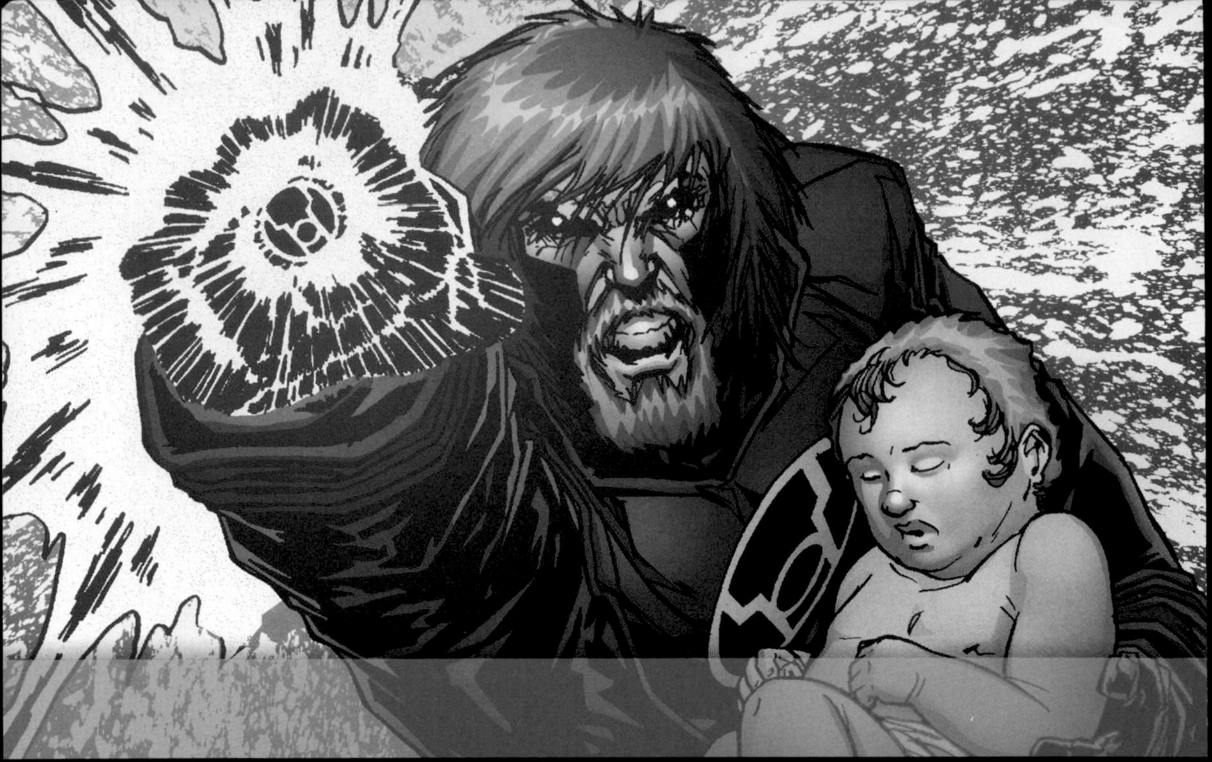

DARREN SHAN Editor - Original Series LIZ ERICKSON Editor ROBBIE BIEDERMAN Publication Design

BOB HARRAS Senior VP - Editor-in-Chief, DC Comics

DIANE NELSON President DAN DIDIO and JIM LEE Co-Publishers GEOFF JOHNS Chief Creative Officer
AMIT DESAI Senior VP - Marketing and Franchise Management
AMY GENKINS Senior VP - Business and Legal Affairs NAIRI GARDINER Senior VP - Finance
JEFF BOISON VP - Publishing Planning MARK CHIARELLO VP - Art Direction and Design
JOHN CUNNINGHAM VP - Marketing TERRI CUNNINGHAM VP - Editorial Administration
LARRY GANEM VP - Talent Relations and Services ALISON GILL Senior VP - Manufacturing and Operations
HANK KANALZ Senior VP - Vertigo and Integrated Publishing JAY KOGAN VP - Business and Legal Affairs, Publishing
JACK MAHAN VP - Business Affairs, Talent NICK NAPOLITANO VP - Manufacturing Administration SUE POHJA VP - Book Sales
FRED RUIZ VP - Manufacturing Operations COURTNEY SIMMONS Senior VP - Publicity BOB WAYNE Senior VP - Sales

RED LANTERNS VOLUME 6: FORGED IN BLOOD

DC Comics, 4000 Warner Blvd., Burbank, CA 91522
A Warner Bros. Entertainment Company.
Printed by RR Donnelley, Owensville, MO USA. 6/26/15. First Printing.

ISBN: 978-1-4012-5484-1

Library of Congress Cataloging-in-Publication Data

Soule, Charles.
Red Lanterns. Volume 6 / Charles Soule ; illustrated by J. Calafiore.
pages cm. — (The New 52!)
Originally published in single magazine form in RED LANTERNS 35-40,
RED LANTERNS FUTURES END 1
ISBN 978-1-4012-5484-1 (paperback)
1. Graphic novels. I. Calafiore, Jim, illustrator. II. Title.
PN6728.R439S7 2015
741.5'973—dc23
2015008048

SUSTAINABLE FORESTRY INITIATIVE
Certified Chain of Custody
20% Certified Forest Content, 80% Certified Sourcing
www.sfiprogram.org
SFI-01042

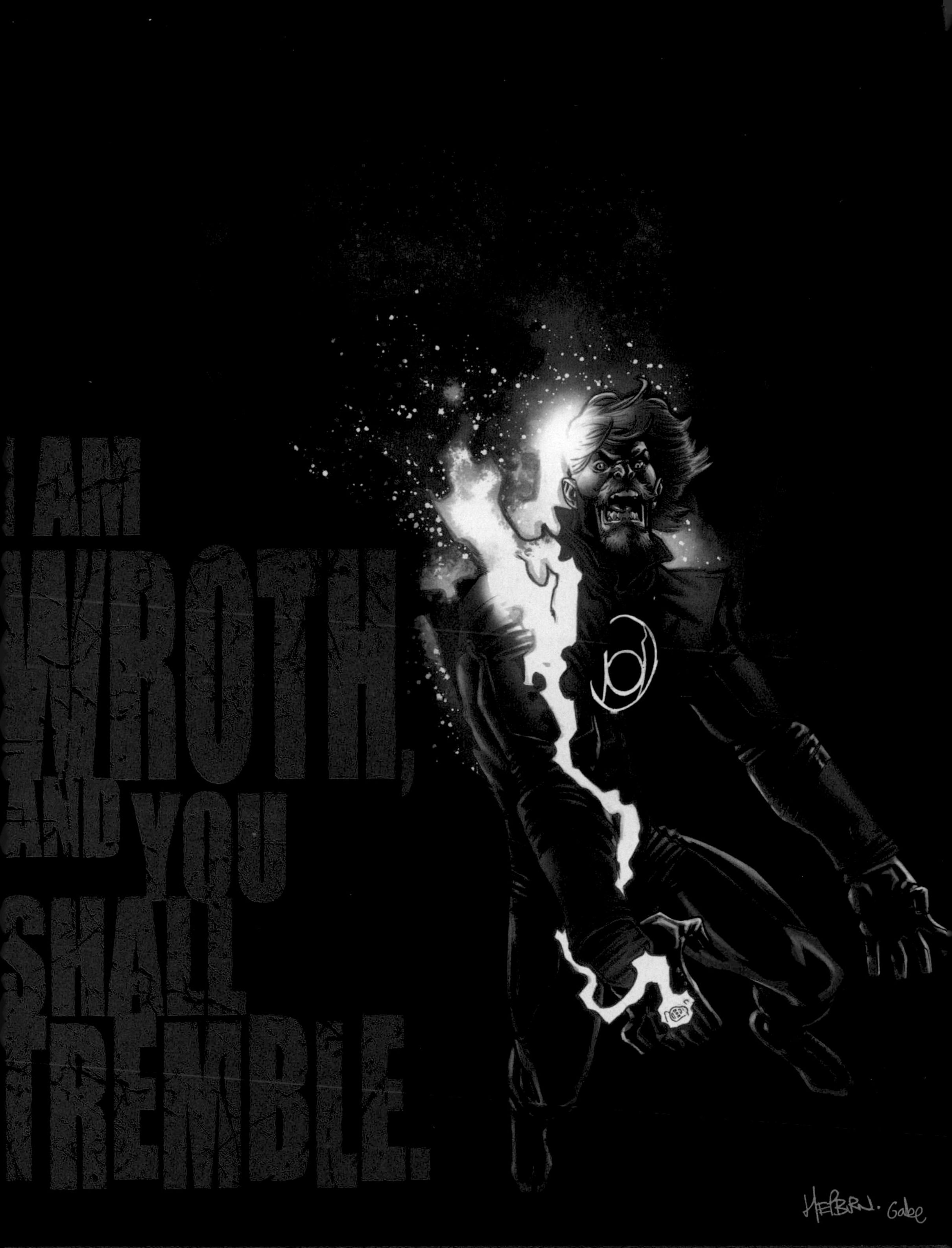
I AM
WROTH,
AND YOU
SHALL
TREMBLE.

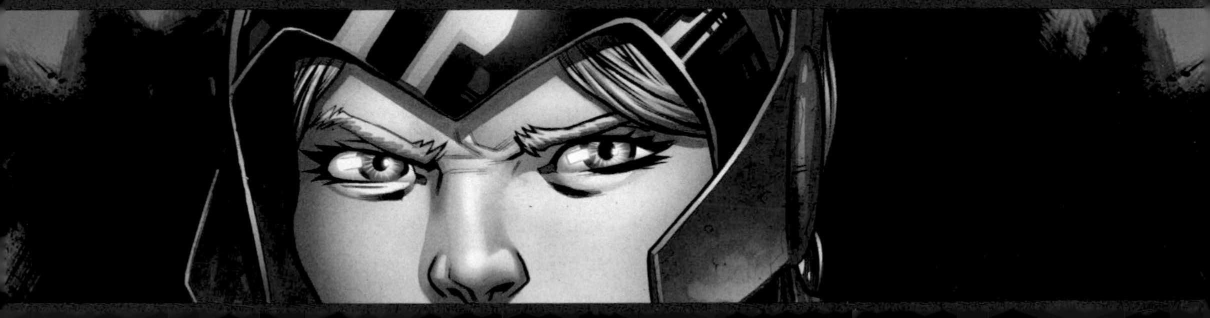

GODHEAD ACT I, PART V: GOD IS RED

CHARLES SOULE writer **J. CALAFIORE** artist **GABE ELTAEB** colorist **DEZI SIENTY TAYLOR ESPOSITO** letterers
cover art by **SCOTT HEPBURN** and **GABE ELTAEB**

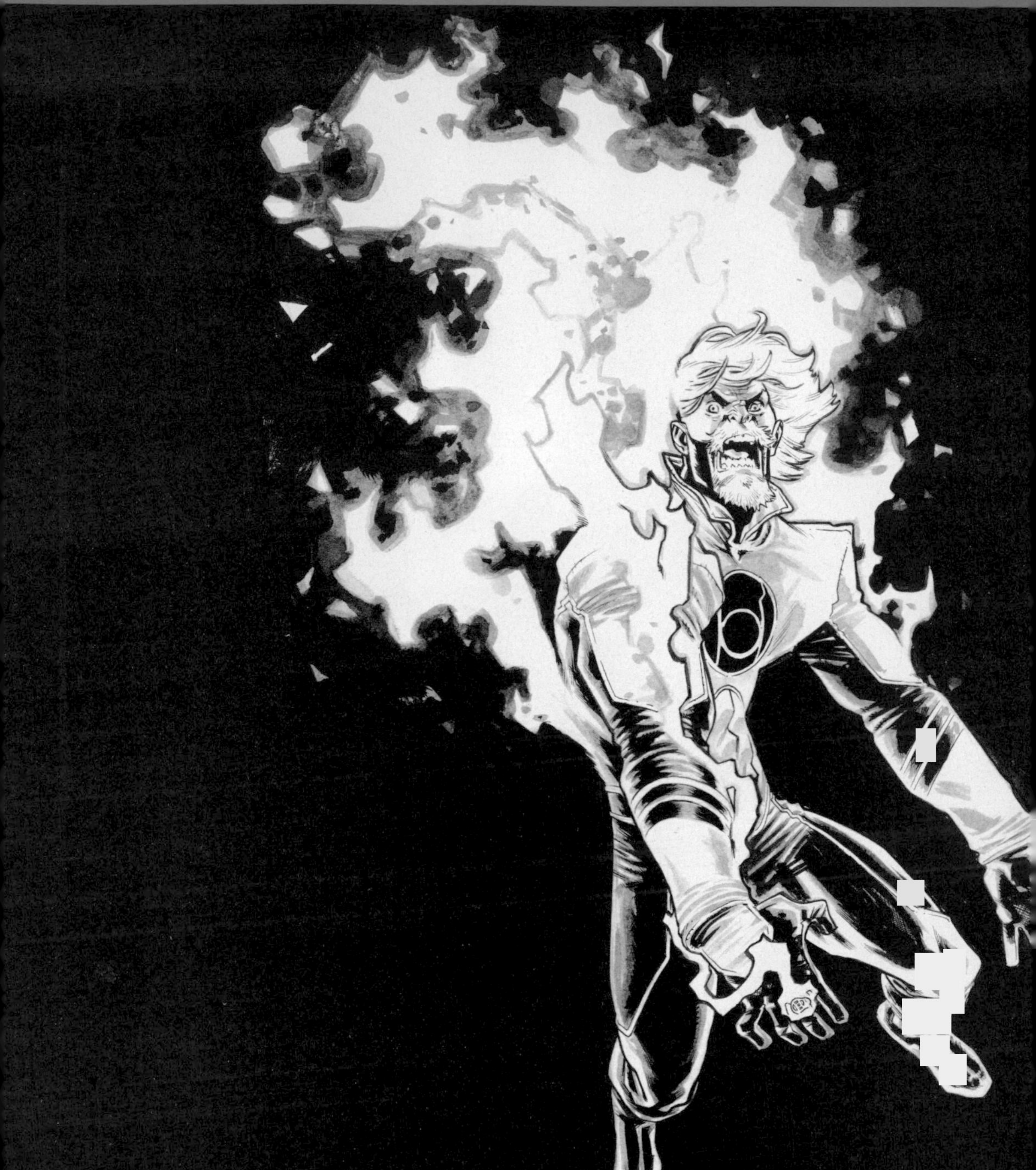

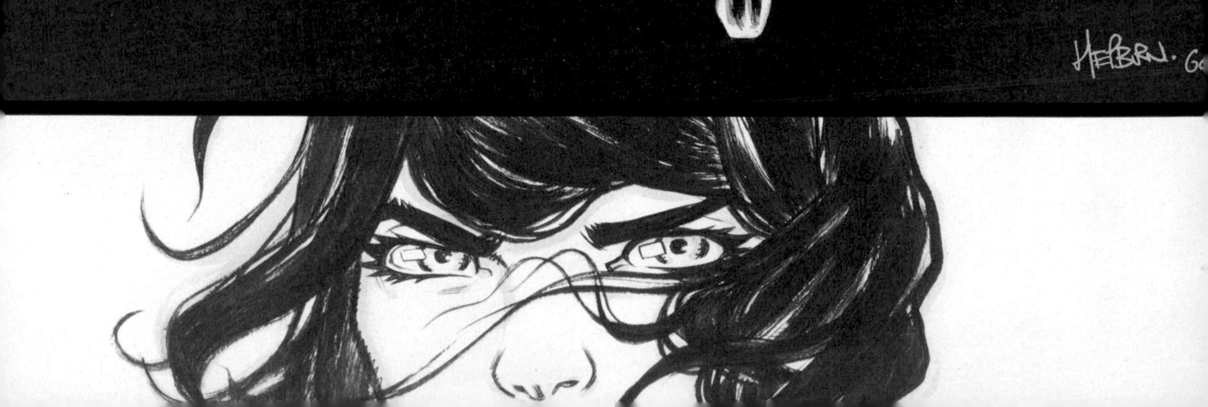

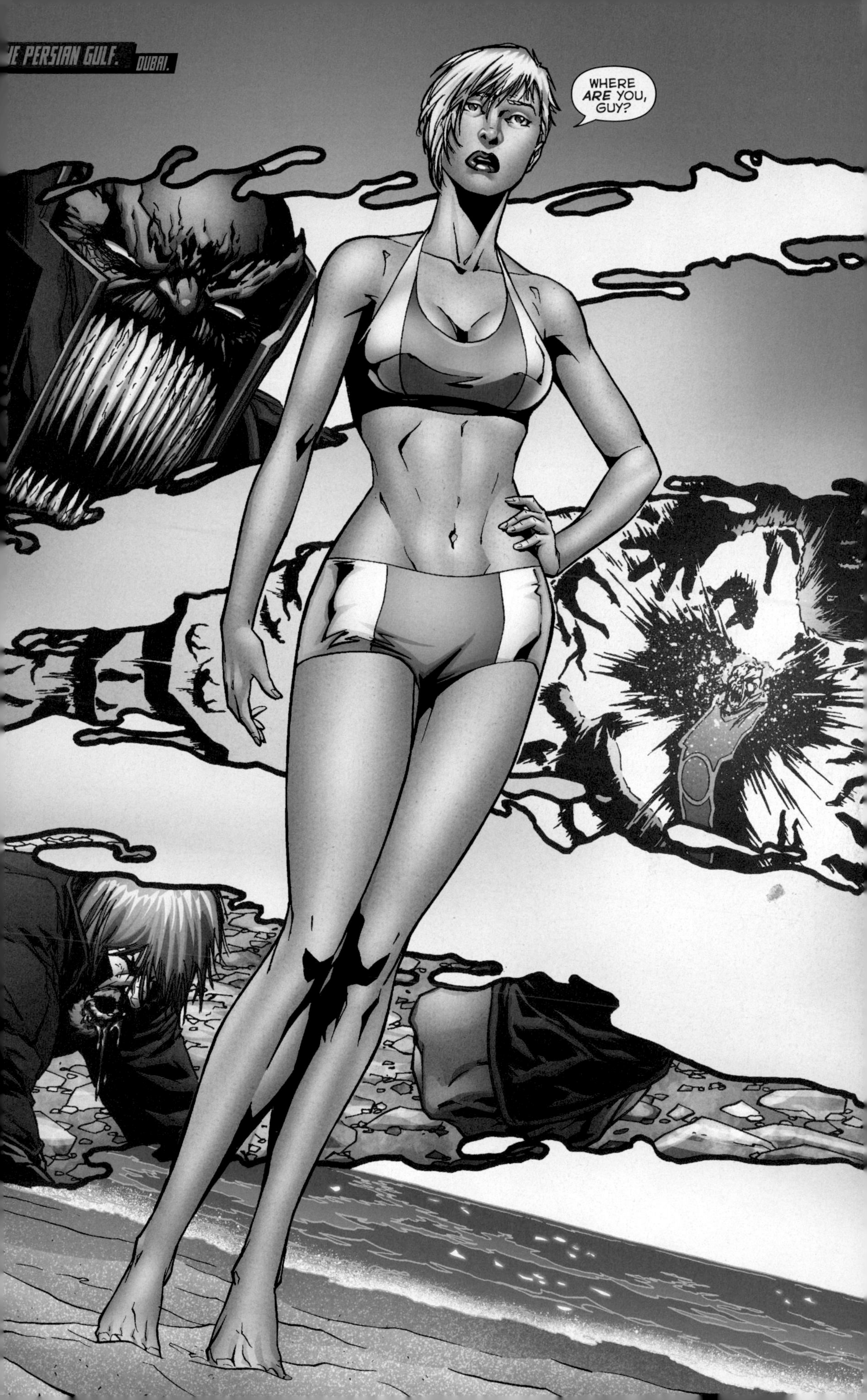
HE PERSIAN GULF.
DUBAI.
WHERE ARE YOU, GUY?

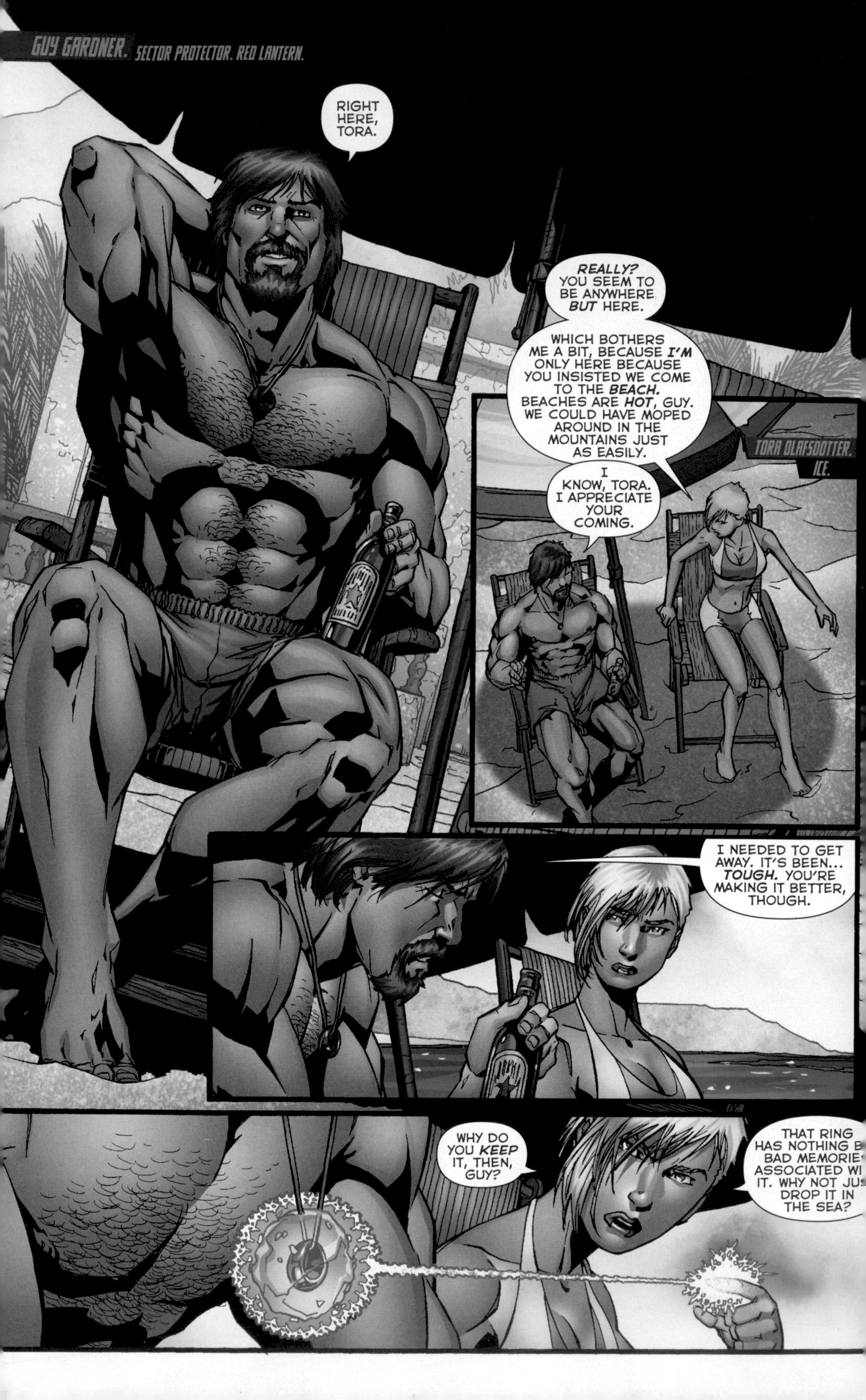
GUY GARDNER. SECTOR PROTECTOR. RED LANTERN.
RIGHT HERE, TORA.
REALLY? YOU SEEM TO BE ANYWHERE BUT HERE.
WHICH BOTHERS ME A BIT, BECAUSE I'M ONLY HERE BECAUSE YOU INSISTED WE COME TO THE BEACH. BEACHES ARE HOT, GUY. WE COULD HAVE MOPED AROUND IN THE MOUNTAINS JUST AS EASILY.
TORA OLAFSDOTTER. ICE.
I KNOW, TORA. I APPRECIATE YOUR COMING.
I NEEDED TO GET AWAY. IT'S BEEN... TOUGH. YOU'RE MAKING IT BETTER, THOUGH.
WHY DO YOU KEEP IT, THEN, GUY?
THAT RING HAS NOTHING B BAD MEMORIE ASSOCIATED WI IT. WHY NOT JU DROP IT IN THE SEA?

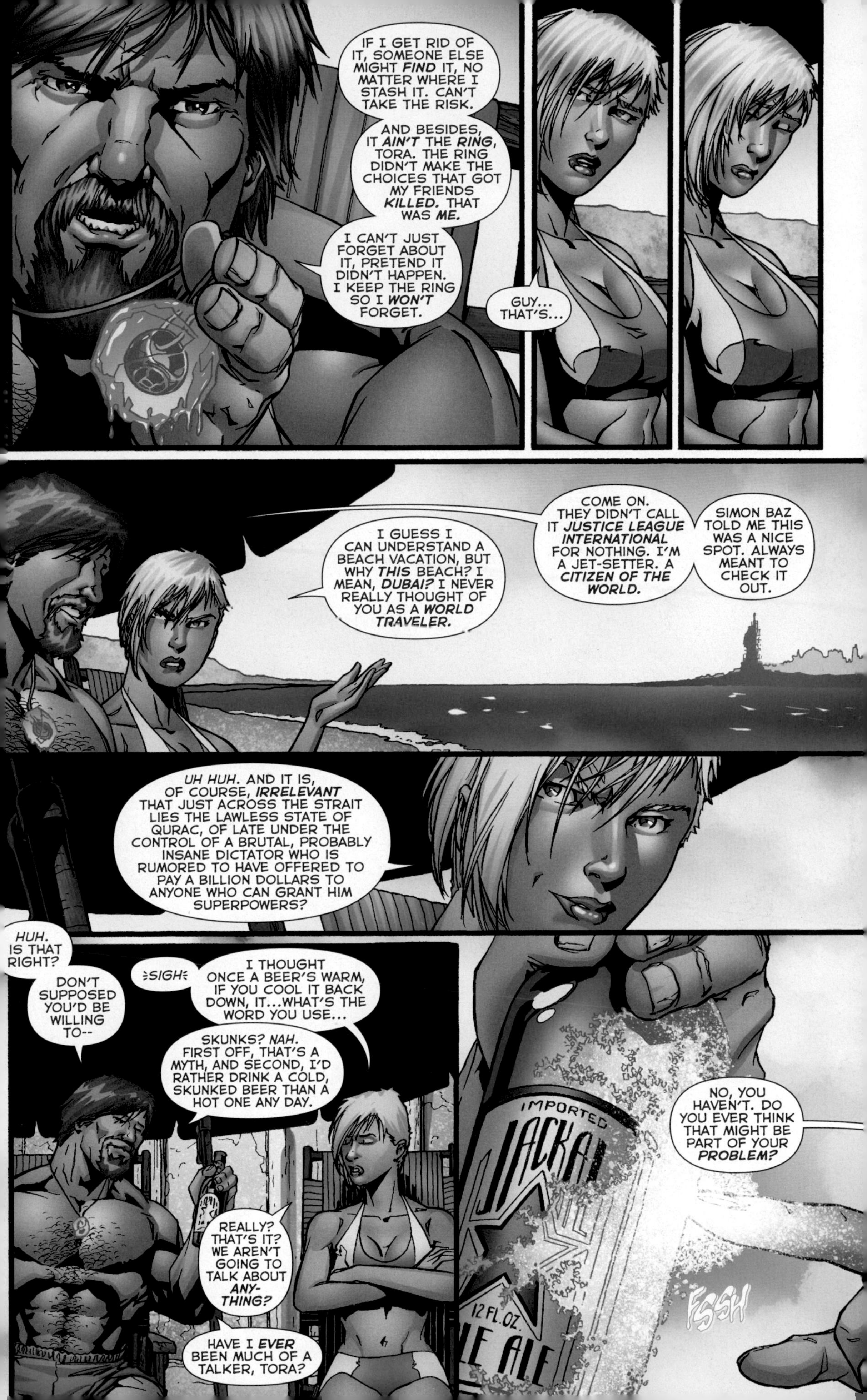
IF I GET RID OF IT, SOMEONE ELSE MIGHT *FIND* IT, NO MATTER WHERE I STASH IT. CAN'T TAKE THE RISK.
AND BESIDES, IT *AIN'T* THE *RING*, TORA. THE RING DIDN'T MAKE THE CHOICES THAT GOT MY FRIENDS *KILLED.* THAT WAS *ME.*
I CAN'T JUST FORGET ABOUT IT, PRETEND IT DIDN'T HAPPEN. I KEEP THE RING SO I *WON'T* FORGET.
GUY... THAT'S...
I GUESS I CAN UNDERSTAND A BEACH VACATION, BUT WHY *THIS* BEACH? I MEAN, *DUBAI?* I NEVER REALLY THOUGHT OF YOU AS A *WORLD TRAVELER.*
COME ON. THEY DIDN'T CALL IT *JUSTICE LEAGUE INTERNATIONAL* FOR NOTHING. I'M A JET-SETTER. A *CITIZEN OF THE WORLD.*
SIMON BAZ TOLD ME THIS WAS A NICE SPOT. ALWAYS MEANT TO CHECK IT OUT.
UH HUH. AND IT IS, OF COURSE, *IRRELEVANT* THAT JUST ACROSS THE STRAIT LIES THE LAWLESS STATE OF QURAC, OF LATE UNDER THE CONTROL OF A BRUTAL, PROBABLY INSANE DICTATOR WHO IS RUMORED TO HAVE OFFERED TO PAY A BILLION DOLLARS TO ANYONE WHO CAN GRANT HIM SUPERPOWERS?
HUH. IS THAT RIGHT?
DON'T SUPPOSED YOU'D BE WILLING TO--
SIGH
I THOUGHT ONCE A BEER'S WARM, IF YOU COOL IT BACK DOWN, IT...WHAT'S THE WORD YOU USE...
SKUNKS? *NAH.* FIRST OFF, THAT'S A MYTH, AND SECOND, I'D RATHER DRINK A COLD, SKUNKED BEER THAN A HOT ONE ANY DAY.
REALLY? THAT'S IT? WE AREN'T GOING TO TALK ABOUT *ANY-THING?*
HAVE I *EVER* BEEN MUCH OF A TALKER, TORA?
IMPORTED
12 FL. OZ.
FSSH
NO, YOU HAVEN'T. DO YOU EVER THINK THAT MIGHT BE PART OF YOUR *PROBLEM?*

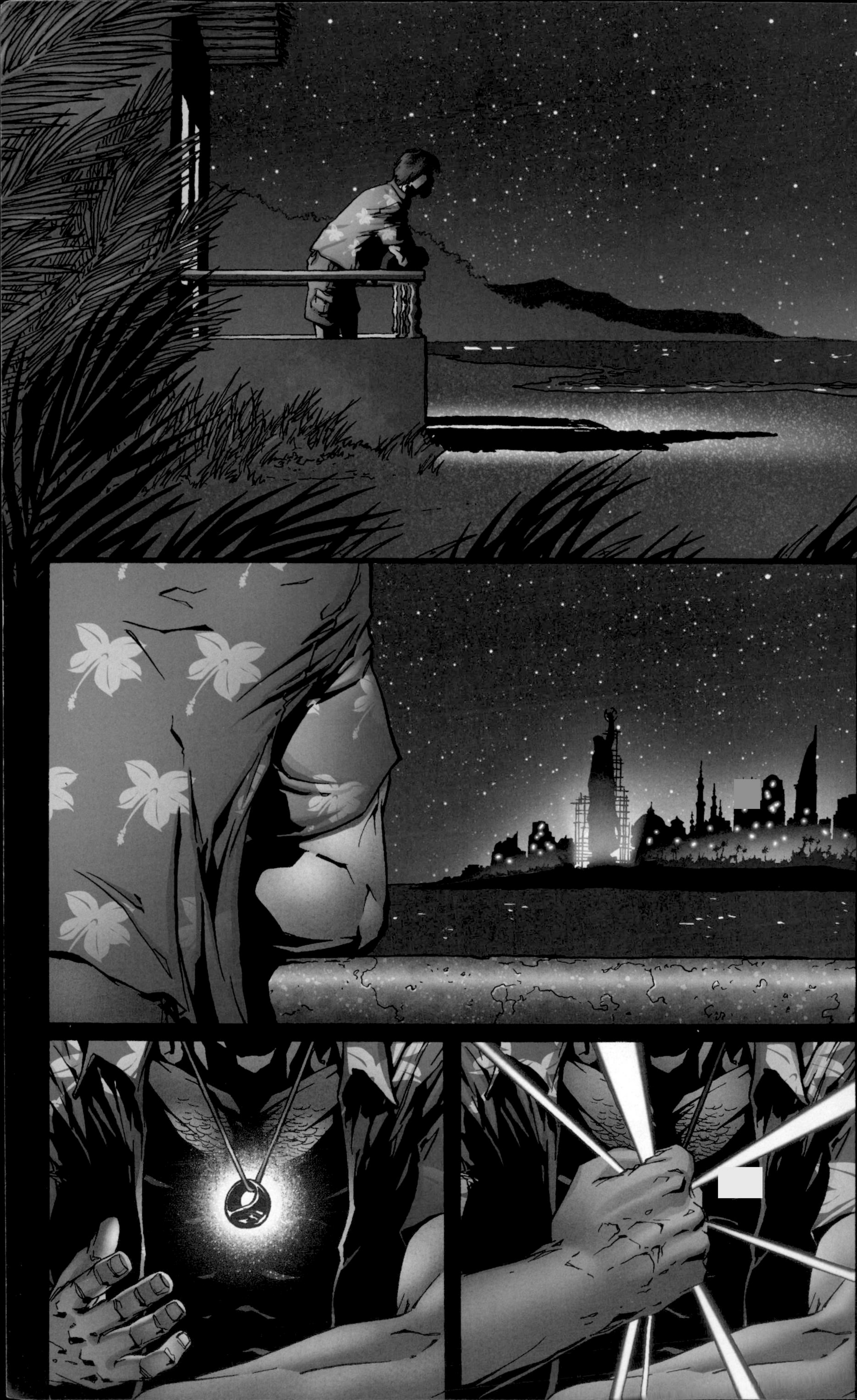

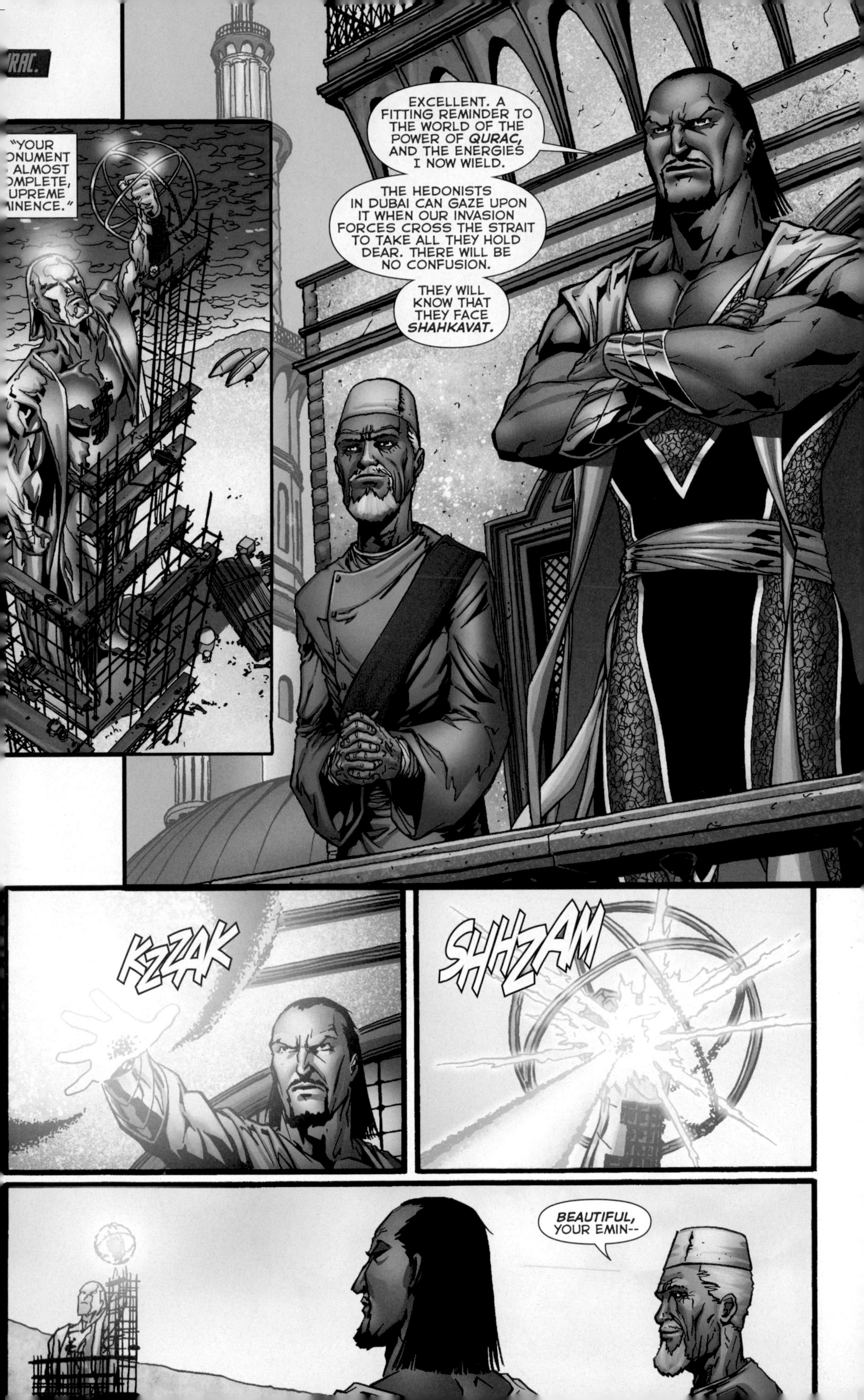

RAC.
"YOUR
ONUMENT
ALMOST
OMPLETE,
UPREME
MINENCE."
EXCELLENT. A FITTING REMINDER TO THE WORLD OF THE POWER OF QURAC, AND THE ENERGIES I NOW WIELD.
THE HEDONISTS IN DUBAI CAN GAZE UPON IT WHEN OUR INVASION FORCES CROSS THE STRAIT TO TAKE ALL THEY HOLD DEAR. THERE WILL BE NO CONFUSION.
THEY WILL KNOW THAT THEY FACE SHAHKAVAT.
KZZAK
SHHZAM
BEAUTIFUL, YOUR EMIN--

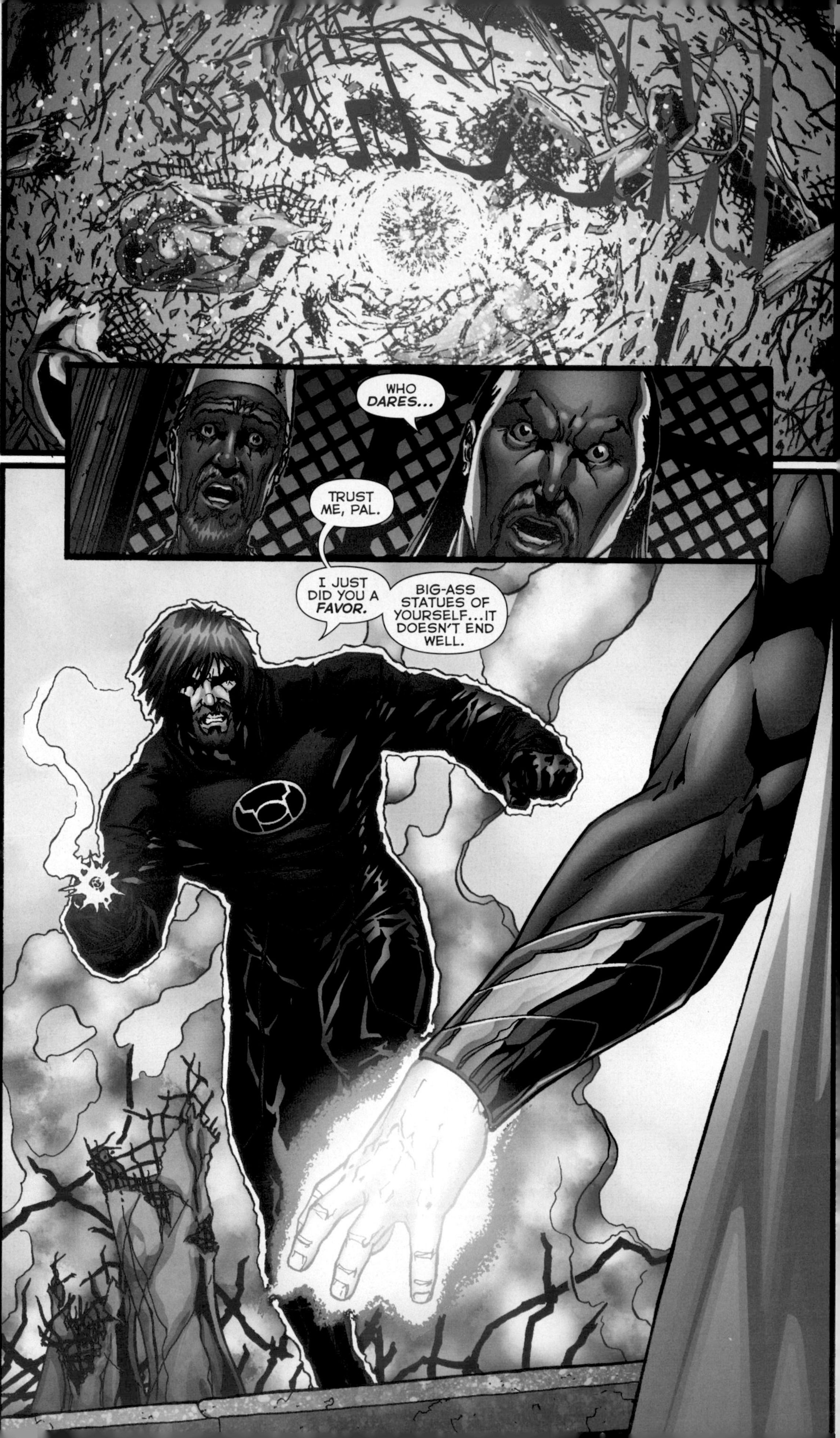
WHO DARES...
TRUST ME, PAL.
I JUST DID YOU A FAVOR.
BIG-ASS STATUES OF YOURSELF...IT DOESN'T END WELL.

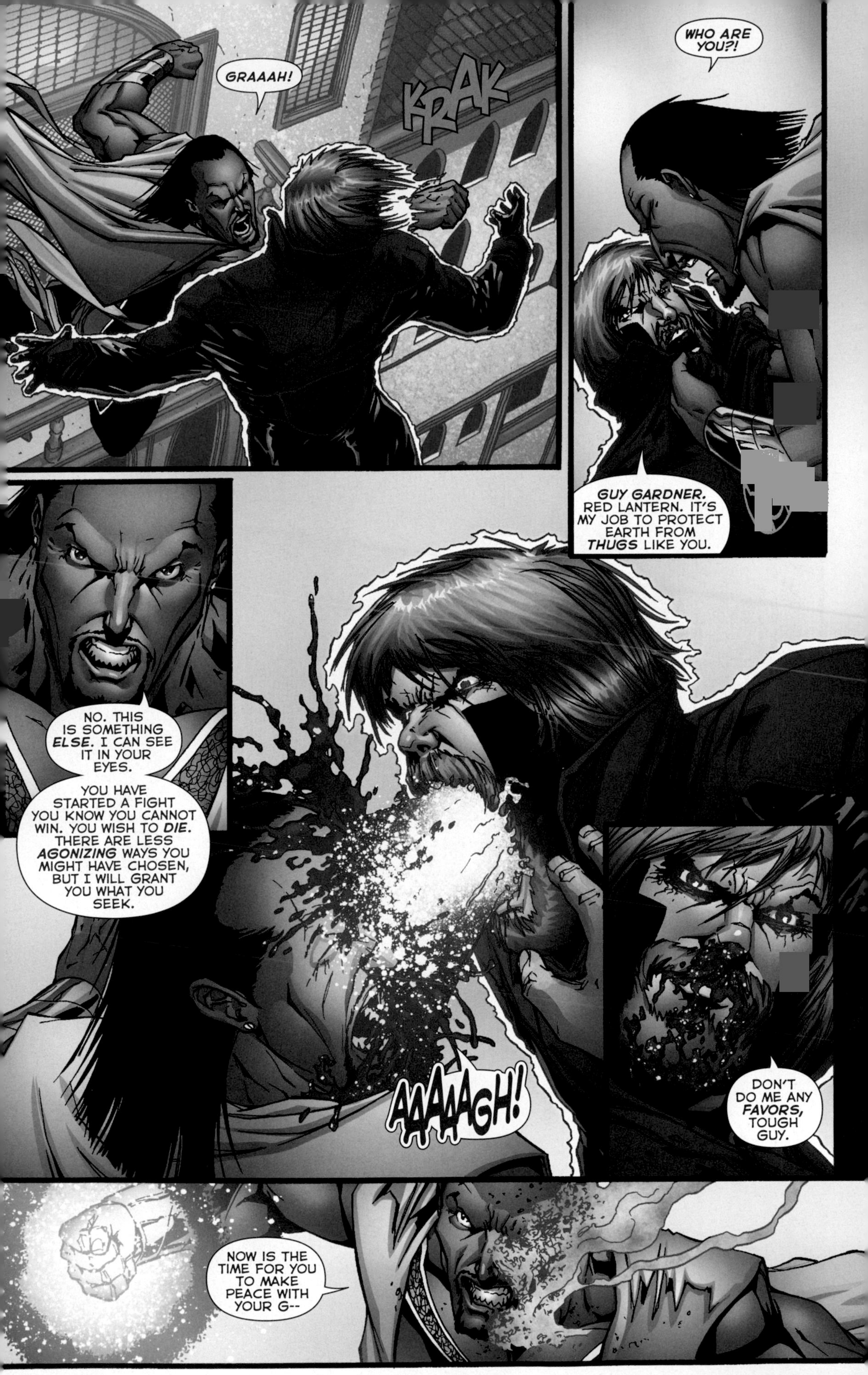
GRAAAH!
KRAK
WHO ARE YOU?!
GUY GARDNER. RED LANTERN. IT'S MY JOB TO PROTECT EARTH FROM THUGS LIKE YOU.
NO. THIS IS SOMETHING ELSE. I CAN SEE IT IN YOUR EYES.
YOU HAVE STARTED A FIGHT YOU KNOW YOU CANNOT WIN. YOU WISH TO DIE. THERE ARE LESS AGONIZING WAYS YOU MIGHT HAVE CHOSEN, BUT I WILL GRANT YOU WHAT YOU SEEK.
AAAAGH!
DON'T DO ME ANY FAVORS, TOUGH GUY.
NOW IS THE TIME FOR YOU TO MAKE PEACE WITH YOUR G--

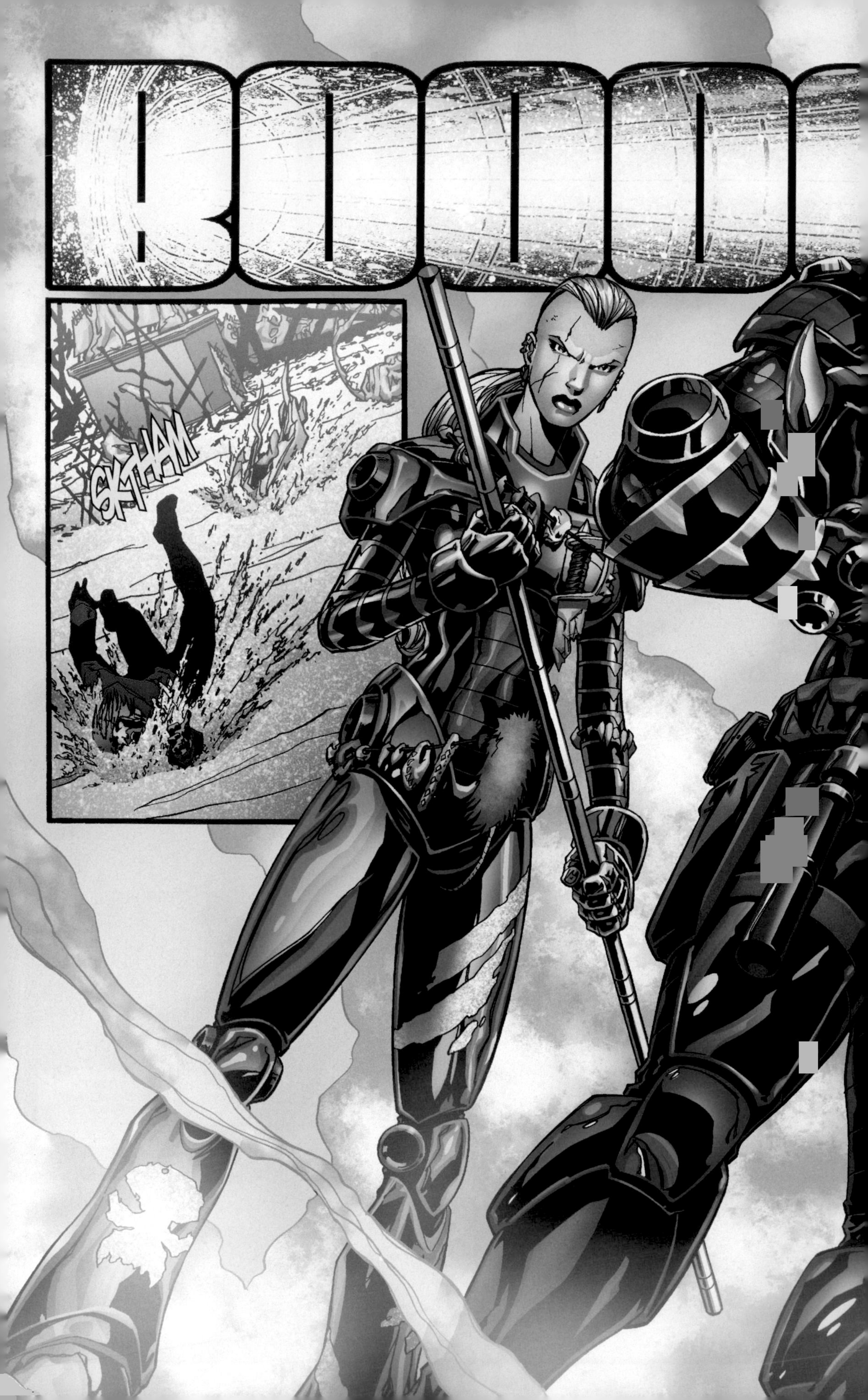
SKTHAM

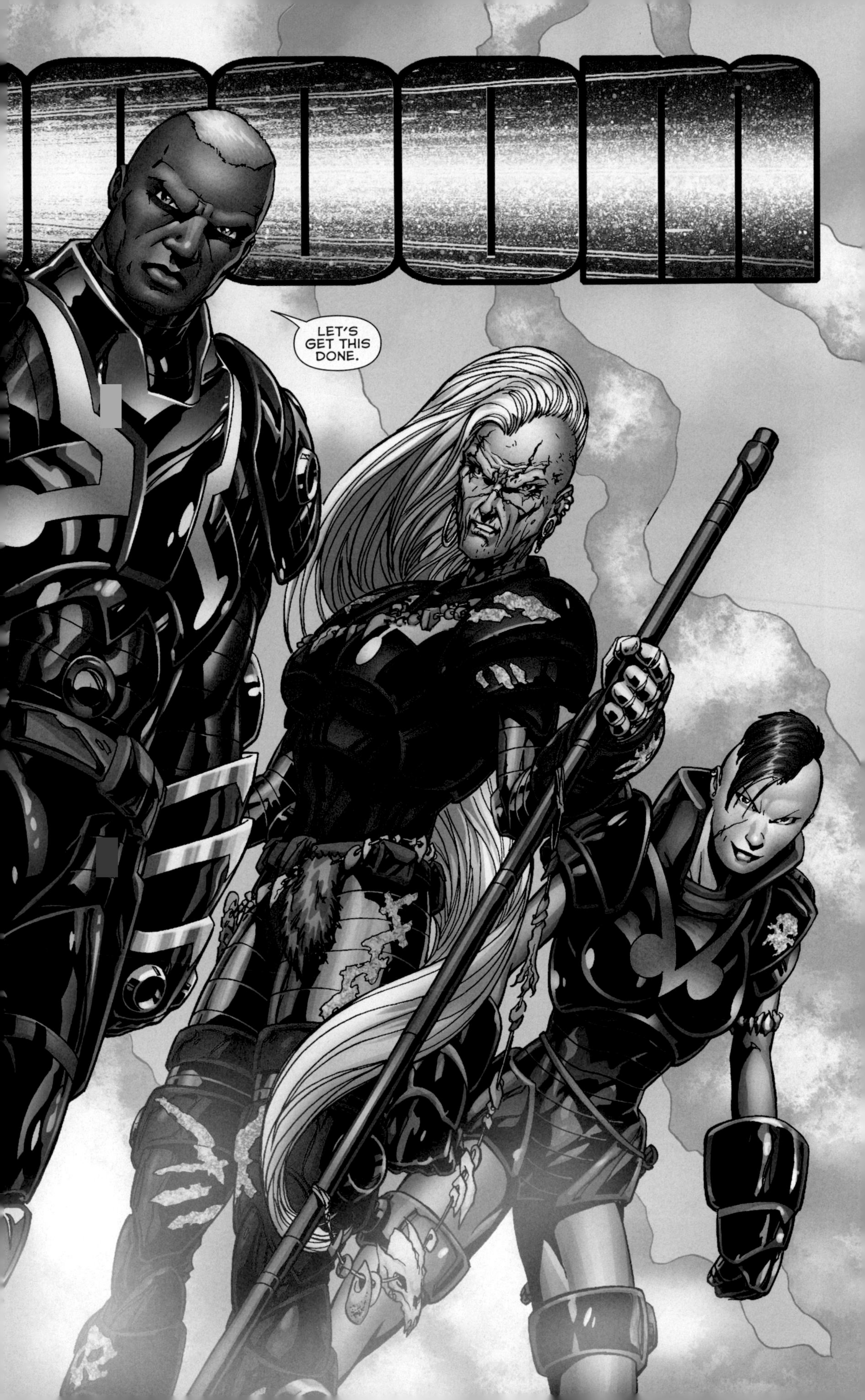
LET'S GET THIS DONE.

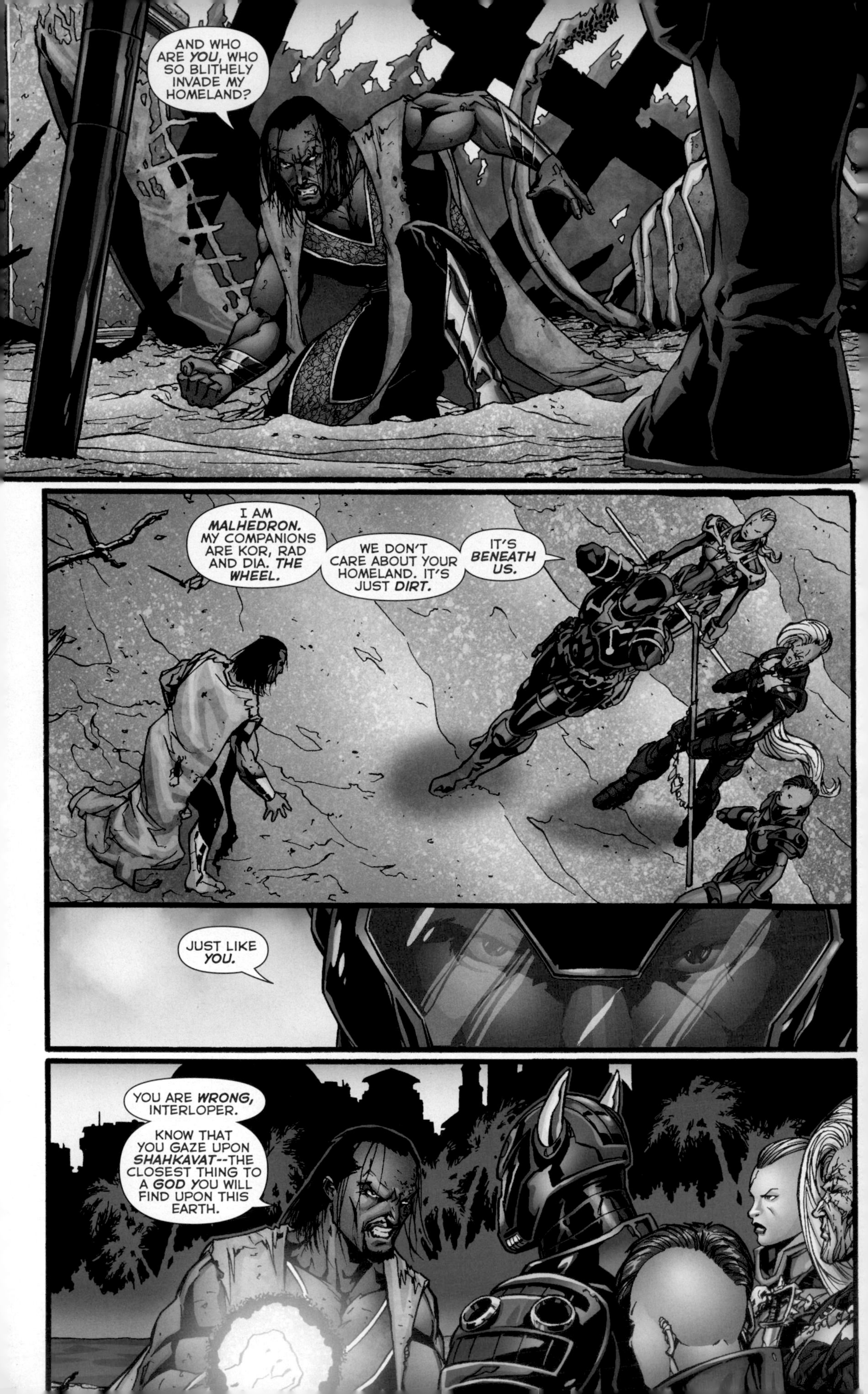
AND WHO ARE YOU, WHO SO BLITHELY INVADE MY HOMELAND?
I AM MALHEDRON. MY COMPANIONS ARE KOR, RAD AND DIA. THE WHEEL.
WE DON'T CARE ABOUT YOUR HOMELAND. IT'S JUST DIRT.
IT'S BENEATH US.
JUST LIKE YOU.
YOU ARE WRONG, INTERLOPER.
KNOW THAT YOU GAZE UPON SHAHKAVAT--THE CLOSEST THING TO A GOD YOU WILL FIND UPON THIS EARTH.

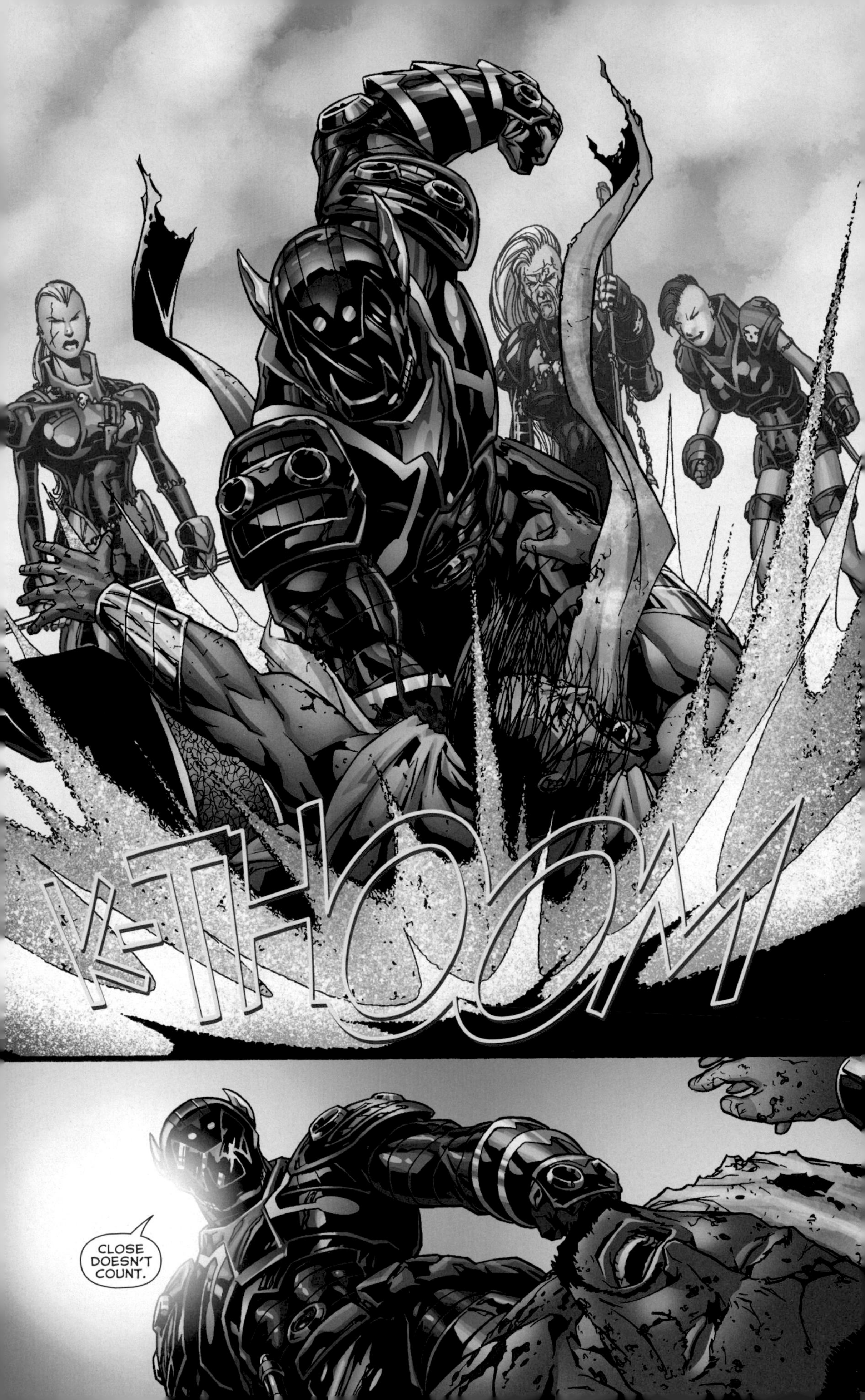
K-THOOM
CLOSE DOESN'T COUNT.

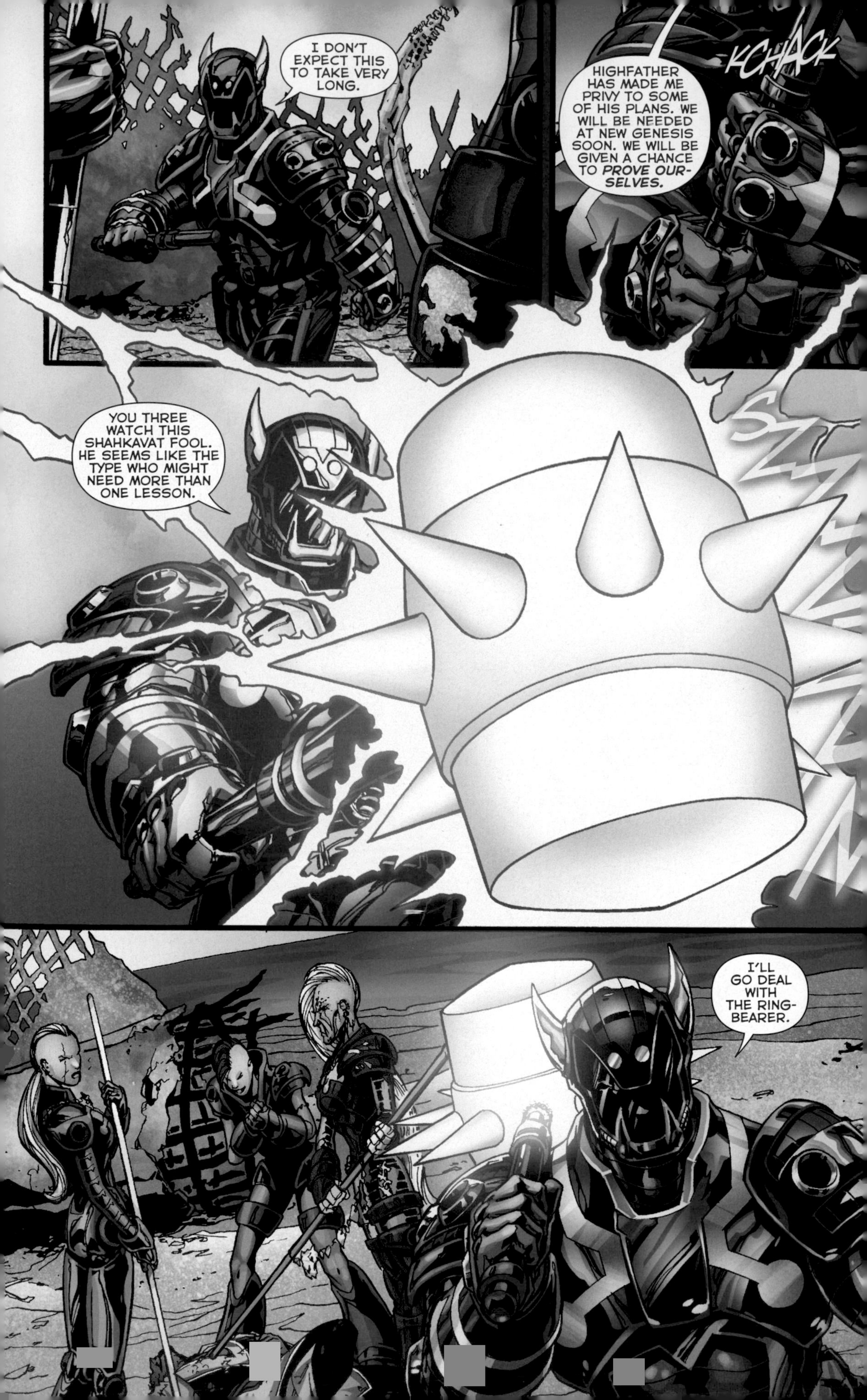
I DON'T EXPECT THIS TO TAKE VERY LONG.
KCHACK
HIGHFATHER HAS MADE ME PRIVY TO SOME OF HIS PLANS. WE WILL BE NEEDED AT NEW GENESIS SOON. WE WILL BE GIVEN A CHANCE TO *PROVE OURSELVES.*
YOU THREE WATCH THIS SHAHKAVAT FOOL. HE SEEMS LIKE THE TYPE WHO MIGHT NEED MORE THAN ONE LESSON.
I'LL GO DEAL WITH THE RING-BEARER.

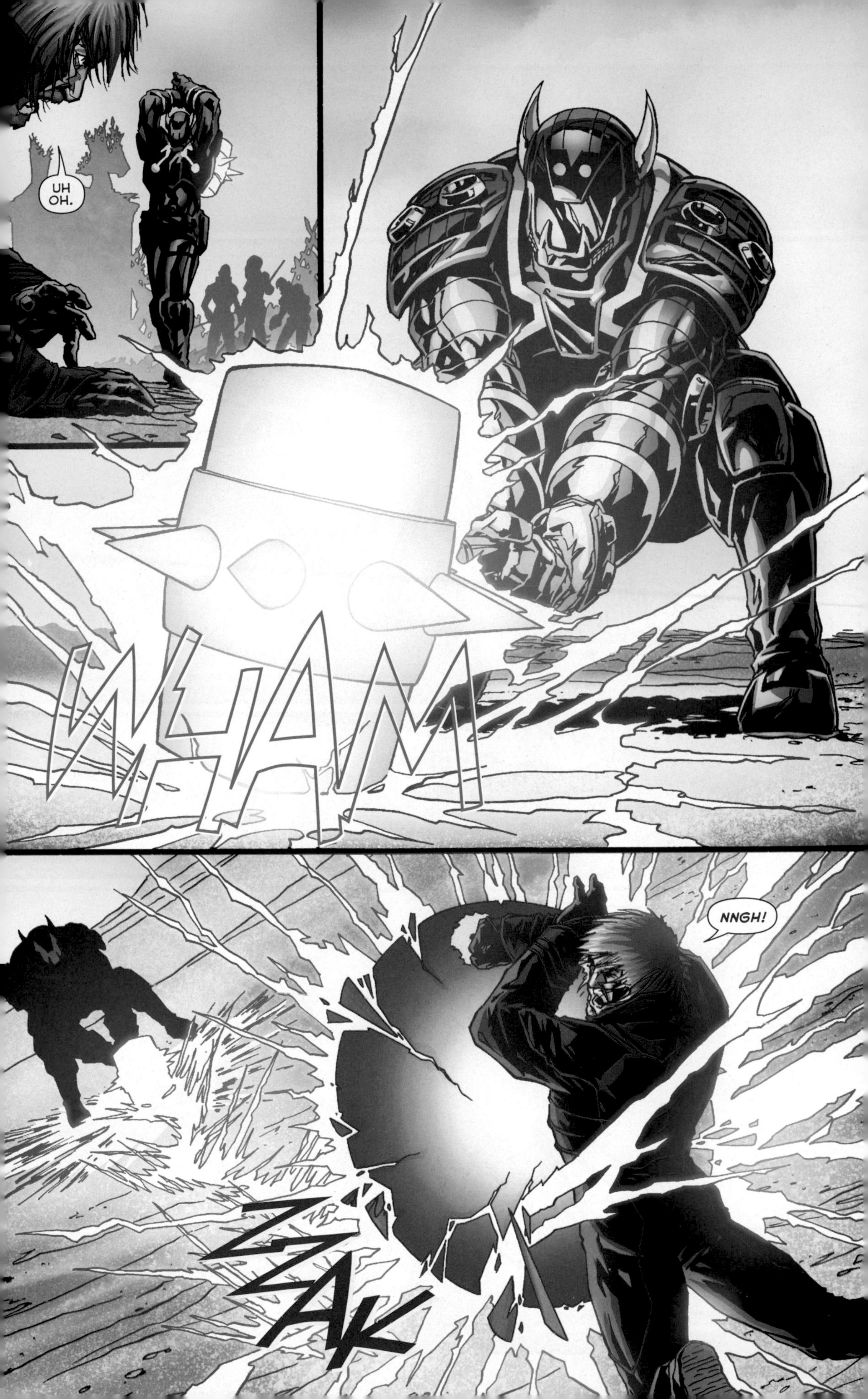
UH OH.
WHAM
NNGH!
ZZAK

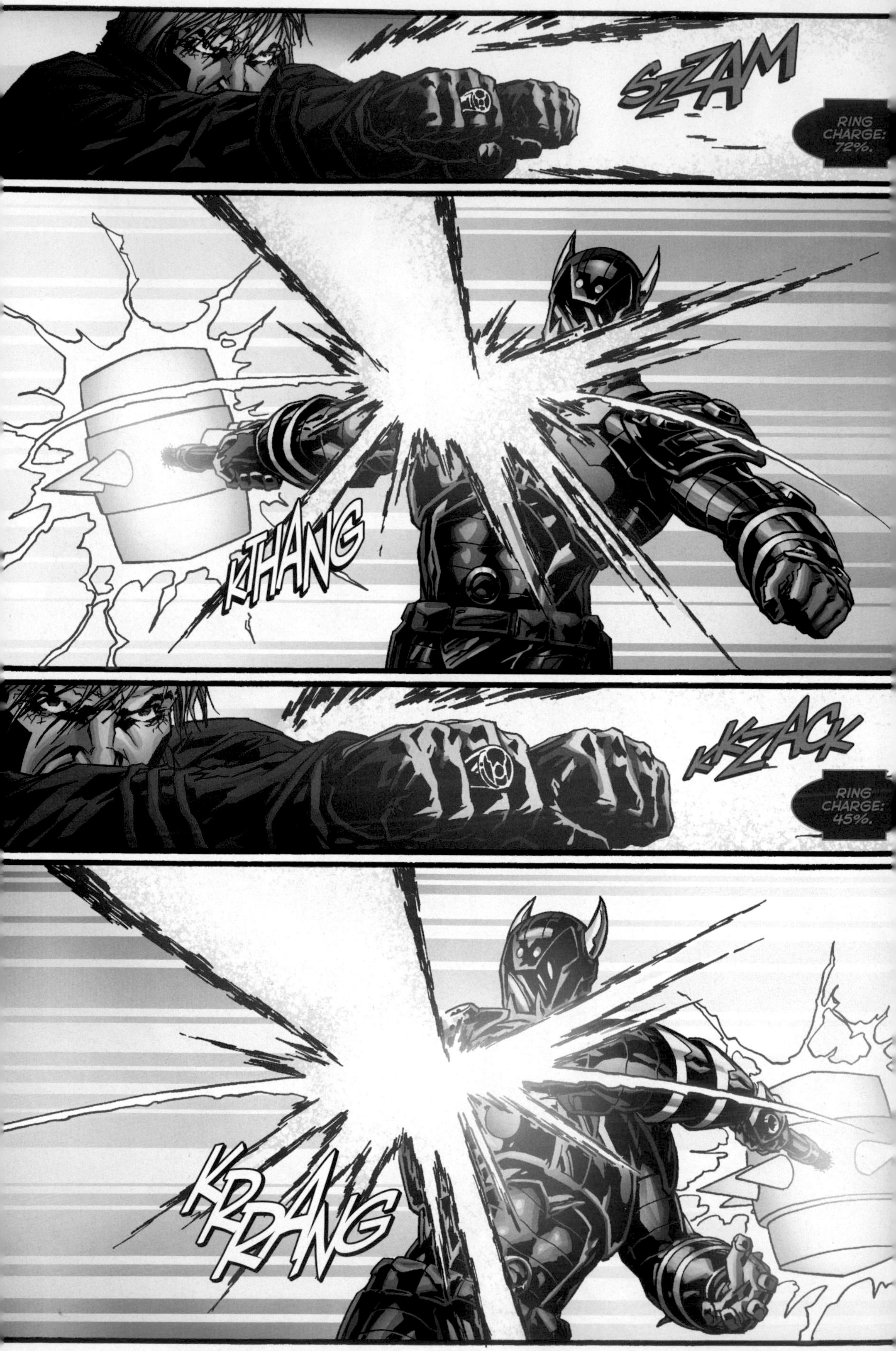
SZZAM
RING CHARGE: 72%.
KTHANG
KKZACK
RING CHARGE: 45%.
KRRANG

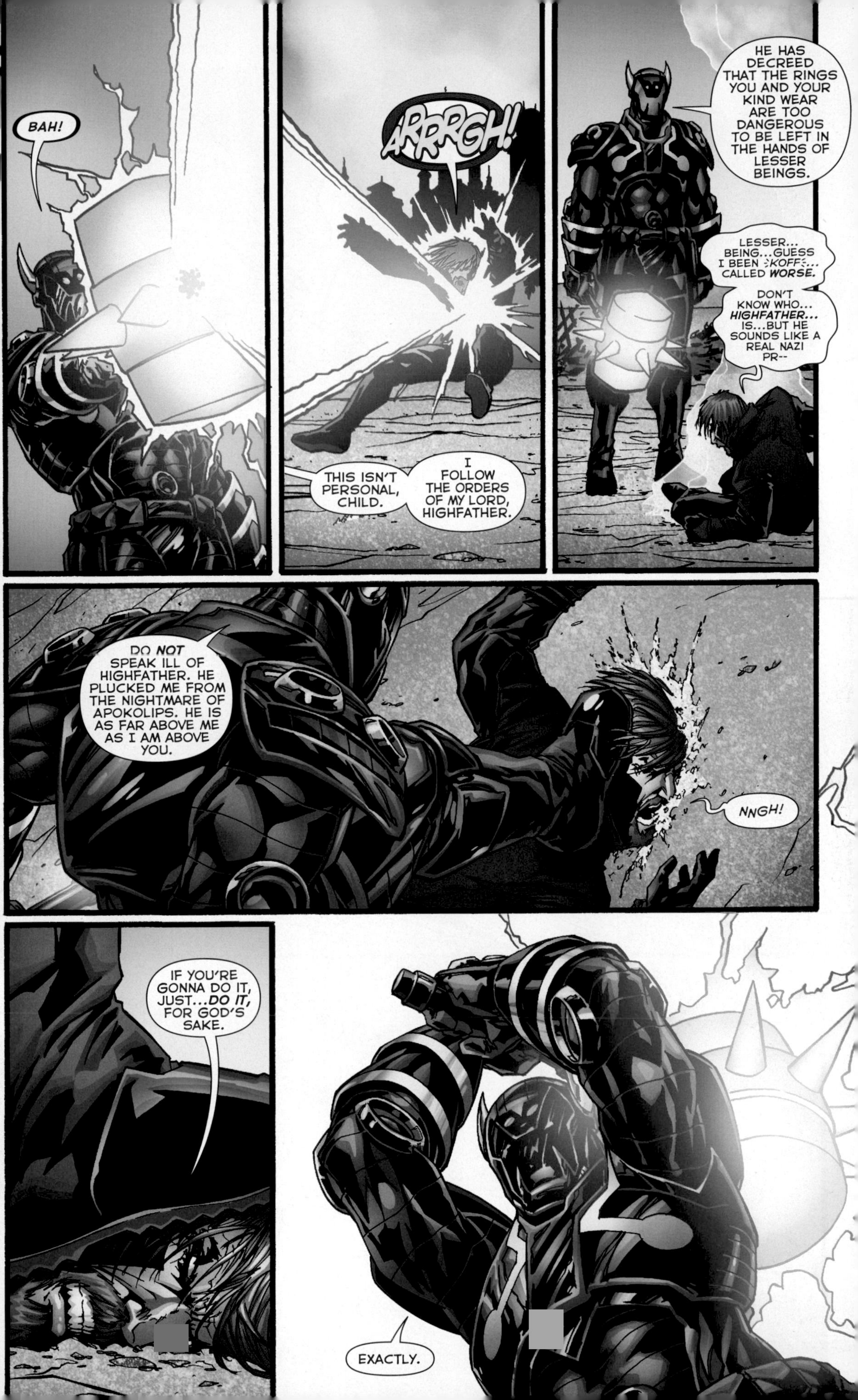
BAH!
ARRRGH!
THIS ISN'T PERSONAL, CHILD.
I FOLLOW THE ORDERS OF MY LORD, HIGHFATHER.
HE HAS DECREED THAT THE RINGS YOU AND YOUR KIND WEAR ARE TOO DANGEROUS TO BE LEFT IN THE HANDS OF LESSER BEINGS.
LESSER... BEING...GUESS I BEEN *KOFF*... CALLED *WORSE.*
DON'T KNOW WHO... *HIGHFATHER...* IS...BUT HE SOUNDS LIKE A REAL NAZI PR--
DO *NOT* SPEAK ILL OF HIGHFATHER. HE PLUCKED ME FROM THE NIGHTMARE OF APOKOLIPS. HE IS AS FAR ABOVE ME AS I AM ABOVE YOU.
NNGH!
IF YOU'RE GONNA DO IT, JUST...*DO IT,* FOR GOD'S SAKE.
EXACTLY.

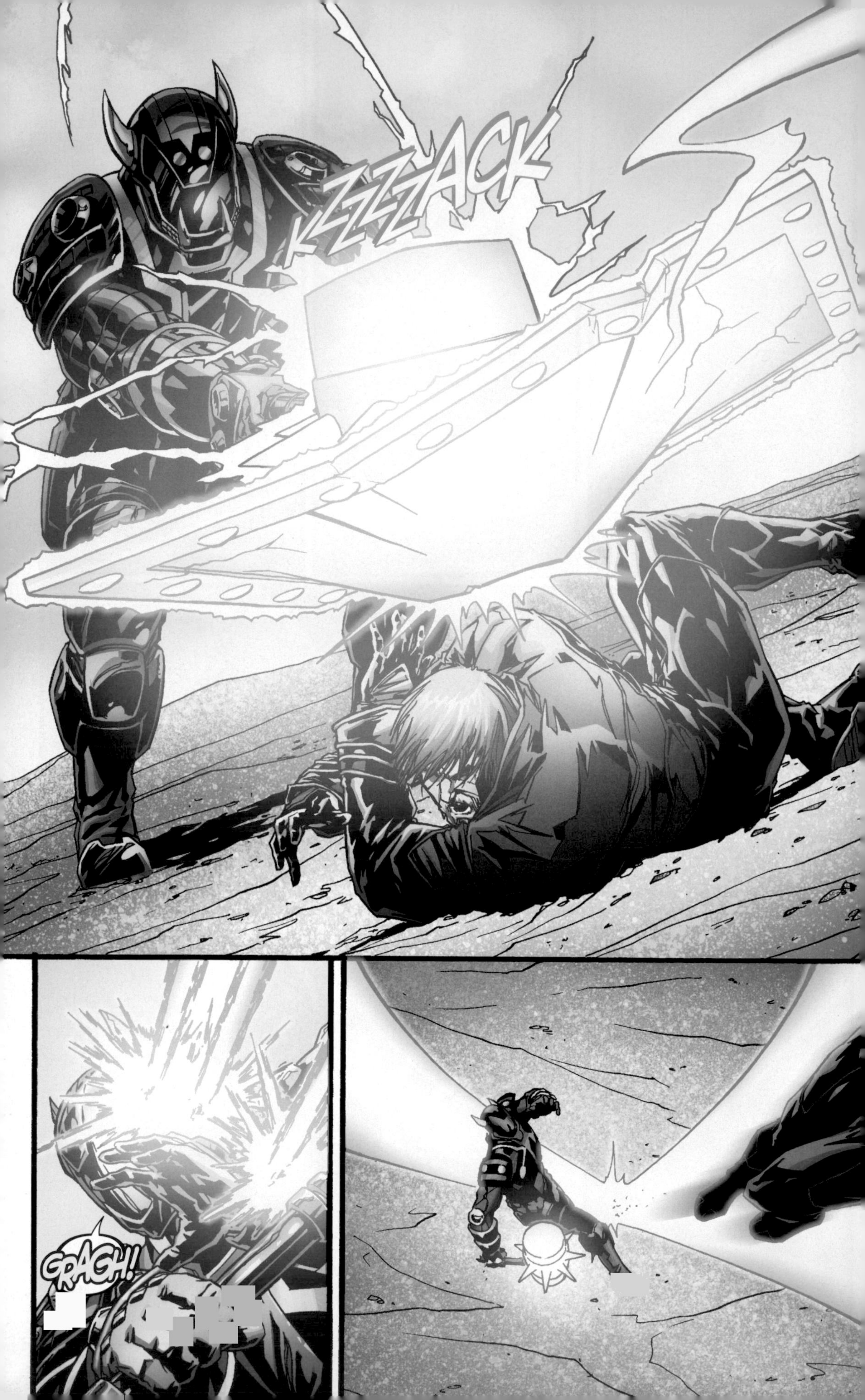
KZZZZACK
GRAGH!

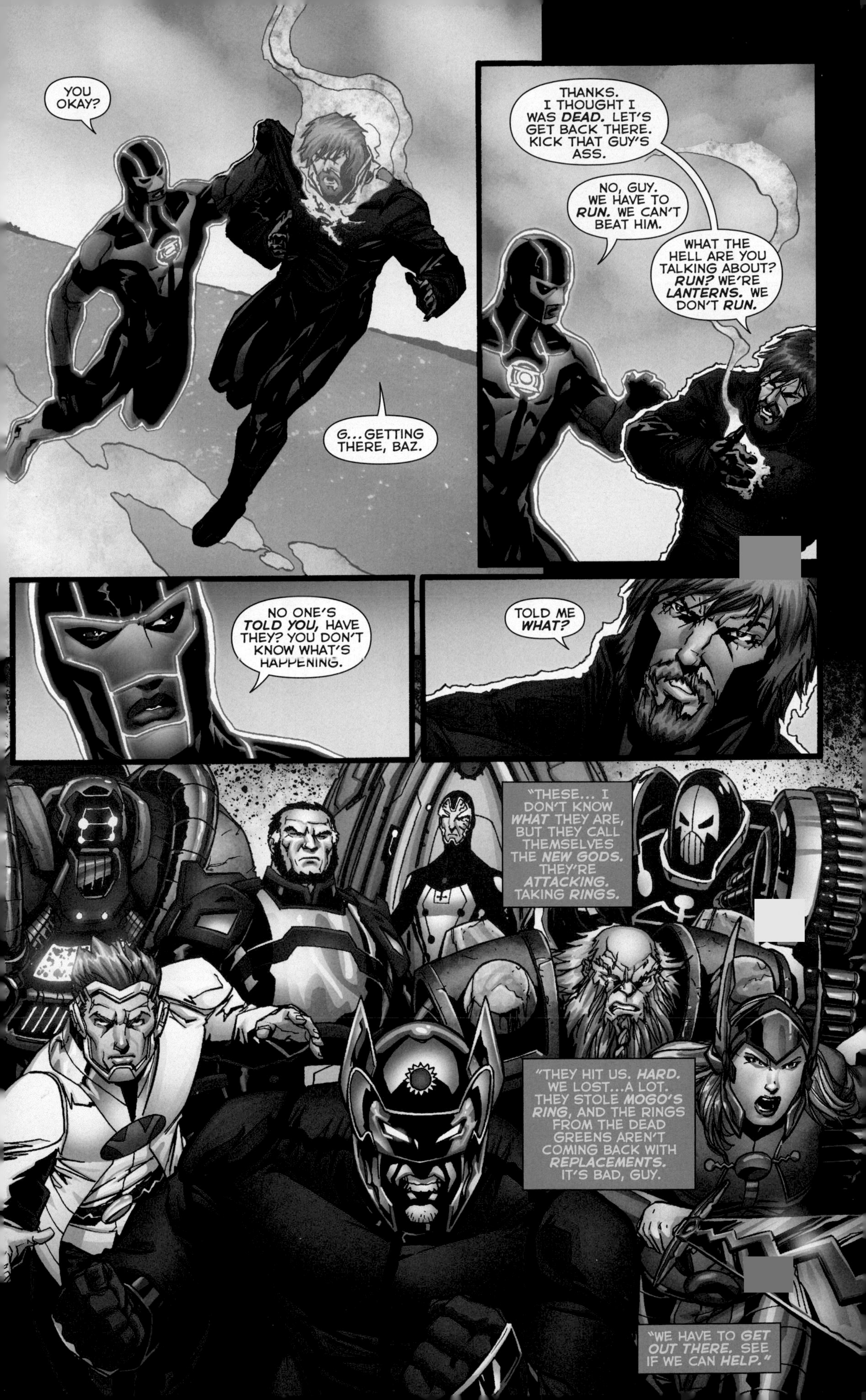

YOU OKAY?
G...GETTING THERE, BAZ.
THANKS. I THOUGHT I WAS DEAD. LET'S GET BACK THERE. KICK THAT GUY'S ASS.
NO, GUY. WE HAVE TO RUN. WE CAN'T BEAT HIM.
WHAT THE HELL ARE YOU TALKING ABOUT? RUN? WE'RE LANTERNS. WE DON'T RUN.
NO ONE'S TOLD YOU, HAVE THEY? YOU DON'T KNOW WHAT'S HAPPENING.
TOLD ME WHAT?
"THESE... I DON'T KNOW WHAT THEY ARE, BUT THEY CALL THEMSELVES THE NEW GODS. THEY'RE ATTACKING. TAKING RINGS.
"THEY HIT US. HARD. WE LOST...A LOT. THEY STOLE MOGO'S RING, AND THE RINGS FROM THE DEAD GREENS AREN'T COMING BACK WITH REPLACEMENTS. IT'S BAD, GUY.
"WE HAVE TO GET OUT THERE. SEE IF WE CAN HELP."

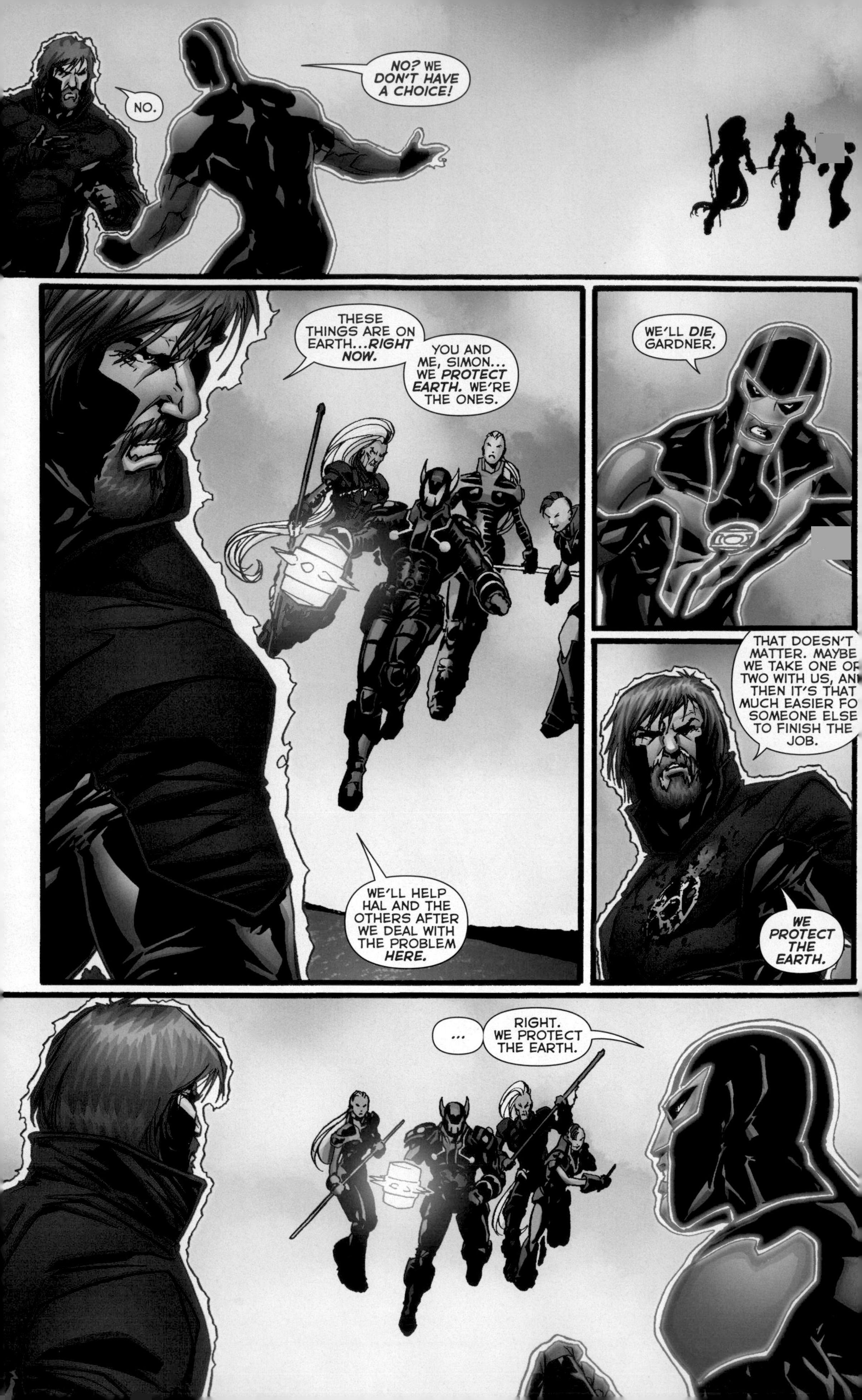
NO.
NO? WE DON'T HAVE A CHOICE!
THESE THINGS ARE ON EARTH...RIGHT NOW.
YOU AND ME, SIMON... WE PROTECT EARTH. WE'RE THE ONES.
WE'LL HELP HAL AND THE OTHERS AFTER WE DEAL WITH THE PROBLEM HERE.
WE'LL DIE, GARDNER.
THAT DOESN'T MATTER. MAYBE WE TAKE ONE OF TWO WITH US, AN THEN IT'S THAT MUCH EASIER FO SOMEONE ELSE TO FINISH THE JOB.
WE PROTECT THE EARTH.
...
RIGHT. WE PROTECT THE EARTH.

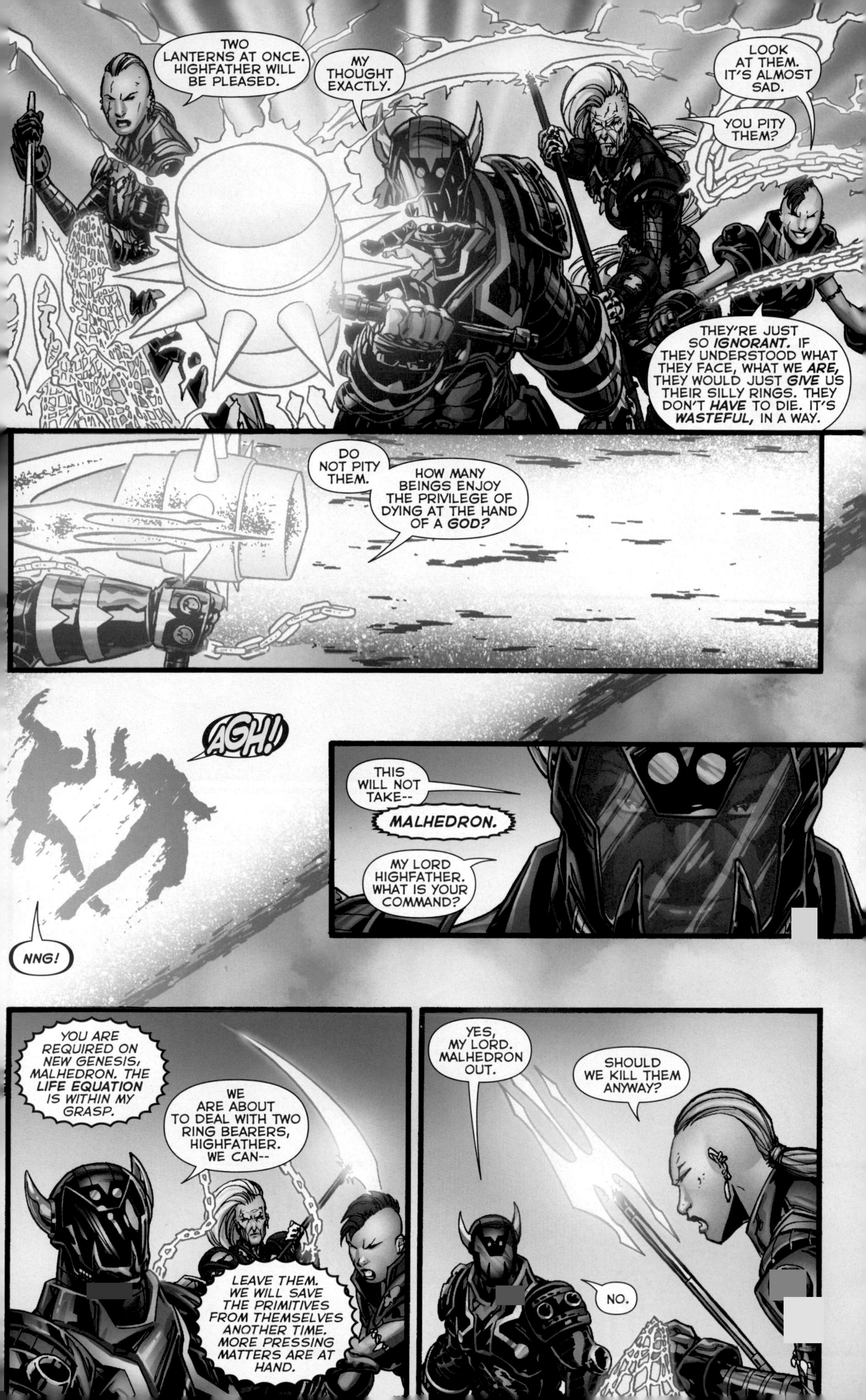
TWO LANTERNS AT ONCE. HIGHFATHER WILL BE PLEASED.
MY THOUGHT EXACTLY.
LOOK AT THEM. IT'S ALMOST SAD.
YOU PITY THEM?
THEY'RE JUST SO *IGNORANT.* IF THEY UNDERSTOOD WHAT THEY FACE, WHAT WE *ARE,* THEY WOULD JUST *GIVE* US THEIR SILLY RINGS. THEY DON'T *HAVE* TO DIE. IT'S *WASTEFUL,* IN A WAY.
DO NOT PITY THEM.
HOW MANY BEINGS ENJOY THE PRIVILEGE OF DYING AT THE HAND OF A *GOD?*
AGH!
NNG!
THIS WILL NOT TAKE--
MALHEDRON.
MY LORD HIGHFATHER. WHAT IS YOUR COMMAND?
*YOU ARE REQUIRED ON NEW GENESIS, MALHEDRON. THE **LIFE EQUATION** IS WITHIN MY GRASP.*
WE ARE ABOUT TO DEAL WITH TWO RING BEARERS, HIGHFATHER. WE CAN--
LEAVE THEM. WE WILL SAVE THE PRIMITIVES FROM THEMSELVES ANOTHER TIME. MORE PRESSING MATTERS ARE AT HAND.
YES, MY LORD. MALHEDRON OUT.
SHOULD WE KILL THEM ANYWAY?
NO.

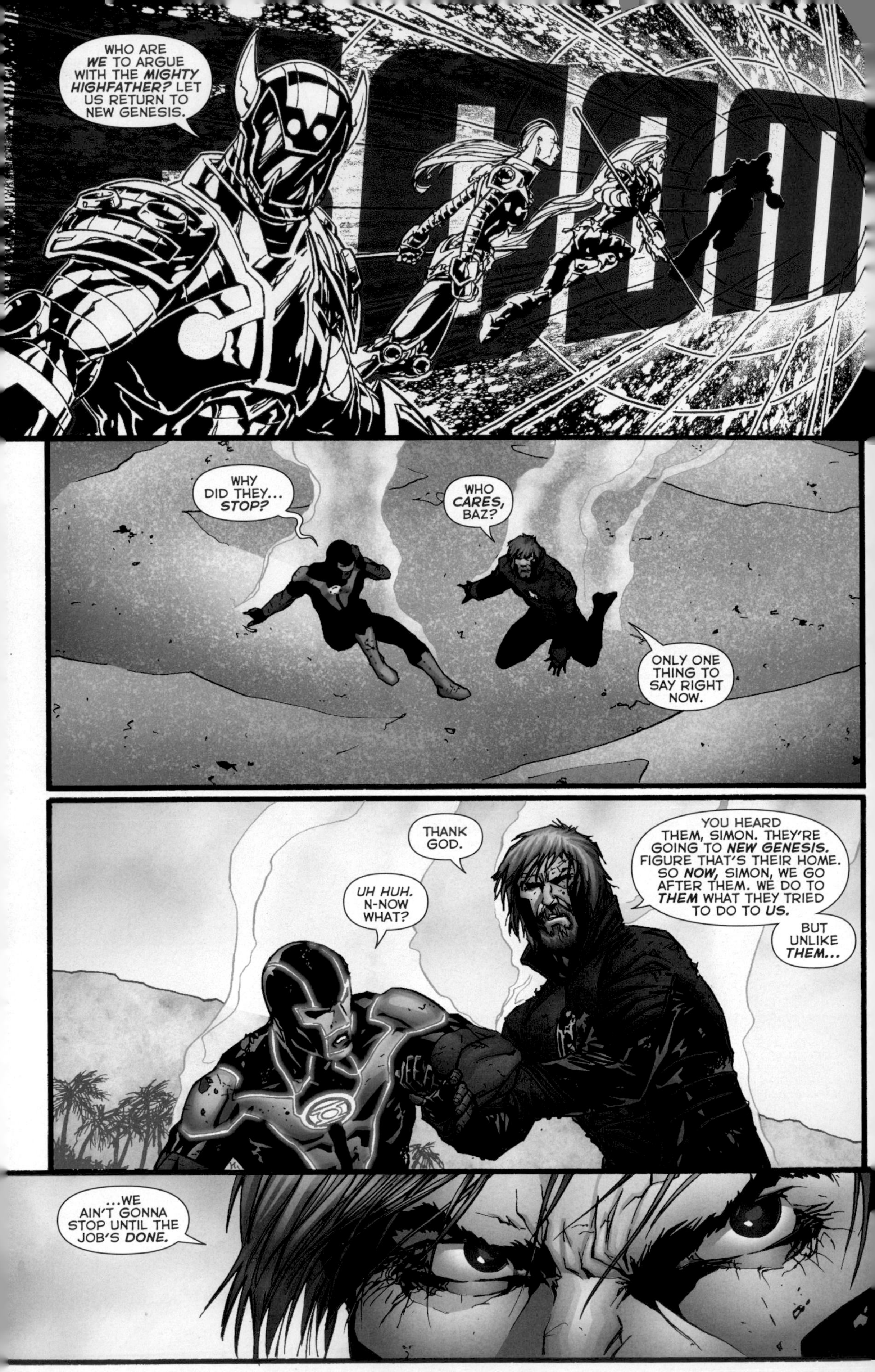
WHO ARE WE TO ARGUE WITH THE MIGHTY HIGHFATHER? LET US RETURN TO NEW GENESIS.
WHY DID THEY... STOP?
WHO CARES, BAZ?
ONLY ONE THING TO SAY RIGHT NOW.
THANK GOD.
UH HUH. N-NOW WHAT?
YOU HEARD THEM, SIMON. THEY'RE GOING TO NEW GENESIS. FIGURE THAT'S THEIR HOME. SO NOW, SIMON, WE GO AFTER THEM. WE DO TO THEM WHAT THEY TRIED TO DO TO US.
BUT UNLIKE THEM...
...WE AIN'T GONNA STOP UNTIL THE JOB'S DONE.

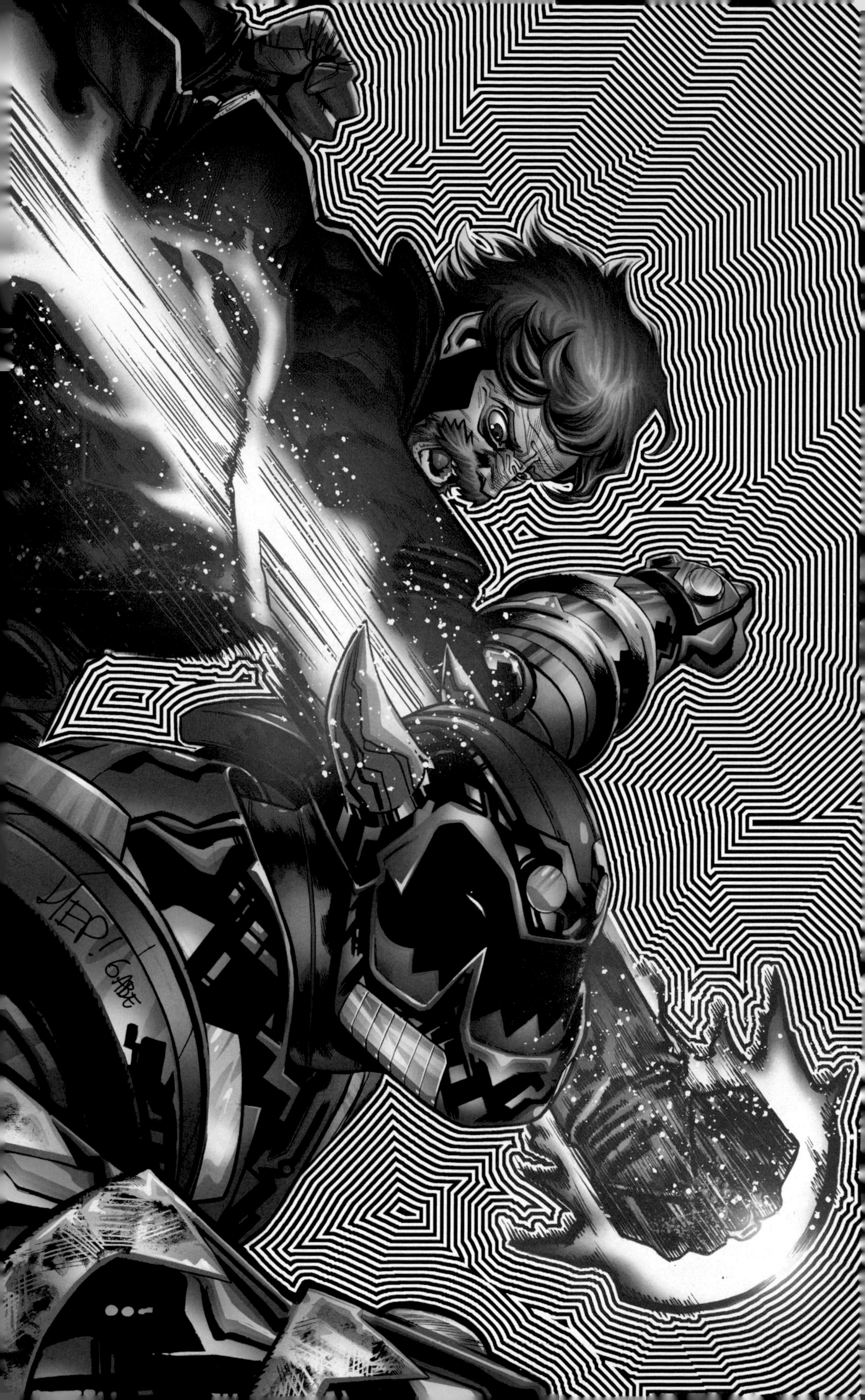

GODHEAD ACT II, PART IV: BOOM

CHARLES SOULE writer **J. CALAFIORE** artist **GABE ELTAEB** colorist **DAVE SHARPE** letterer
cover art by **SCOTT HEPBURN** and **GABE ELTAEB**

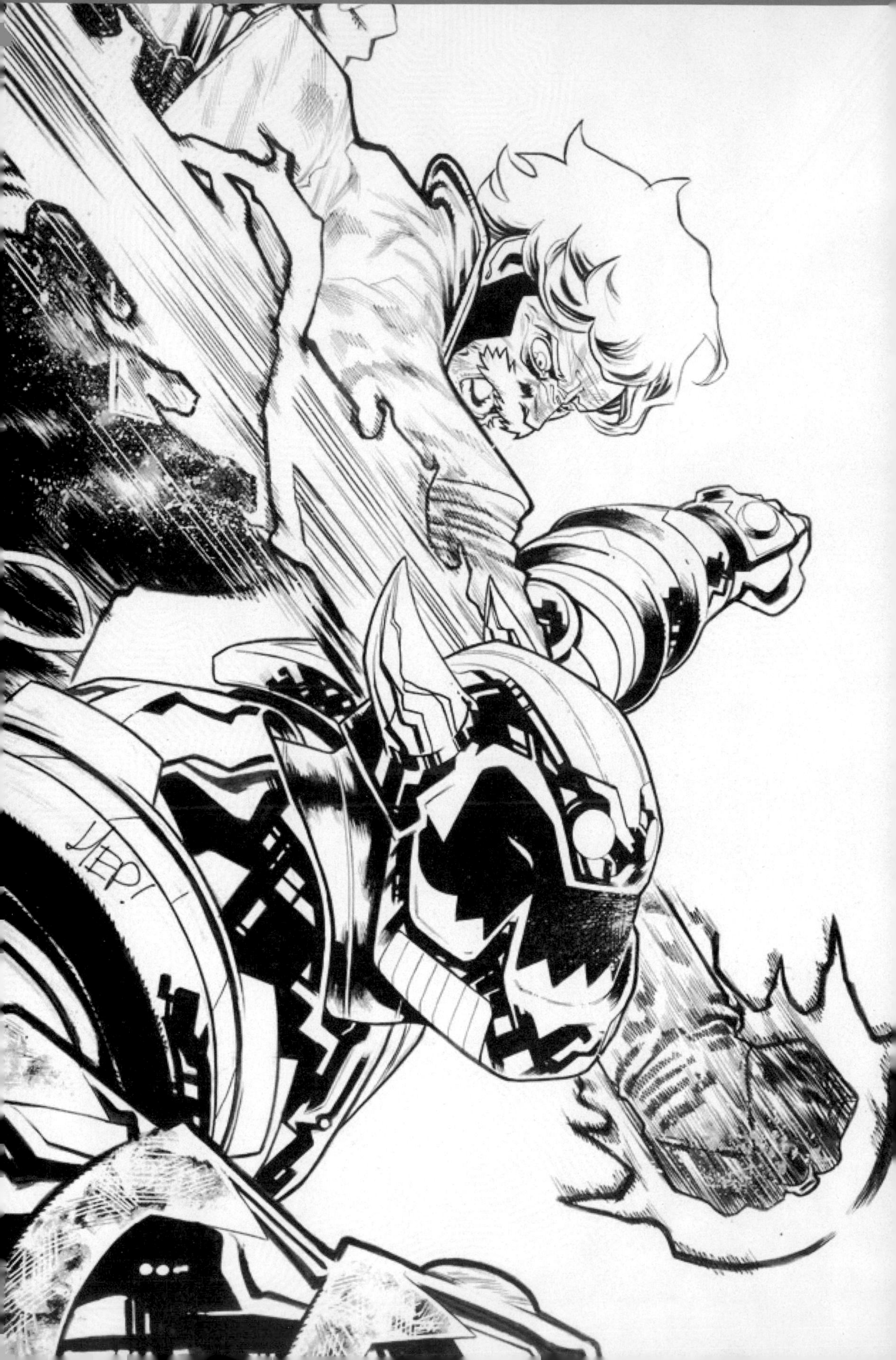

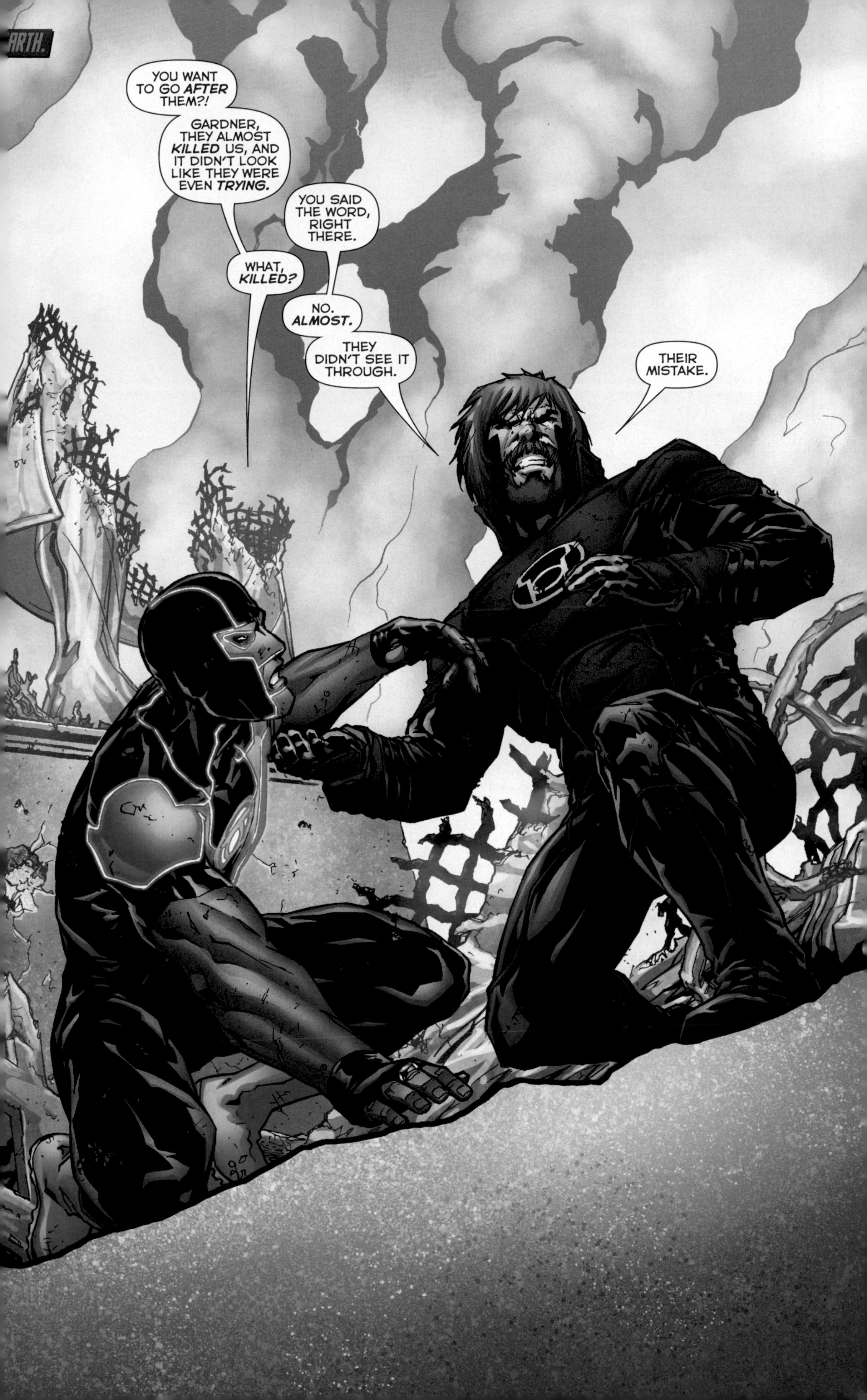

ARTH.
YOU WANT TO GO AFTER THEM?!
GARDNER, THEY ALMOST KILLED US, AND IT DIDN'T LOOK LIKE THEY WERE EVEN TRYING.
YOU SAID THE WORD, RIGHT THERE.
WHAT, KILLED?
NO. ALMOST.
THEY DIDN'T SEE IT THROUGH.
THEIR MISTAKE.

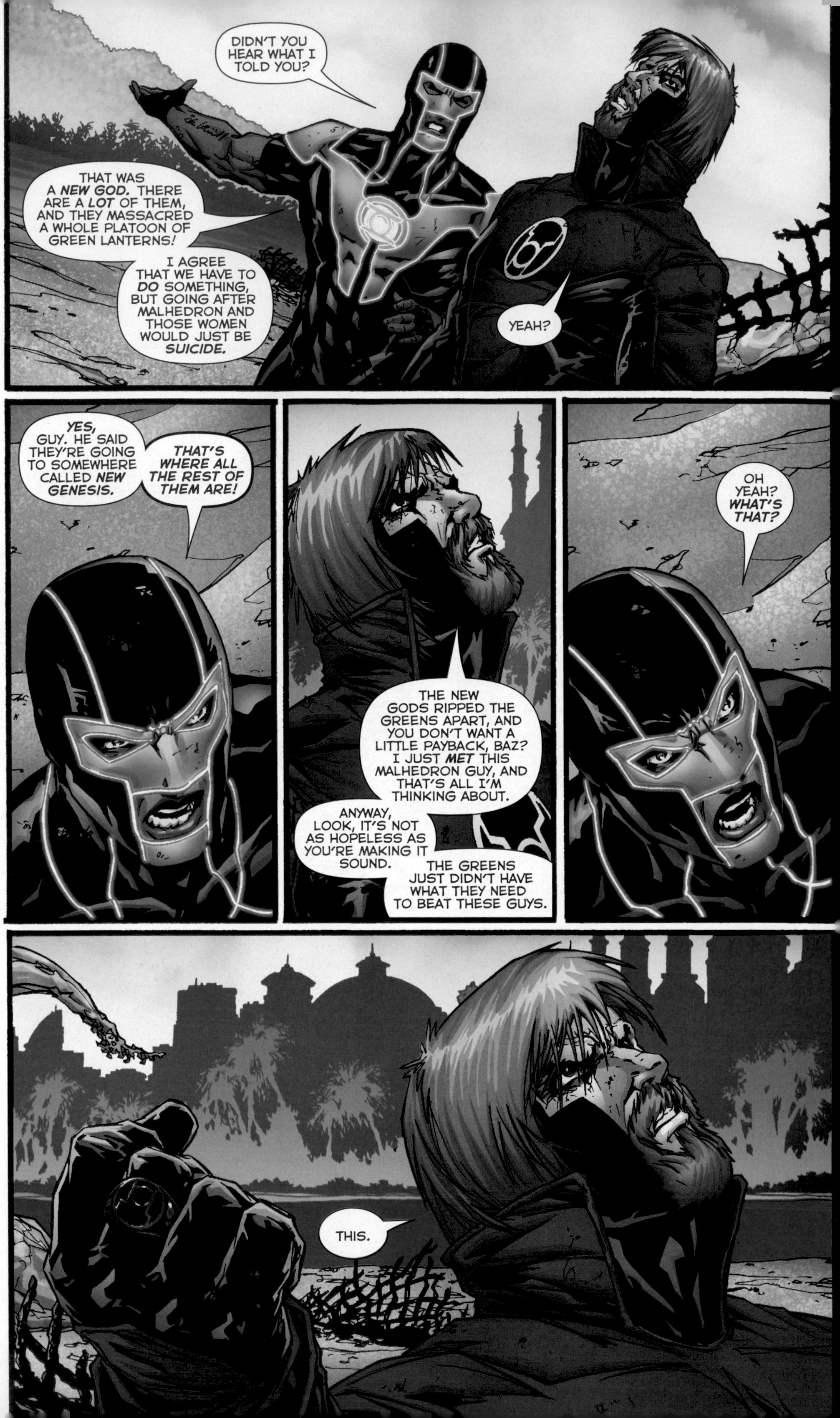
DIDN'T YOU HEAR WHAT I TOLD YOU?
THAT WAS A NEW GOD. THERE ARE A LOT OF THEM, AND THEY MASSACRED A WHOLE PLATOON OF GREEN LANTERNS!
I AGREE THAT WE HAVE TO DO SOMETHING, BUT GOING AFTER MALHEDRON AND THOSE WOMEN WOULD JUST BE SUICIDE.
YEAH?
YES, GUY. HE SAID THEY'RE GOING TO SOMEWHERE CALLED NEW GENESIS.
THAT'S WHERE ALL THE REST OF THEM ARE!
THE NEW GODS RIPPED THE GREENS APART, AND YOU DON'T WANT A LITTLE PAYBACK, BAZ? I JUST MET THIS MALHEDRON GUY, AND THAT'S ALL I'M THINKING ABOUT.
ANYWAY, LOOK, IT'S NOT AS HOPELESS AS YOU'RE MAKING IT SOUND.
THE GREENS JUST DIDN'T HAVE WHAT THEY NEED TO BEAT THESE GUYS.
OH YEAH? WHAT'S THAT?
THIS.

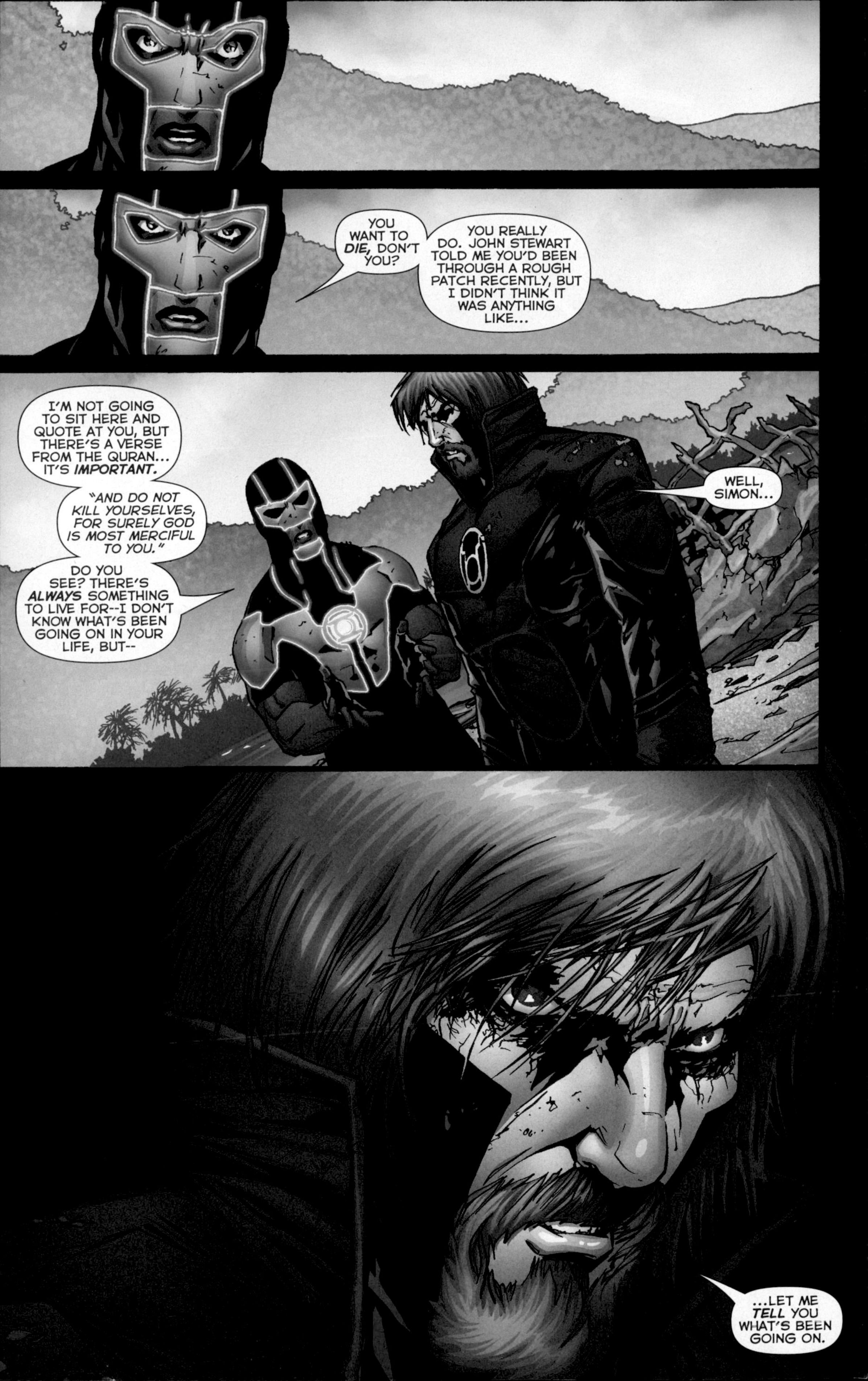
YOU WANT TO *DIE*, DON'T YOU?
YOU REALLY DO. JOHN STEWART TOLD ME YOU'D BEEN THROUGH A ROUGH PATCH RECENTLY, BUT I DIDN'T THINK IT WAS ANYTHING LIKE...
I'M NOT GOING TO SIT HERE AND QUOTE AT YOU, BUT THERE'S A VERSE FROM THE QURAN... IT'S *IMPORTANT.*
"AND DO NOT KILL YOURSELVES, FOR SURELY GOD IS MOST MERCIFUL TO YOU."
DO YOU SEE? THERE'S *ALWAYS* SOMETHING TO LIVE FOR--I DON'T KNOW WHAT'S BEEN GOING ON IN YOUR LIFE, BUT--
WELL, SIMON...
...LET ME *TELL* YOU WHAT'S BEEN GOING ON.

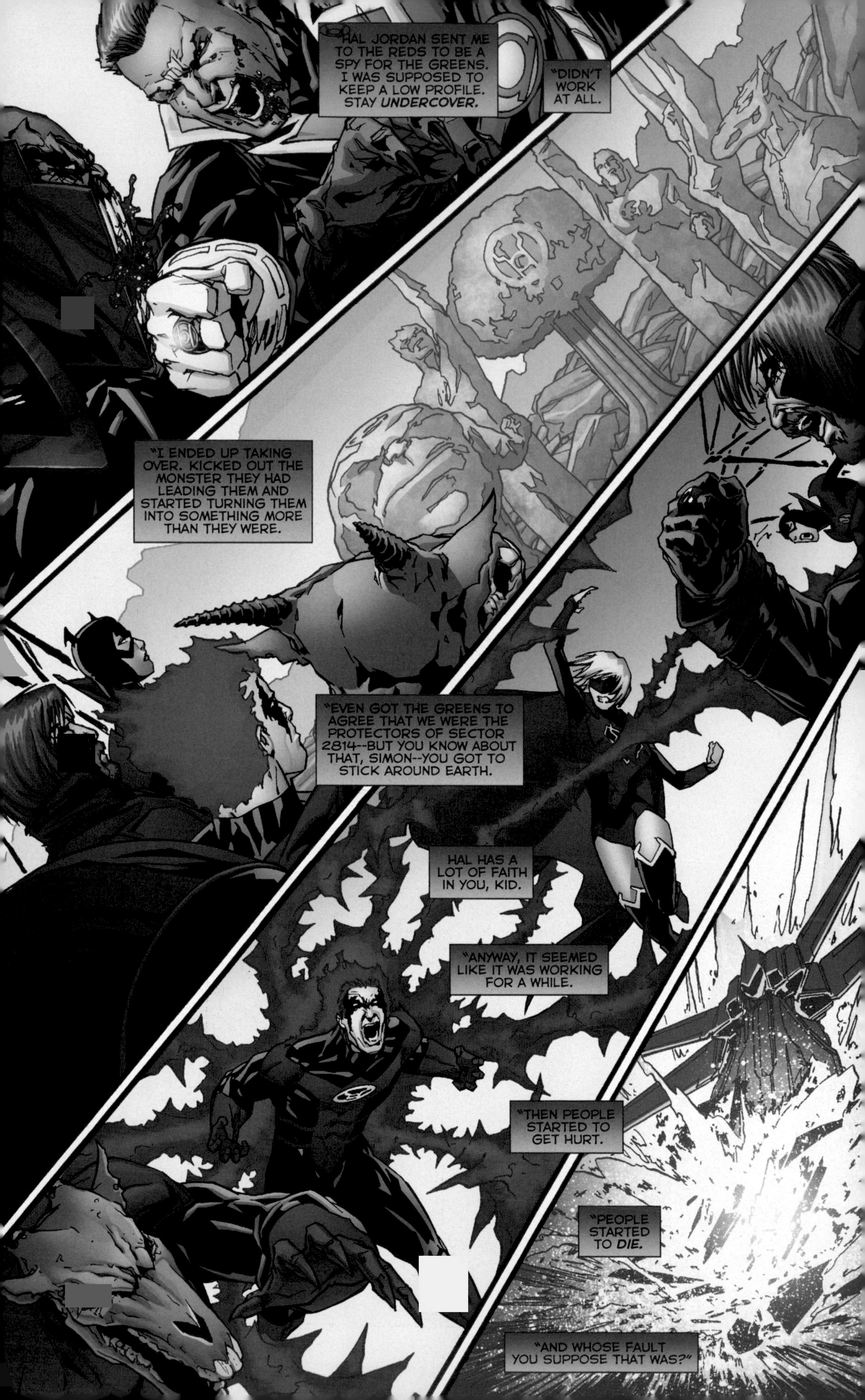
"HAL JORDAN SENT ME TO THE REDS TO BE A SPY FOR THE GREENS. I WAS SUPPOSED TO KEEP A LOW PROFILE. STAY *UNDERCOVER.*
"DIDN'T WORK AT ALL.
"I ENDED UP TAKING OVER. KICKED OUT THE MONSTER THEY HAD LEADING THEM AND STARTED TURNING THEM INTO SOMETHING MORE THAN THEY WERE.
"EVEN GOT THE GREENS TO AGREE THAT WE WERE THE PROTECTORS OF SECTOR 2814--BUT YOU KNOW ABOUT THAT, SIMON--YOU GOT TO STICK AROUND EARTH.
HAL HAS A LOT OF FAITH IN YOU, KID.
"ANYWAY, IT SEEMED LIKE IT WAS WORKING FOR A WHILE.
"THEN PEOPLE STARTED TO GET HURT.
"PEOPLE STARTED TO *DIE.*
"AND WHOSE FAULT YOU SUPPOSE THAT WAS?"

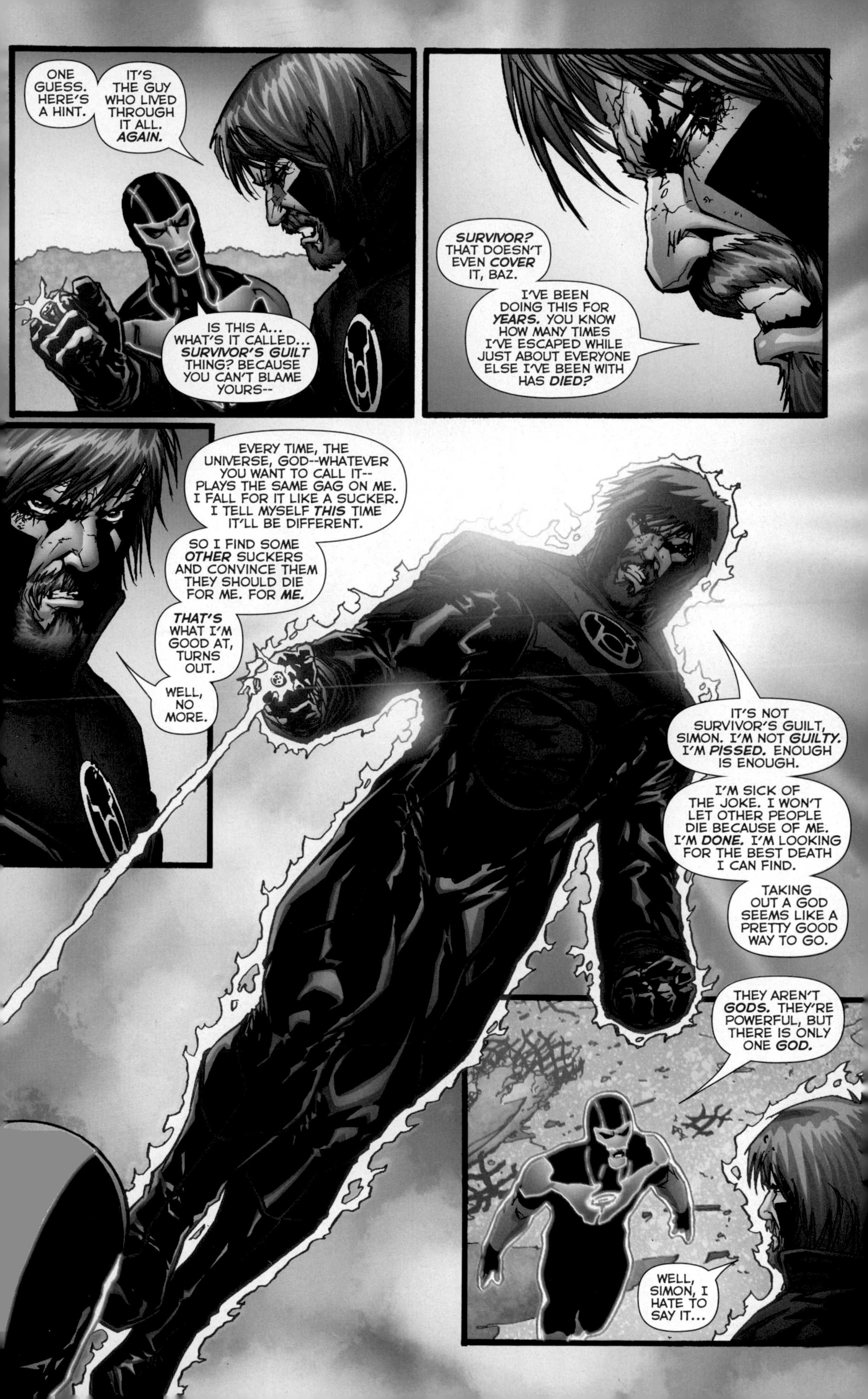
ONE GUESS. HERE'S A HINT.
IT'S THE GUY WHO LIVED THROUGH IT ALL. AGAIN.
IS THIS A... WHAT'S IT CALLED... SURVIVOR'S GUILT THING? BECAUSE YOU CAN'T BLAME YOURS--
SURVIVOR? THAT DOESN'T EVEN COVER IT, BAZ.
I'VE BEEN DOING THIS FOR YEARS. YOU KNOW HOW MANY TIMES I'VE ESCAPED WHILE JUST ABOUT EVERYONE ELSE I'VE BEEN WITH HAS DIED?
EVERY TIME, THE UNIVERSE, GOD--WHATEVER YOU WANT TO CALL IT-- PLAYS THE SAME GAG ON ME. I FALL FOR IT LIKE A SUCKER. I TELL MYSELF THIS TIME IT'LL BE DIFFERENT.
SO I FIND SOME OTHER SUCKERS AND CONVINCE THEM THEY SHOULD DIE FOR ME. FOR ME.
THAT'S WHAT I'M GOOD AT, TURNS OUT.
WELL, NO MORE.
IT'S NOT SURVIVOR'S GUILT, SIMON. I'M NOT GUILTY. I'M PISSED. ENOUGH IS ENOUGH.
I'M SICK OF THE JOKE. I WON'T LET OTHER PEOPLE DIE BECAUSE OF ME. I'M DONE. I'M LOOKING FOR THE BEST DEATH I CAN FIND.
TAKING OUT A GOD SEEMS LIKE A PRETTY GOOD WAY TO GO.
THEY AREN'T GODS. THEY'RE POWERFUL, BUT THERE IS ONLY ONE GOD.
WELL, SIMON, I HATE TO SAY IT...

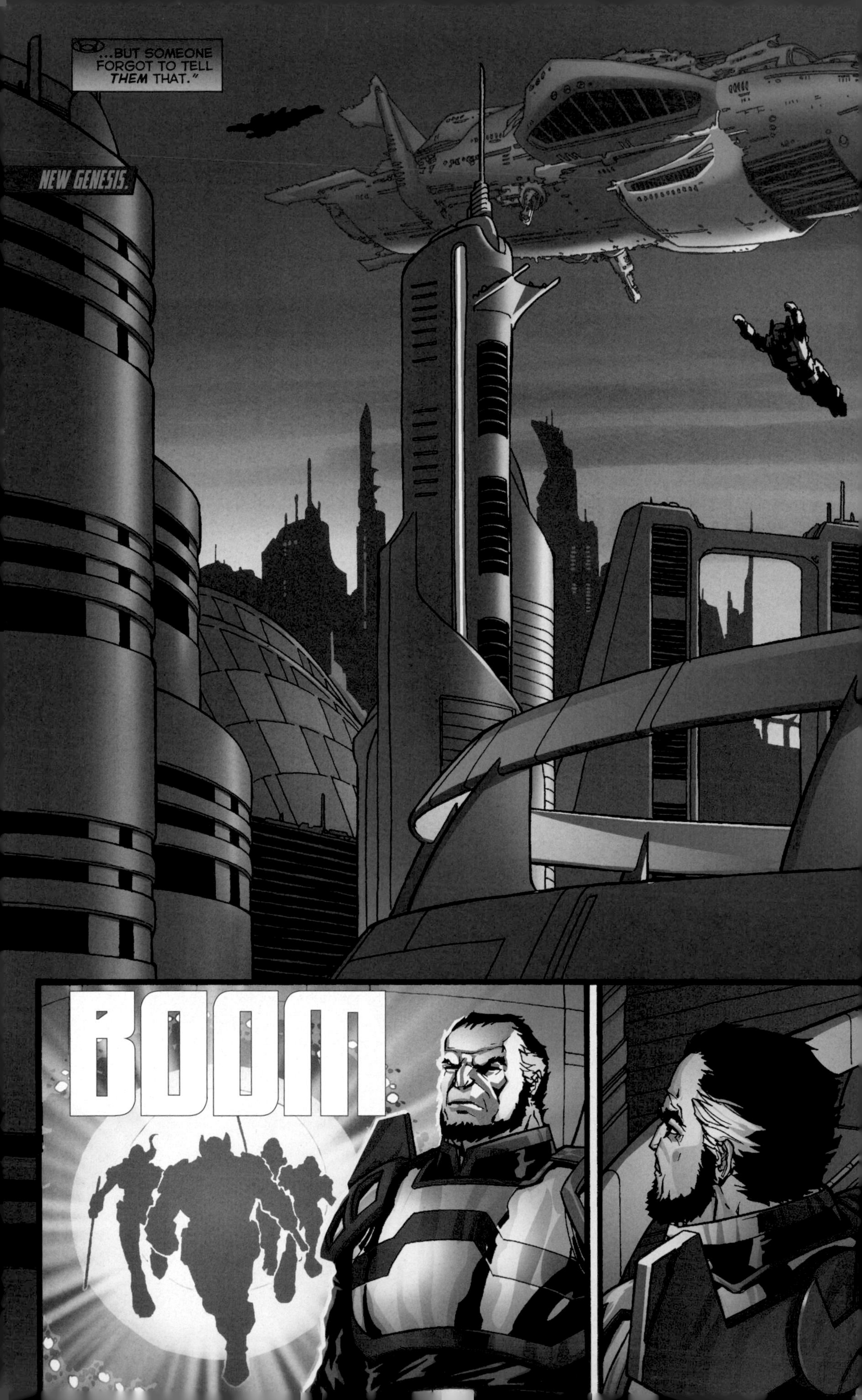

...BUT SOMEONE FORGOT TO TELL THEM THAT."
NEW GENESIS.
BOOM

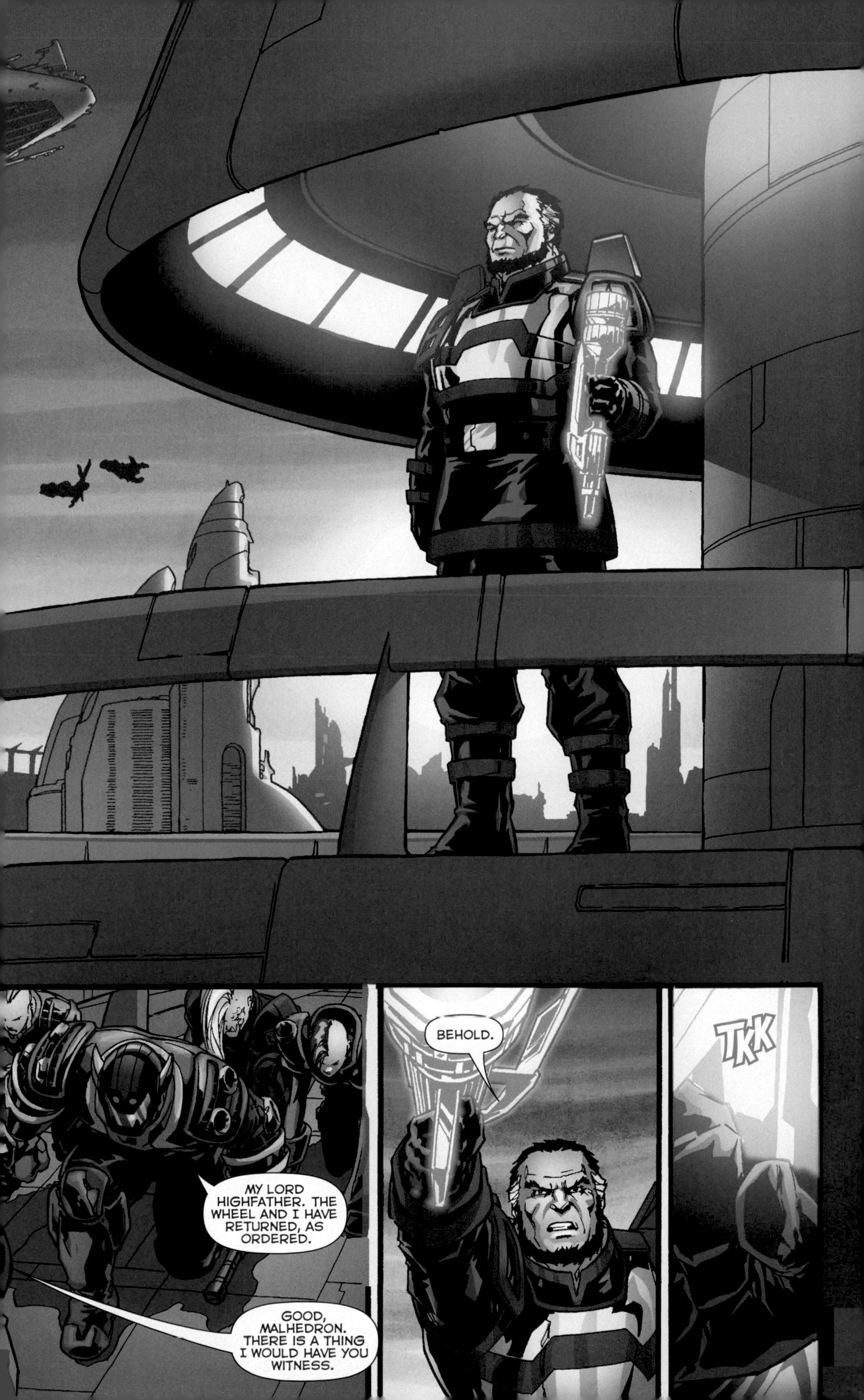
MY LORD HIGHFATHER. THE WHEEL AND I HAVE RETURNED, AS ORDERED.
GOOD, MALHEDRON. THERE IS A THING I WOULD HAVE YOU WITNESS.
BEHOLD.
TKK

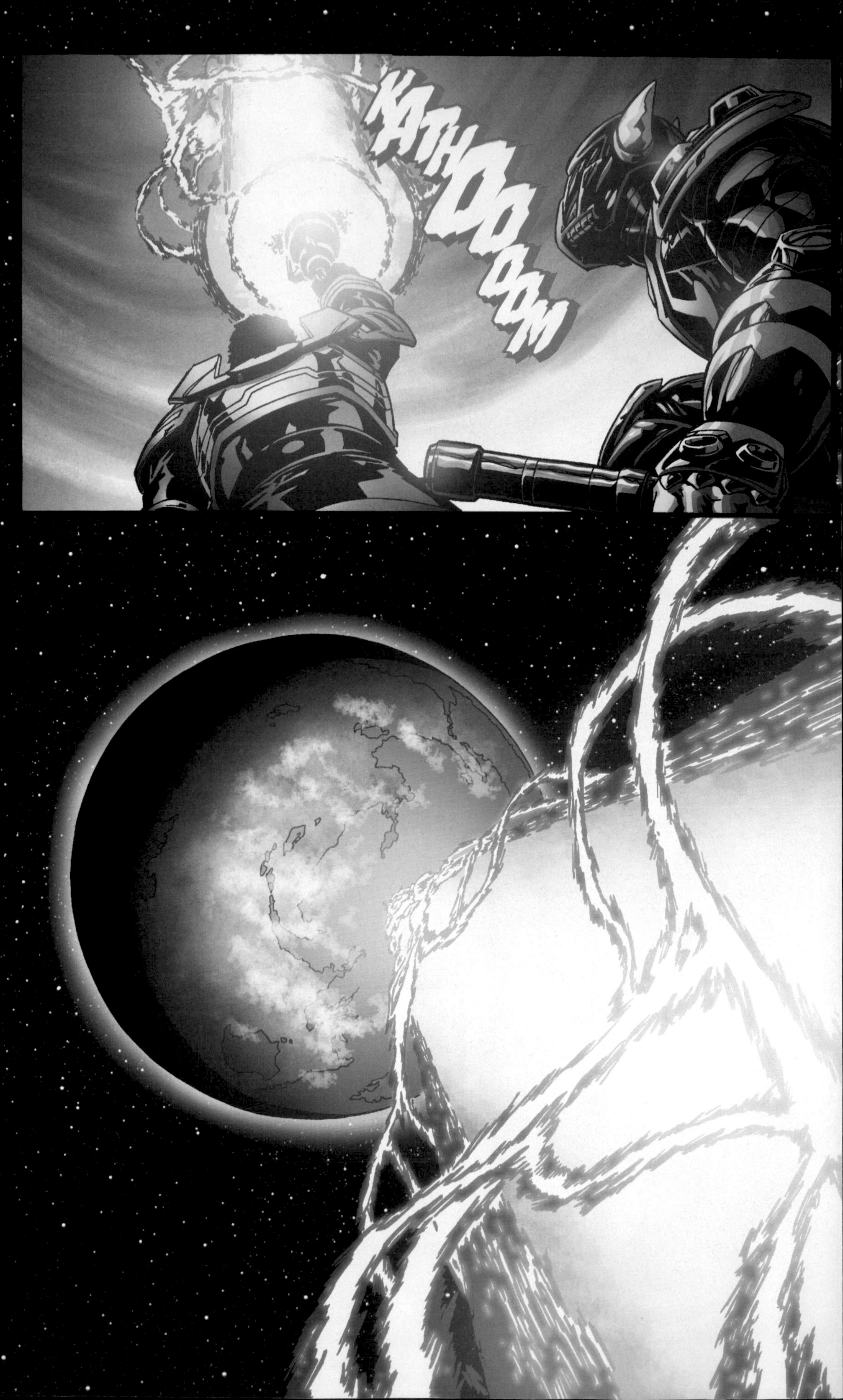
KATHOOOOM

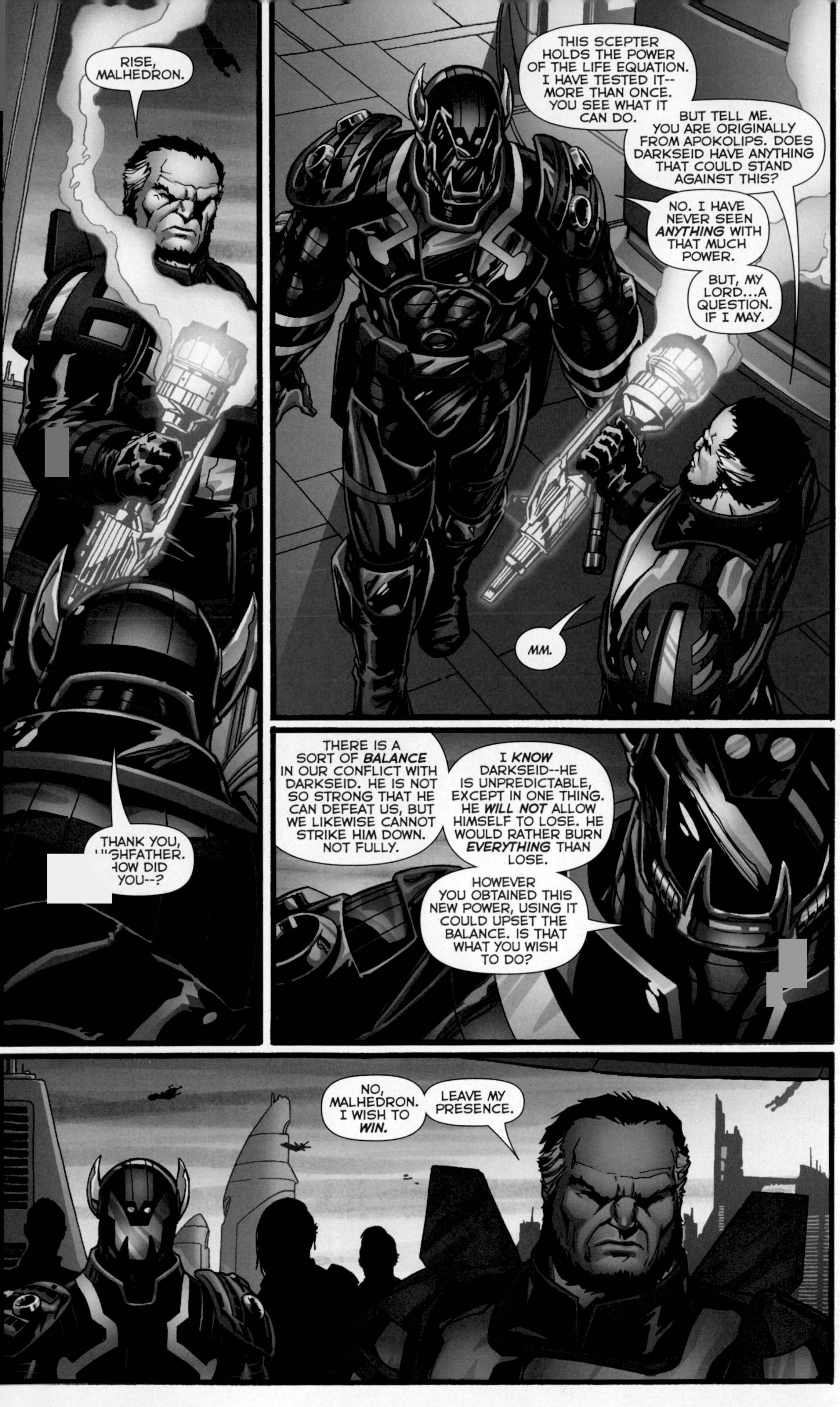
RISE, MALHEDRON.
THANK YOU, HIGHFATHER. HOW DID YOU--?
THIS SCEPTER HOLDS THE POWER OF THE LIFE EQUATION. I HAVE TESTED IT-- MORE THAN ONCE. YOU SEE WHAT IT CAN DO.
BUT TELL ME. YOU ARE ORIGINALLY FROM APOKOLIPS. DOES DARKSEID HAVE ANYTHING THAT COULD STAND AGAINST THIS?
NO. I HAVE NEVER SEEN *ANYTHING* WITH THAT MUCH POWER.
BUT, MY LORD...A QUESTION. IF I MAY.
MM.
THERE IS A SORT OF *BALANCE* IN OUR CONFLICT WITH DARKSEID. HE IS NOT SO STRONG THAT HE CAN DEFEAT US, BUT WE LIKEWISE CANNOT STRIKE HIM DOWN. NOT FULLY.
I *KNOW* DARKSEID--HE IS UNPREDICTABLE, EXCEPT IN ONE THING. HE *WILL NOT* ALLOW HIMSELF TO LOSE. HE WOULD RATHER BURN *EVERYTHING* THAN LOSE.
HOWEVER YOU OBTAINED THIS NEW POWER, USING IT COULD UPSET THE BALANCE. IS THAT WHAT YOU WISH TO DO?
NO, MALHEDRON. I WISH TO *WIN.*
LEAVE MY PRESENCE.

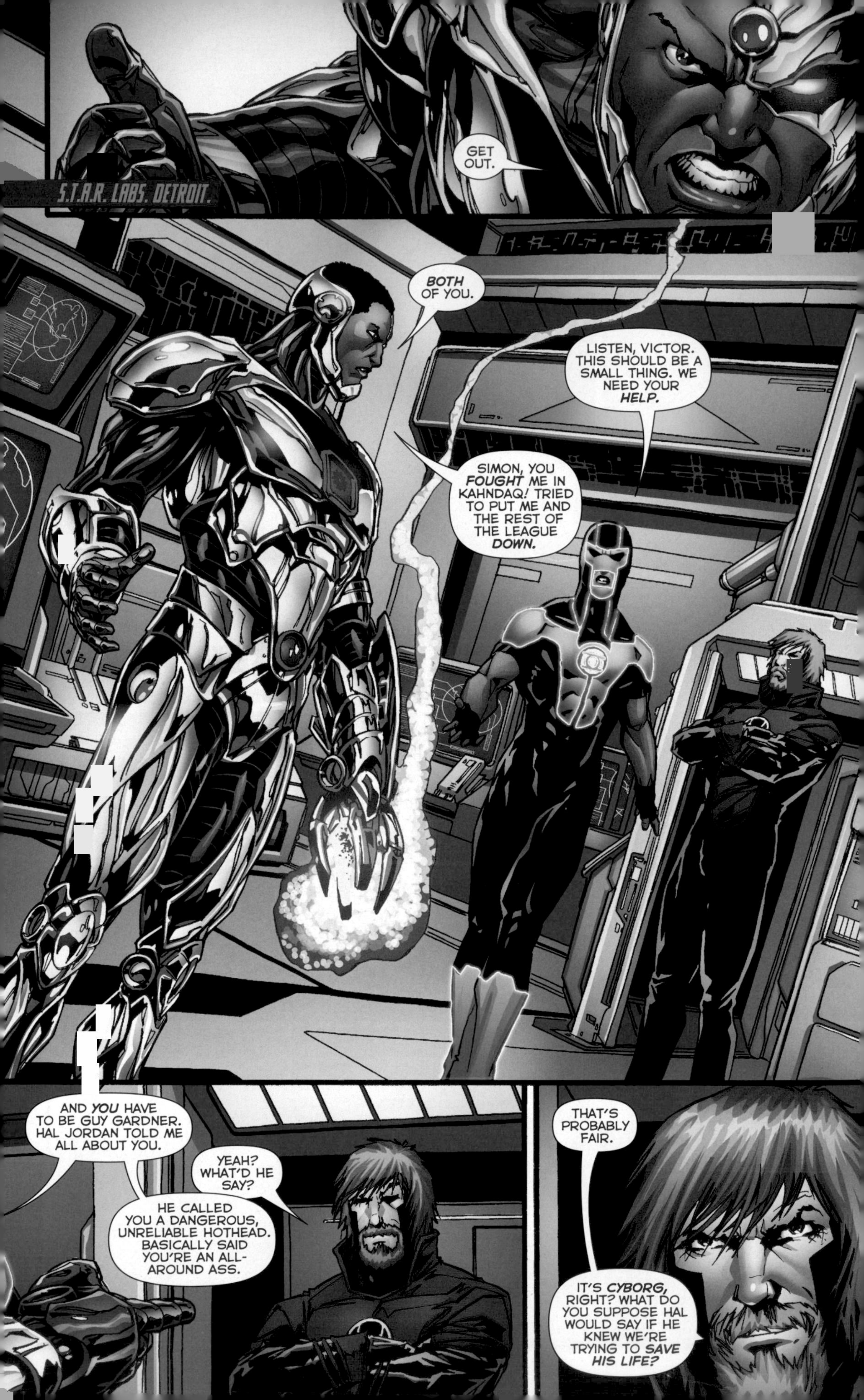
S.T.A.R. LABS. DETROIT.
GET OUT.
BOTH OF YOU.
LISTEN, VICTOR. THIS SHOULD BE A SMALL THING. WE NEED YOUR HELP.
SIMON, YOU FOUGHT ME IN KAHNDAQ! TRIED TO PUT ME AND THE REST OF THE LEAGUE DOWN.
AND YOU HAVE TO BE GUY GARDNER. HAL JORDAN TOLD ME ALL ABOUT YOU.
YEAH? WHAT'D HE SAY?
HE CALLED YOU A DANGEROUS, UNRELIABLE HOTHEAD. BASICALLY SAID YOU'RE AN ALL-AROUND ASS.
THAT'S PROBABLY FAIR.
IT'S CYBORG, RIGHT? WHAT DO YOU SUPPOSE HAL WOULD SAY IF HE KNEW WE'RE TRYING TO SAVE HIS LIFE?

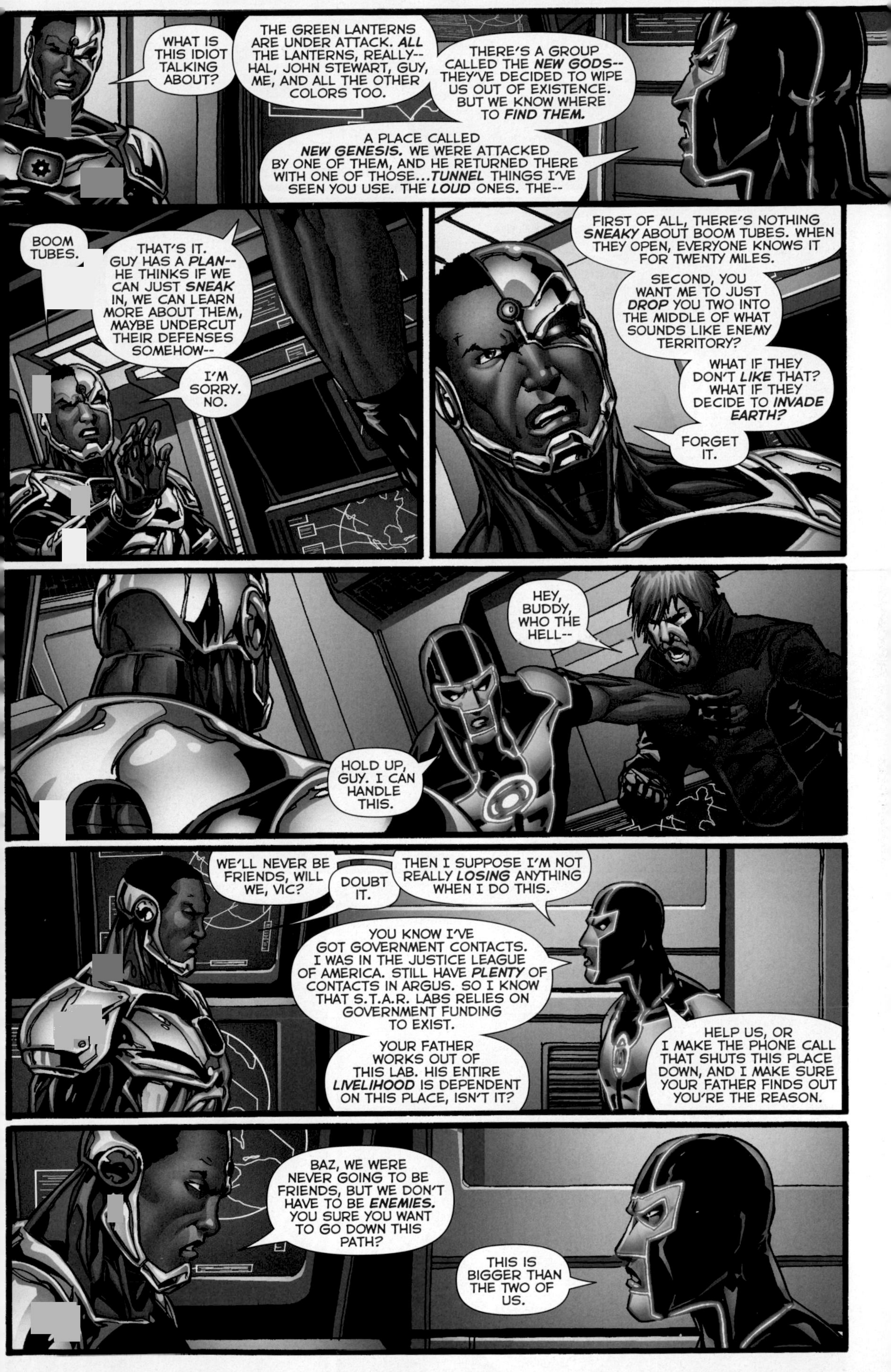
WHAT IS THIS IDIOT TALKING ABOUT?
THE GREEN LANTERNS ARE UNDER ATTACK. ALL THE LANTERNS, REALLY--HAL, JOHN STEWART, GUY, ME, AND ALL THE OTHER COLORS TOO.
THERE'S A GROUP CALLED THE NEW GODS--THEY'VE DECIDED TO WIPE US OUT OF EXISTENCE. BUT WE KNOW WHERE TO FIND THEM.
A PLACE CALLED NEW GENESIS. WE WERE ATTACKED BY ONE OF THEM, AND HE RETURNED THERE WITH ONE OF THOSE...TUNNEL THINGS I'VE SEEN YOU USE. THE LOUD ONES. THE--
BOOM TUBES.
THAT'S IT. GUY HAS A PLAN--HE THINKS IF WE CAN JUST SNEAK IN, WE CAN LEARN MORE ABOUT THEM, MAYBE UNDERCUT THEIR DEFENSES SOMEHOW--
I'M SORRY. NO.
FIRST OF ALL, THERE'S NOTHING SNEAKY ABOUT BOOM TUBES. WHEN THEY OPEN, EVERYONE KNOWS IT FOR TWENTY MILES.
SECOND, YOU WANT ME TO JUST DROP YOU TWO INTO THE MIDDLE OF WHAT SOUNDS LIKE ENEMY TERRITORY?
WHAT IF THEY DON'T LIKE THAT? WHAT IF THEY DECIDE TO INVADE EARTH?
FORGET IT.
HEY, BUDDY, WHO THE HELL--
HOLD UP, GUY. I CAN HANDLE THIS.
WE'LL NEVER BE FRIENDS, WILL WE, VIC?
DOUBT IT.
THEN I SUPPOSE I'M NOT REALLY LOSING ANYTHING WHEN I DO THIS.
YOU KNOW I'VE GOT GOVERNMENT CONTACTS. I WAS IN THE JUSTICE LEAGUE OF AMERICA. STILL HAVE PLENTY OF CONTACTS IN ARGUS. SO I KNOW THAT S.T.A.R. LABS RELIES ON GOVERNMENT FUNDING TO EXIST.
YOUR FATHER WORKS OUT OF THIS LAB. HIS ENTIRE LIVELIHOOD IS DEPENDENT ON THIS PLACE, ISN'T IT?
HELP US, OR I MAKE THE PHONE CALL THAT SHUTS THIS PLACE DOWN, AND I MAKE SURE YOUR FATHER FINDS OUT YOU'RE THE REASON.
BAZ, WE WERE NEVER GOING TO BE FRIENDS, BUT WE DON'T HAVE TO BE ENEMIES. YOU SURE YOU WANT TO GO DOWN THIS PATH?
THIS IS BIGGER THAN THE TWO OF US.

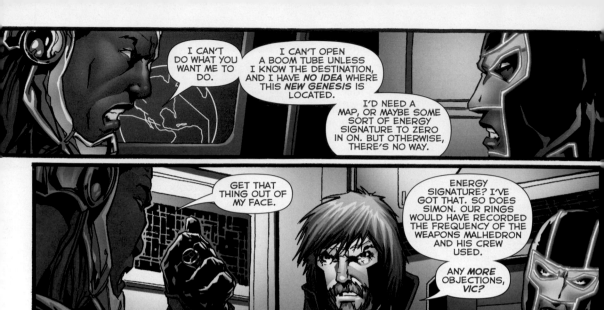

I CAN'T DO WHAT YOU WANT ME TO DO.

I CAN'T OPEN A BOOM TUBE UNLESS I KNOW THE DESTINATION, AND I HAVE *NO IDEA* WHERE THIS *NEW GENESIS* IS LOCATED.

I'D NEED A MAP, OR MAYBE SOME SORT OF ENERGY SIGNATURE TO ZERO IN ON. BUT OTHERWISE, THERE'S NO WAY.

GET THAT THING OUT OF MY FACE.

ENERGY SIGNATURE? I'VE GOT THAT. SO DOES SIMON. OUR RINGS WOULD HAVE RECORDED THE FREQUENCY OF THE WEAPONS MALHEDRON AND HIS CREW USED.

ANY *MORE* OBJECTIONS, *VIC*?

FINE. BUT YOU NEED TO KNOW IT WOULD BE A ONE-WAY TRIP. I CAN'T KEEP THE BOOM TUBE OPEN FOR MORE THAN HALF A SECOND--THE RISK OF SOMETHING COMING BACK THROUGH IS TOO BIG.

AND UNLESS YOU FIND ANOTHER WAY HOME, YOU'RE STUCK THERE.

HMM. GUY, MAYBE WE SHOULD--

THAT'S FINE, CYBORG. GET IT READY.

KEEP EARTH SAFE WHILE I'M GONE, BAZ. WOULDN'T WANT WORD GETTING OUT THAT THE REDS CAN'T DO THEIR *JOBS.*

I'M COMING WITH YOU, GUY.

I *TOLD* YOU, I'M DONE--

IT'S *MY* DECISION. NOT YOURS. BUT WE STILL NEED SOMEONE TO PROTECT THE EARTH.

WHAT DO YOU THINK *I'M* HERE FOR? NOT TO MENTION THE REST OF THE LEAGUE.

I'VE GOT IT.

I'M SURE YOU'RE *REAL TOUGH,* PAL, BUT NO OFFENSE--

--YOU AIN'T A LANTERN.

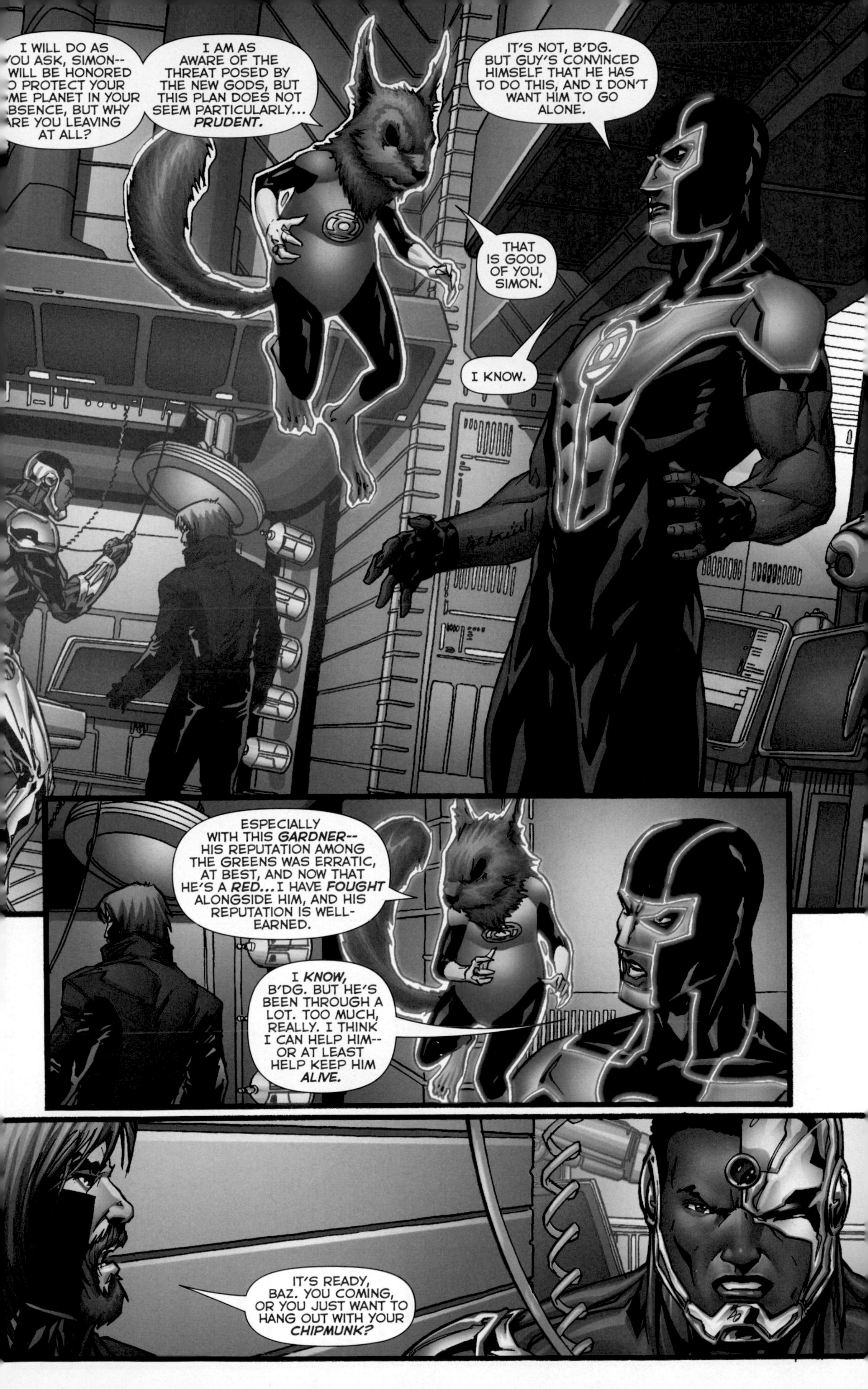
I WILL DO AS OU ASK, SIMON-- WILL BE HONORED O PROTECT YOUR ME PLANET IN YOUR BSENCE, BUT WHY ARE YOU LEAVING AT ALL?
I AM AS AWARE OF THE THREAT POSED BY THE NEW GODS, BUT THIS PLAN DOES NOT SEEM PARTICULARLY... PRUDENT.
IT'S NOT, B'DG. BUT GUY'S CONVINCED HIMSELF THAT HE HAS TO DO THIS, AND I DON'T WANT HIM TO GO ALONE.
THAT IS GOOD OF YOU, SIMON.
I KNOW.
ESPECIALLY WITH THIS GARDNER-- HIS REPUTATION AMONG THE GREENS WAS ERRATIC, AT BEST, AND NOW THAT HE'S A RED... I HAVE FOUGHT ALONGSIDE HIM, AND HIS REPUTATION IS WELL-EARNED.
I KNOW, B'DG. BUT HE'S BEEN THROUGH A LOT. TOO MUCH, REALLY. I THINK I CAN HELP HIM-- OR AT LEAST HELP KEEP HIM ALIVE.
IT'S READY, BAZ. YOU COMING, OR YOU JUST WANT TO HANG OUT WITH YOUR CHIPMUNK?

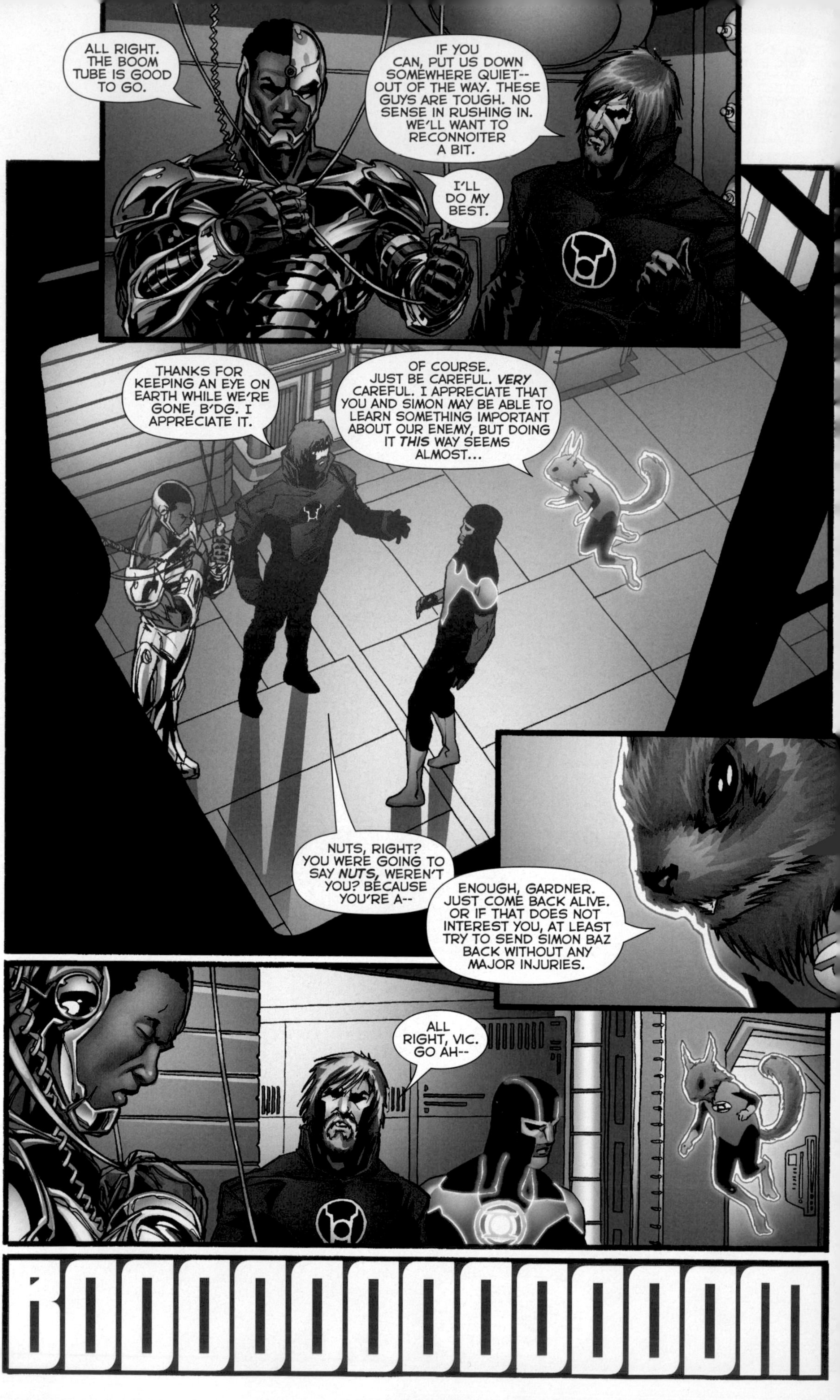
ALL RIGHT. THE BOOM TUBE IS GOOD TO GO.
IF YOU CAN, PUT US DOWN SOMEWHERE QUIET-- OUT OF THE WAY. THESE GUYS ARE TOUGH. NO SENSE IN RUSHING IN. WE'LL WANT TO RECONNOITER A BIT.
I'LL DO MY BEST.
THANKS FOR KEEPING AN EYE ON EARTH WHILE WE'RE GONE, B'DG. I APPRECIATE IT.
OF COURSE. JUST BE CAREFUL. *VERY* CAREFUL. I APPRECIATE THAT YOU AND SIMON MAY BE ABLE TO LEARN SOMETHING IMPORTANT ABOUT OUR ENEMY, BUT DOING IT *THIS* WAY SEEMS ALMOST...
NUTS, RIGHT? YOU WERE GOING TO SAY *NUTS,* WEREN'T YOU? BECAUSE YOU'RE A--
ENOUGH, GARDNER. JUST COME BACK ALIVE. OR IF THAT DOES NOT INTEREST YOU, AT LEAST TRY TO SEND SIMON BAZ BACK WITHOUT ANY MAJOR INJURIES.
ALL RIGHT, VIC. GO AH--
BOOOOOOOOOOOOOM

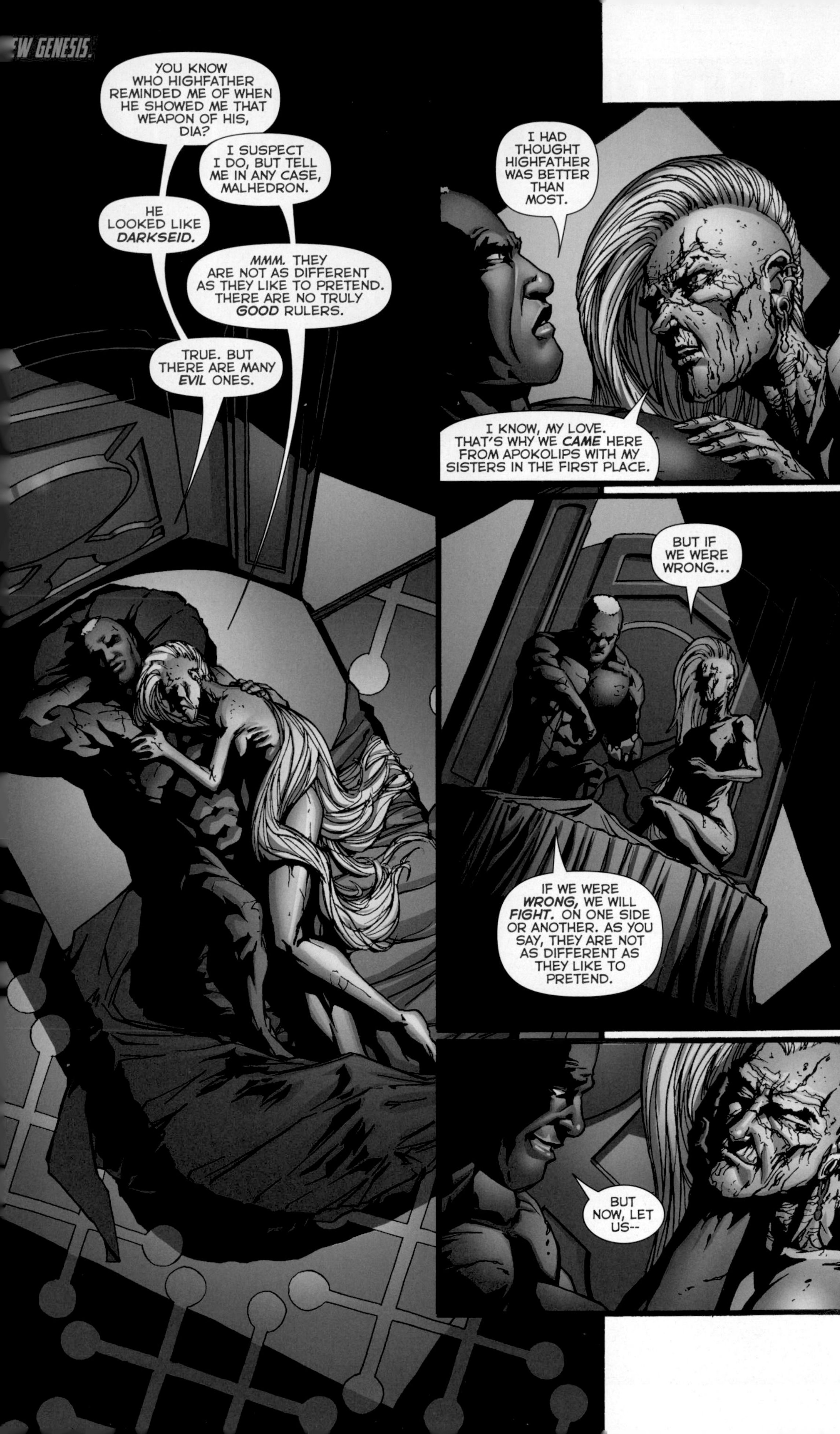

EW GENESIS.
YOU KNOW WHO HIGHFATHER REMINDED ME OF WHEN HE SHOWED ME THAT WEAPON OF HIS, DIA?
I SUSPECT I DO, BUT TELL ME IN ANY CASE, MALHEDRON.
HE LOOKED LIKE DARKSEID.
MMM. THEY ARE NOT AS DIFFERENT AS THEY LIKE TO PRETEND. THERE ARE NO TRULY GOOD RULERS.
TRUE. BUT THERE ARE MANY EVIL ONES.
I HAD THOUGHT HIGHFATHER WAS BETTER THAN MOST.
I KNOW, MY LOVE. THAT'S WHY WE CAME HERE FROM APOKOLIPS WITH MY SISTERS IN THE FIRST PLACE.
BUT IF WE WERE WRONG...
IF WE WERE WRONG, WE WILL FIGHT. ON ONE SIDE OR ANOTHER. AS YOU SAY, THEY ARE NOT AS DIFFERENT AS THEY LIKE TO PRETEND.
BUT NOW, LET US--

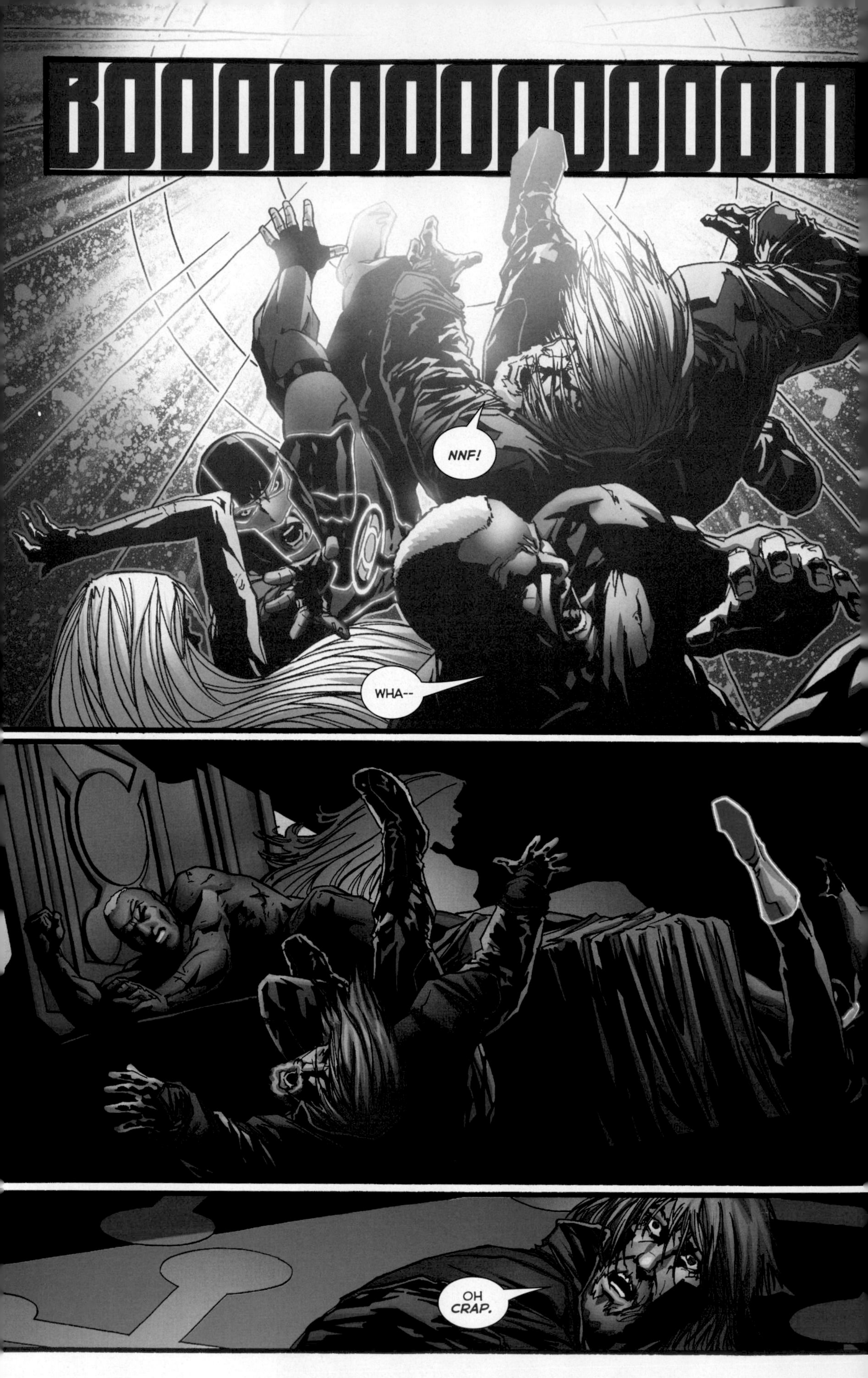
BOOOOOOOOOOOOOM
NNF!
WHA--
OH CRAP.

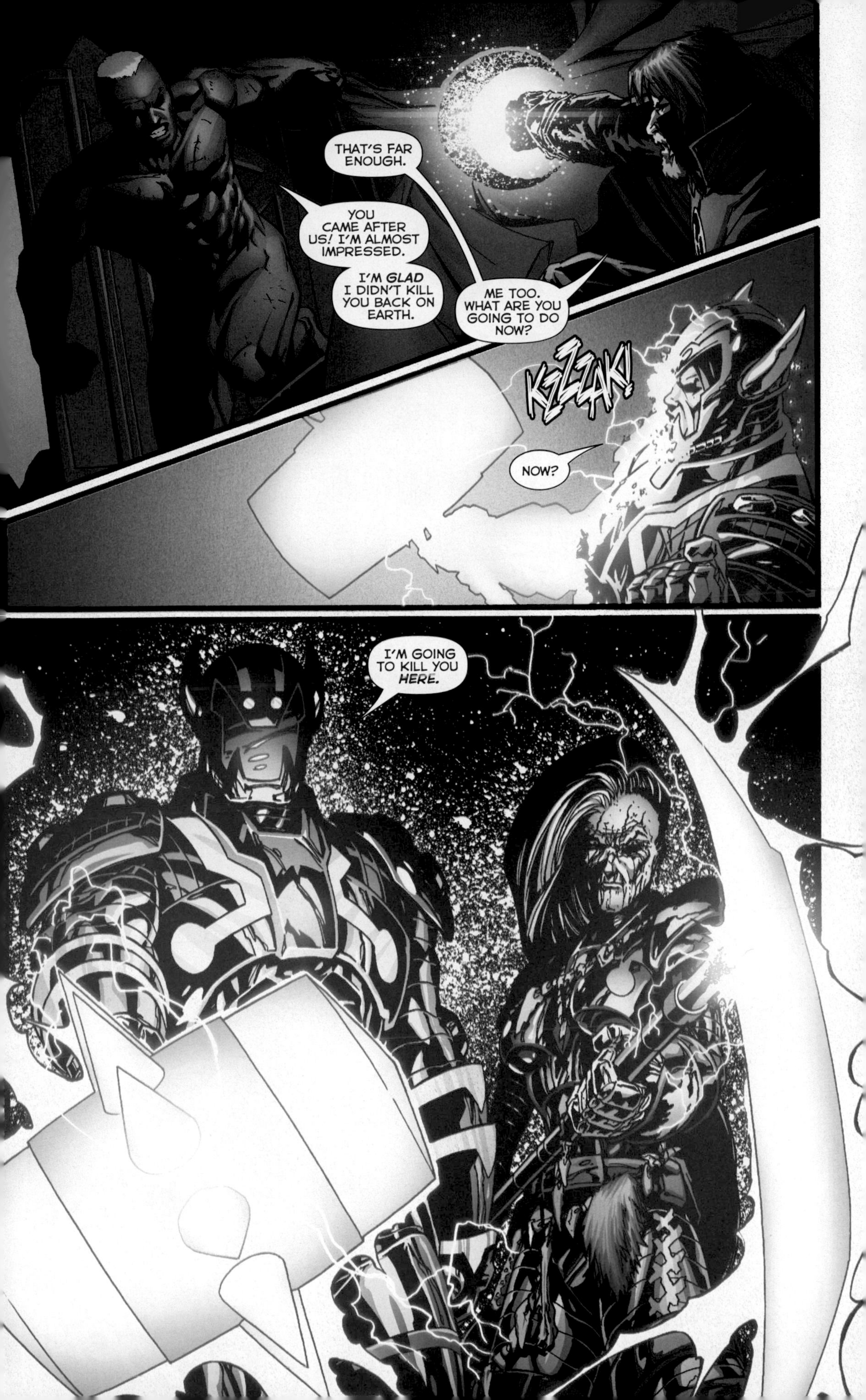
THAT'S FAR ENOUGH.
YOU CAME AFTER US! I'M ALMOST IMPRESSED.
I'M *GLAD* I DIDN'T KILL YOU BACK ON EARTH.
ME TOO. WHAT ARE YOU GOING TO DO NOW?
KZZZAK!
NOW?
I'M GOING TO KILL YOU *HERE.*

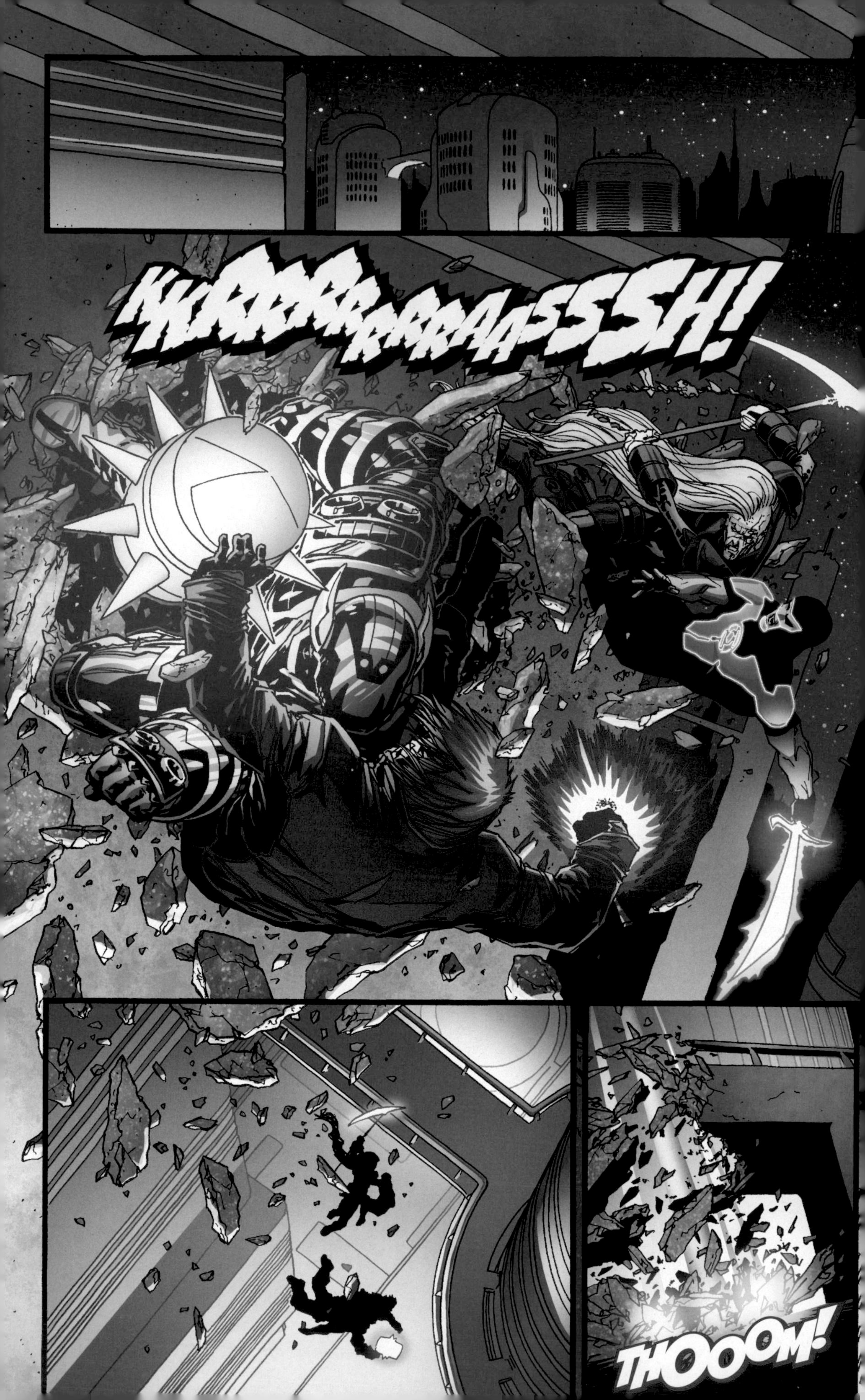
KKRRRRRRRAASSSH!
THOOOM!

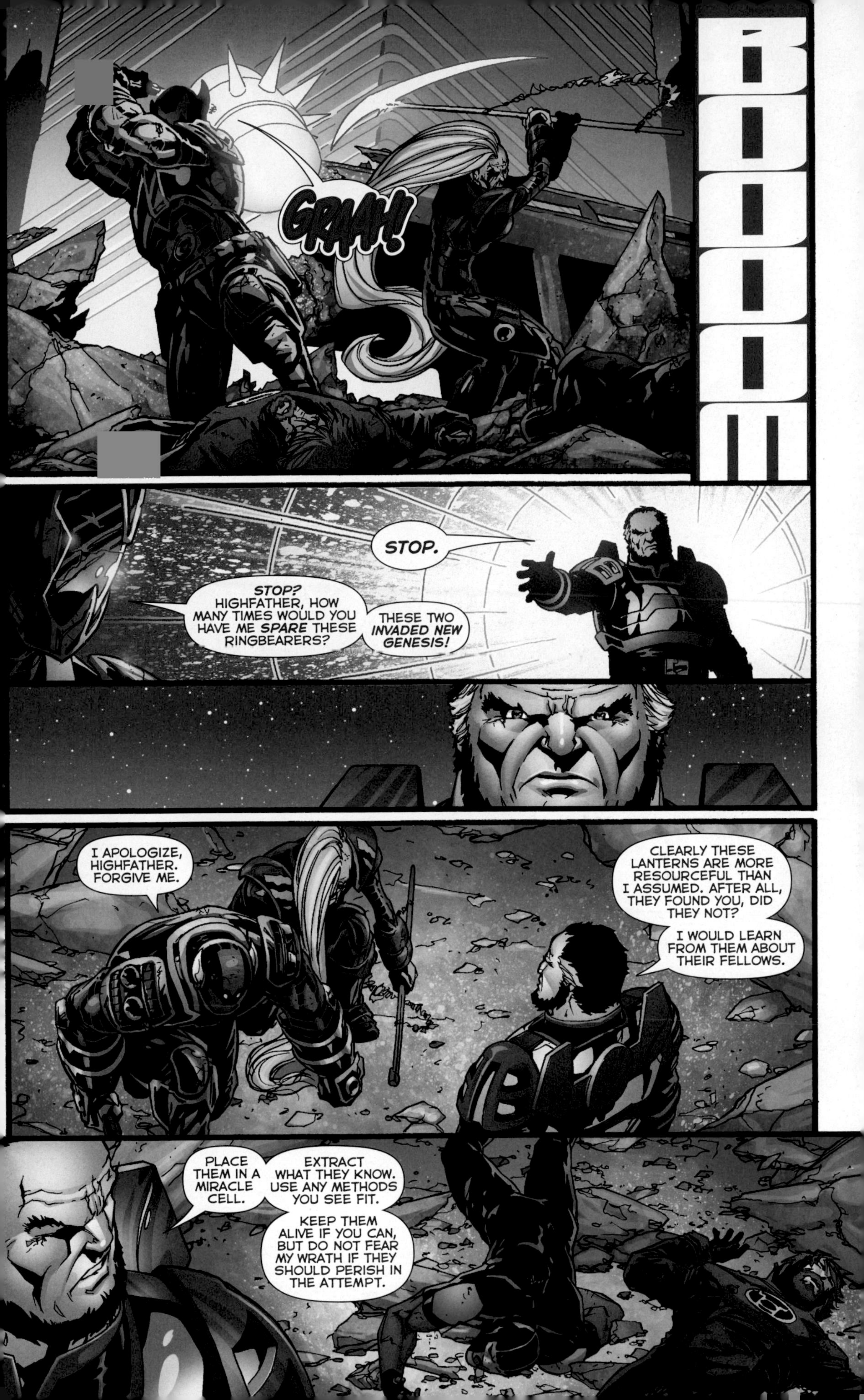

GRAAAH!
BOOOOM
STOP.
STOP? HIGHFATHER, HOW MANY TIMES WOULD YOU HAVE ME SPARE THESE RINGBEARERS?
THESE TWO INVADED NEW GENESIS!
I APOLOGIZE, HIGHFATHER. FORGIVE ME.
CLEARLY THESE LANTERNS ARE MORE RESOURCEFUL THAN I ASSUMED. AFTER ALL, THEY FOUND YOU, DID THEY NOT?
I WOULD LEARN FROM THEM ABOUT THEIR FELLOWS.
PLACE THEM IN A MIRACLE CELL.
EXTRACT WHAT THEY KNOW. USE ANY METHODS YOU SEE FIT.
KEEP THEM ALIVE IF YOU CAN, BUT DO NOT FEAR MY WRATH IF THEY SHOULD PERISH IN THE ATTEMPT.

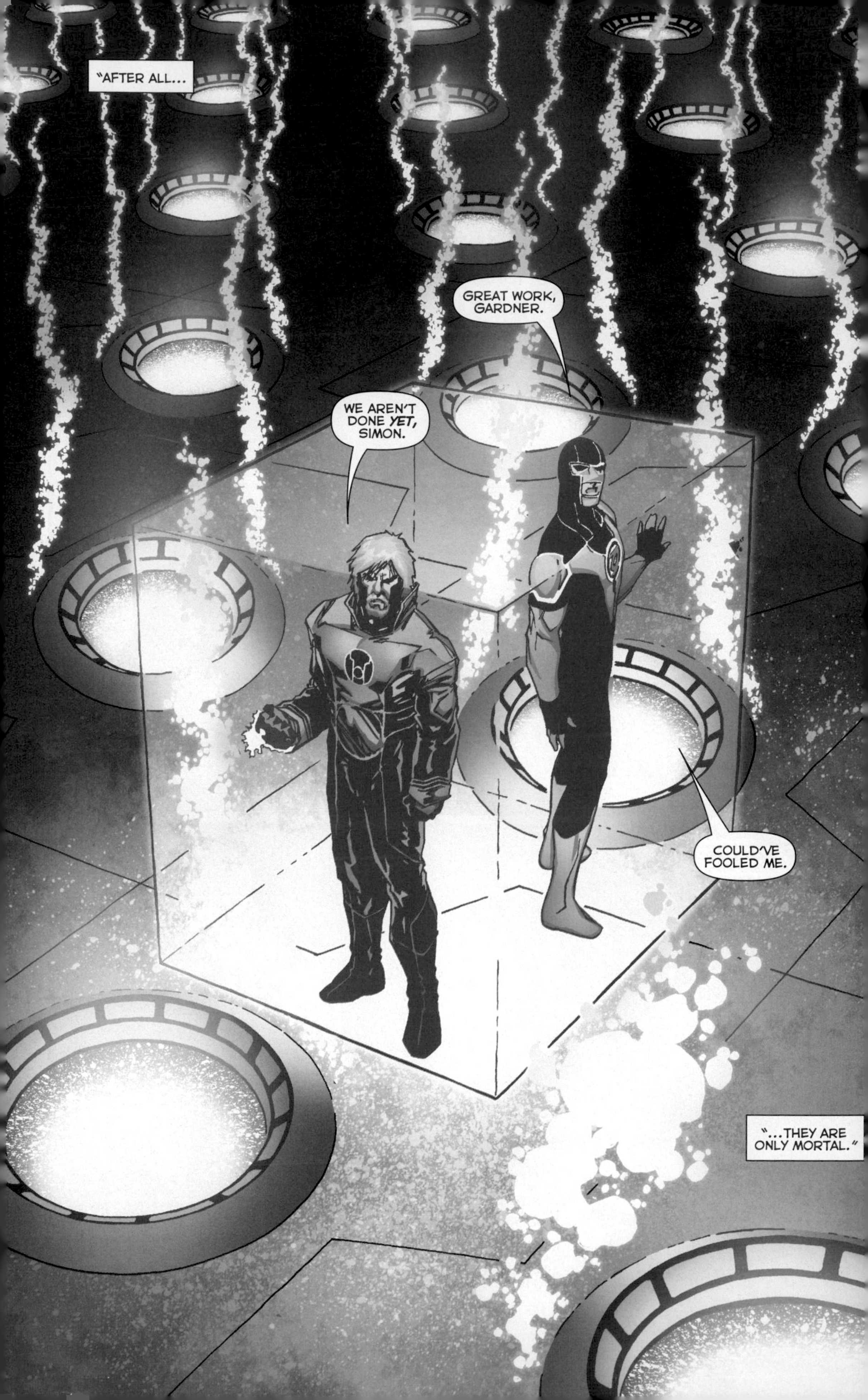
"AFTER ALL...
GREAT WORK, GARDNER.
WE AREN'T DONE *YET,* SIMON.
COULD'VE FOOLED ME.
"...THEY ARE ONLY MORTAL."

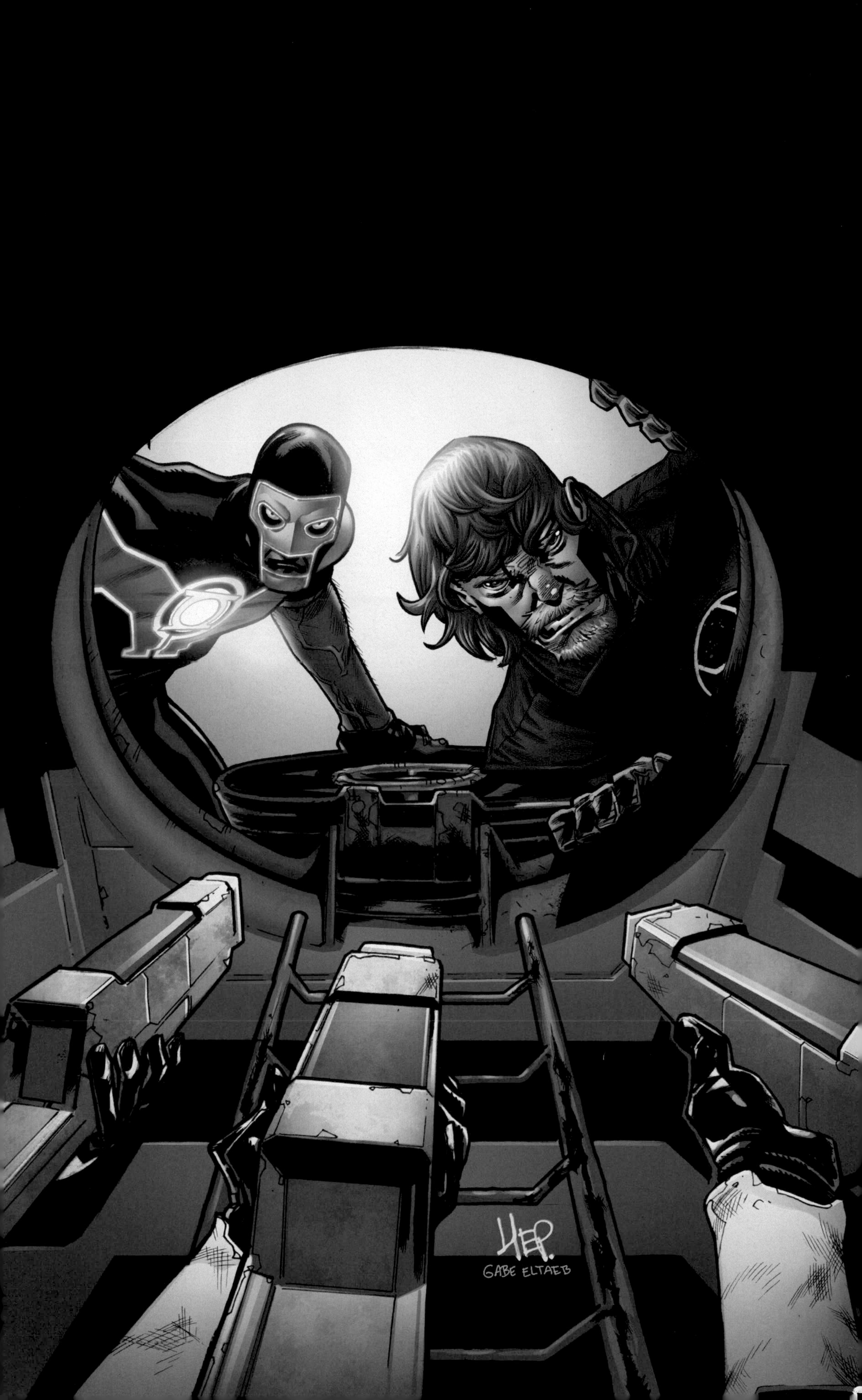
GABE ELTAEB

GODHEAD ACT III, PART IV: FORGED IN BLOOD

CHARLES SOULE writer **J. CALAFIORE** artist **GABE ELTAEB** colorist **DAVE SHARPE** letterer
cover art by **SCOTT HEPBURN** and **GABE ELTAEB**

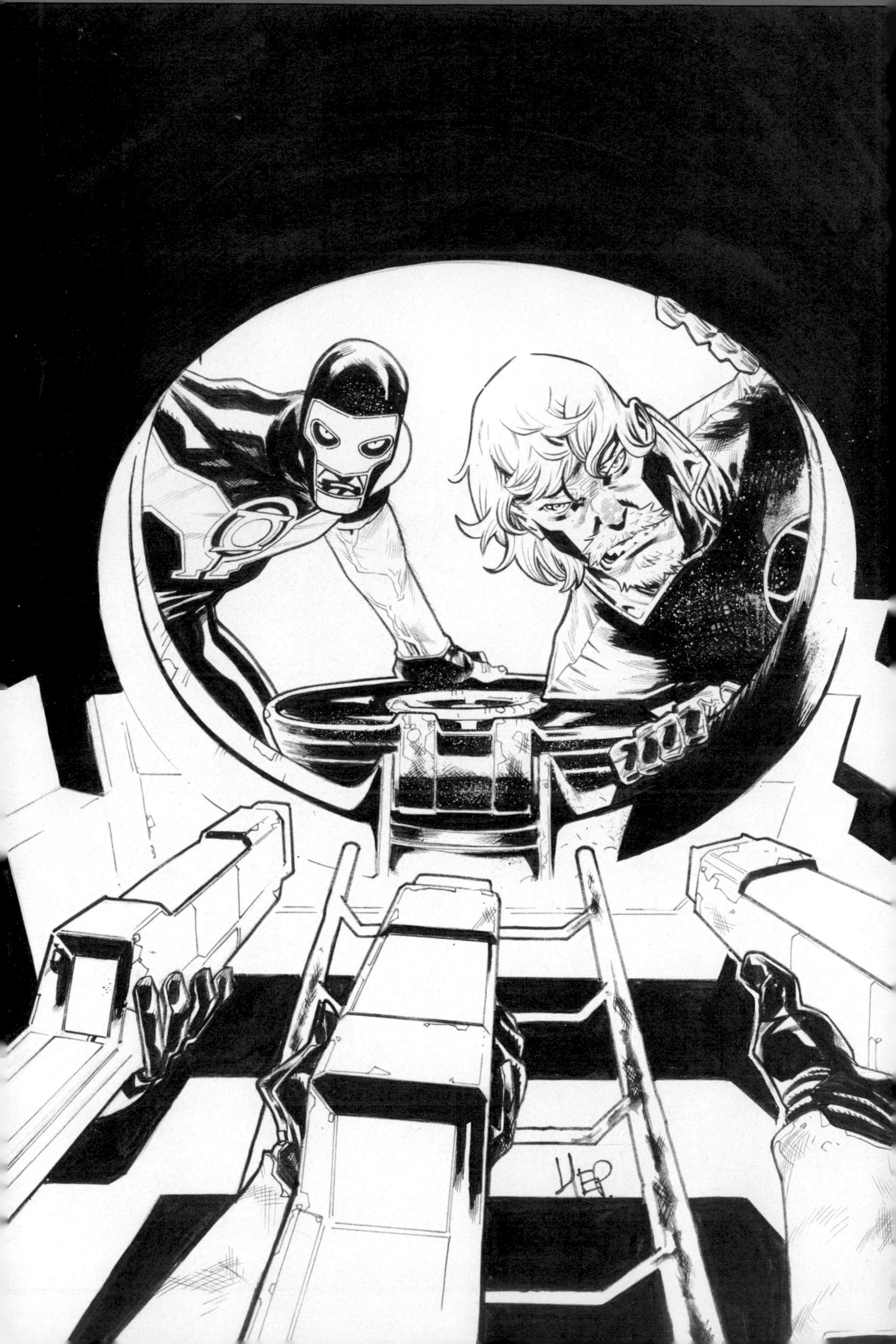

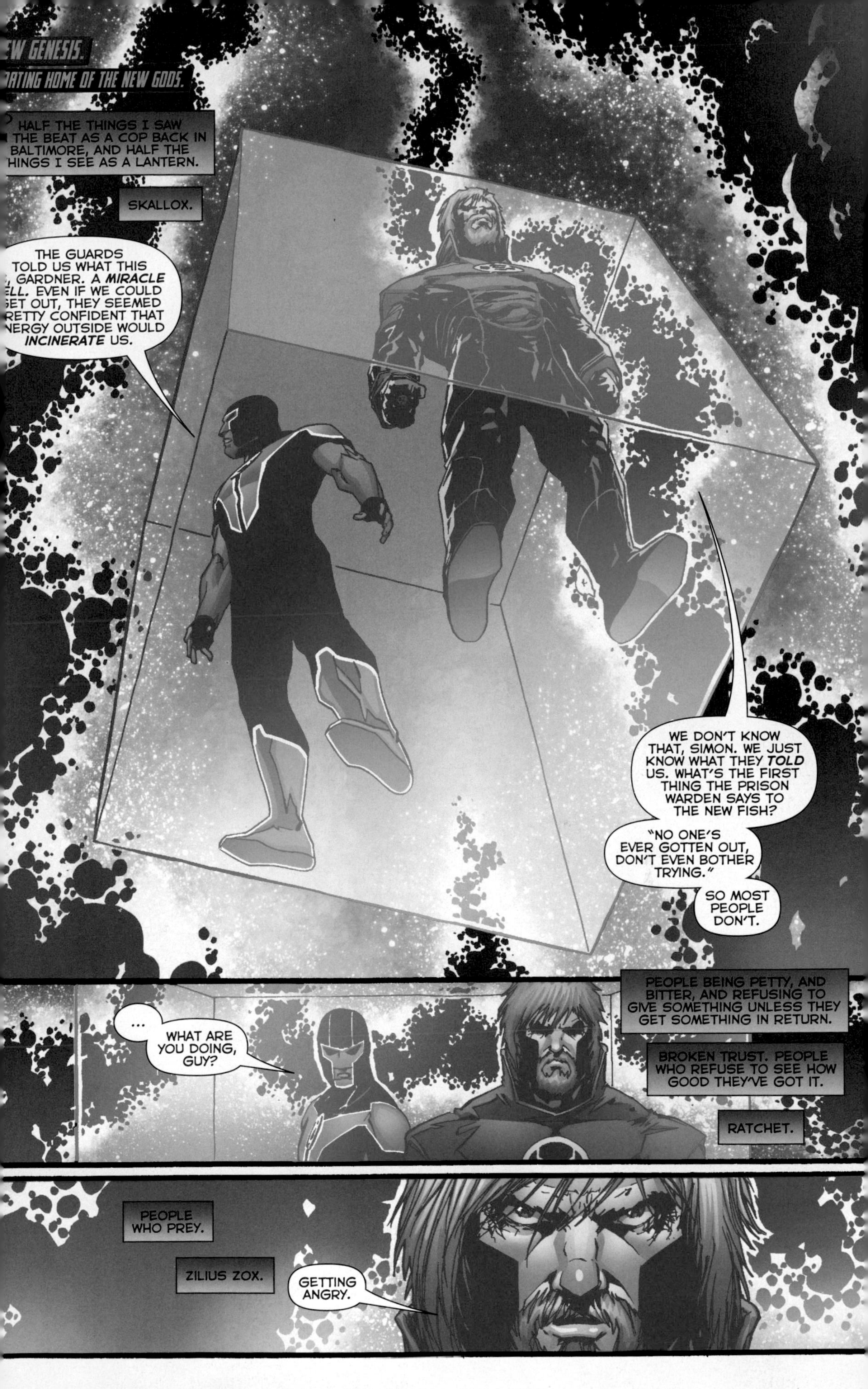
EW GENESIS.
ATING HOME OF THE NEW GODS.
HALF THE THINGS I SAW THE BEAT AS A COP BACK IN BALTIMORE, AND HALF THE HINGS I SEE AS A LANTERN.
SKALLOX.
THE GUARDS TOLD US WHAT THIS , GARDNER. A *MIRACLE* ELL. EVEN IF WE COULD ET OUT, THEY SEEMED RETTY CONFIDENT THAT NERGY OUTSIDE WOULD *INCINERATE* US.
WE DON'T KNOW THAT, SIMON. WE JUST KNOW WHAT THEY *TOLD* US. WHAT'S THE FIRST THING THE PRISON WARDEN SAYS TO THE NEW FISH?
"NO ONE'S EVER GOTTEN OUT, DON'T EVEN BOTHER TRYING."
SO MOST PEOPLE DON'T.
PEOPLE BEING PETTY, AND BITTER, AND REFUSING TO GIVE SOMETHING UNLESS THEY GET SOMETHING IN RETURN.
...
WHAT ARE YOU DOING, GUY?
BROKEN TRUST. PEOPLE WHO REFUSE TO SEE HOW GOOD THEY'VE GOT IT.
RATCHET.
PEOPLE WHO PREY.
ZILIUS ZOX.
GETTING ANGRY.

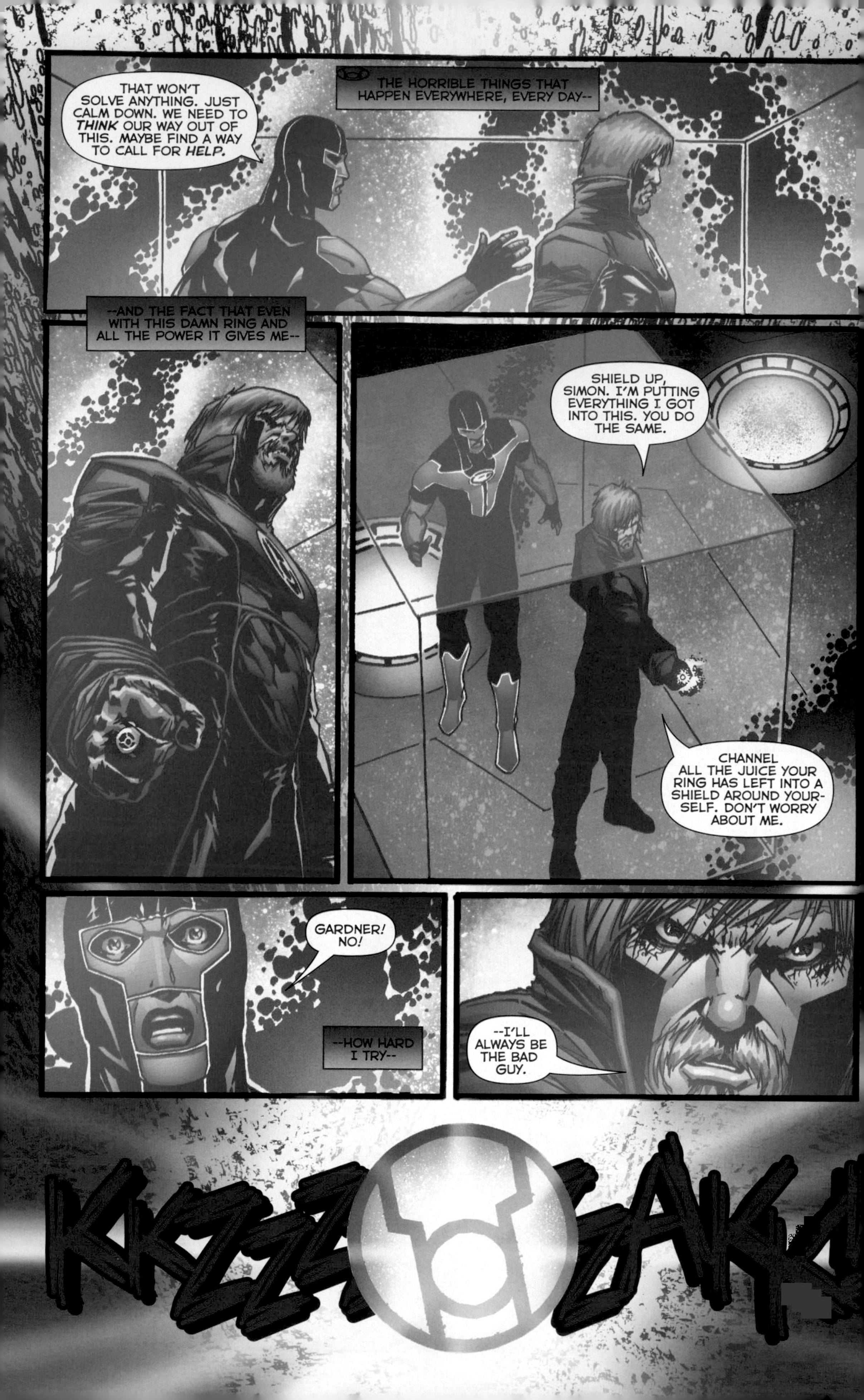
THE HORRIBLE THINGS THAT HAPPEN EVERYWHERE, EVERY DAY--
THAT WON'T SOLVE ANYTHING. JUST CALM DOWN. WE NEED TO THINK OUR WAY OUT OF THIS. MAYBE FIND A WAY TO CALL FOR HELP.
--AND THE FACT THAT EVEN WITH THIS DAMN RING AND ALL THE POWER IT GIVES ME--
SHIELD UP, SIMON. I'M PUTTING EVERYTHING I GOT INTO THIS. YOU DO THE SAME.
CHANNEL ALL THE JUICE YOUR RING HAS LEFT INTO A SHIELD AROUND YOURSELF. DON'T WORRY ABOUT ME.
GARDNER! NO!
--HOW HARD I TRY--
--I'LL ALWAYS BE THE BAD GUY.
KKZZZ ZAKK

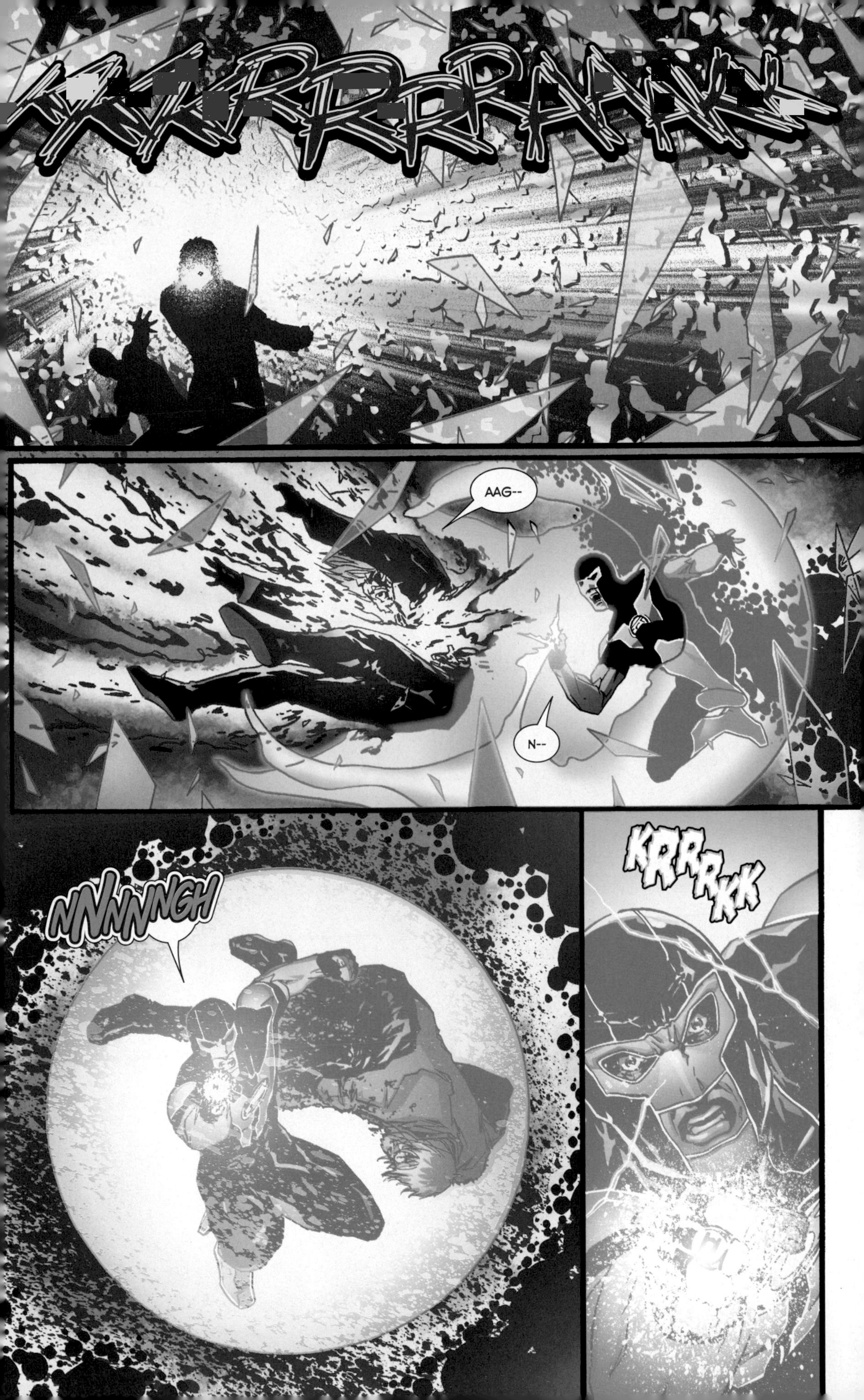
AAG--
N--
NNNNNGH
KRRRKK

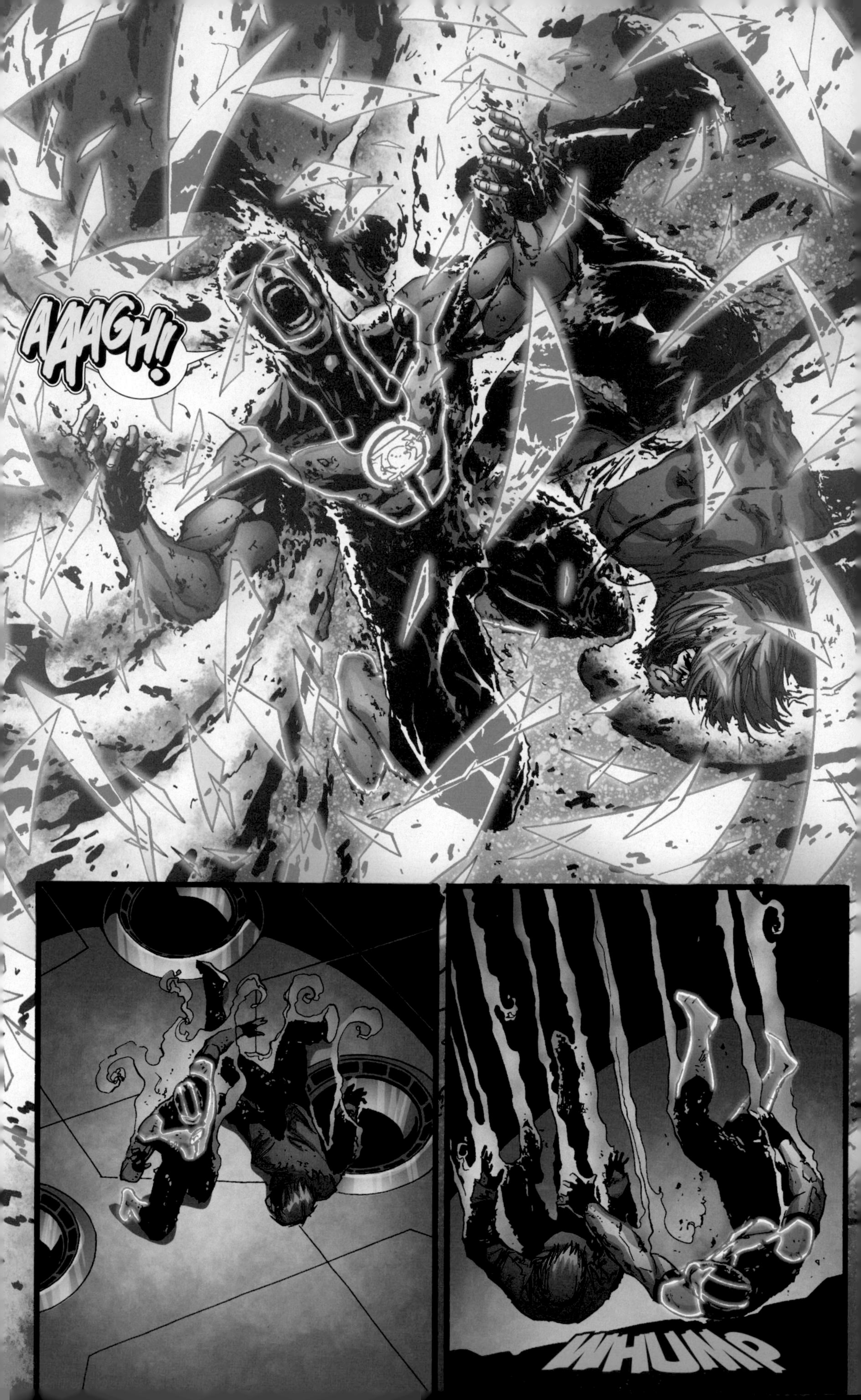
AAAGH!
WHUMP

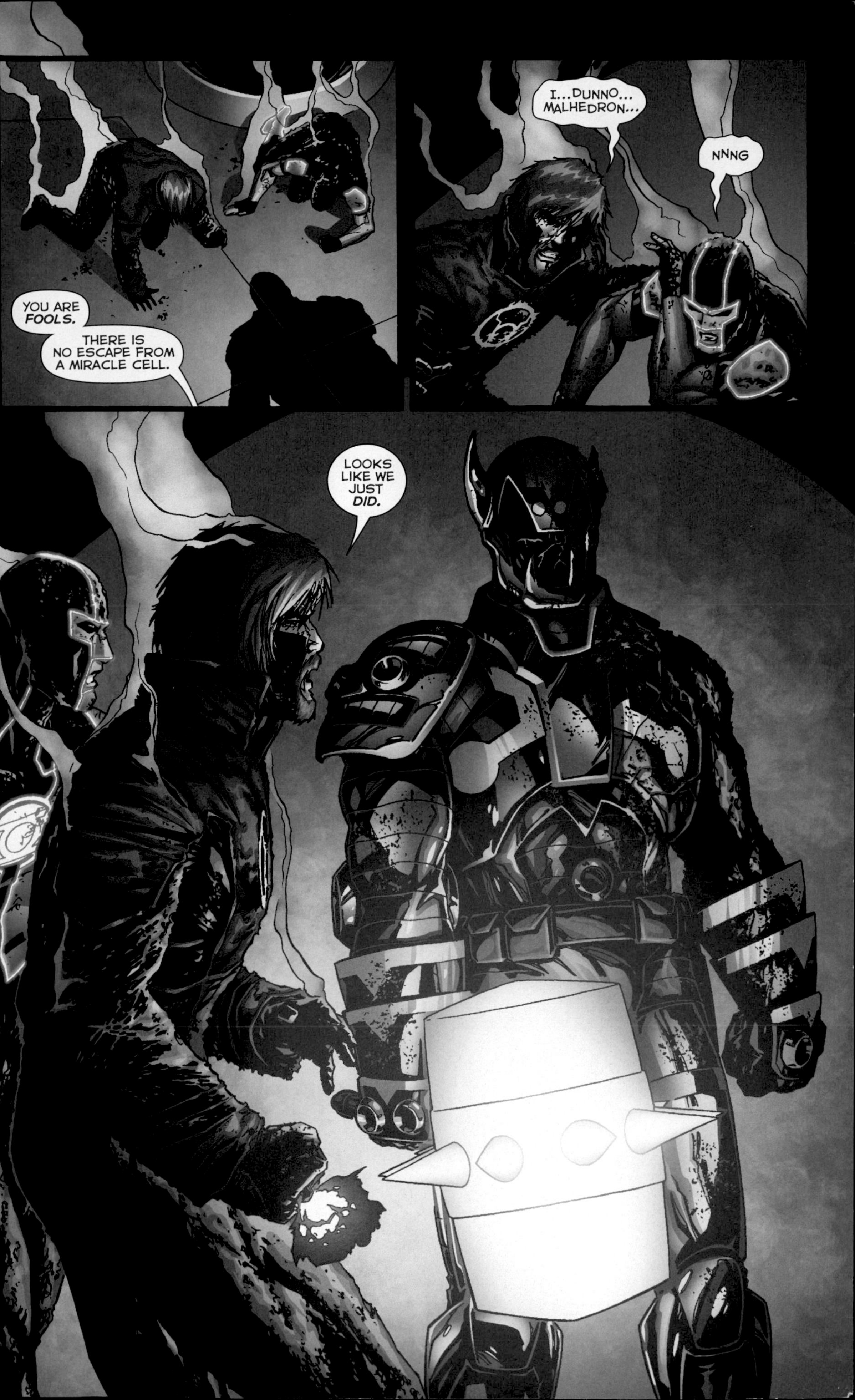
YOU ARE FOOLS.
THERE IS NO ESCAPE FROM A MIRACLE CELL.
I...DUNNO... MALHEDRON...
NNNG
LOOKS LIKE WE JUST DID.

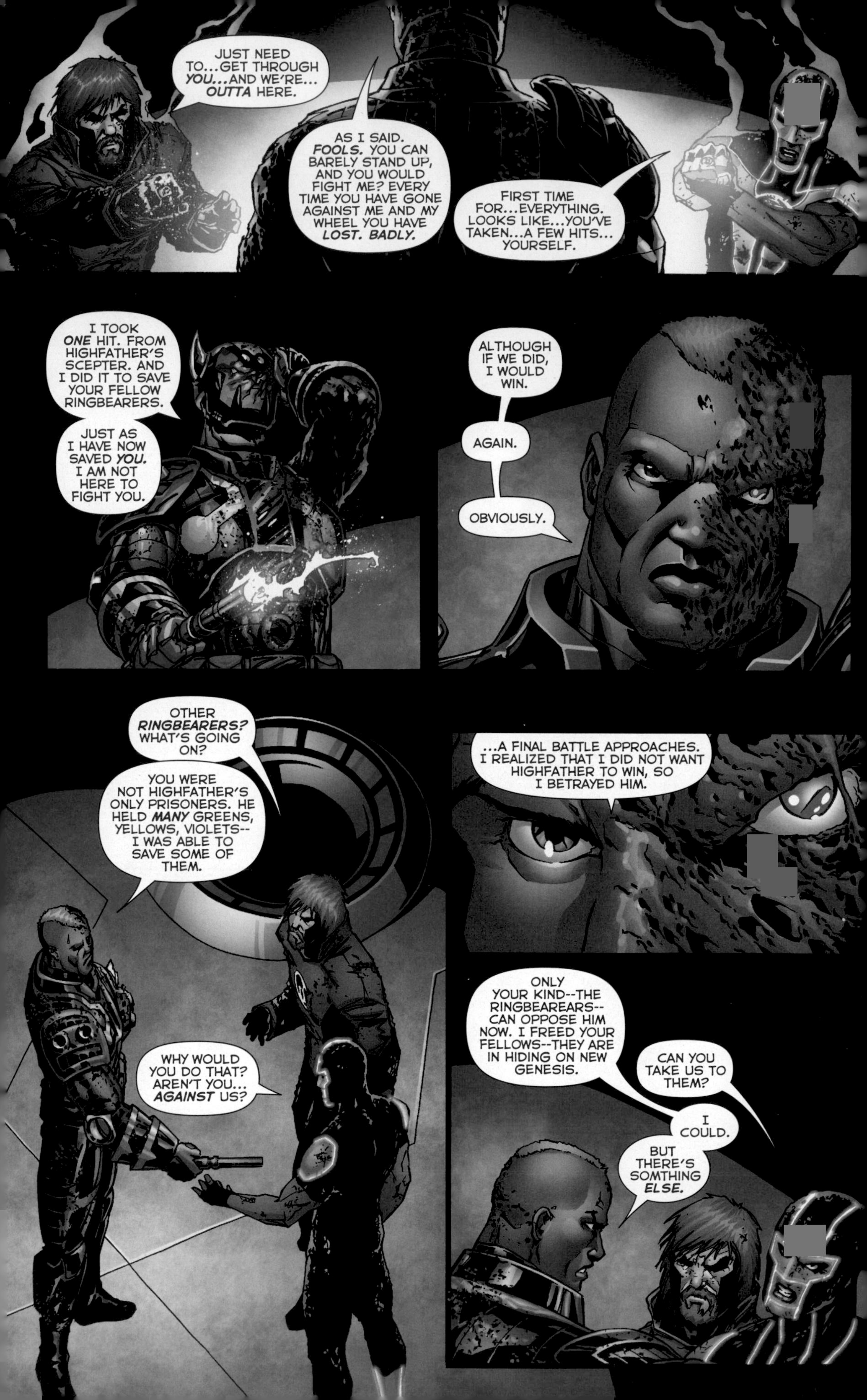
JUST NEED TO...GET THROUGH YOU...AND WE'RE... OUTTA HERE.
AS I SAID. FOOLS. YOU CAN BARELY STAND UP, AND YOU WOULD FIGHT ME? EVERY TIME YOU HAVE GONE AGAINST ME AND MY WHEEL YOU HAVE LOST. BADLY.
FIRST TIME FOR...EVERYTHING. LOOKS LIKE...YOU'VE TAKEN...A FEW HITS... YOURSELF.
I TOOK ONE HIT. FROM HIGHFATHER'S SCEPTER. AND I DID IT TO SAVE YOUR FELLOW RINGBEARERS.
JUST AS I HAVE NOW SAVED YOU. I AM NOT HERE TO FIGHT YOU.
ALTHOUGH IF WE DID, I WOULD WIN.
AGAIN.
OBVIOUSLY.
OTHER RINGBEARERS? WHAT'S GOING ON?
YOU WERE NOT HIGHFATHER'S ONLY PRISONERS. HE HELD MANY GREENS, YELLOWS, VIOLETS-- I WAS ABLE TO SAVE SOME OF THEM.
WHY WOULD YOU DO THAT? AREN'T YOU... AGAINST US?
...A FINAL BATTLE APPROACHES. I REALIZED THAT I DID NOT WANT HIGHFATHER TO WIN, SO I BETRAYED HIM.
ONLY YOUR KIND--THE RINGBEARERS--CAN OPPOSE HIM NOW. I FREED YOUR FELLOWS--THEY ARE IN HIDING ON NEW GENESIS.
CAN YOU TAKE US TO THEM?
I COULD.
BUT THERE'S SOMTHING ELSE.

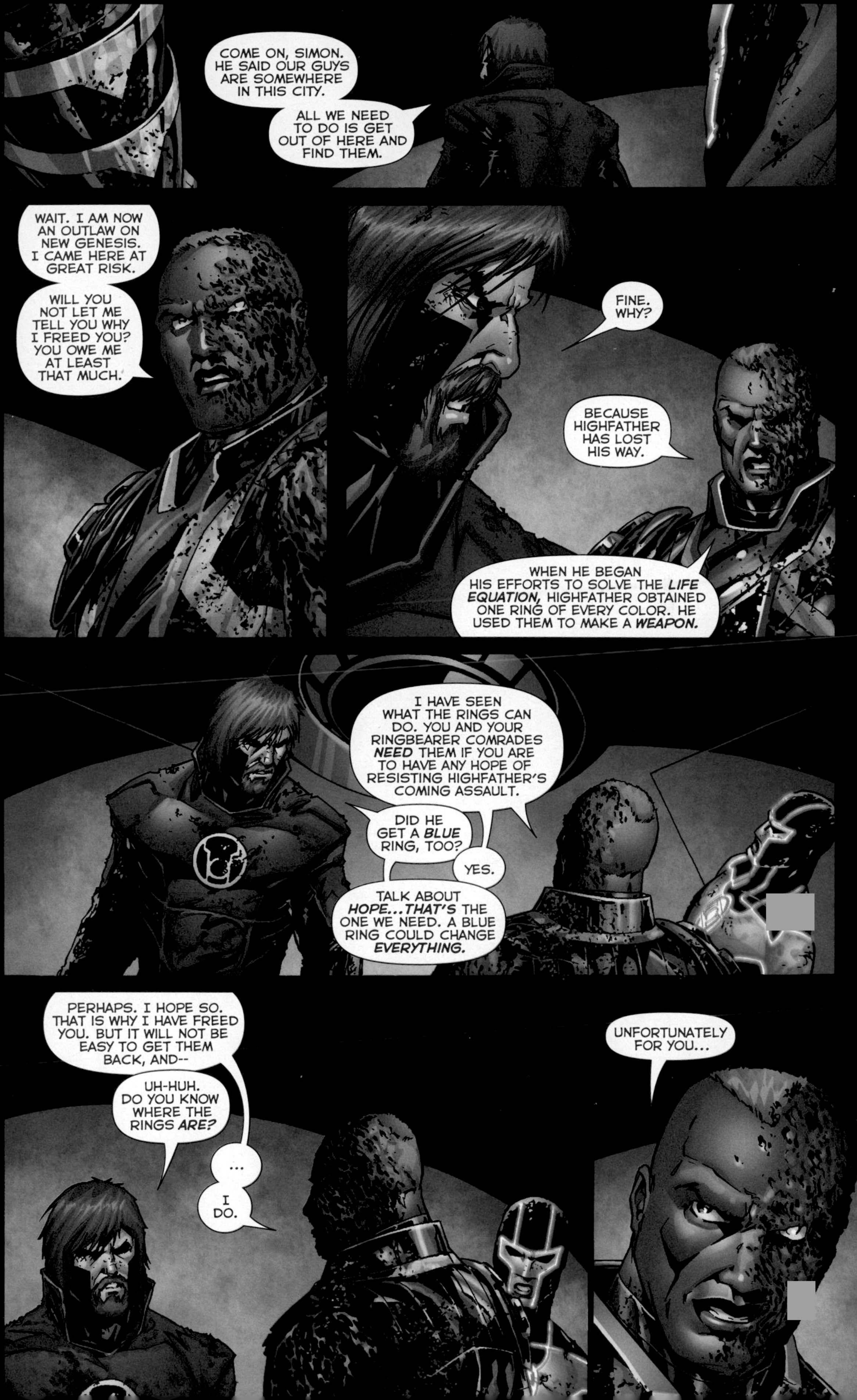
COME ON, SIMON. HE SAID OUR GUYS ARE SOMEWHERE IN THIS CITY.
ALL WE NEED TO DO IS GET OUT OF HERE AND FIND THEM.
WAIT. I AM NOW AN OUTLAW ON NEW GENESIS. I CAME HERE AT GREAT RISK.
WILL YOU NOT LET ME TELL YOU WHY I FREED YOU? YOU OWE ME AT LEAST THAT MUCH.
FINE. WHY?
BECAUSE HIGHFATHER HAS LOST HIS WAY.
WHEN HE BEGAN HIS EFFORTS TO SOLVE THE *LIFE EQUATION,* HIGHFATHER OBTAINED ONE RING OF EVERY COLOR. HE USED THEM TO MAKE A *WEAPON.*
I HAVE SEEN WHAT THE RINGS CAN DO. YOU AND YOUR RINGBEARER COMRADES *NEED* THEM IF YOU ARE TO HAVE ANY HOPE OF RESISTING HIGHFATHER'S COMING ASSAULT.
DID HE GET A *BLUE* RING, TOO?
YES.
TALK ABOUT *HOPE...THAT'S* THE ONE WE NEED. A BLUE RING COULD CHANGE *EVERYTHING.*
PERHAPS. I HOPE SO. THAT IS WHY I HAVE FREED YOU. BUT IT WILL NOT BE EASY TO GET THEM BACK, AND--
UH-HUH. DO YOU KNOW WHERE THE RINGS *ARE?*
...
I DO.
UNFORTUNATELY FOR YOU...

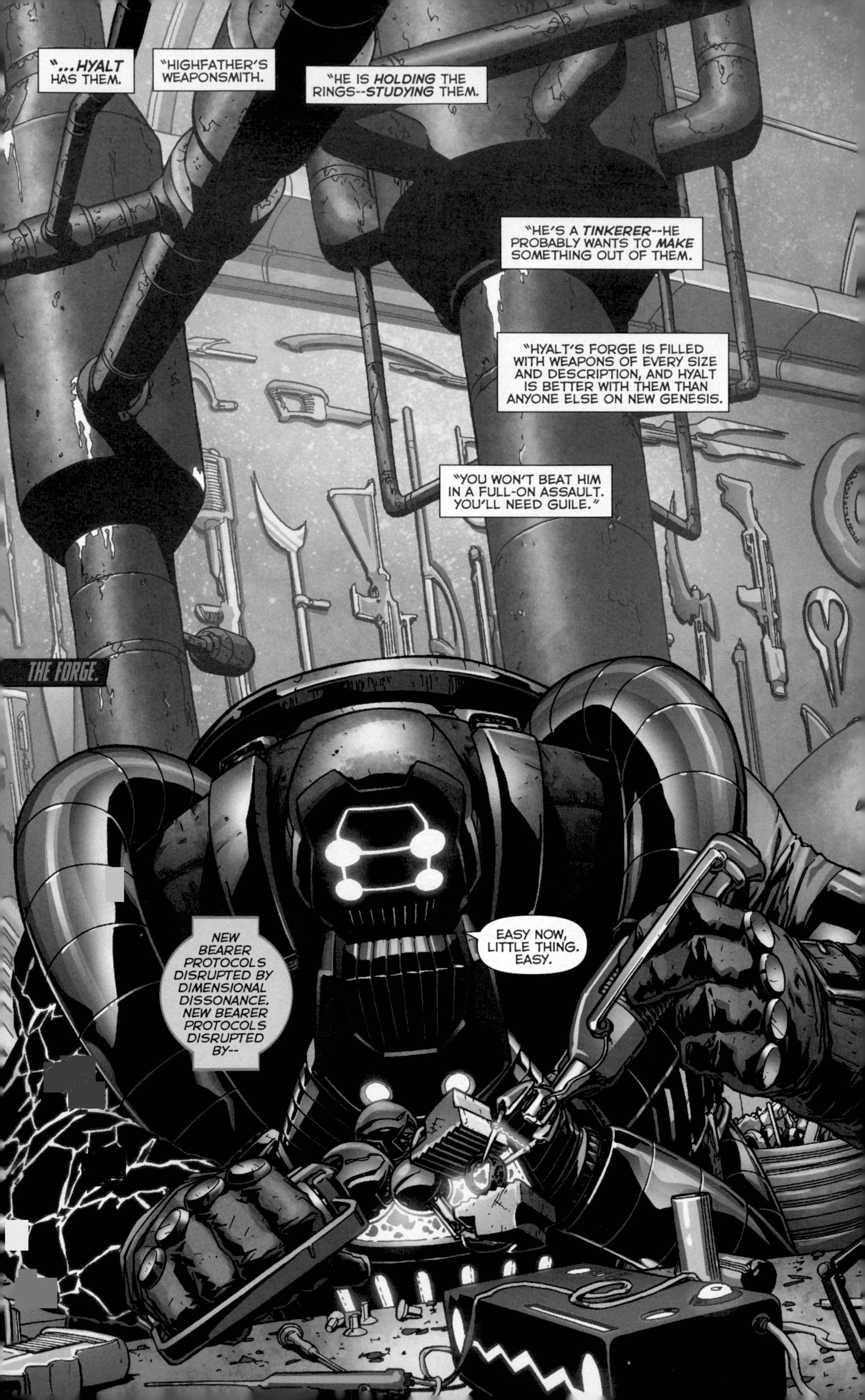
"...HYALT HAS THEM.
"HIGHFATHER'S WEAPONSMITH.
"HE IS HOLDING THE RINGS--STUDYING THEM.
"HE'S A TINKERER--HE PROBABLY WANTS TO MAKE SOMETHING OUT OF THEM.
"HYALT'S FORGE IS FILLED WITH WEAPONS OF EVERY SIZE AND DESCRIPTION, AND HYALT IS BETTER WITH THEM THAN ANYONE ELSE ON NEW GENESIS.
"YOU WON'T BEAT HIM IN A FULL-ON ASSAULT. YOU'LL NEED GUILE."
THE FORGE.
NEW BEARER PROTOCOLS DISRUPTED BY DIMENSIONAL DISSONANCE. NEW BEARER PROTOCOLS DISRUPTED BY--
EASY NOW, LITTLE THING. EASY.

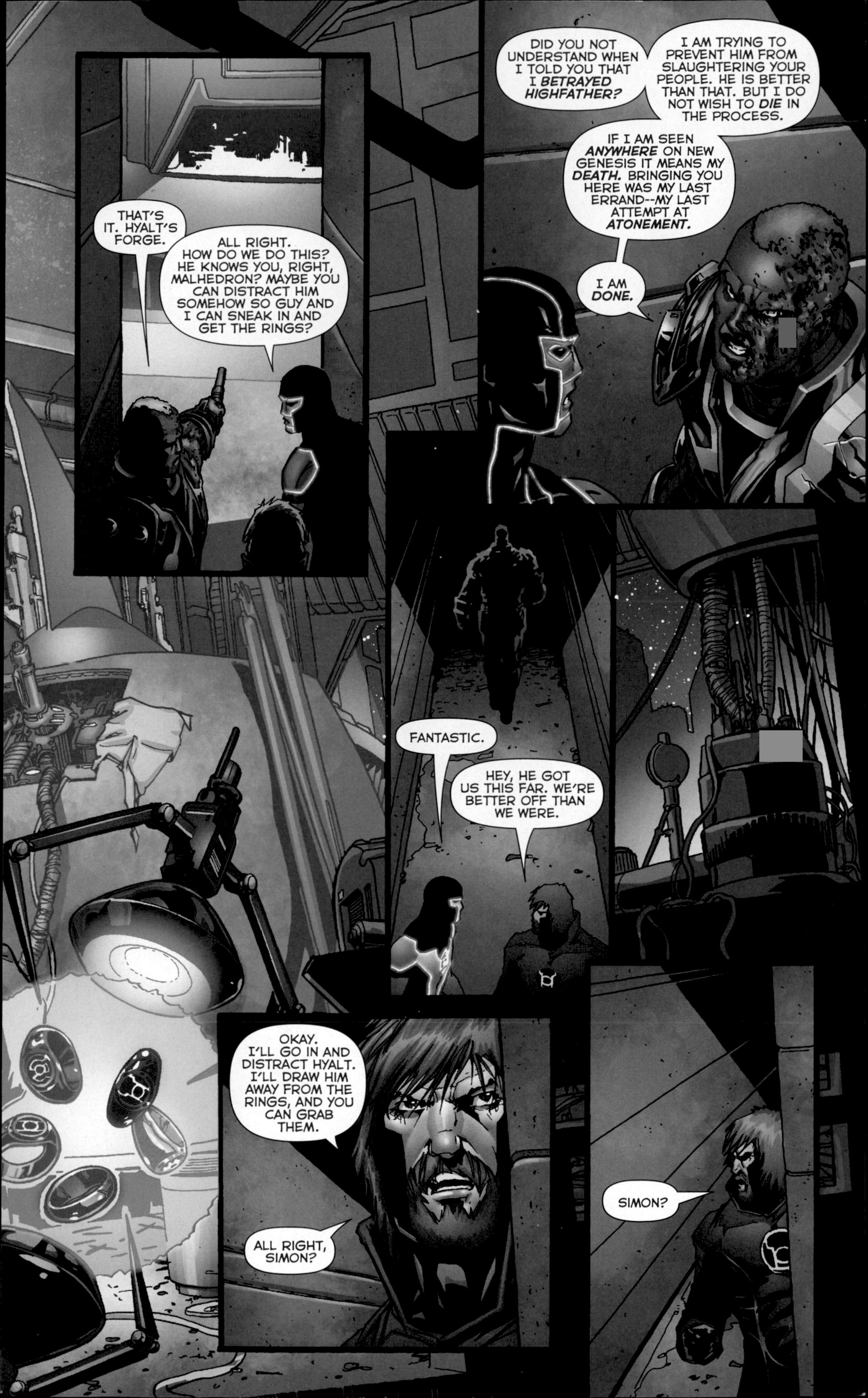

THAT'S IT. HYALT'S FORGE.
ALL RIGHT. HOW DO WE DO THIS? HE KNOWS YOU, RIGHT, MALHEDRON? MAYBE YOU CAN DISTRACT HIM SOMEHOW SO GUY AND I CAN SNEAK IN AND GET THE RINGS?
DID YOU NOT UNDERSTAND WHEN I TOLD YOU THAT I BETRAYED HIGHFATHER?
I AM TRYING TO PREVENT HIM FROM SLAUGHTERING YOUR PEOPLE. HE IS BETTER THAN THAT. BUT I DO NOT WISH TO DIE IN THE PROCESS.
IF I AM SEEN ANYWHERE ON NEW GENESIS IT MEANS MY DEATH. BRINGING YOU HERE WAS MY LAST ERRAND--MY LAST ATTEMPT AT ATONEMENT.
I AM DONE.
FANTASTIC.
HEY, HE GOT US THIS FAR. WE'RE BETTER OFF THAN WE WERE.
OKAY. I'LL GO IN AND DISTRACT HYALT. I'LL DRAW HIM AWAY FROM THE RINGS, AND YOU CAN GRAB THEM.
ALL RIGHT, SIMON?
SIMON?

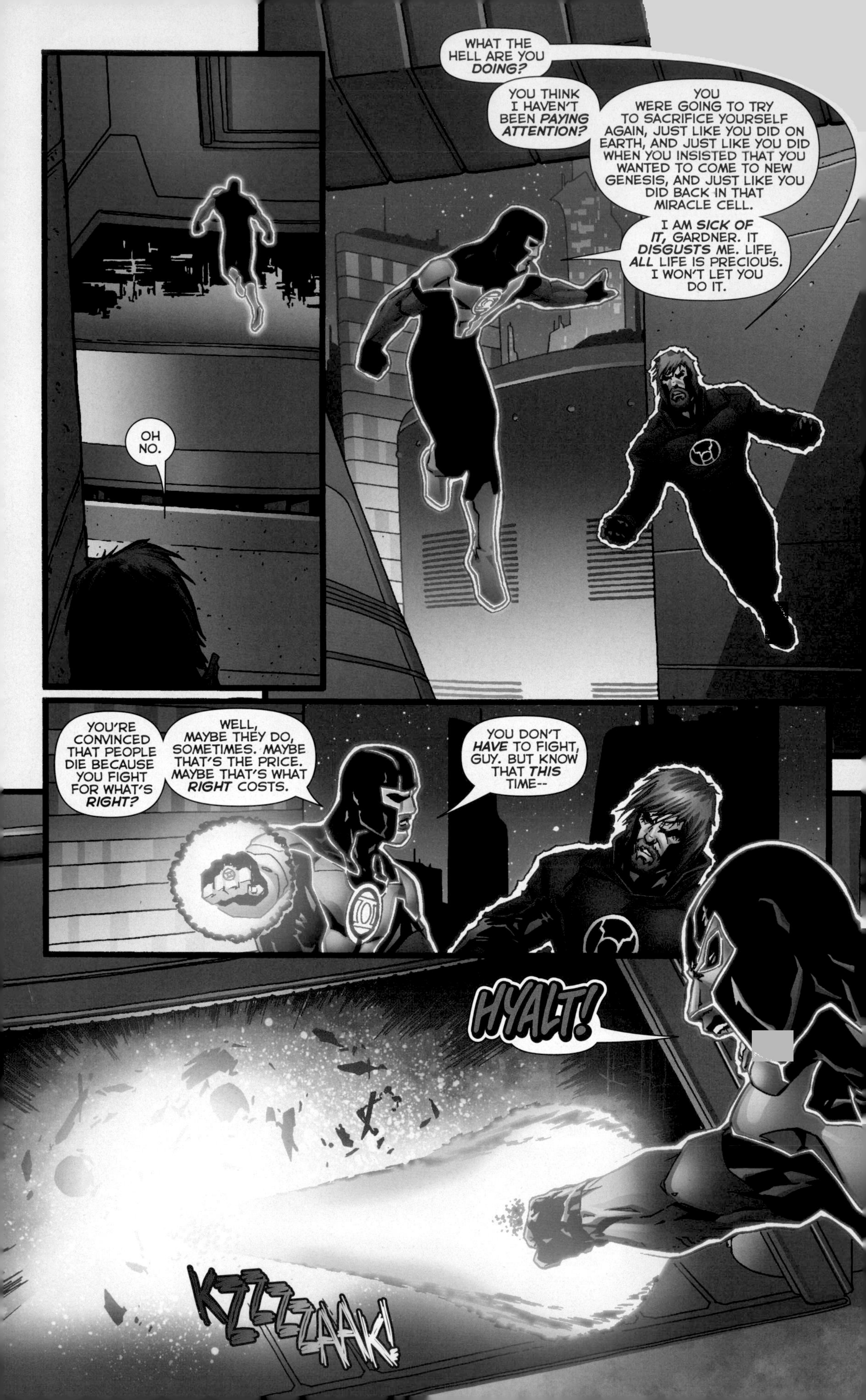
WHAT THE HELL ARE YOU *DOING?*
YOU THINK I HAVEN'T BEEN *PAYING ATTENTION?*
YOU WERE GOING TO TRY TO SACRIFICE YOURSELF AGAIN, JUST LIKE YOU DID ON EARTH, AND JUST LIKE YOU DID WHEN YOU INSISTED THAT YOU WANTED TO COME TO NEW GENESIS, AND JUST LIKE YOU DID BACK IN THAT MIRACLE CELL.
I AM *SICK OF IT,* GARDNER. IT *DISGUSTS* ME. LIFE, *ALL* LIFE IS PRECIOUS. I WON'T LET YOU DO IT.
OH NO.
YOU'RE CONVINCED THAT PEOPLE DIE BECAUSE YOU FIGHT FOR WHAT'S *RIGHT?*
WELL, MAYBE THEY DO, SOMETIMES. MAYBE THAT'S THE PRICE. MAYBE THAT'S WHAT *RIGHT* COSTS.
YOU DON'T *HAVE* TO FIGHT, GUY. BUT KNOW THAT *THIS* TIME--
HYALT!
KZZZZAAK!

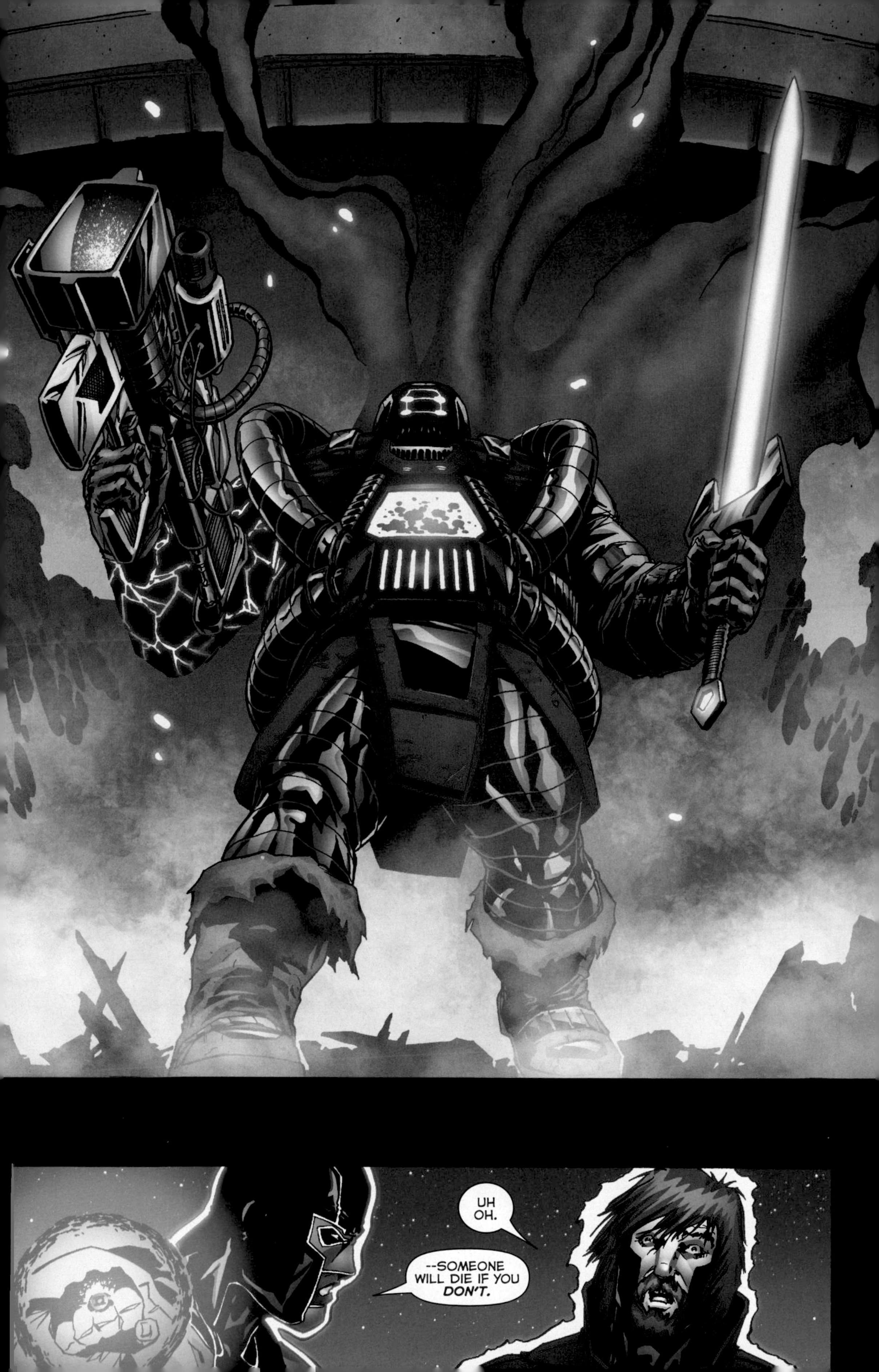
UH OH.
--SOMEONE WILL DIE IF YOU ***DON'T.***

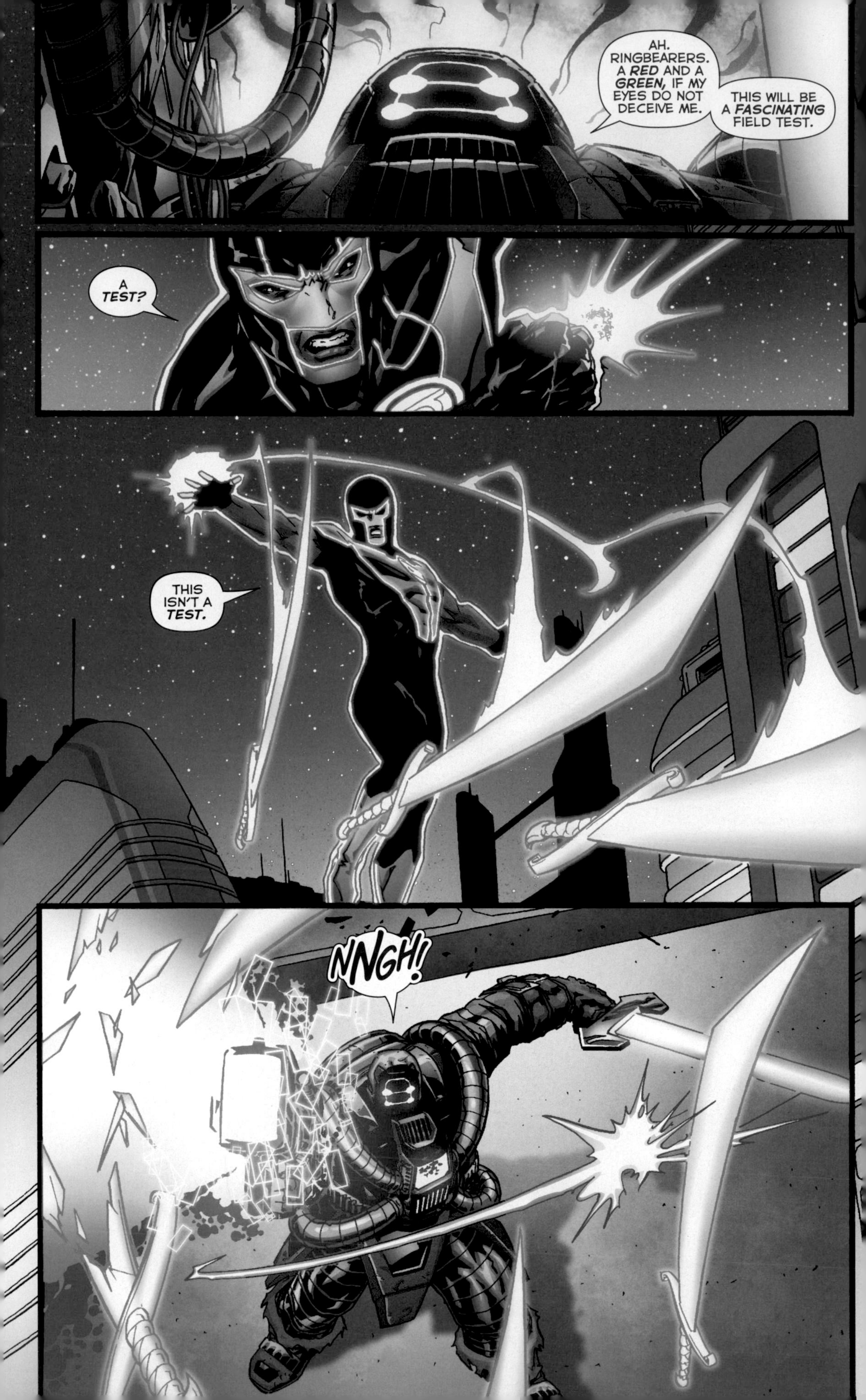

AH. RINGBEARERS. A RED AND A GREEN, IF MY EYES DO NOT DECEIVE ME.
THIS WILL BE A FASCINATING FIELD TEST.
A TEST?
THIS ISN'T A TEST.
NNGH!

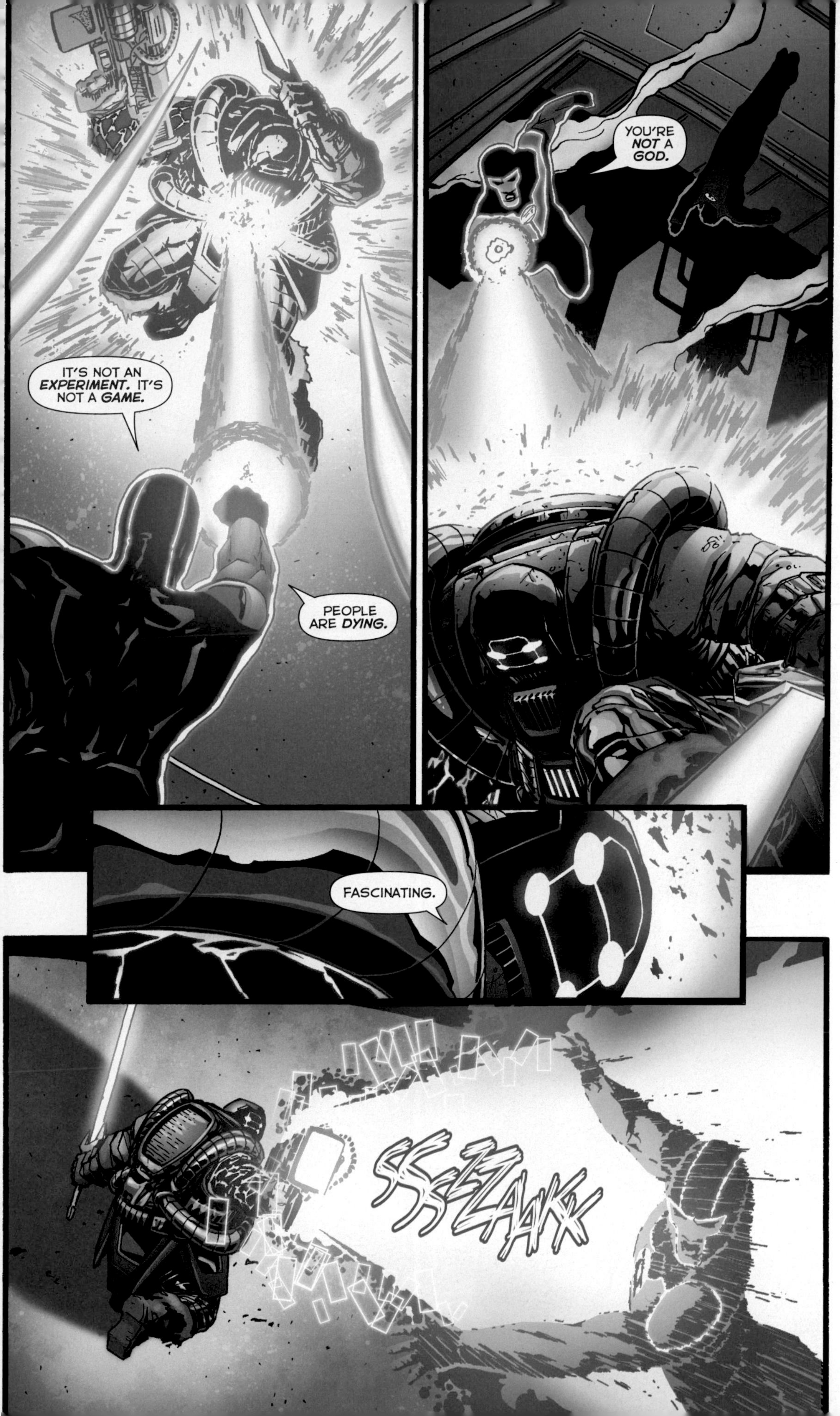
IT'S NOT AN EXPERIMENT. IT'S NOT A GAME.
PEOPLE ARE DYING.
YOU'RE NOT A GOD.
FASCINATING.
SSSZZZAAKKK

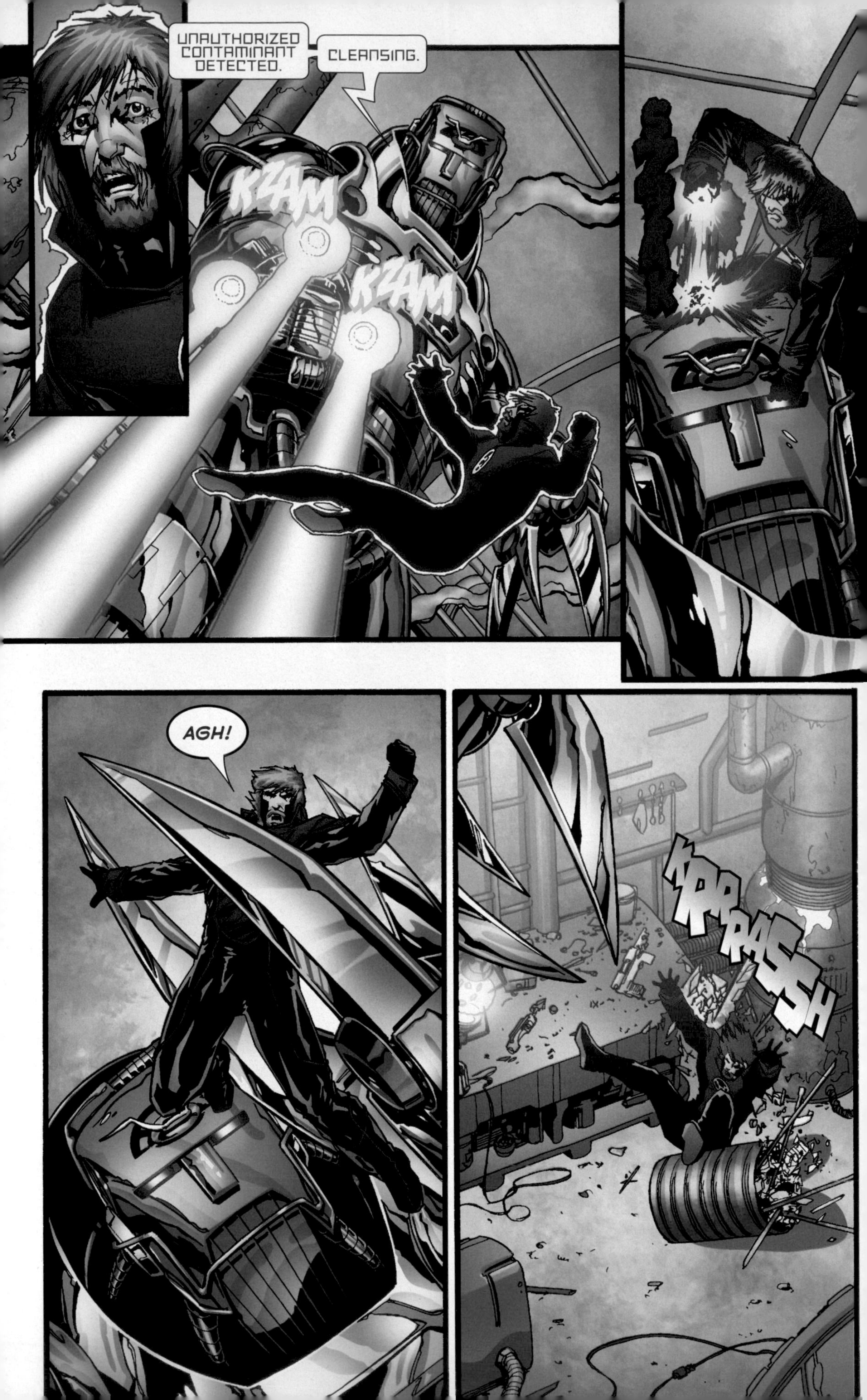
UNAUTHORIZED CONTAMINANT DETECTED.
CLEANSING.
KZAM
KZAM
AGH!
KRRRASSH

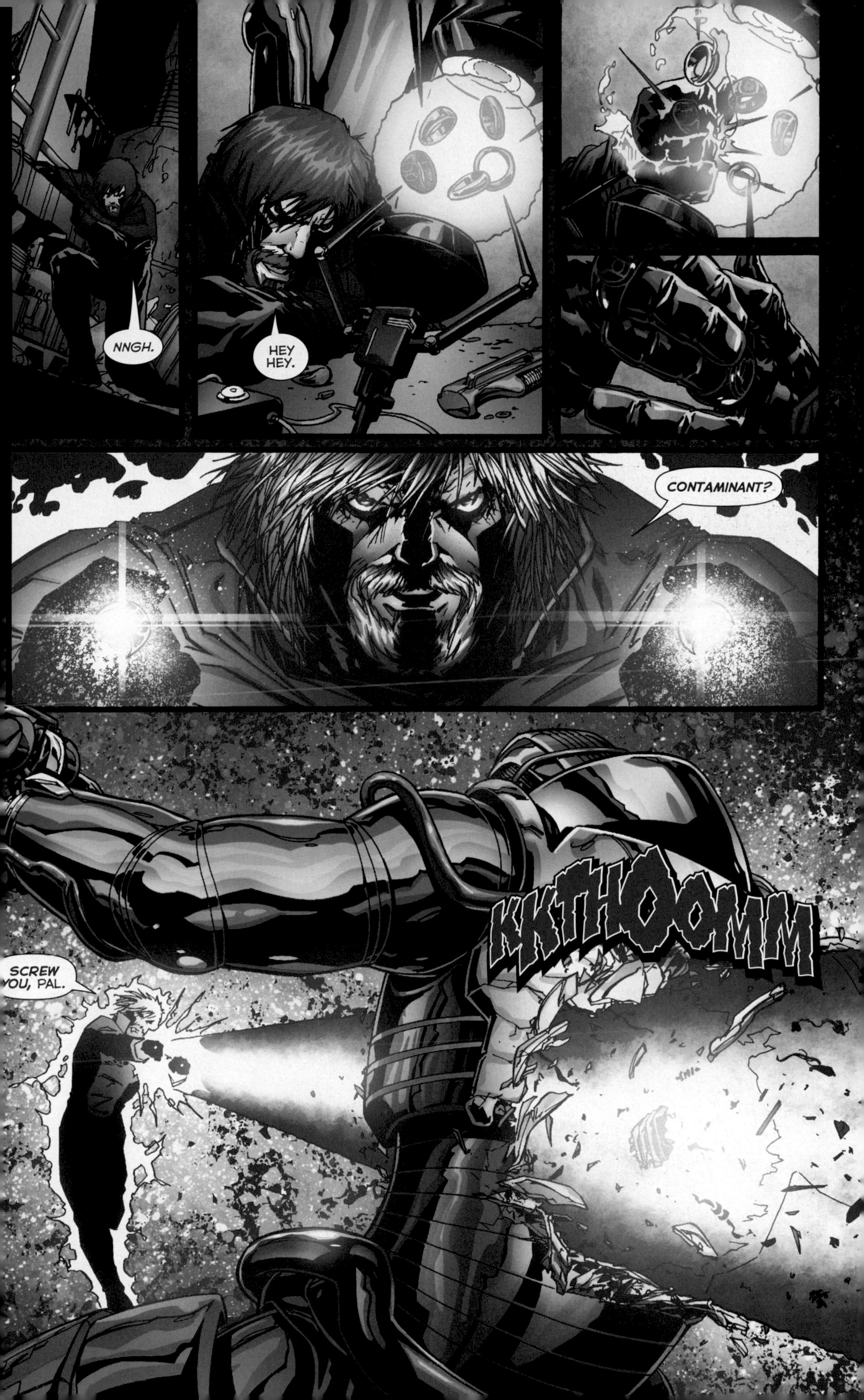
NNGH.
HEY HEY.
CONTAMINANT?
KKTHOOMM
SCREW YOU, PAL.

MOST OF MY OBSERVATIONS OF THESE *RINGS* OF YOURS SUGGEST THEY ARE PRIMARILY USED AS *WEAPONS*.

THIS SEEMS *WASTEFUL*. DO YOU NOT REALIZE THEY MIGHT WORK EQUALLY WELL FOR ANY NUMBER OF PURPOSES?

KLAN NG

FOR INSTANCE, THE *BLUE* RING APPEARS TO INSTILL A SENSE OF *HOPE*. IMAGINE SUCH A DEVICE USED IN CONJUNCTION WITH AN ATTEMPT TO PACIFY AN UNRULY POPULATION?

HOPE IS A POWERFUL INTOXICANT INDEED. WHY--

SHUT *UP!*

THAT WAS VERY RUDE OF YOU. YOU ARE SUCH AN *IMPOLITE* SPEC--

KORASSH

SPLAATH

GAH!!

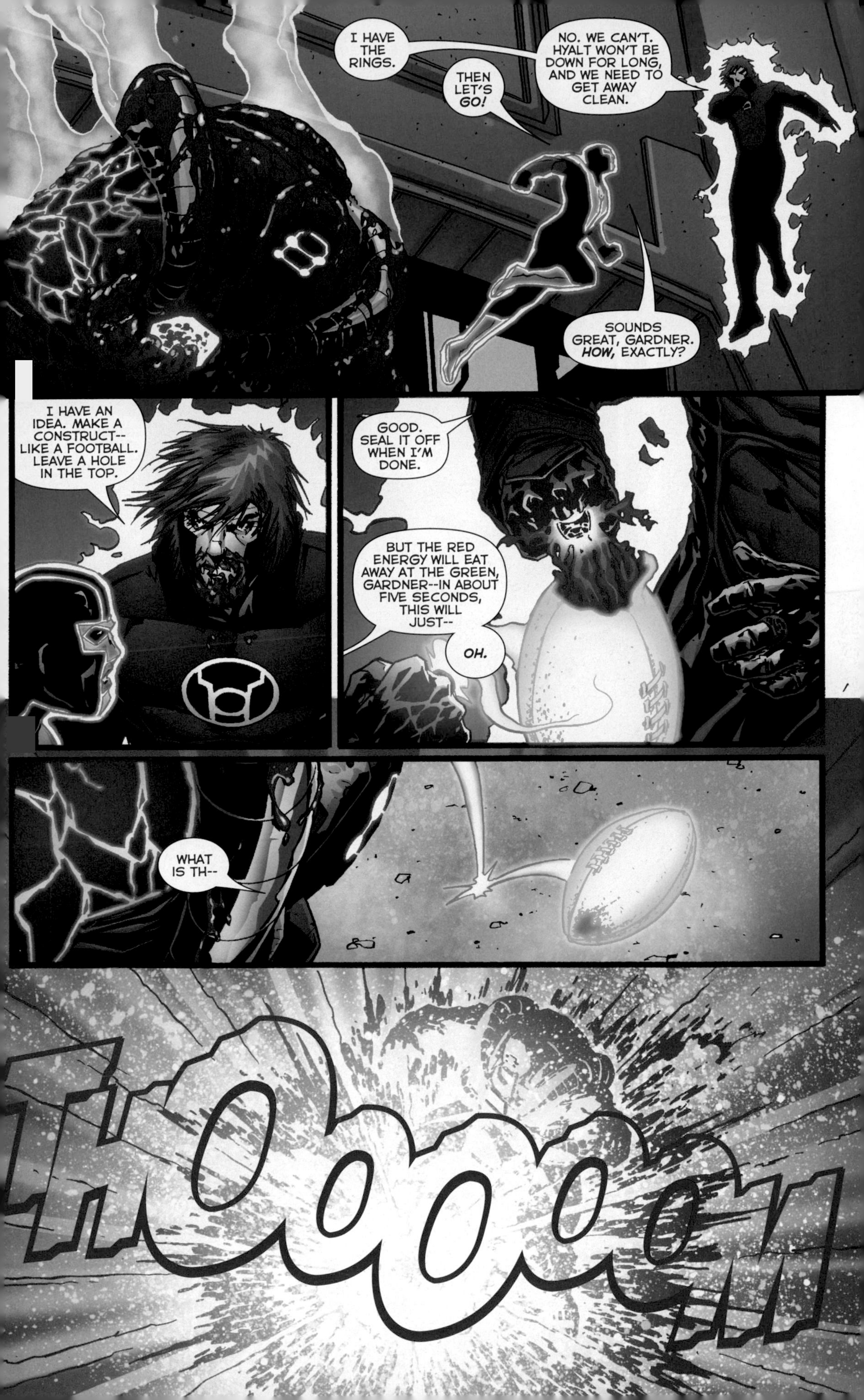
I HAVE THE RINGS.
NO. WE CAN'T. HYALT WON'T BE DOWN FOR LONG, AND WE NEED TO GET AWAY CLEAN.
THEN LET'S GO!
SOUNDS GREAT, GARDNER. HOW, EXACTLY?
I HAVE AN IDEA. MAKE A CONSTRUCT-- LIKE A FOOTBALL. LEAVE A HOLE IN THE TOP.
GOOD. SEAL IT OFF WHEN I'M DONE.
BUT THE RED ENERGY WILL EAT AWAY AT THE GREEN, GARDNER--IN ABOUT FIVE SECONDS, THIS WILL JUST--
OH.
WHAT IS TH--

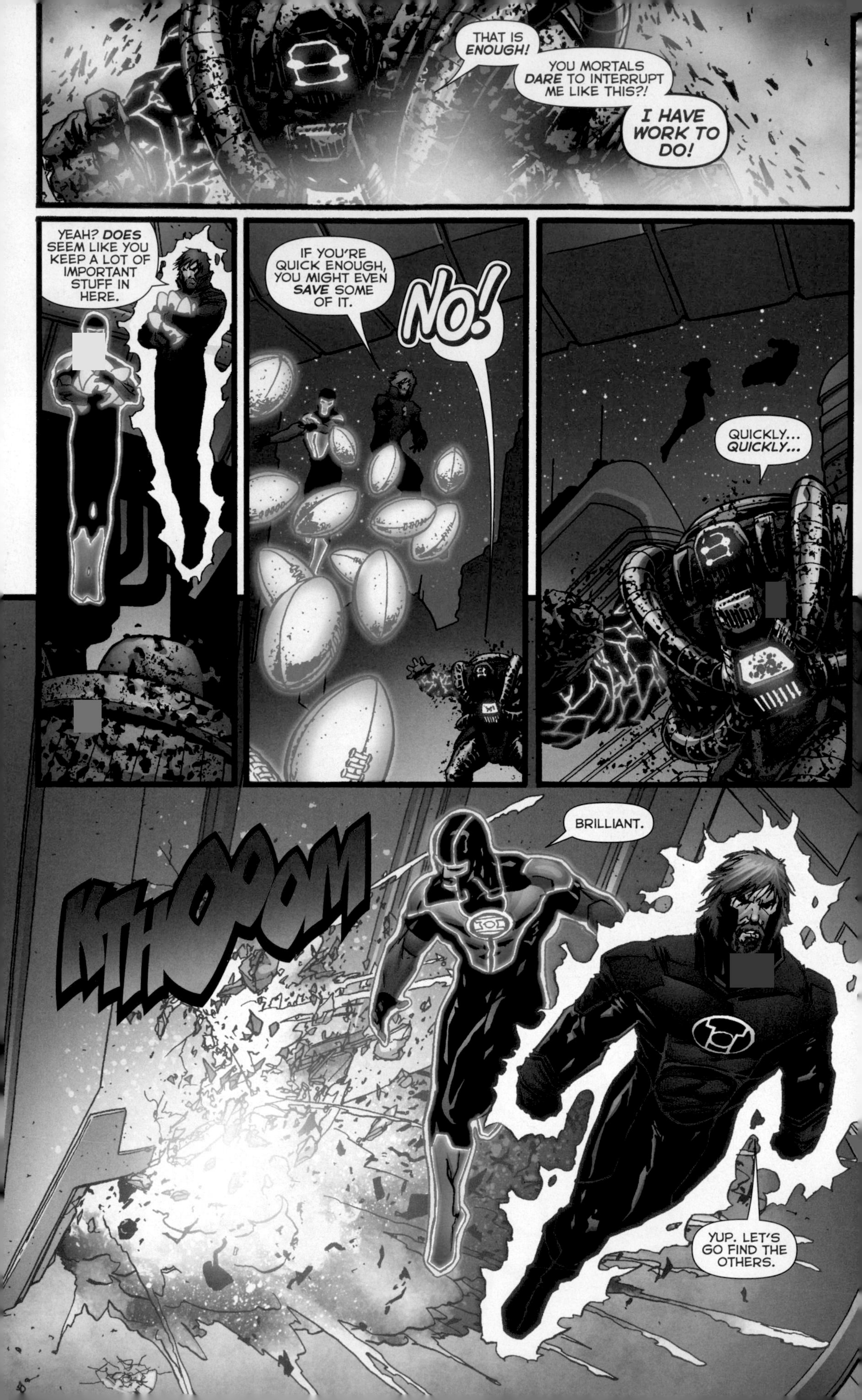
THAT IS ENOUGH!
YOU MORTALS DARE TO INTERRUPT ME LIKE THIS?!
I HAVE WORK TO DO!
YEAH? DOES SEEM LIKE YOU KEEP A LOT OF IMPORTANT STUFF IN HERE.
IF YOU'RE QUICK ENOUGH, YOU MIGHT EVEN SAVE SOME OF IT.
NO!
QUICKLY... QUICKLY...
KTHOOOM
BRILLIANT.
YUP. LET'S GO FIND THE OTHERS.

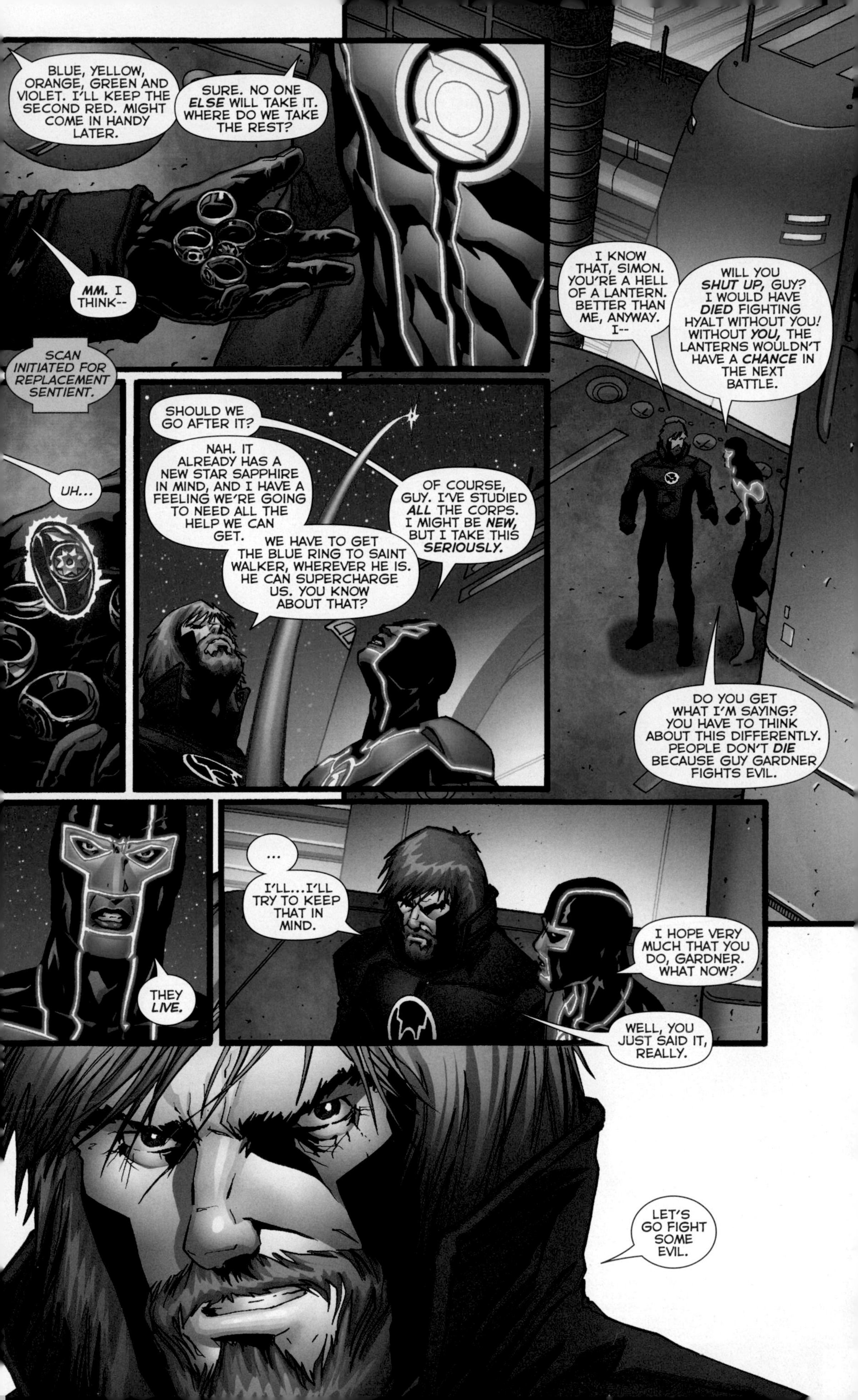
BLUE, YELLOW, ORANGE, GREEN AND VIOLET. I'LL KEEP THE SECOND RED. MIGHT COME IN HANDY LATER.
SURE. NO ONE *ELSE* WILL TAKE IT. WHERE DO WE TAKE THE REST?
MM. I THINK--
SCAN INITIATED FOR REPLACEMENT SENTIENT.
UH...
SHOULD WE GO AFTER IT?
NAH. IT ALREADY HAS A NEW STAR SAPPHIRE IN MIND, AND I HAVE A FEELING WE'RE GOING TO NEED ALL THE HELP WE CAN GET.
WE HAVE TO GET THE BLUE RING TO SAINT WALKER, WHEREVER HE IS. HE CAN SUPERCHARGE US. YOU KNOW ABOUT THAT?
OF COURSE, GUY. I'VE STUDIED *ALL* THE CORPS. I MIGHT BE *NEW,* BUT I TAKE THIS *SERIOUSLY.*
I KNOW THAT, SIMON. YOU'RE A HELL OF A LANTERN. BETTER THAN ME, ANYWAY. I--
WILL YOU *SHUT UP,* GUY? I WOULD HAVE *DIED* FIGHTING HYALT WITHOUT YOU! WITHOUT *YOU,* THE LANTERNS WOULDN'T HAVE A *CHANCE* IN THE NEXT BATTLE.
DO YOU GET WHAT I'M SAYING? YOU HAVE TO THINK ABOUT THIS DIFFERENTLY. PEOPLE DON'T *DIE* BECAUSE GUY GARDNER FIGHTS EVIL.
THEY *LIVE.*
...
I'LL...I'LL TRY TO KEEP THAT IN MIND.
I HOPE VERY MUCH THAT YOU DO, GARDNER. WHAT NOW?
WELL, YOU JUST SAID IT, REALLY.
LET'S GO FIGHT SOME EVIL.

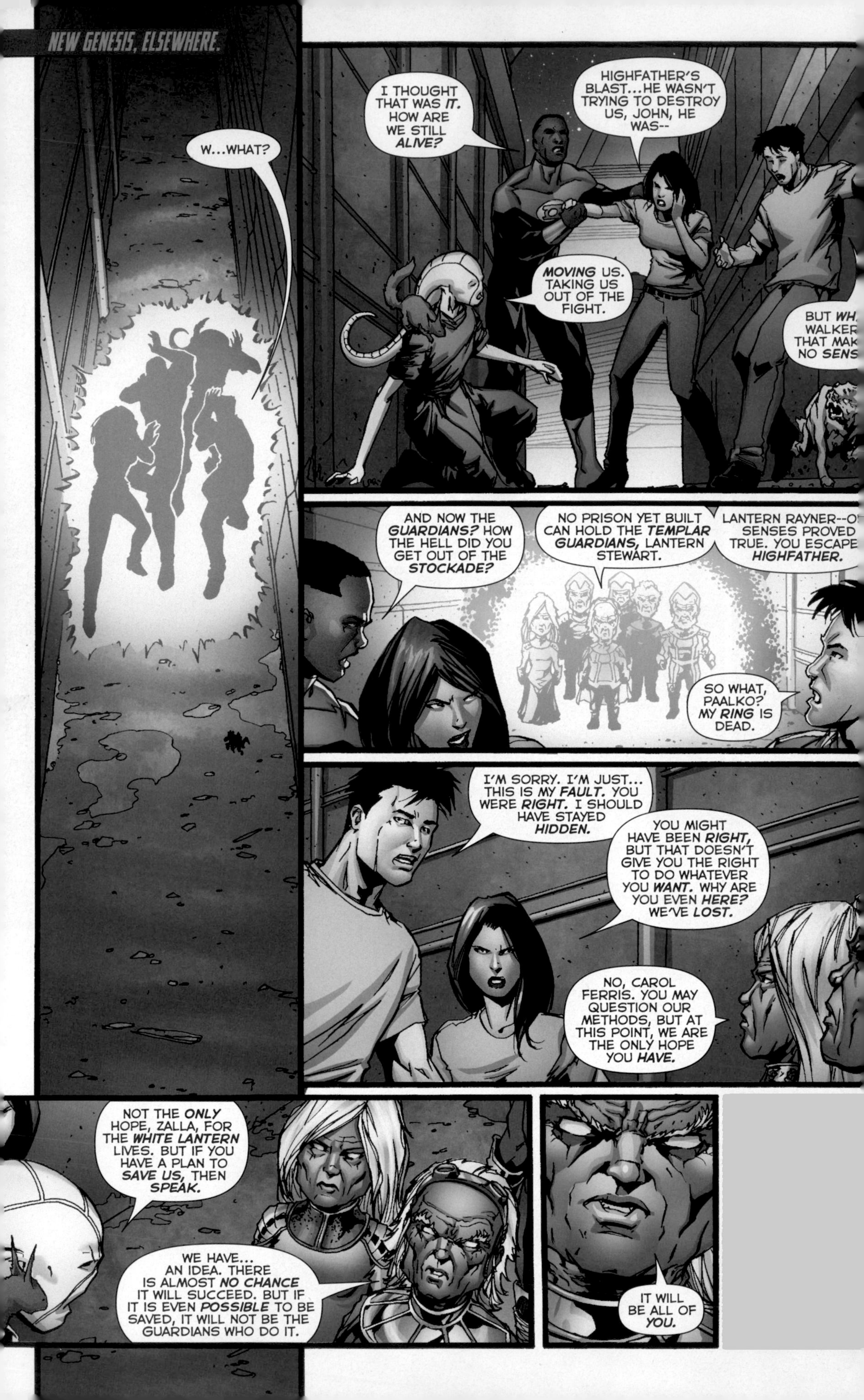
NEW GENESIS, ELSEWHERE.
W...WHAT?
I THOUGHT THAT WAS IT. HOW ARE WE STILL ALIVE?
HIGHFATHER'S BLAST...HE WASN'T TRYING TO DESTROY US, JOHN, HE WAS--
MOVING US. TAKING US OUT OF THE FIGHT.
BUT WH WALKER THAT MAK NO SENS
AND NOW THE GUARDIANS? HOW THE HELL DID YOU GET OUT OF THE STOCKADE?
NO PRISON YET BUILT CAN HOLD THE TEMPLAR GUARDIANS, LANTERN STEWART.
LANTERN RAYNER--O SENSES PROVED TRUE. YOU ESCAPE HIGHFATHER.
SO WHAT, PAALKO? MY RING IS DEAD.
I'M SORRY. I'M JUST... THIS IS MY FAULT. YOU WERE RIGHT. I SHOULD HAVE STAYED HIDDEN.
YOU MIGHT HAVE BEEN RIGHT, BUT THAT DOESN'T GIVE YOU THE RIGHT TO DO WHATEVER YOU WANT. WHY ARE YOU EVEN HERE? WE'VE LOST.
NO, CAROL FERRIS. YOU MAY QUESTION OUR METHODS, BUT AT THIS POINT, WE ARE THE ONLY HOPE YOU HAVE.
NOT THE ONLY HOPE, ZALLA, FOR THE WHITE LANTERN LIVES. BUT IF YOU HAVE A PLAN TO SAVE US, THEN SPEAK.
WE HAVE... AN IDEA. THERE IS ALMOST NO CHANCE IT WILL SUCCEED. BUT IF IT IS EVEN POSSIBLE TO BE SAVED, IT WILL NOT BE THE GUARDIANS WHO DO IT.
IT WILL BE ALL OF YOU.

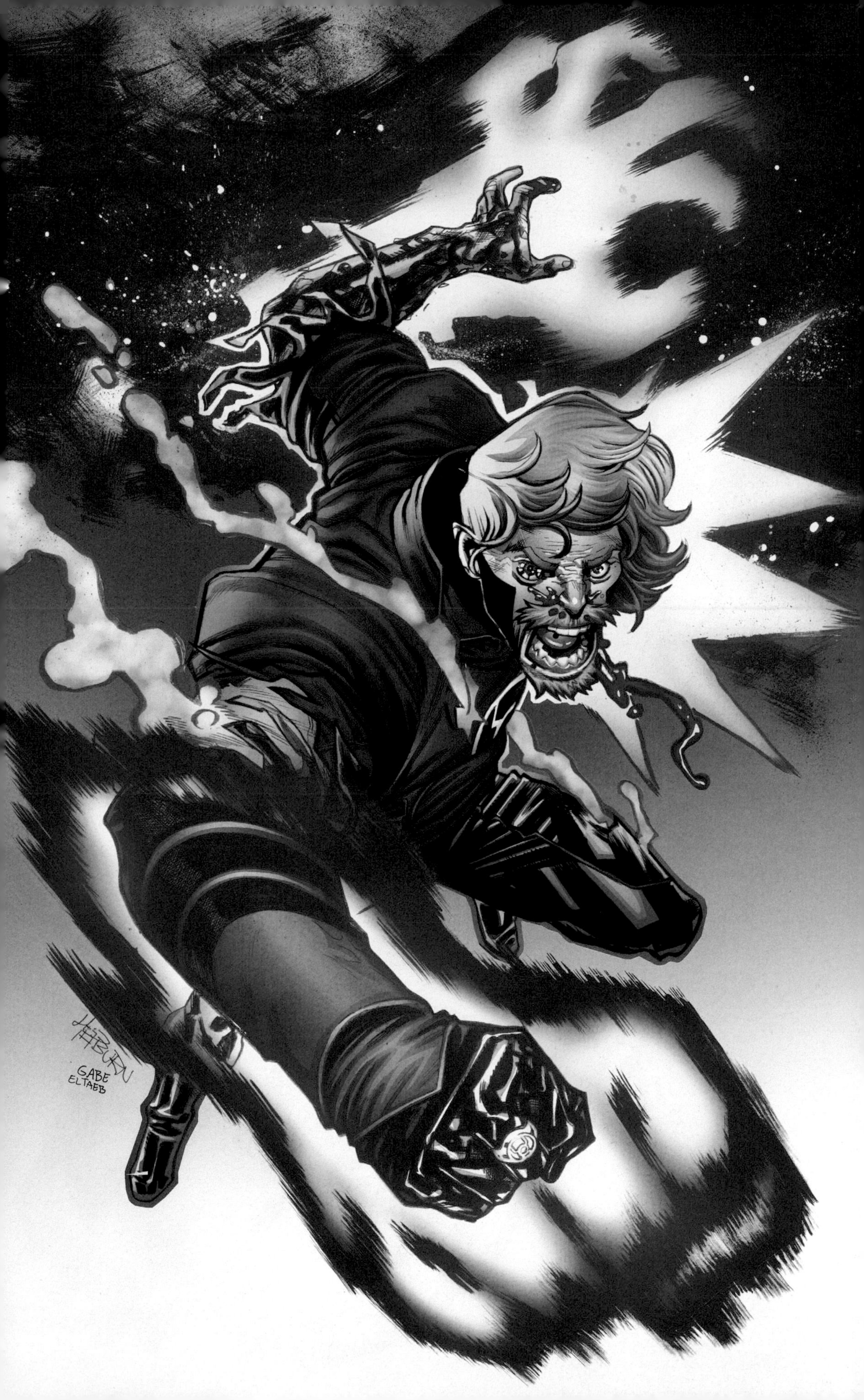
GABE
ELTAEB

RAGE

LANDRY Q. WALKER writer **J. CALAFIORE** artist **GABE ELTAEB** colorist **DAVE SHARPE** letterer
cover art by **SCOTT HEPBURN** and **GABE ELTAEB**

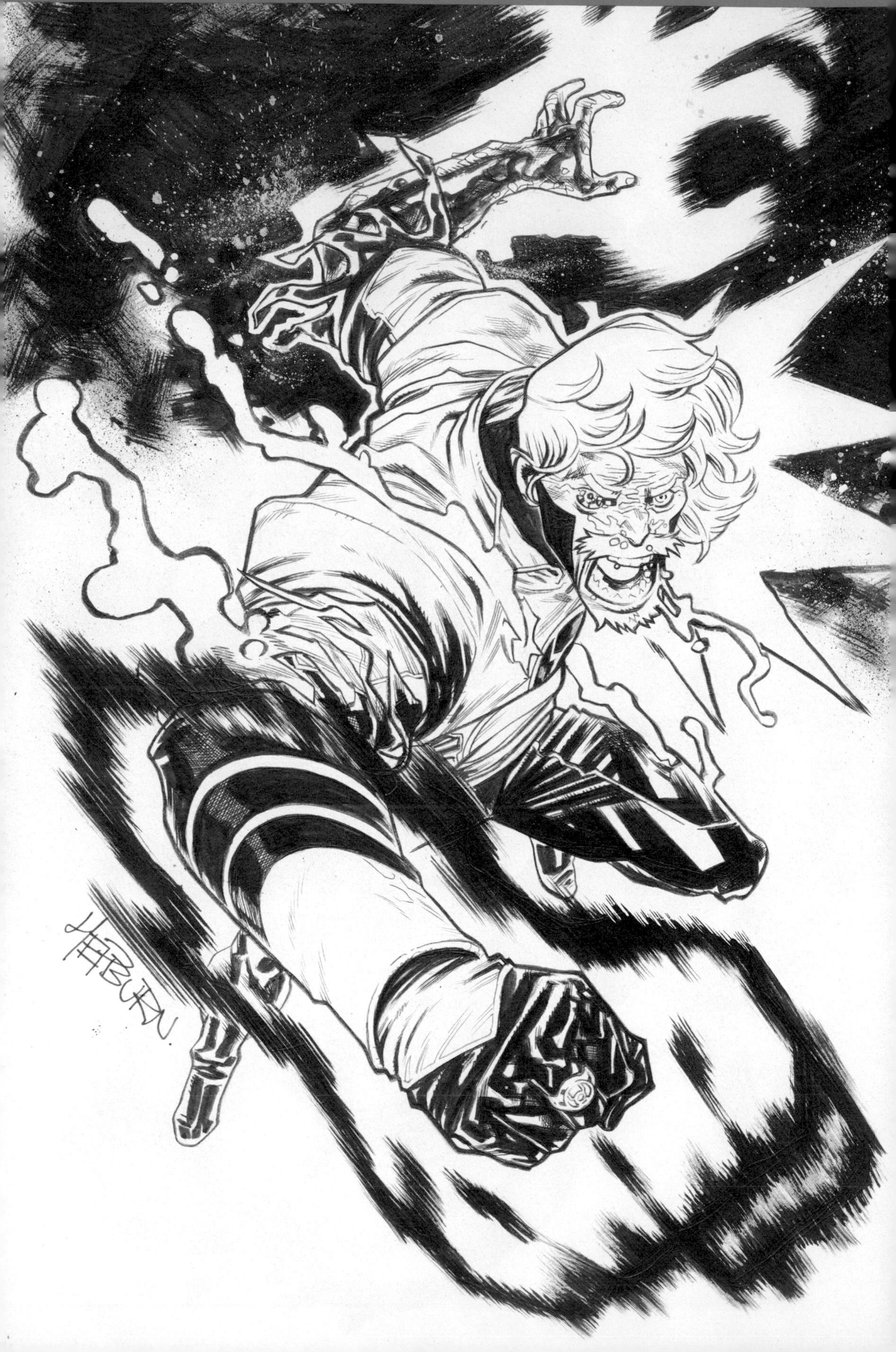

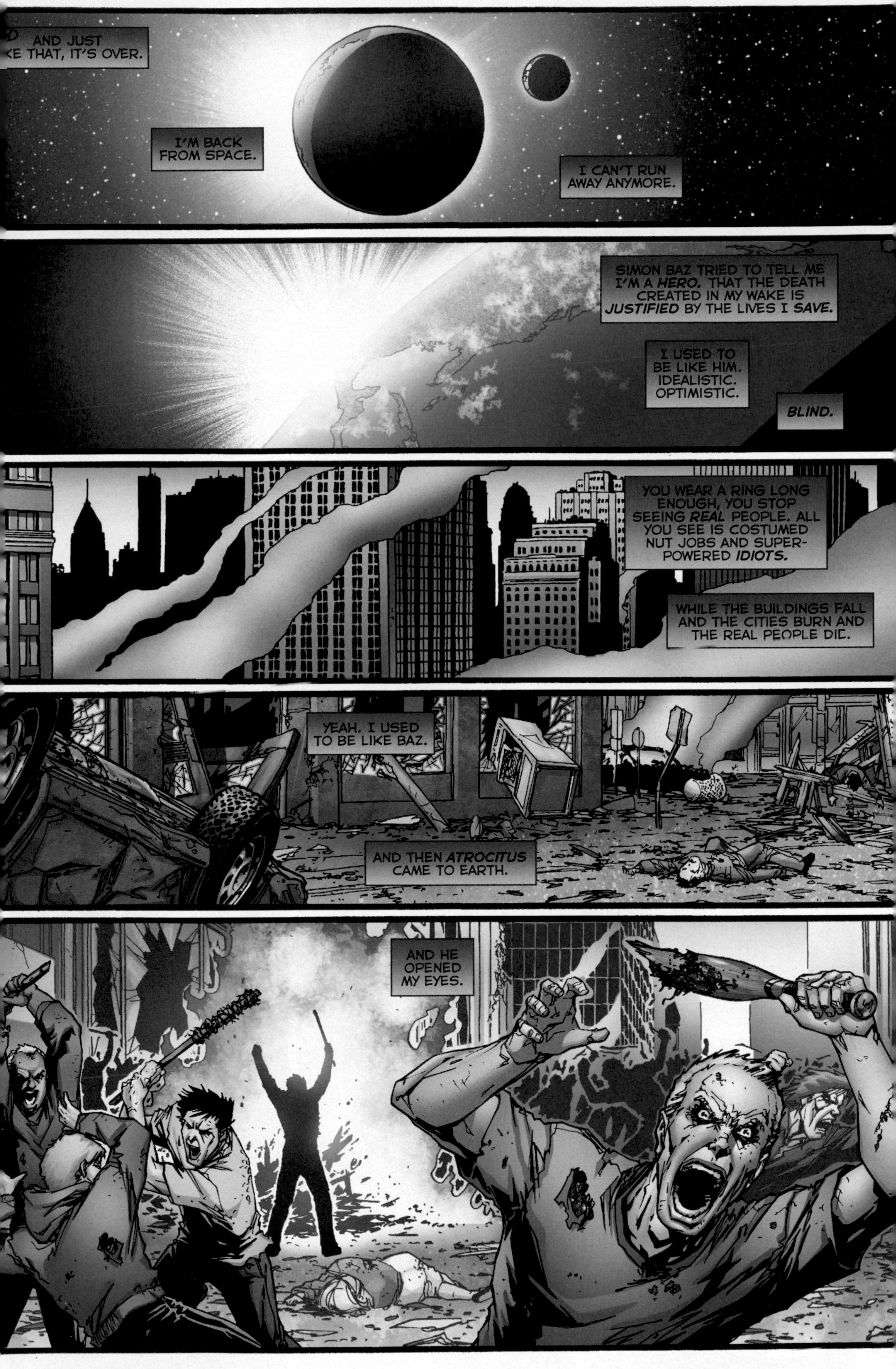

AND JUST
KE THAT, IT'S OVER.
I'M BACK FROM SPACE.
I CAN'T RUN AWAY ANYMORE.
SIMON BAZ TRIED TO TELL ME I'M A *HERO.* THAT THE DEATH CREATED IN MY WAKE IS *JUSTIFIED* BY THE LIVES I *SAVE.*
I USED TO BE LIKE HIM. IDEALISTIC. OPTIMISTIC.
BLIND.
YOU WEAR A RING LONG ENOUGH, YOU STOP SEEING *REAL* PEOPLE. ALL YOU SEE IS COSTUMED NUT JOBS AND SUPER-POWERED *IDIOTS.*
WHILE THE BUILDINGS FALL AND THE CITIES BURN AND THE REAL PEOPLE DIE.
YEAH. I USED TO BE LIKE BAZ.
AND THEN *ATROCITUS* CAME TO EARTH.
AND HE OPENED MY EYES.

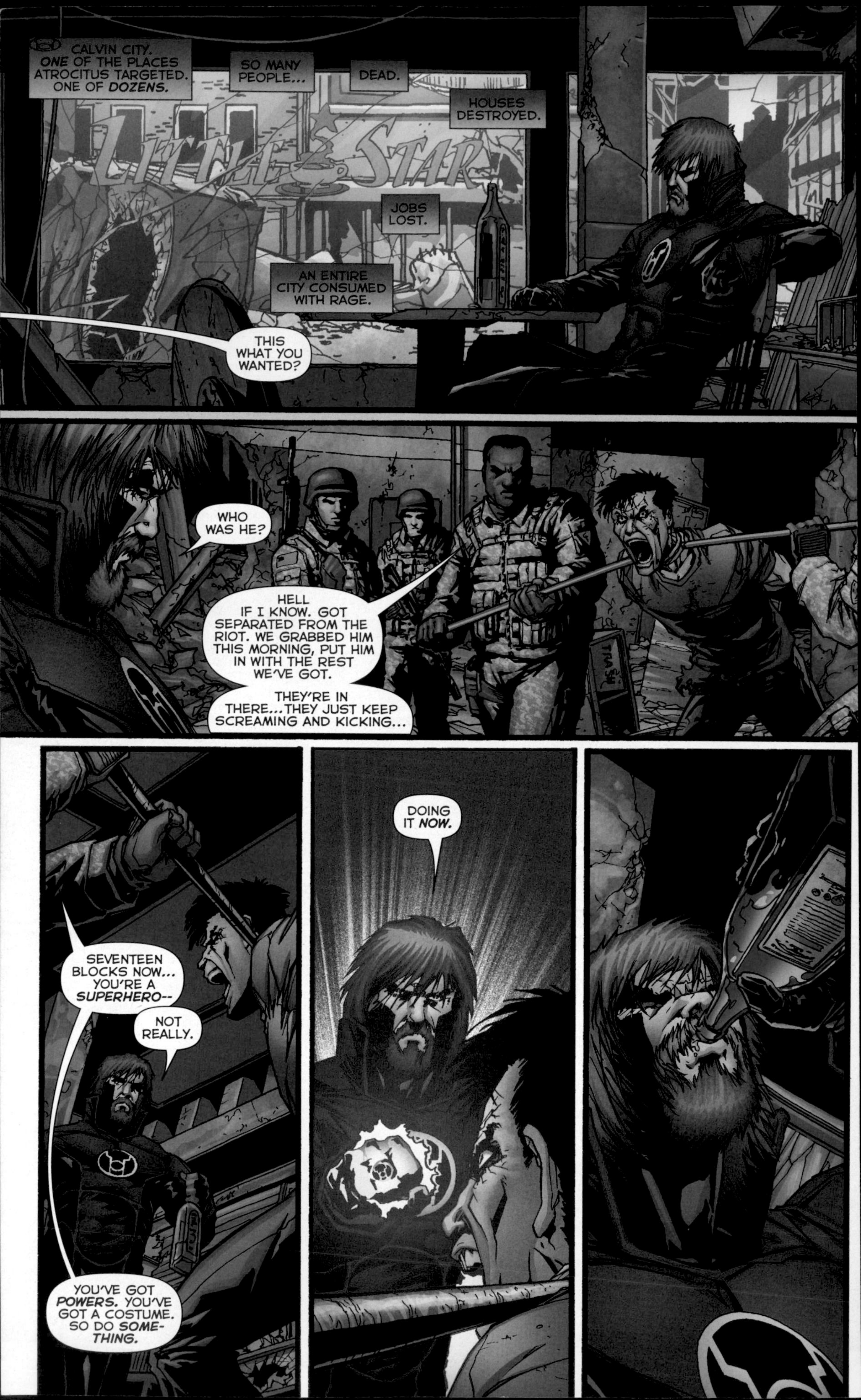
CALVIN CITY. ONE OF THE PLACES ATROCITUS TARGETED. ONE OF DOZENS.
SO MANY PEOPLE...
DEAD.
HOUSES DESTROYED.
LITTLE STAR
JOBS LOST.
AN ENTIRE CITY CONSUMED WITH RAGE.
THIS WHAT YOU WANTED?
WHO WAS HE?
HELL IF I KNOW. GOT SEPARATED FROM THE RIOT. WE GRABBED HIM THIS MORNING, PUT HIM IN WITH THE REST WE'VE GOT.
THEY'RE IN THERE...THEY JUST KEEP SCREAMING AND KICKING...
SEVENTEEN BLOCKS NOW... YOU'RE A SUPERHERO--
NOT REALLY.
YOU'VE GOT POWERS. YOU'VE GOT A COSTUME. SO DO SOME-THING.
DOING IT NOW.

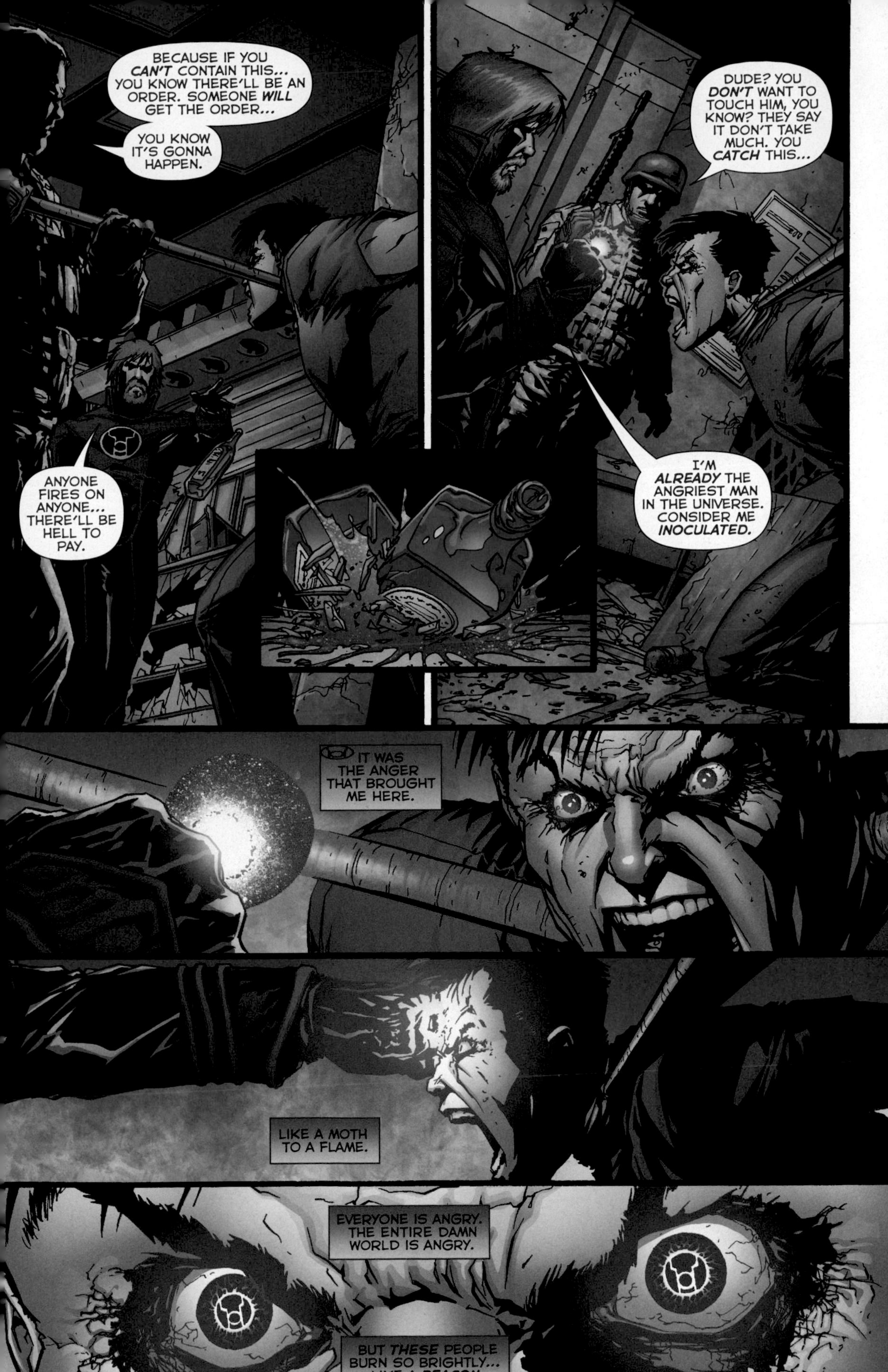
BECAUSE IF YOU *CAN'T* CONTAIN THIS... YOU KNOW THERE'LL BE AN ORDER. SOMEONE *WILL* GET THE ORDER...
YOU KNOW IT'S GONNA HAPPEN.
ANYONE FIRES ON ANYONE... THERE'LL BE HELL TO PAY.
DUDE? YOU *DON'T* WANT TO TOUCH HIM, YOU KNOW? THEY SAY IT DON'T TAKE MUCH. YOU *CATCH* THIS...
I'M *ALREADY* THE ANGRIEST MAN IN THE UNIVERSE. CONSIDER ME *INOCULATED.*
IT WAS THE ANGER THAT BROUGHT ME HERE.
LIKE A MOTH TO A FLAME.
EVERYONE IS ANGRY. THE ENTIRE DAMN WORLD IS ANGRY.
BUT *THESE* PEOPLE BURN SO BRIGHTLY... LIKE A *BEACON.*

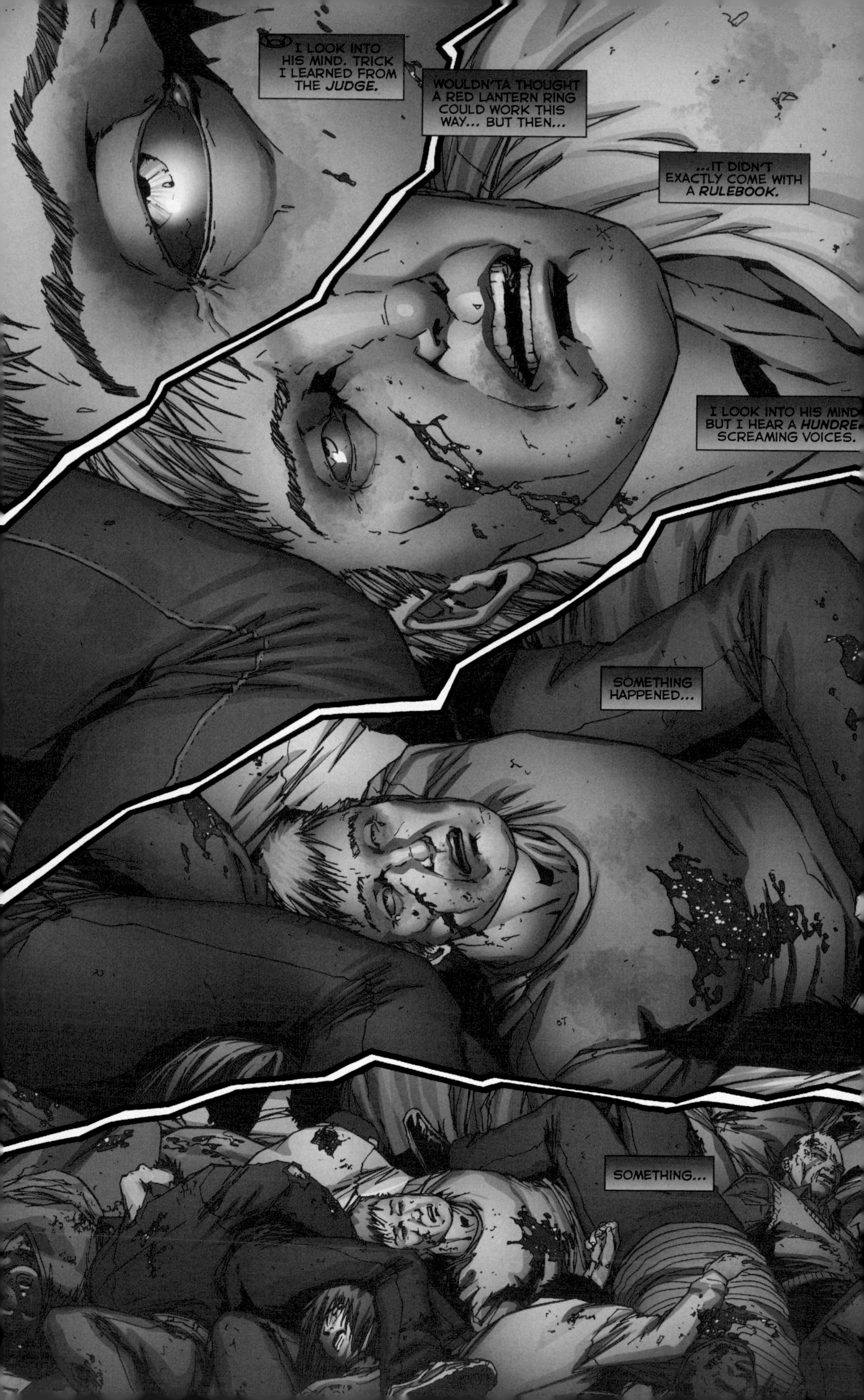
I LOOK INTO HIS MIND. TRICK I LEARNED FROM THE JUDGE.
WOULDN'TA THOUGHT A RED LANTERN RING COULD WORK THIS WAY... BUT THEN...
...IT DIDN'T EXACTLY COME WITH A RULEBOOK.
I LOOK INTO HIS MIND BUT I HEAR A HUNDRE
SCREAMING VOICES.
SOMETHING HAPPENED...
SOMETHING...

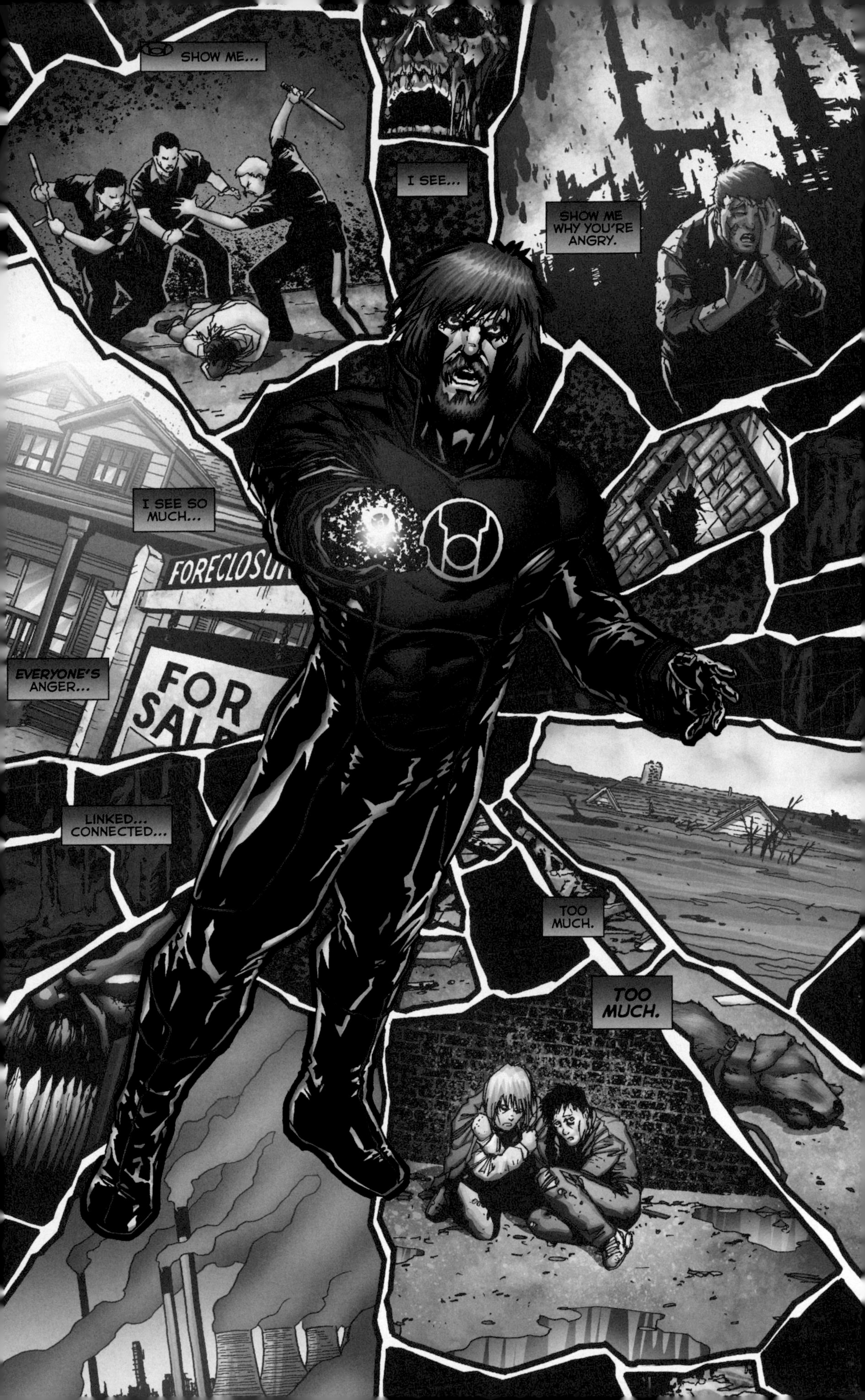

SHOW ME...
I SEE...
SHOW ME WHY YOU'RE ANGRY.
I SEE SO MUCH...
FORECLOSU
FOR SAL
EVERYONE'S ANGER...
LINKED... CONNECTED...
TOO MUCH.
TOO MUCH.

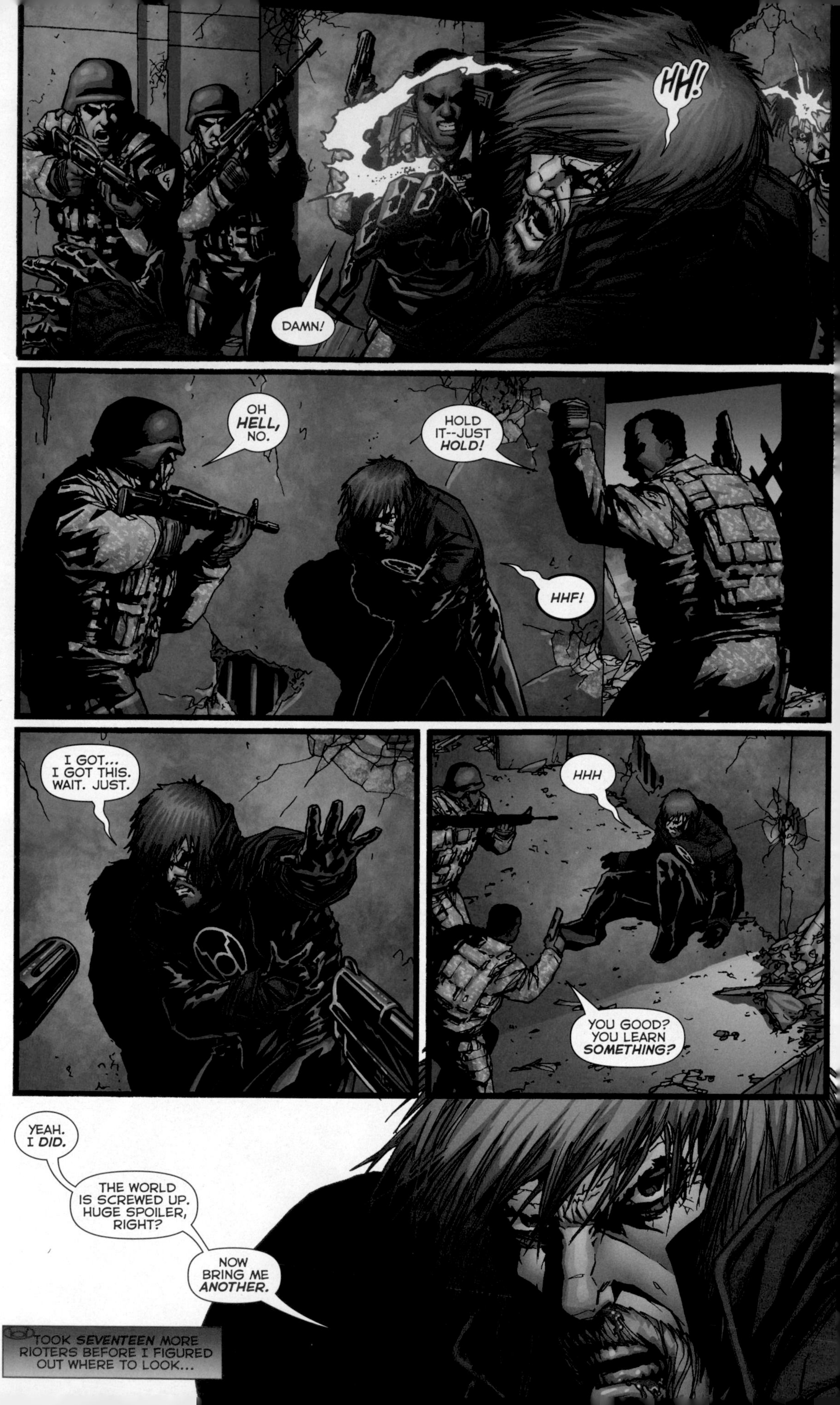
HH!
DAMN!
OH HELL, NO.
HOLD IT--JUST HOLD!
HHF!
I GOT... I GOT THIS. WAIT. JUST.
HHH
YOU GOOD? YOU LEARN SOMETHING?
YEAH. I DID.
THE WORLD IS SCREWED UP. HUGE SPOILER, RIGHT?
NOW BRING ME ANOTHER.
TOOK SEVENTEEN MORE RIOTERS BEFORE I FIGURED OUT WHERE TO LOOK...

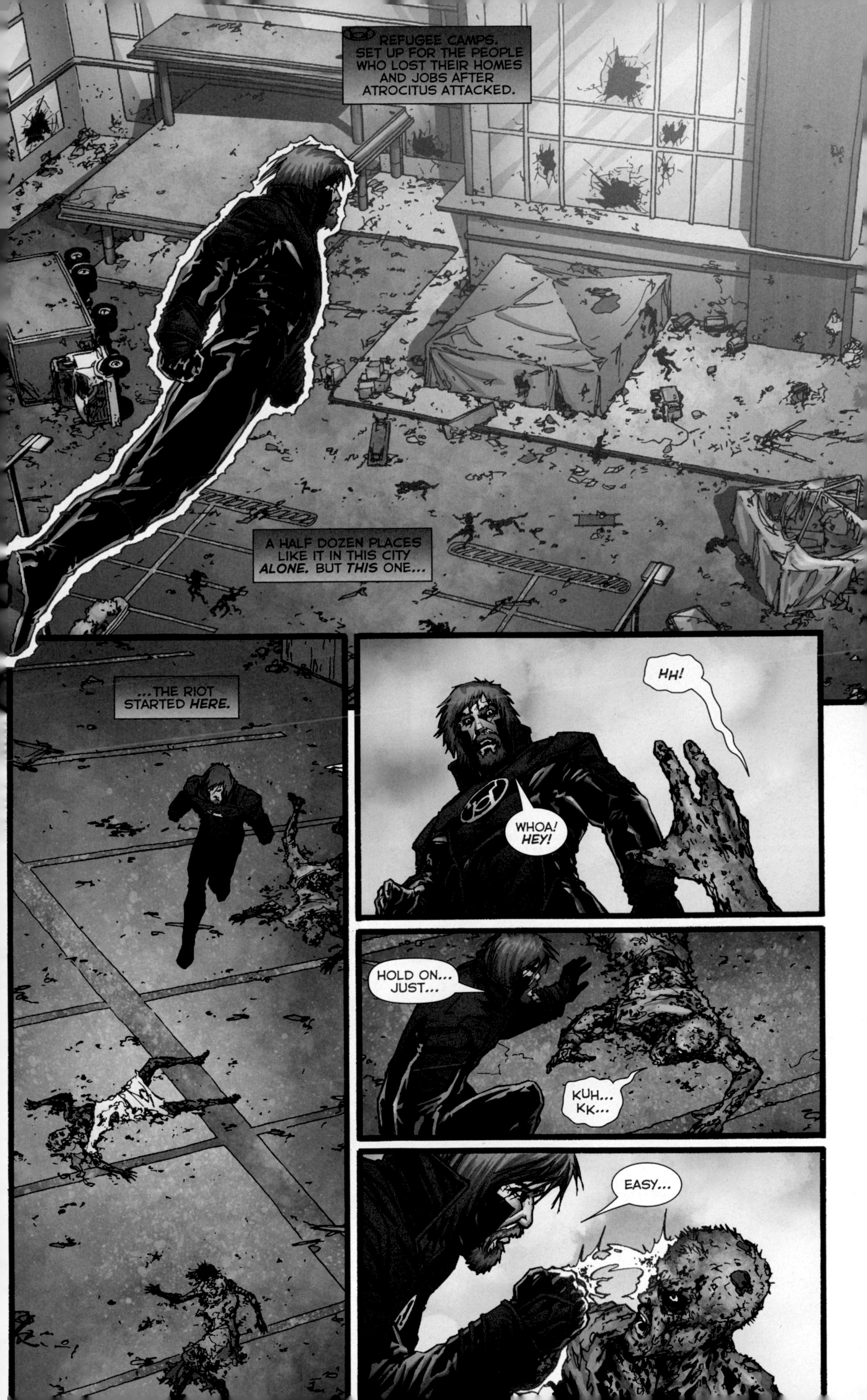
REFUGEE CAMPS. SET UP FOR THE PEOPLE WHO LOST THEIR HOMES AND JOBS AFTER ATROCITUS ATTACKED.
A HALF DOZEN PLACES LIKE IT IN THIS CITY *ALONE*. BUT *THIS* ONE...
...THE RIOT STARTED *HERE*.
HH!
WHOA! *HEY!*
HOLD ON... JUST...
KUH... KK...
EASY...

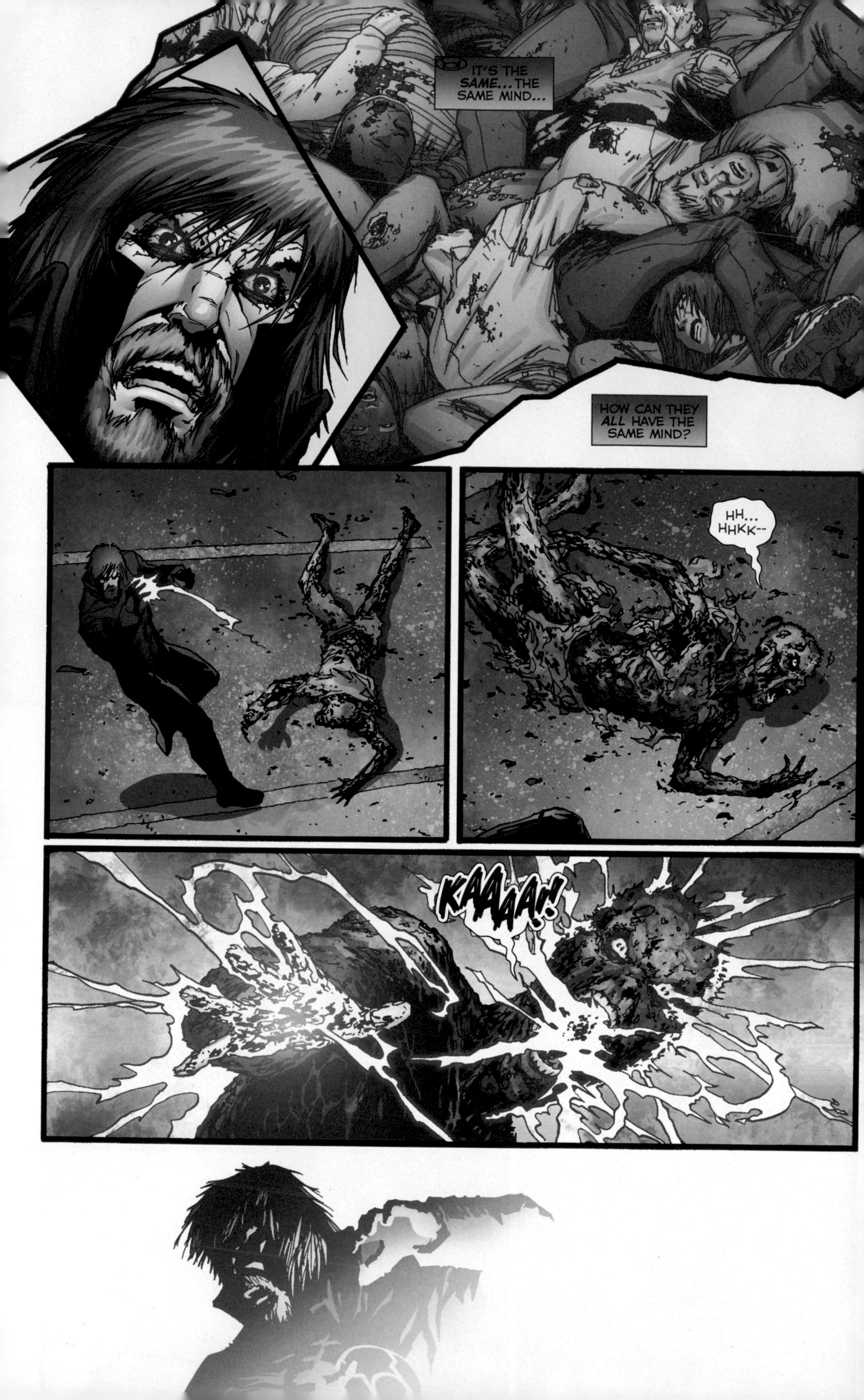
IT'S THE SAME... THE SAME MIND...
HOW CAN THEY ALL HAVE THE SAME MIND?
HH... HHKK--
KAAAAA!!

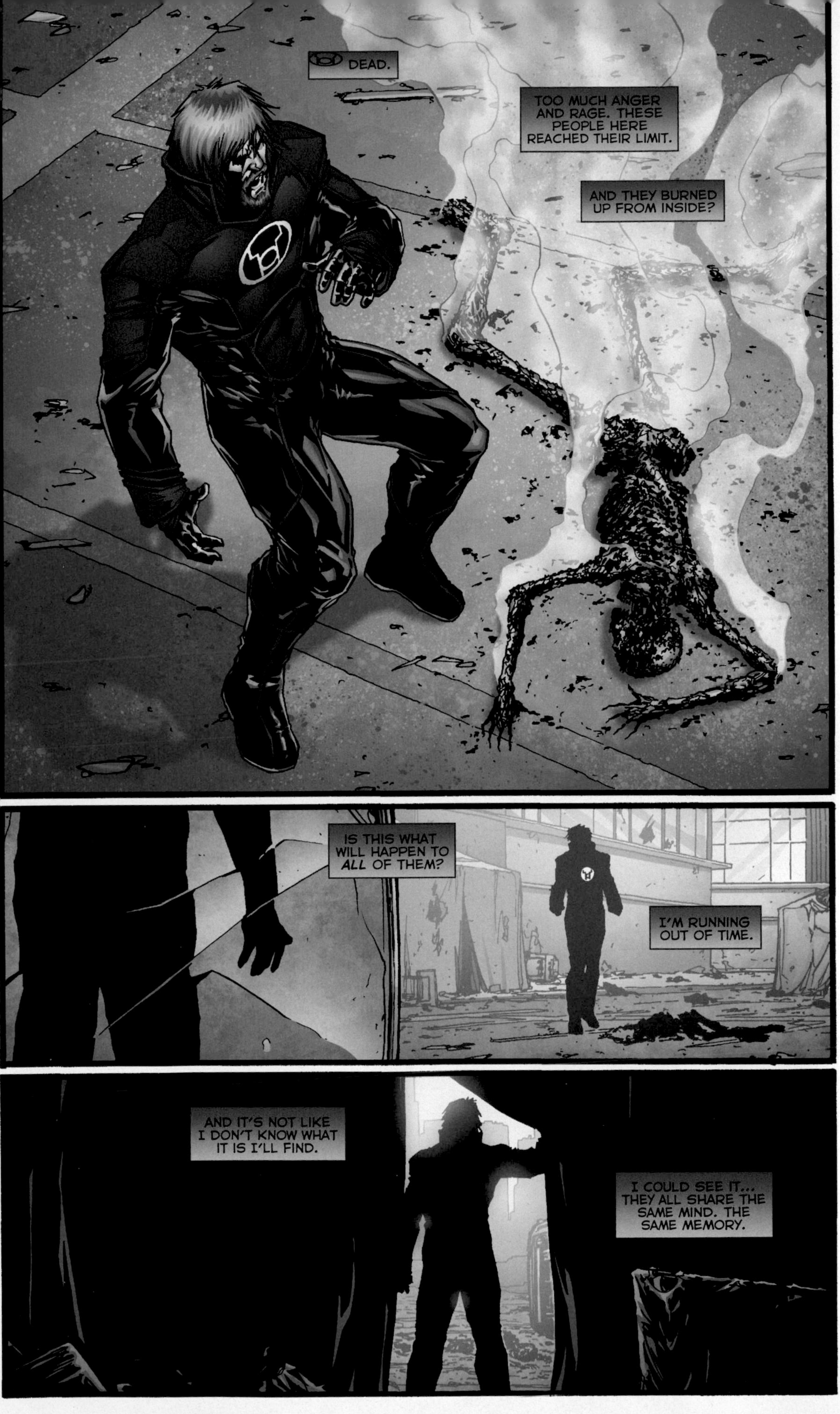
DEAD.
TOO MUCH ANGER AND RAGE. THESE PEOPLE HERE REACHED THEIR LIMIT.
AND THEY BURNED UP FROM INSIDE?
IS THIS WHAT WILL HAPPEN TO *ALL* OF THEM?
I'M RUNNING OUT OF TIME.
AND IT'S NOT LIKE I DON'T KNOW WHAT IT IS I'LL FIND.
I COULD SEE IT... THEY ALL SHARE THE SAME MIND. THE SAME MEMORY.

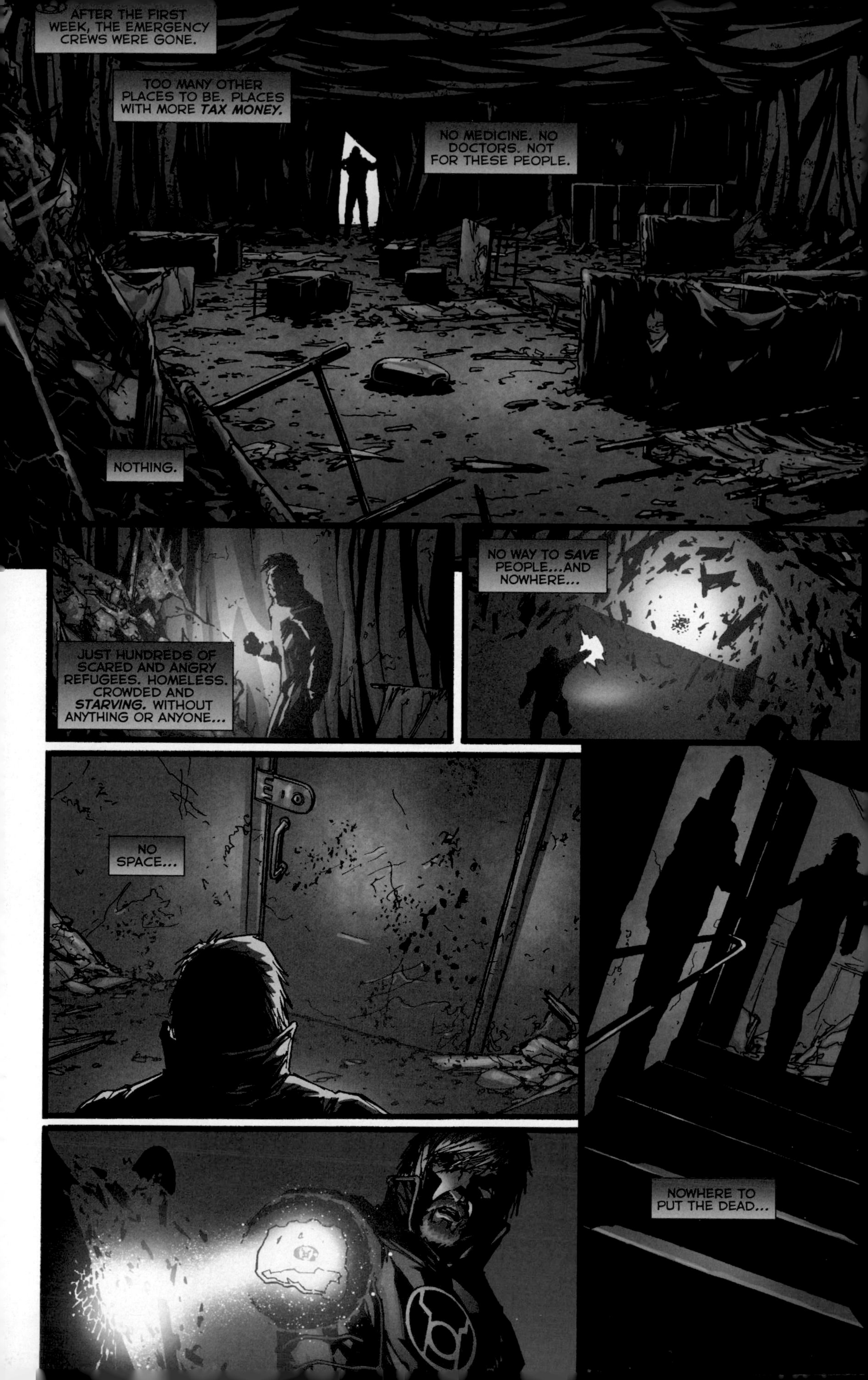
AFTER THE FIRST WEEK, THE EMERGENCY CREWS WERE GONE.
TOO MANY OTHER PLACES TO BE. PLACES WITH MORE TAX MONEY.
NO MEDICINE. NO DOCTORS. NOT FOR THESE PEOPLE.
NOTHING.
JUST HUNDREDS OF SCARED AND ANGRY REFUGEES. HOMELESS. CROWDED AND STARVING. WITHOUT ANYTHING OR ANYONE...
NO WAY TO SAVE PEOPLE...AND NOWHERE...
NO SPACE...
NOWHERE TO PUT THE DEAD...

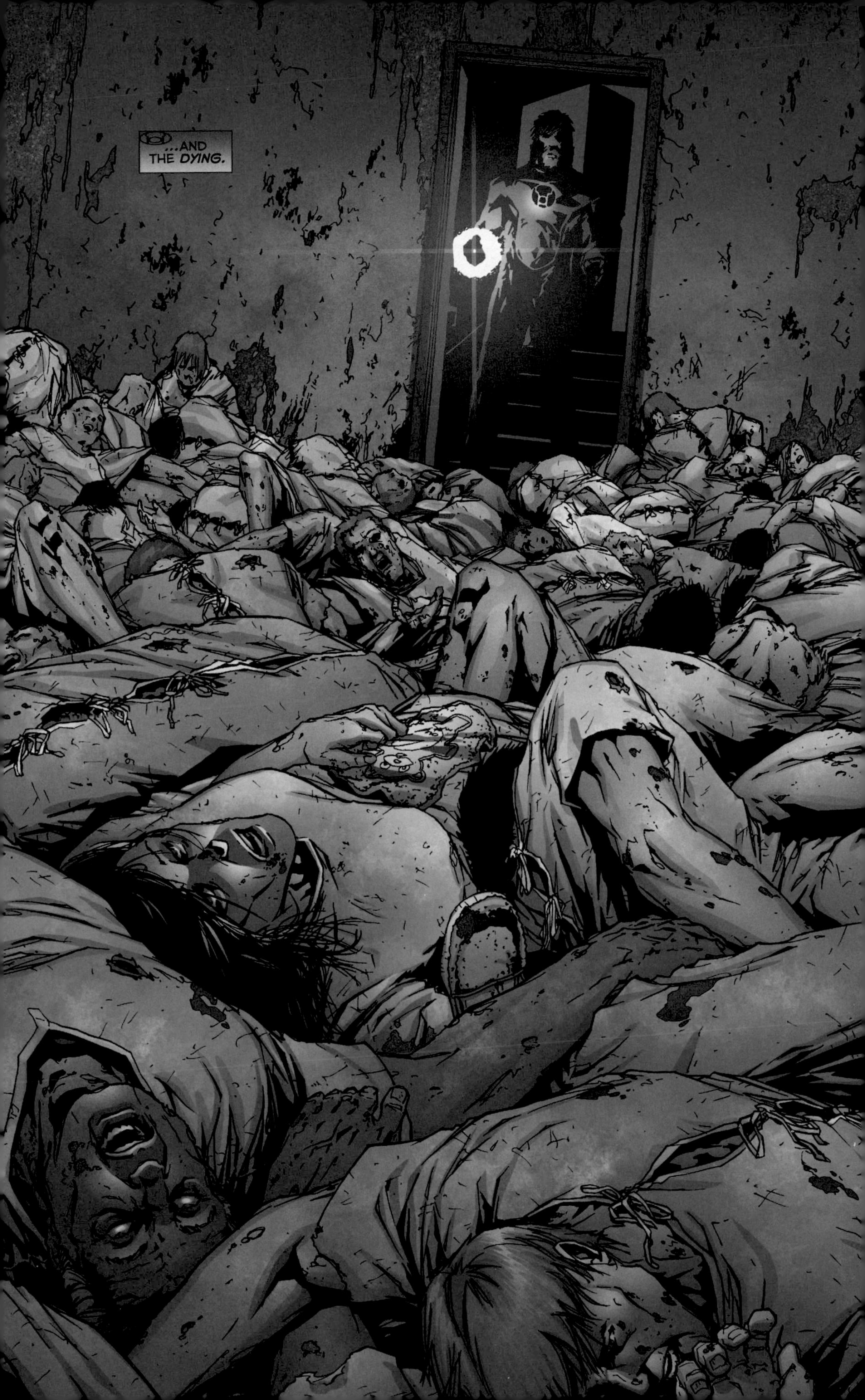
...AND THE DYING.

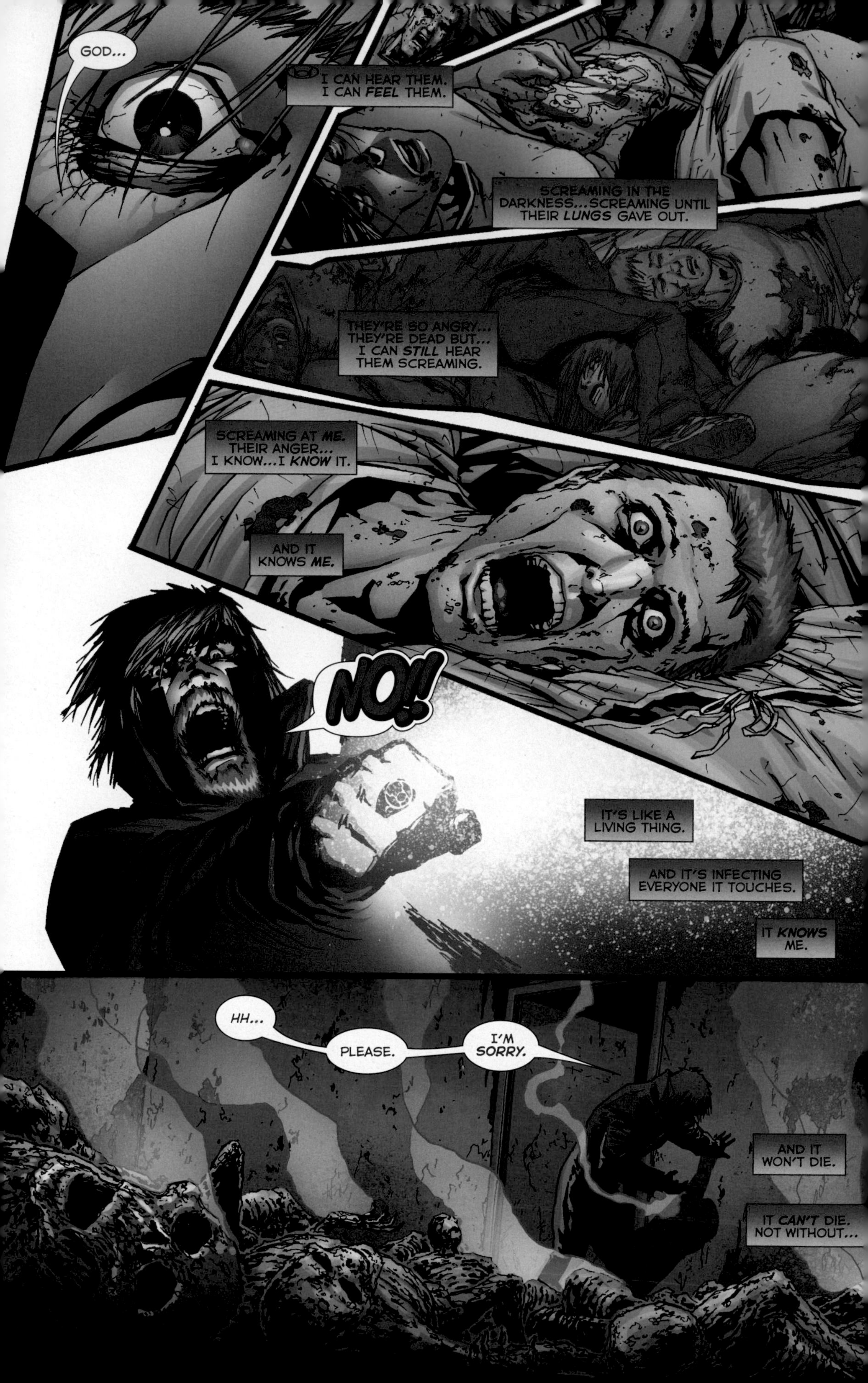
GOD...
I CAN HEAR THEM. I CAN FEEL THEM.
SCREAMING IN THE DARKNESS...SCREAMING UNTIL THEIR LUNGS GAVE OUT.
THEY'RE SO ANGRY... THEY'RE DEAD BUT... I CAN STILL HEAR THEM SCREAMING.
SCREAMING AT ME. THEIR ANGER... I KNOW...I KNOW IT.
AND IT KNOWS ME.
NO!!
IT'S LIKE A LIVING THING.
AND IT'S INFECTING EVERYONE IT TOUCHES.
IT KNOWS ME.
HH...
PLEASE.
I'M SORRY.
AND IT WON'T DIE.
IT CAN'T DIE. NOT WITHOUT...

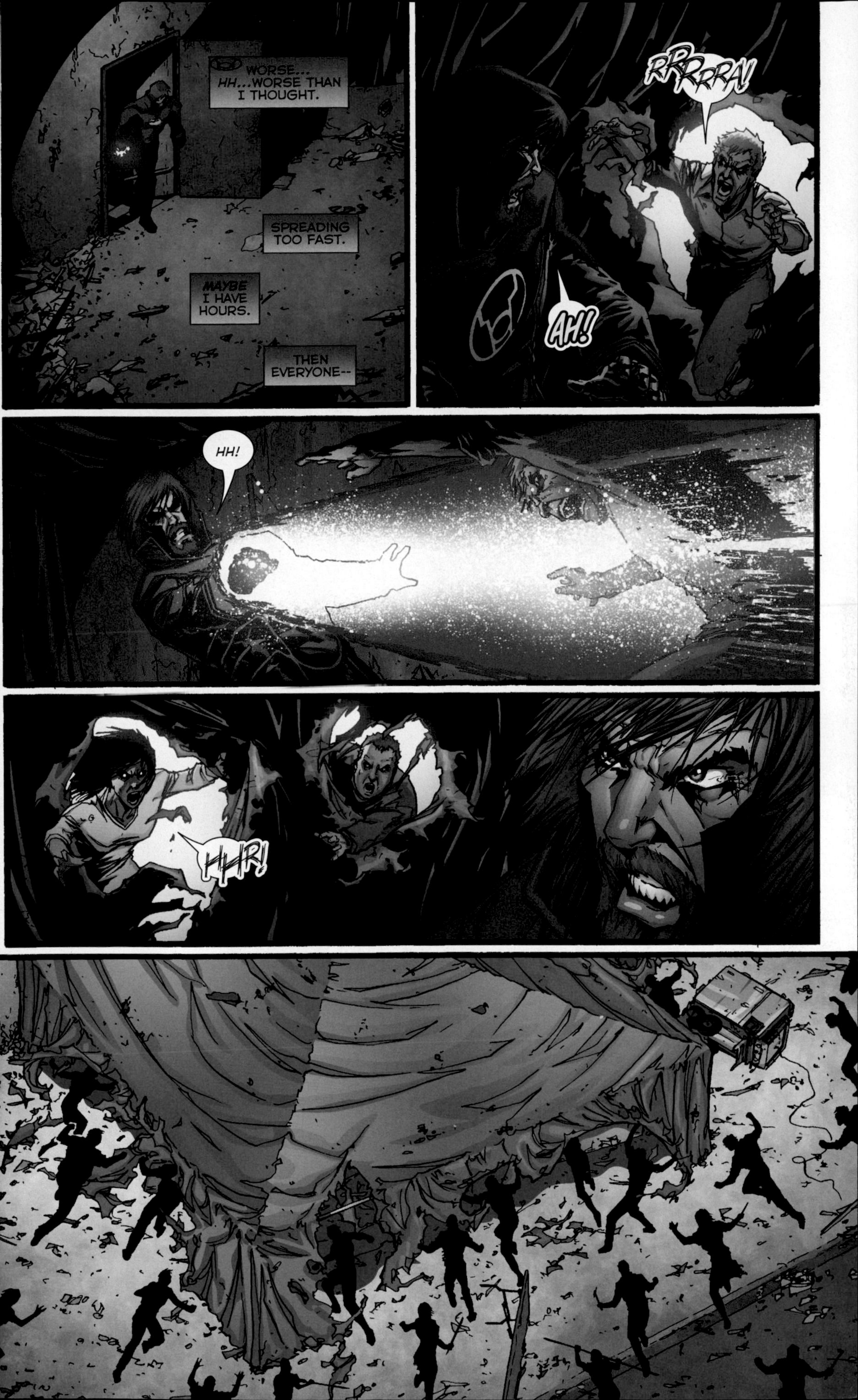
WORSE... HH...WORSE THAN I THOUGHT.
SPREADING TOO FAST.
MAYBE I HAVE HOURS.
THEN EVERYONE--
RRRRRRA!
AH!
HH!
HHR!

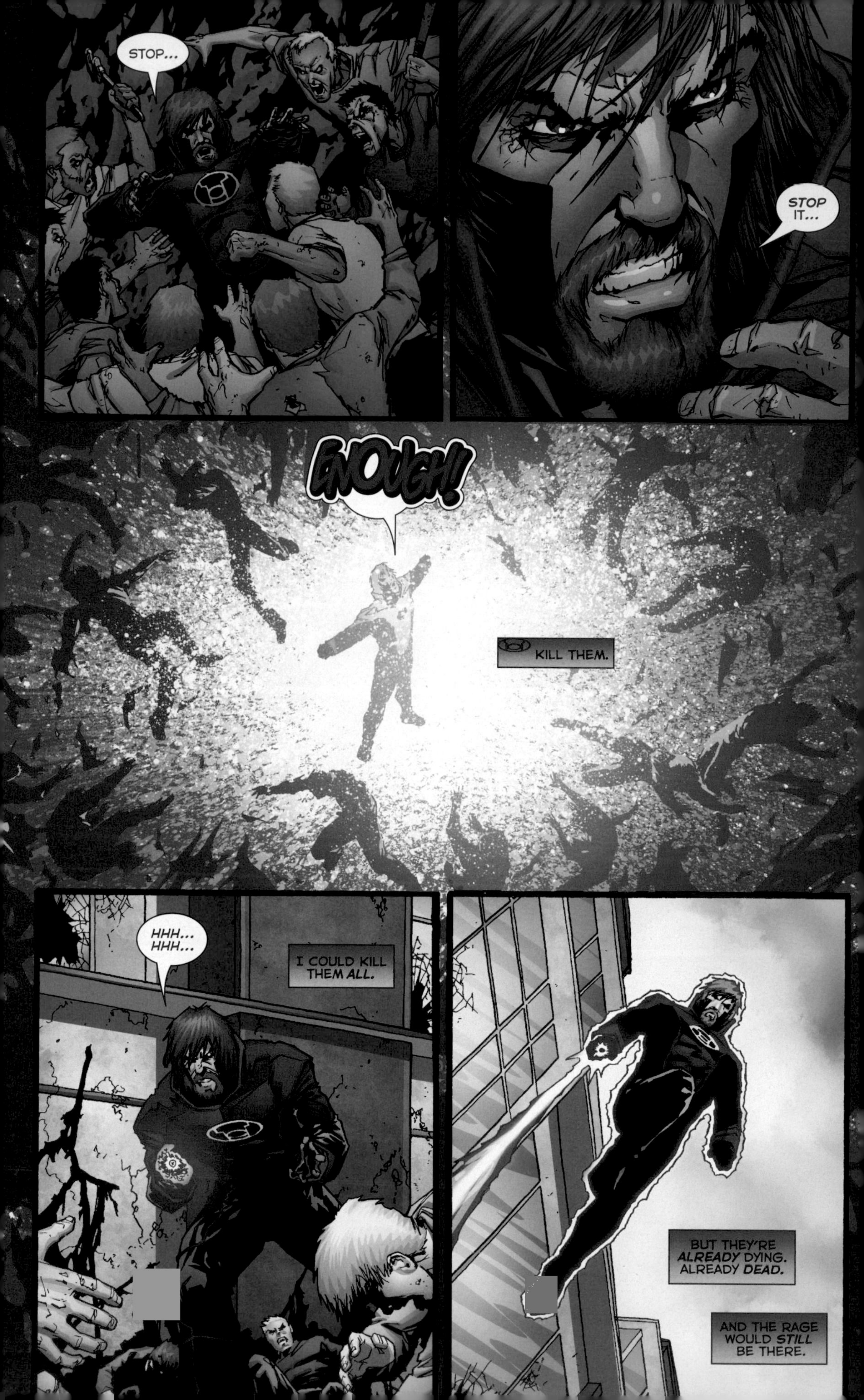
STOP...
STOP IT...
ENOUGH!
KILL THEM.
HHH... HHH...
I COULD KILL THEM ALL.
BUT THEY'RE ALREADY DYING. ALREADY DEAD.
AND THE RAGE WOULD STILL BE THERE.

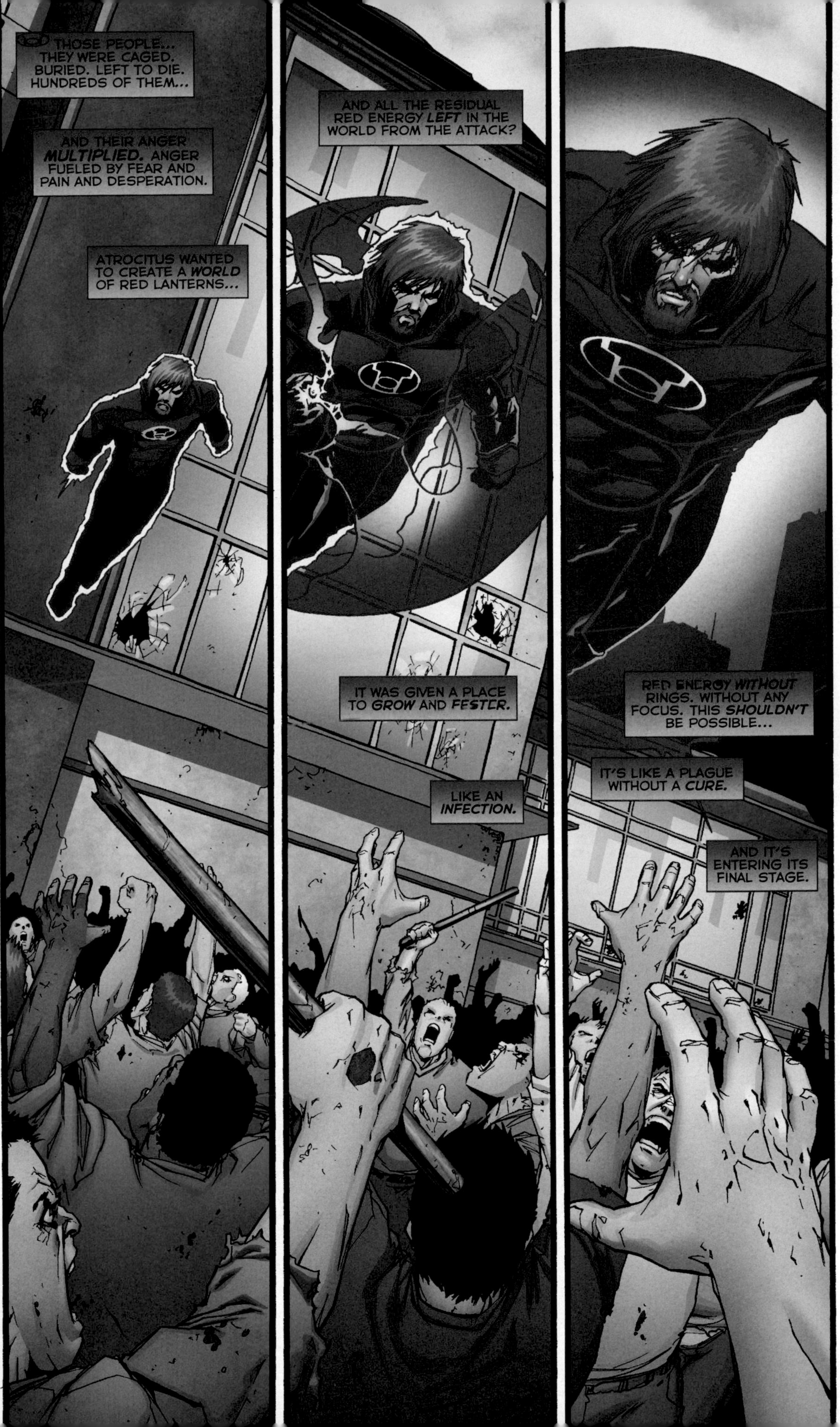
THOSE PEOPLE... THEY WERE CAGED. BURIED. LEFT TO DIE. HUNDREDS OF THEM...
AND THEIR ANGER MULTIPLIED. ANGER FUELED BY FEAR AND PAIN AND DESPERATION.
ATROCITUS WANTED TO CREATE A WORLD OF RED LANTERNS...
AND ALL THE RESIDUAL RED ENERGY LEFT IN THE WORLD FROM THE ATTACK?
IT WAS GIVEN A PLACE TO GROW AND FESTER.
LIKE AN INFECTION.
RED ENERGY WITHOUT RINGS. WITHOUT ANY FOCUS. THIS SHOULDN'T BE POSSIBLE...
IT'S LIKE A PLAGUE WITHOUT A CURE.
AND IT'S ENTERING ITS FINAL STAGE.

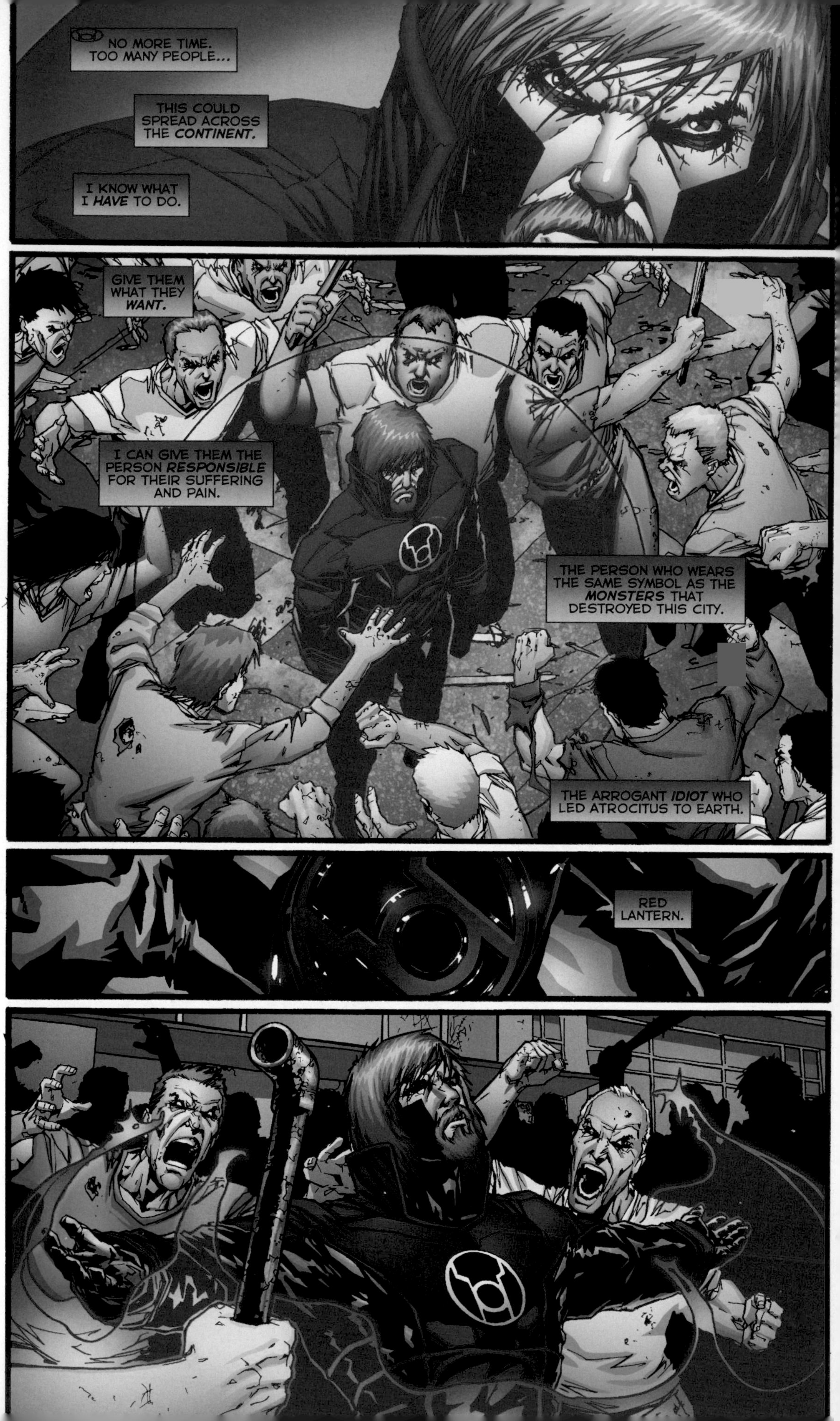
NO MORE TIME. TOO MANY PEOPLE...
THIS COULD SPREAD ACROSS THE CONTINENT.
I KNOW WHAT I HAVE TO DO.
GIVE THEM WHAT THEY WANT.
I CAN GIVE THEM THE PERSON RESPONSIBLE FOR THEIR SUFFERING AND PAIN.
THE PERSON WHO WEARS THE SAME SYMBOL AS THE MONSTERS THAT DESTROYED THIS CITY.
THE ARROGANT IDIOT WHO LED ATROCITUS TO EARTH.
RED LANTERN.

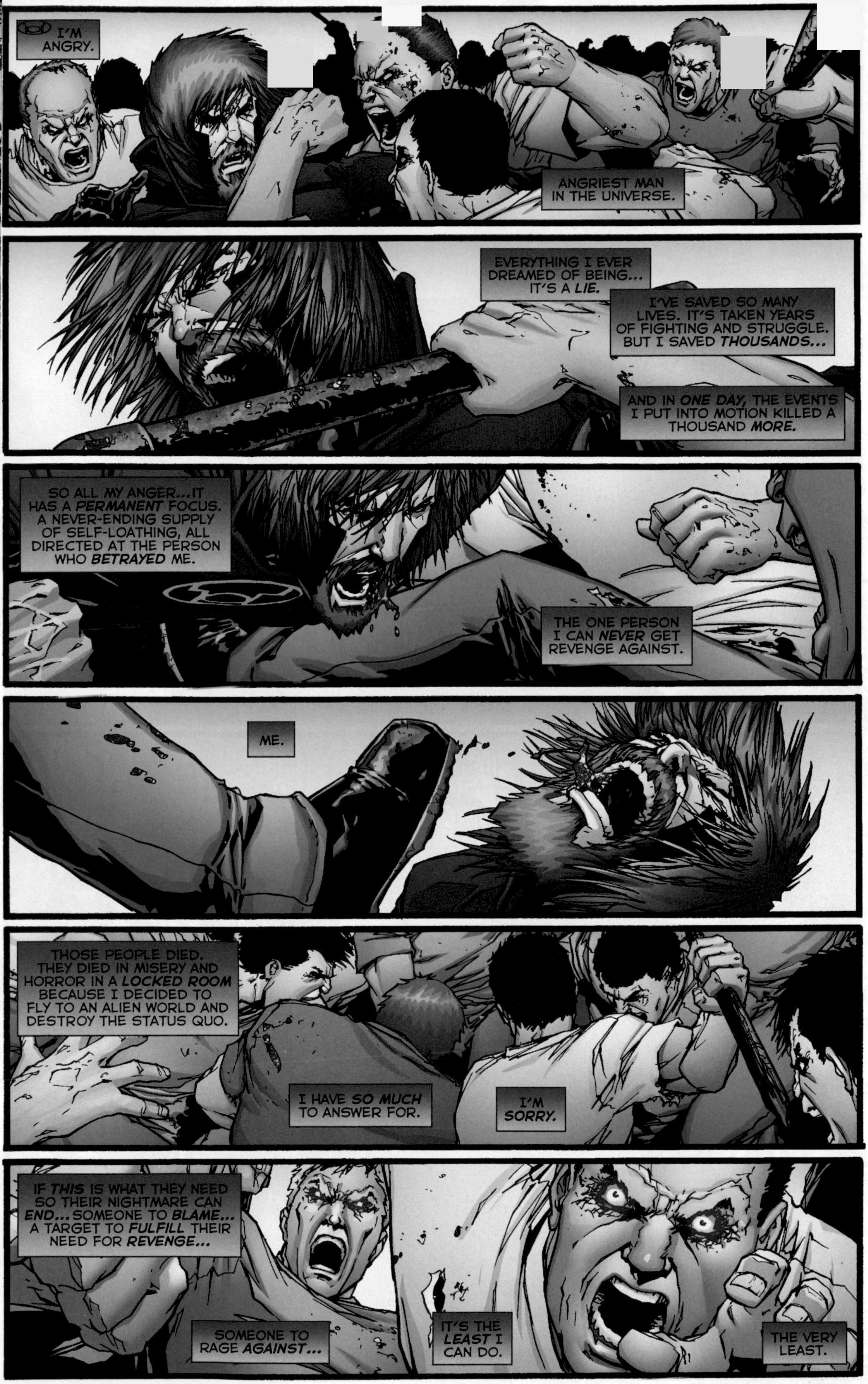
I'M ANGRY.
ANGRIEST MAN IN THE UNIVERSE.
EVERYTHING I EVER DREAMED OF BEING... IT'S A LIE.
I'VE SAVED SO MANY LIVES. IT'S TAKEN YEARS OF FIGHTING AND STRUGGLE. BUT I SAVED THOUSANDS...
AND IN ONE DAY, THE EVENTS I PUT INTO MOTION KILLED A THOUSAND MORE.
SO ALL MY ANGER...IT HAS A PERMANENT FOCUS. A NEVER-ENDING SUPPLY OF SELF-LOATHING, ALL DIRECTED AT THE PERSON WHO BETRAYED ME.
THE ONE PERSON I CAN NEVER GET REVENGE AGAINST.
ME.
THOSE PEOPLE DIED. THEY DIED IN MISERY AND HORROR IN A LOCKED ROOM BECAUSE I DECIDED TO FLY TO AN ALIEN WORLD AND DESTROY THE STATUS QUO.
I HAVE SO MUCH TO ANSWER FOR.
I'M SORRY.
IF THIS IS WHAT THEY NEED SO THEIR NIGHTMARE CAN END...SOMEONE TO BLAME... A TARGET TO FULFILL THEIR NEED FOR REVENGE...
SOMEONE TO RAGE AGAINST...
IT'S THE LEAST I CAN DO.
THE VERY LEAST.

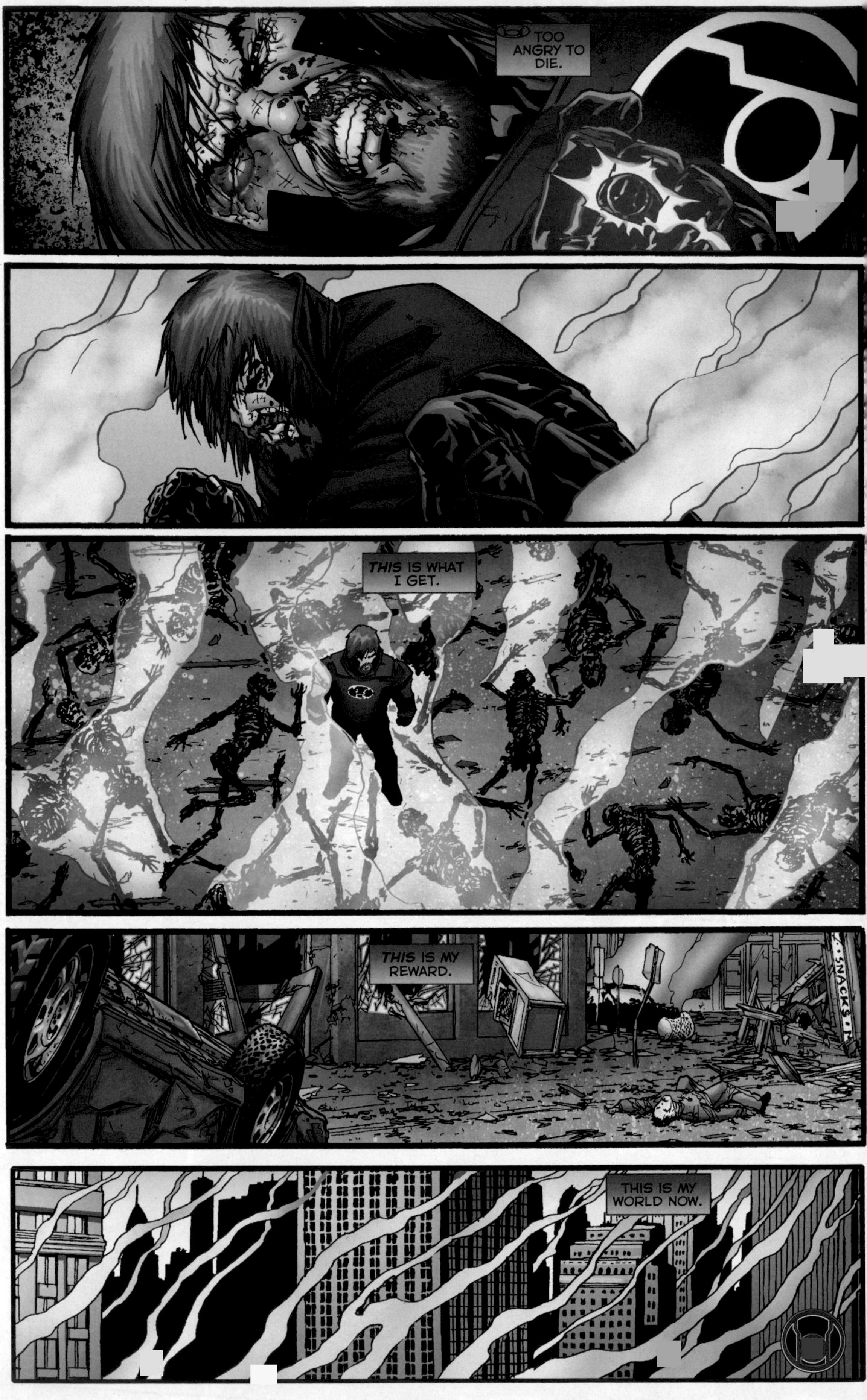
TOO ANGRY TO DIE.
THIS IS WHAT I GET.
THIS IS MY REWARD.
SNACKS
THIS IS MY WORLD NOW.

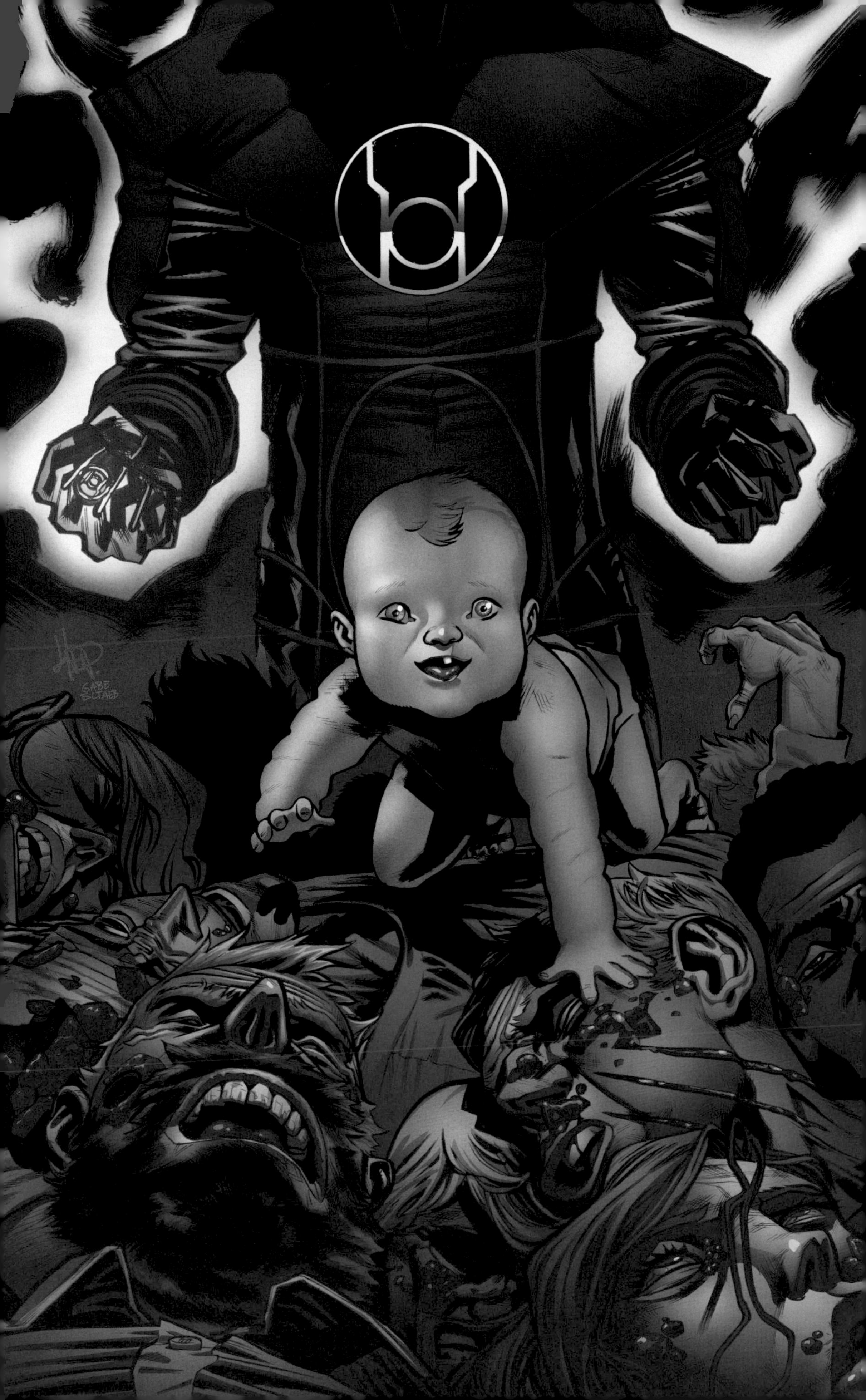

HUSH LI'L BABY

LANDRY Q. WALKER writer **J. CALAFIORE** artist **GABE ELTAEB** colorist **DAVE SHARPE** letterer
cover art by **SCOTT HEPBURN** and **GABE ELTAEB**

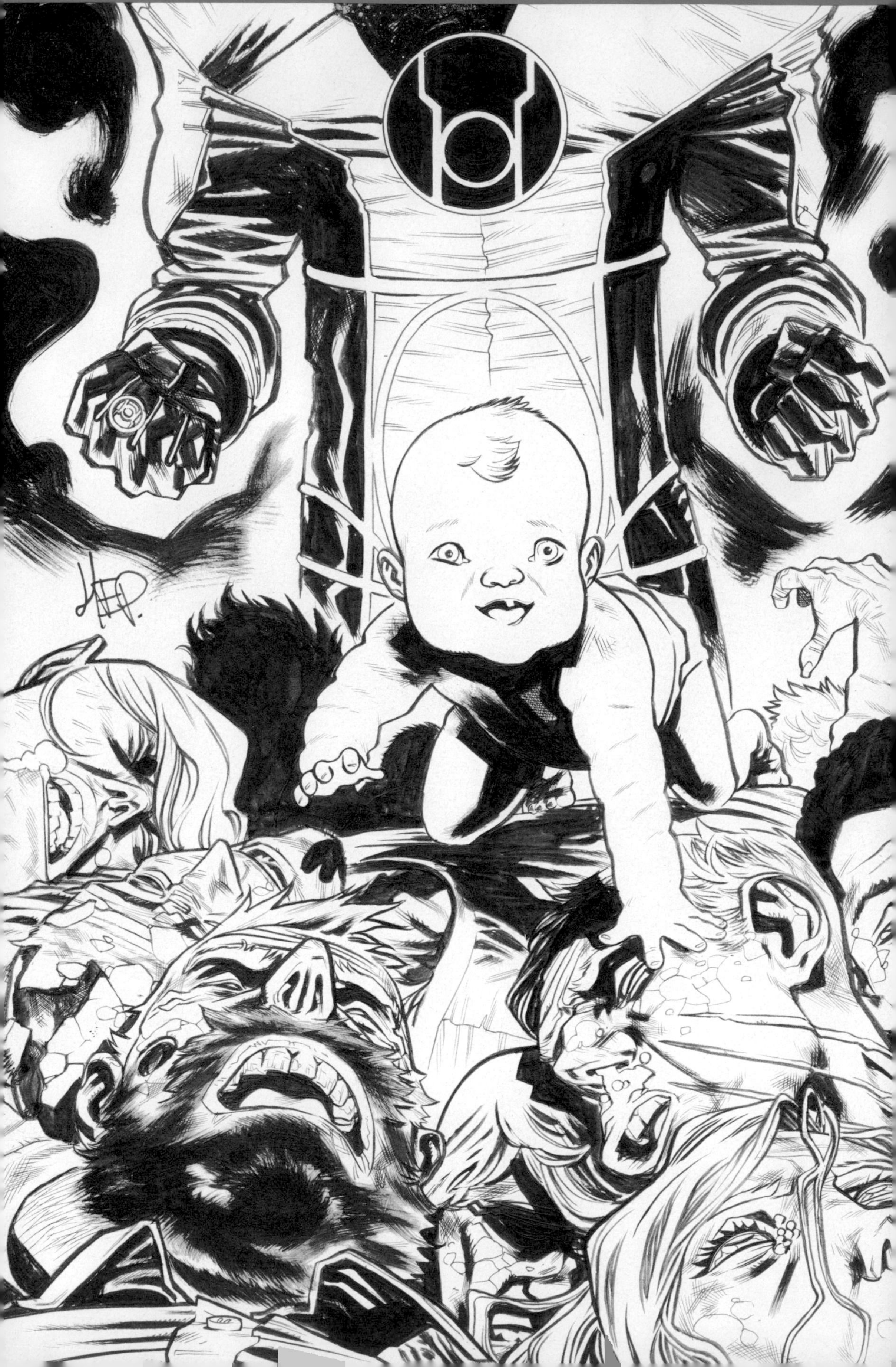

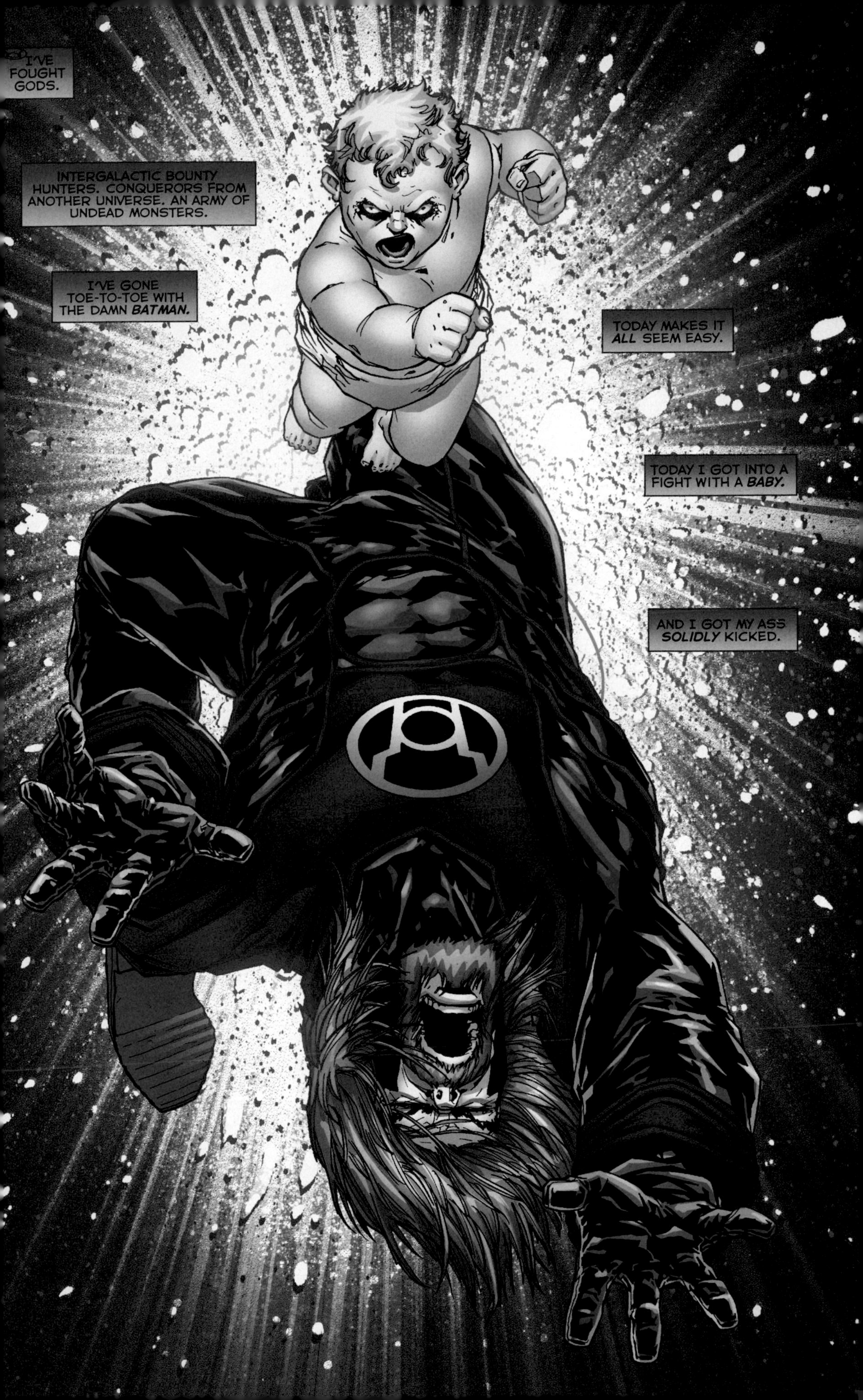
I'VE FOUGHT GODS.
INTERGALACTIC BOUNTY HUNTERS. CONQUERORS FROM ANOTHER UNIVERSE. AN ARMY OF UNDEAD MONSTERS.
I'VE GONE TOE-TO-TOE WITH THE DAMN BATMAN.
TODAY MAKES IT ALL SEEM EASY.
TODAY I GOT INTO A FIGHT WITH A BABY.
AND I GOT MY ASS SOLIDLY KICKED.

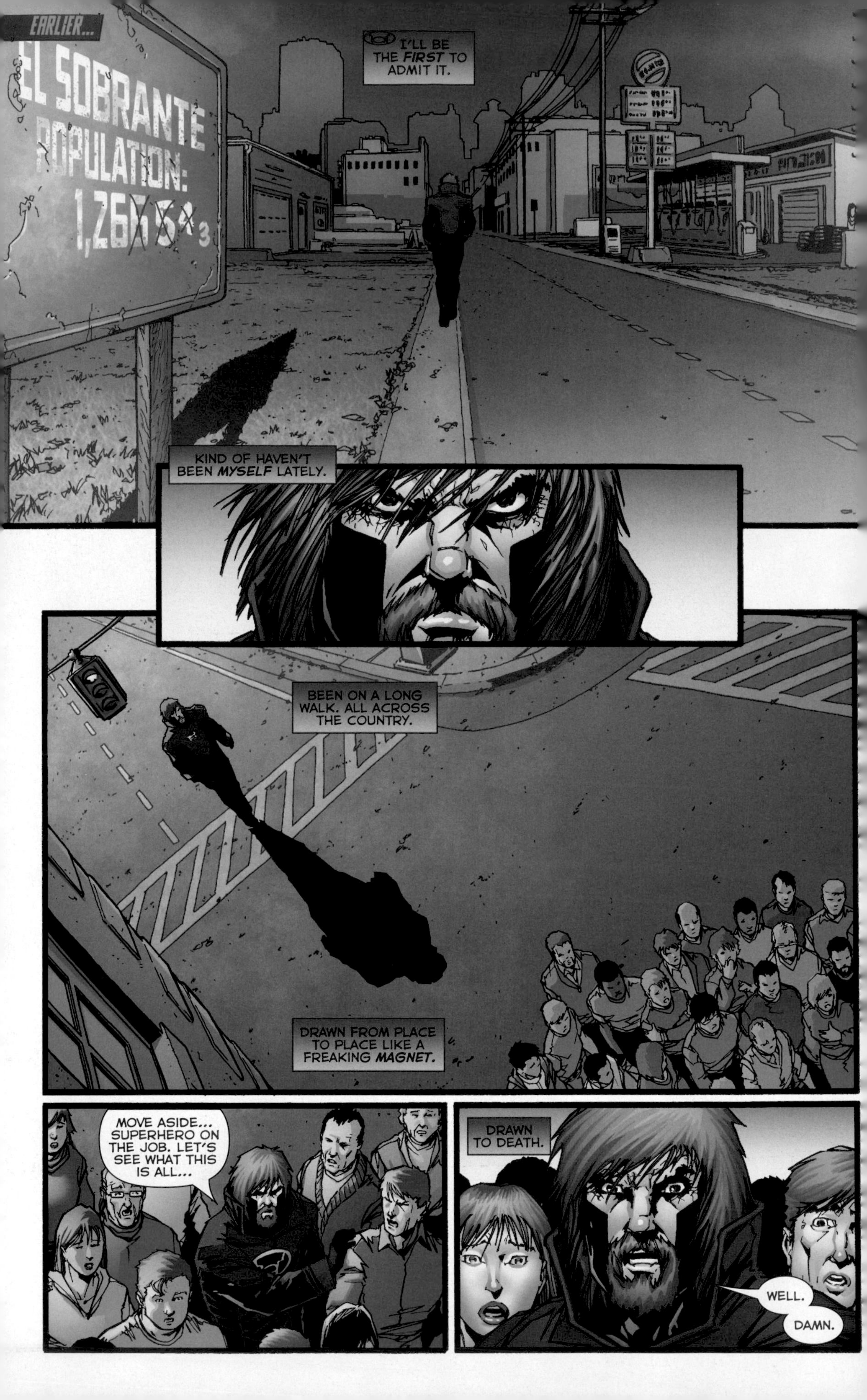
EARLIER...
EL SOBRANTE POPULATION: 1,263
I'LL BE THE FIRST TO ADMIT IT.
KIND OF HAVEN'T BEEN MYSELF LATELY.
BEEN ON A LONG WALK. ALL ACROSS THE COUNTRY.
DRAWN FROM PLACE TO PLACE LIKE A FREAKING MAGNET.
MOVE ASIDE... SUPERHERO ON THE JOB. LET'S SEE WHAT THIS IS ALL...
DRAWN TO DEATH.
WELL.
DAMN.

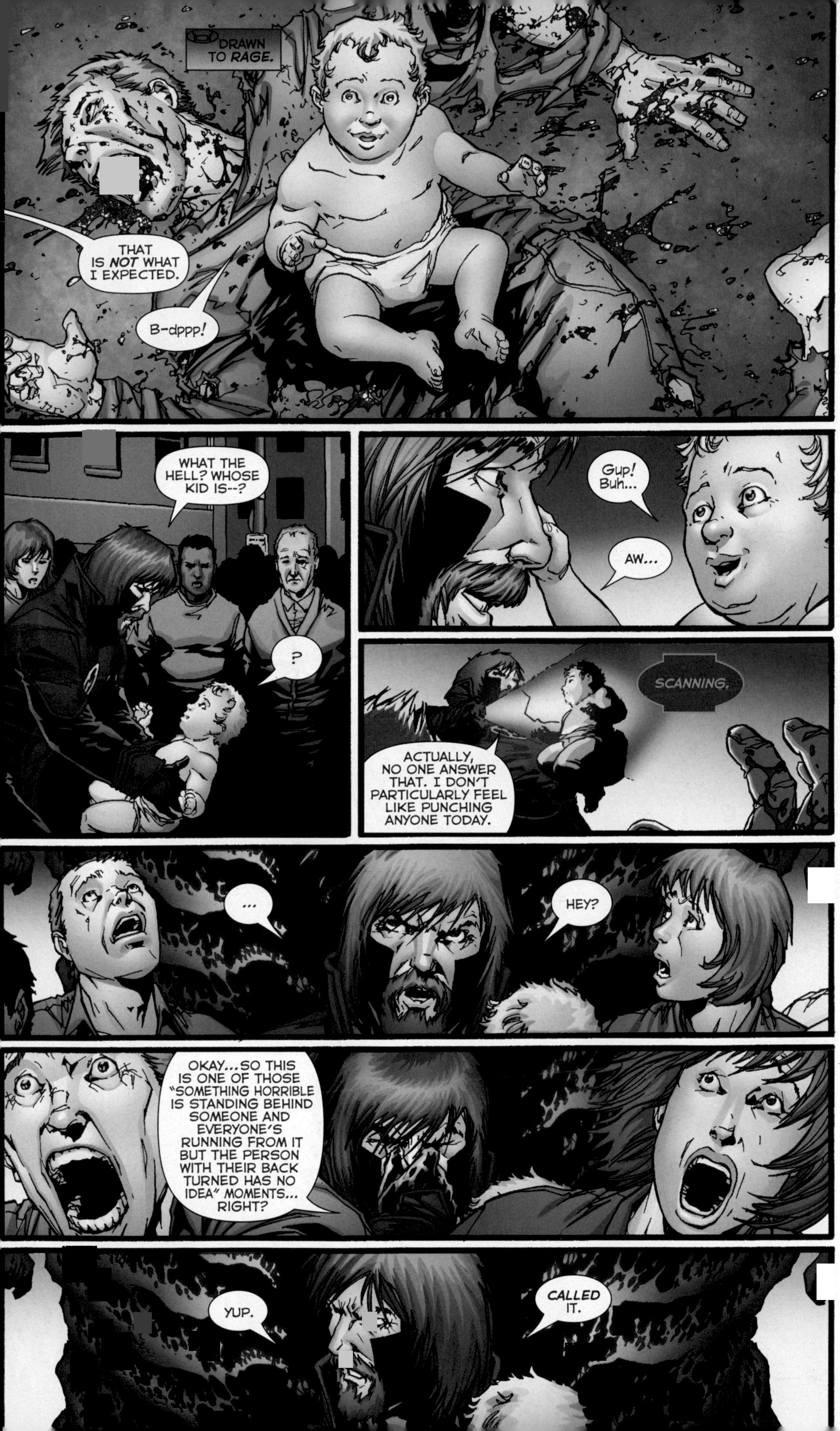
DRAWN TO RAGE.
THAT IS NOT WHAT I EXPECTED.
B-dppp!
WHAT THE HELL? WHOSE KID IS--?
?
Gup! Buh...
AW...
SCANNING.
ACTUALLY, NO ONE ANSWER THAT. I DON'T PARTICULARLY FEEL LIKE PUNCHING ANYONE TODAY.
...
HEY?
OKAY...SO THIS IS ONE OF THOSE "SOMETHING HORRIBLE IS STANDING BEHIND SOMEONE AND EVERYONE'S RUNNING FROM IT BUT THE PERSON WITH THEIR BACK TURNED HAS NO IDEA" MOMENTS... RIGHT?
YUP.
CALLED IT.

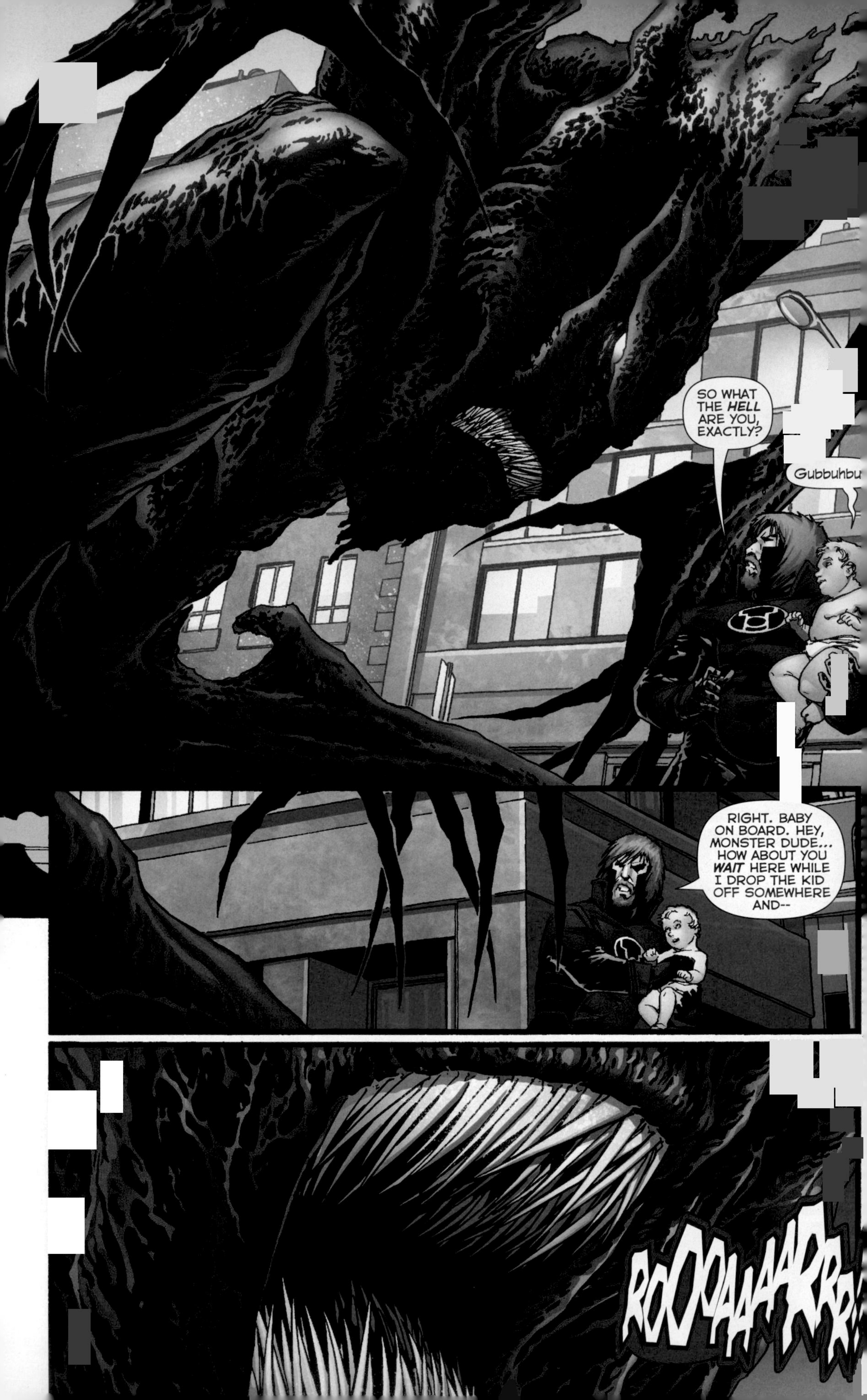
SO WHAT THE *HELL* ARE YOU, EXACTLY?
Gubbuhbu
RIGHT. BABY ON BOARD. HEY, MONSTER DUDE... HOW ABOUT YOU *WAIT* HERE WHILE I DROP THE KID OFF SOMEWHERE AND--
ROOOAAARRR!

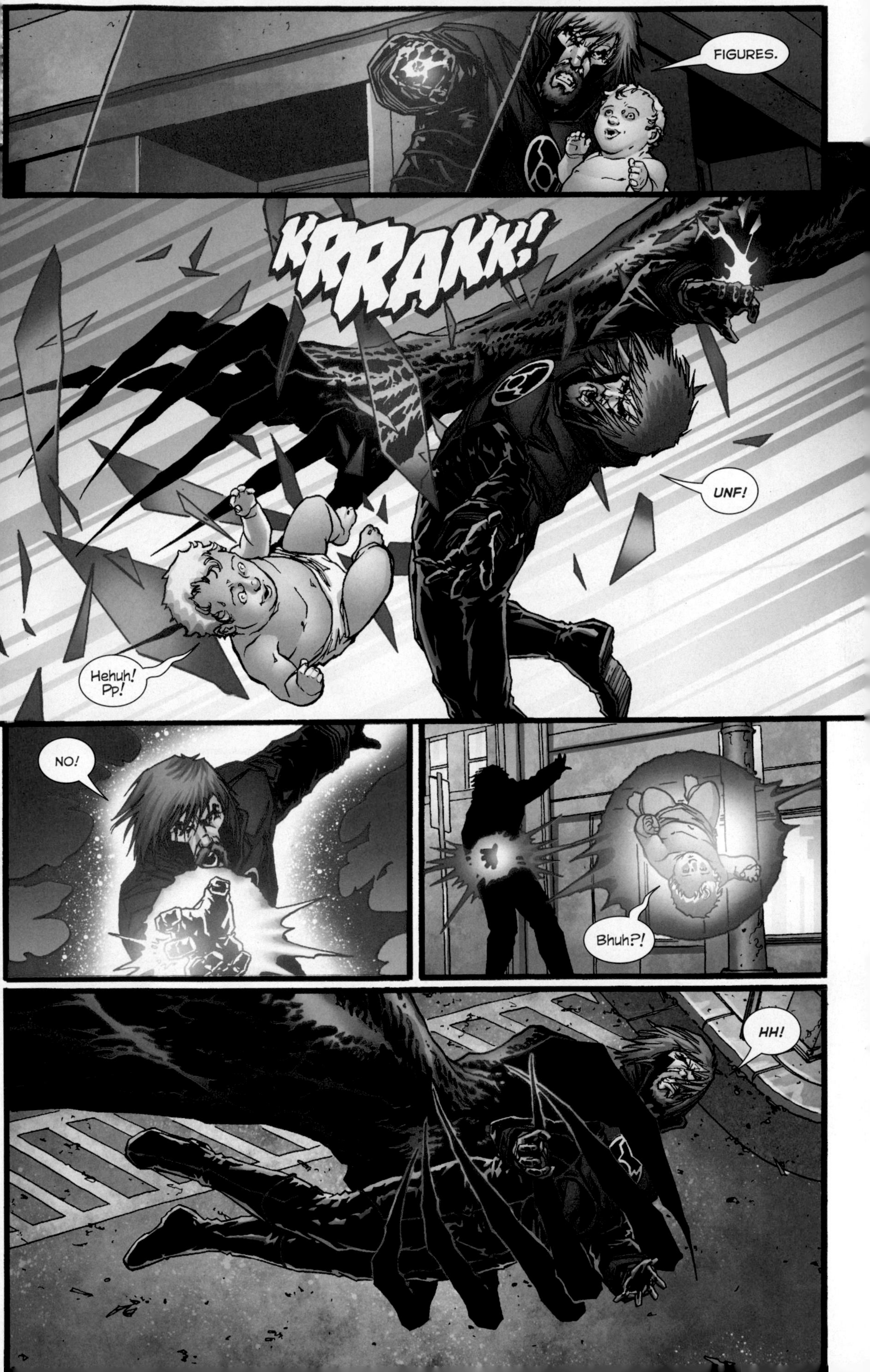
FIGURES.
KRRAKK!
UNF!
Hehuh! Pp!
NO!
Bhuh?!
HH!

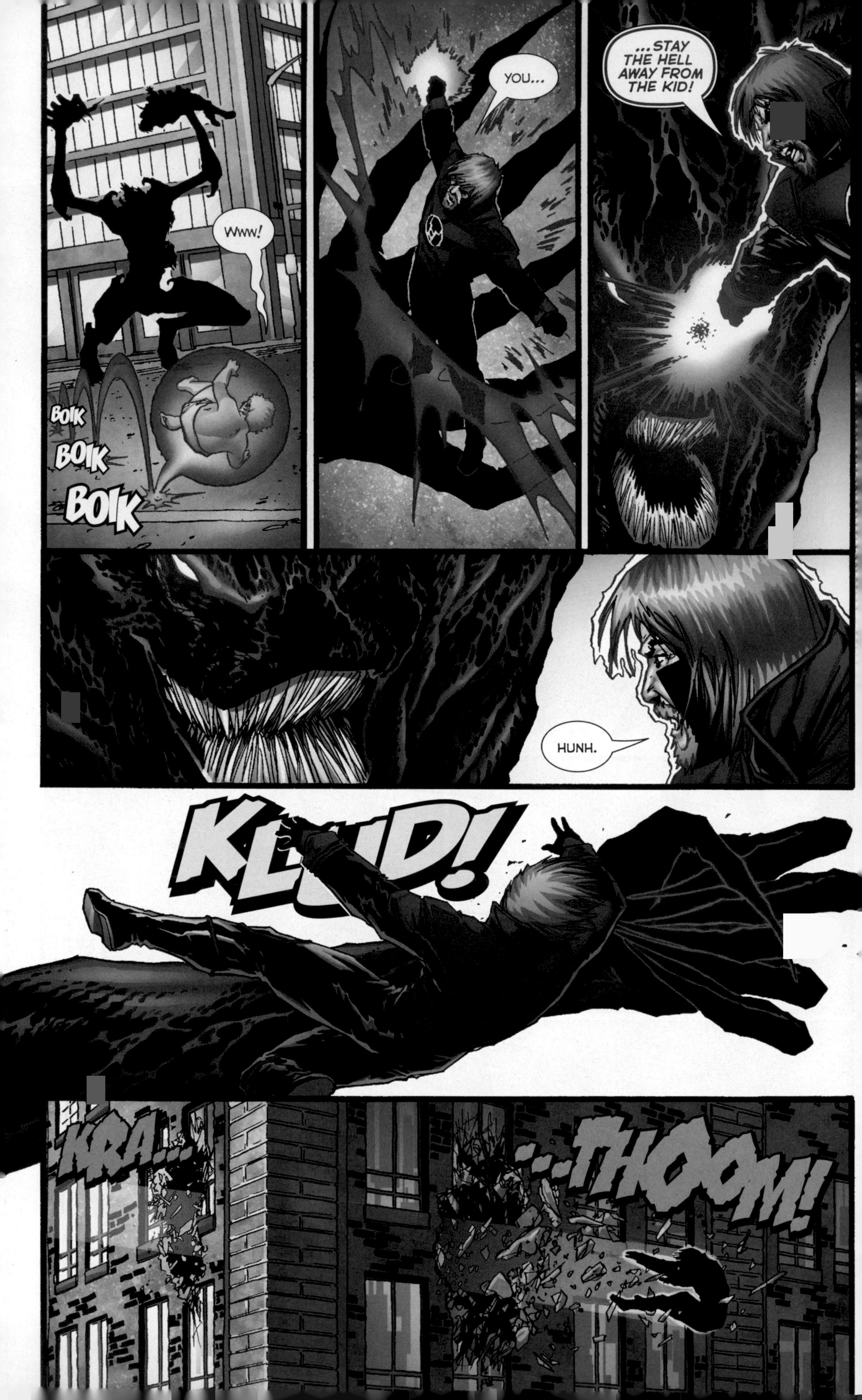
WWW!
BOIK
BOIK
BOIK
YOU...
...STAY THE HELL AWAY FROM THE KID!
HUNH.
KLUD!
KRA...
...THOOM!

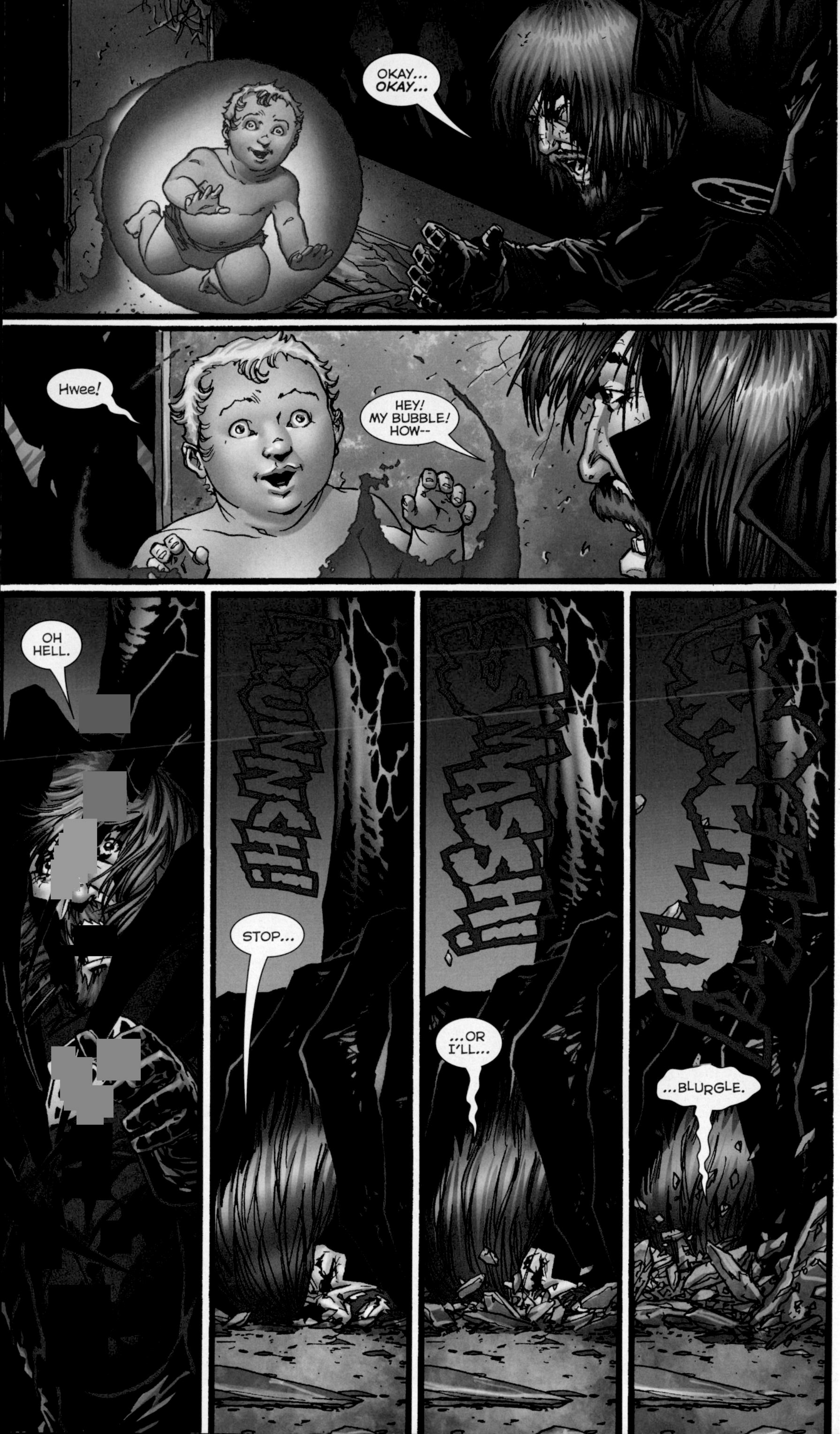
OKAY... OKAY...
Hwee!
HEY! MY BUBBLE! HOW--
OH HELL.
STOP...
...OR I'LL...
...BLURGLE.

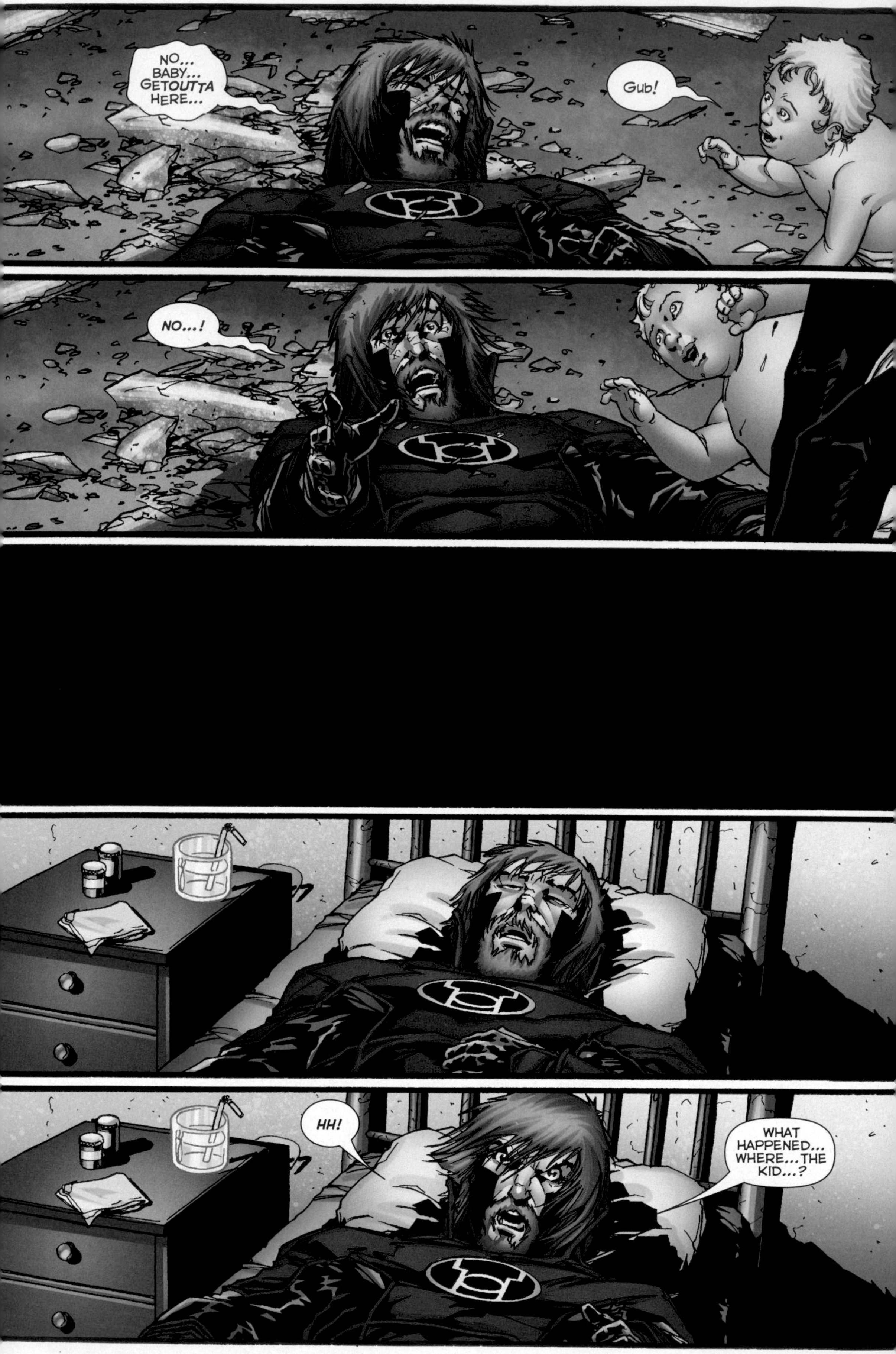
NO... BABY... GETOUTTA HERE...
Gub!
NO...!
HH!
WHAT HAPPENED... WHERE...THE KID...?

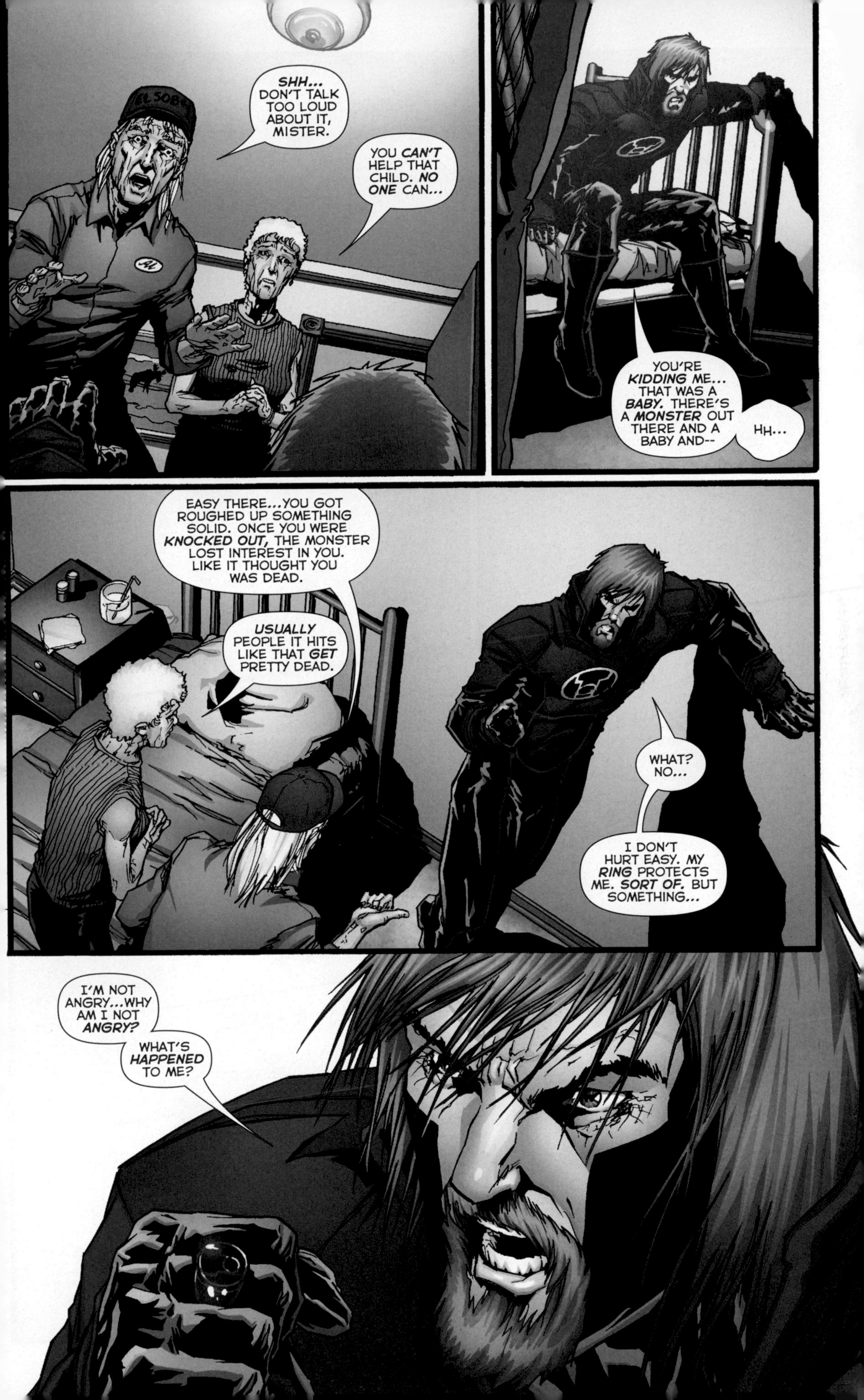

SHH... DON'T TALK TOO LOUD ABOUT IT, MISTER.
YOU CAN'T HELP THAT CHILD. NO ONE CAN...
YOU'RE KIDDING ME... THAT WAS A BABY. THERE'S A MONSTER OUT THERE AND A BABY AND--
HH...
EASY THERE...YOU GOT ROUGHED UP SOMETHING SOLID. ONCE YOU WERE KNOCKED OUT, THE MONSTER LOST INTEREST IN YOU. LIKE IT THOUGHT YOU WAS DEAD.
USUALLY PEOPLE IT HITS LIKE THAT GET PRETTY DEAD.
WHAT? NO...
I DON'T HURT EASY. MY RING PROTECTS ME. SORT OF. BUT SOMETHING...
I'M NOT ANGRY...WHY AM I NOT ANGRY?
WHAT'S HAPPENED TO ME?

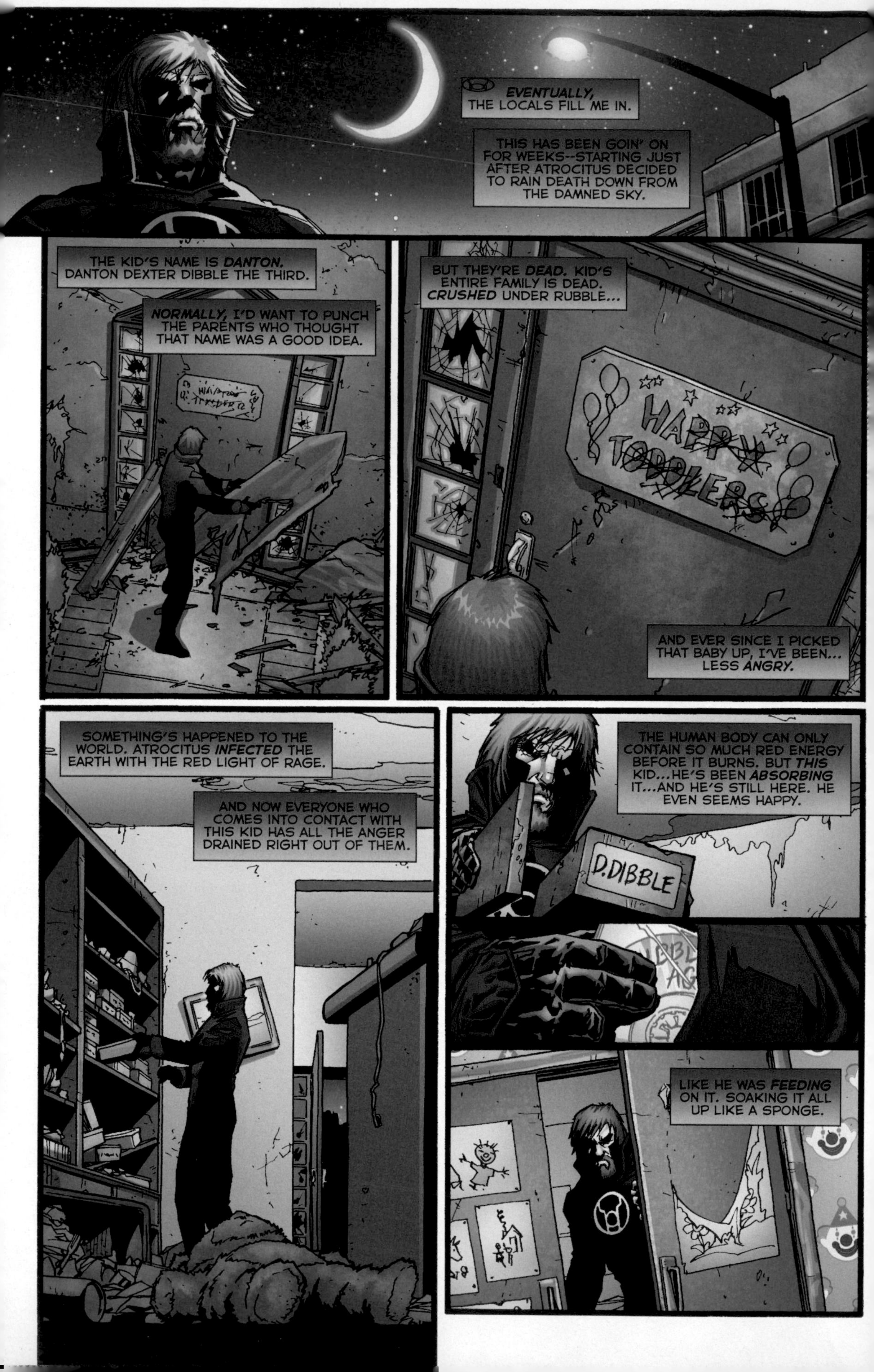
EVENTUALLY, THE LOCALS FILL ME IN.
THIS HAS BEEN GOIN' ON FOR WEEKS--STARTING JUST AFTER ATROCITUS DECIDED TO RAIN DEATH DOWN FROM THE DAMNED SKY.
THE KID'S NAME IS DANTON. DANTON DEXTER DIBBLE THE THIRD.
NORMALLY, I'D WANT TO PUNCH THE PARENTS WHO THOUGHT THAT NAME WAS A GOOD IDEA.
BUT THEY'RE DEAD. KID'S ENTIRE FAMILY IS DEAD. CRUSHED UNDER RUBBLE...
HAPPY TODDLERS
AND EVER SINCE I PICKED THAT BABY UP, I'VE BEEN... LESS ANGRY.
SOMETHING'S HAPPENED TO THE WORLD. ATROCITUS INFECTED THE EARTH WITH THE RED LIGHT OF RAGE.
AND NOW EVERYONE WHO COMES INTO CONTACT WITH THIS KID HAS ALL THE ANGER DRAINED RIGHT OUT OF THEM.
THE HUMAN BODY CAN ONLY CONTAIN SO MUCH RED ENERGY BEFORE IT BURNS. BUT THIS KID...HE'S BEEN ABSORBING IT...AND HE'S STILL HERE. HE EVEN SEEMS HAPPY.
D.DIBBLE
LIKE HE WAS FEEDING ON IT. SOAKING IT ALL UP LIKE A SPONGE.

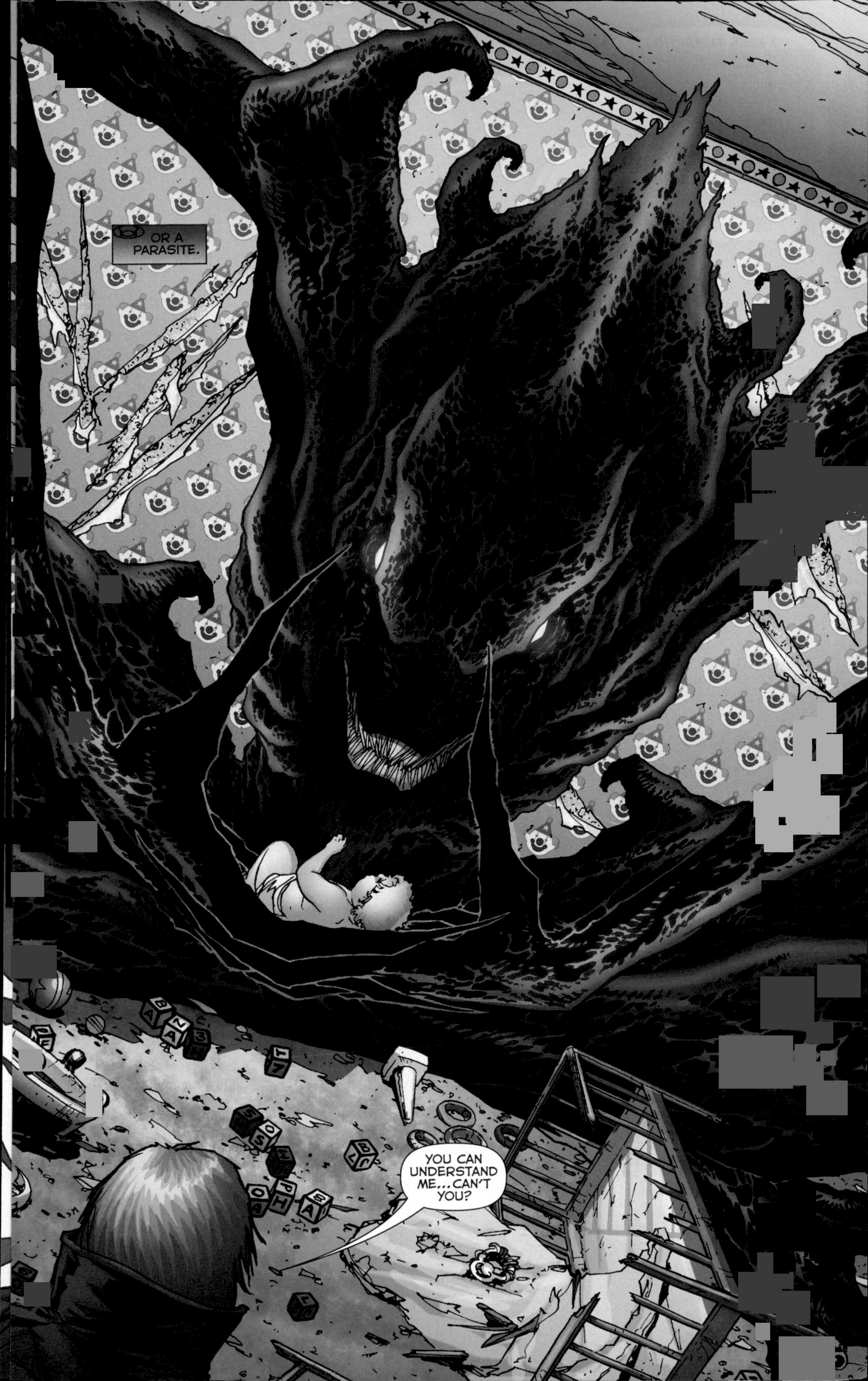
OR A PARASITE.
YOU CAN UNDERSTAND ME...CAN'T YOU?

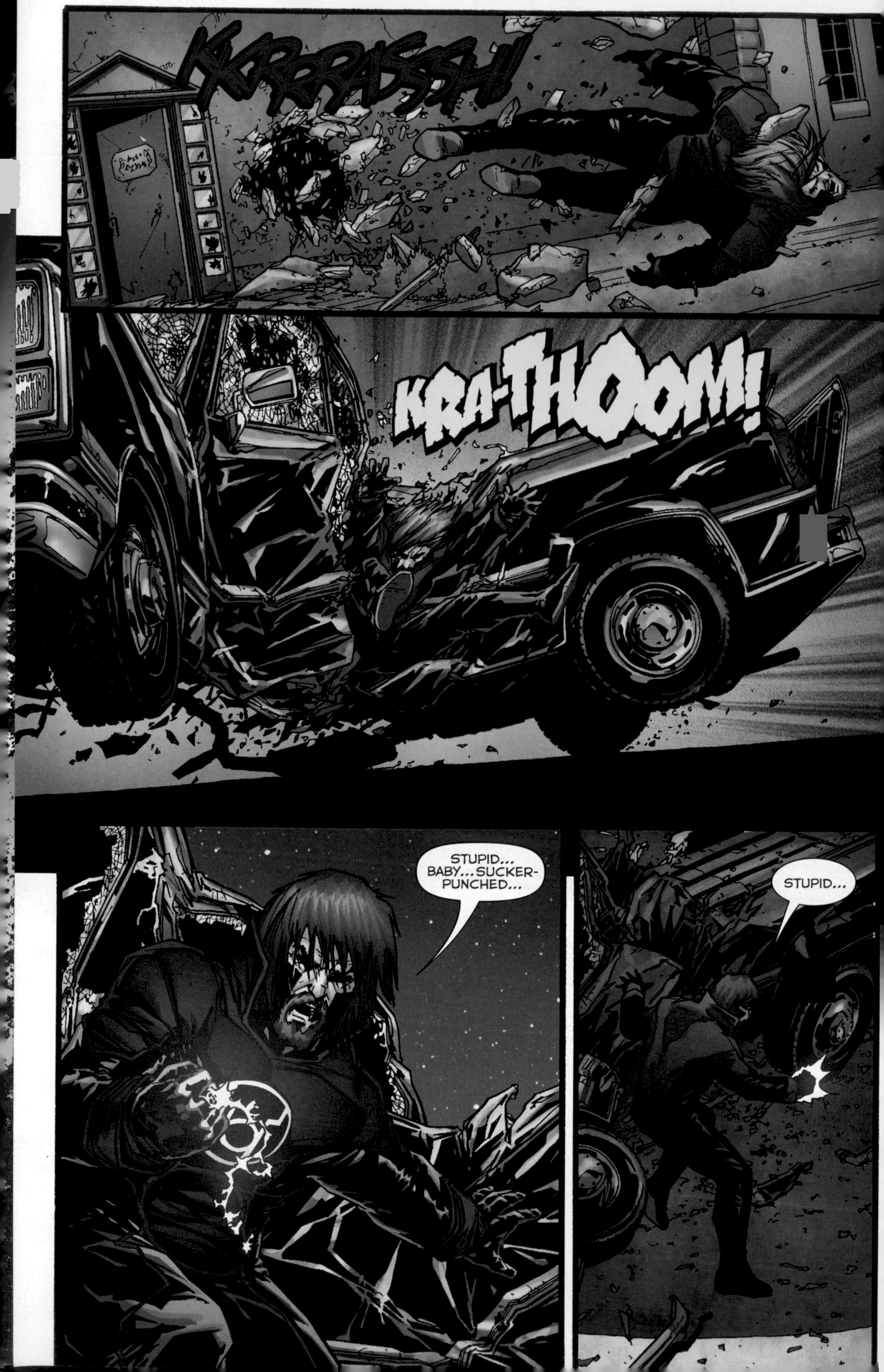
KKRRRASSSH!
KRA-THOOM!
STUPID... BABY... SUCKER-PUNCHED...
STUPID...

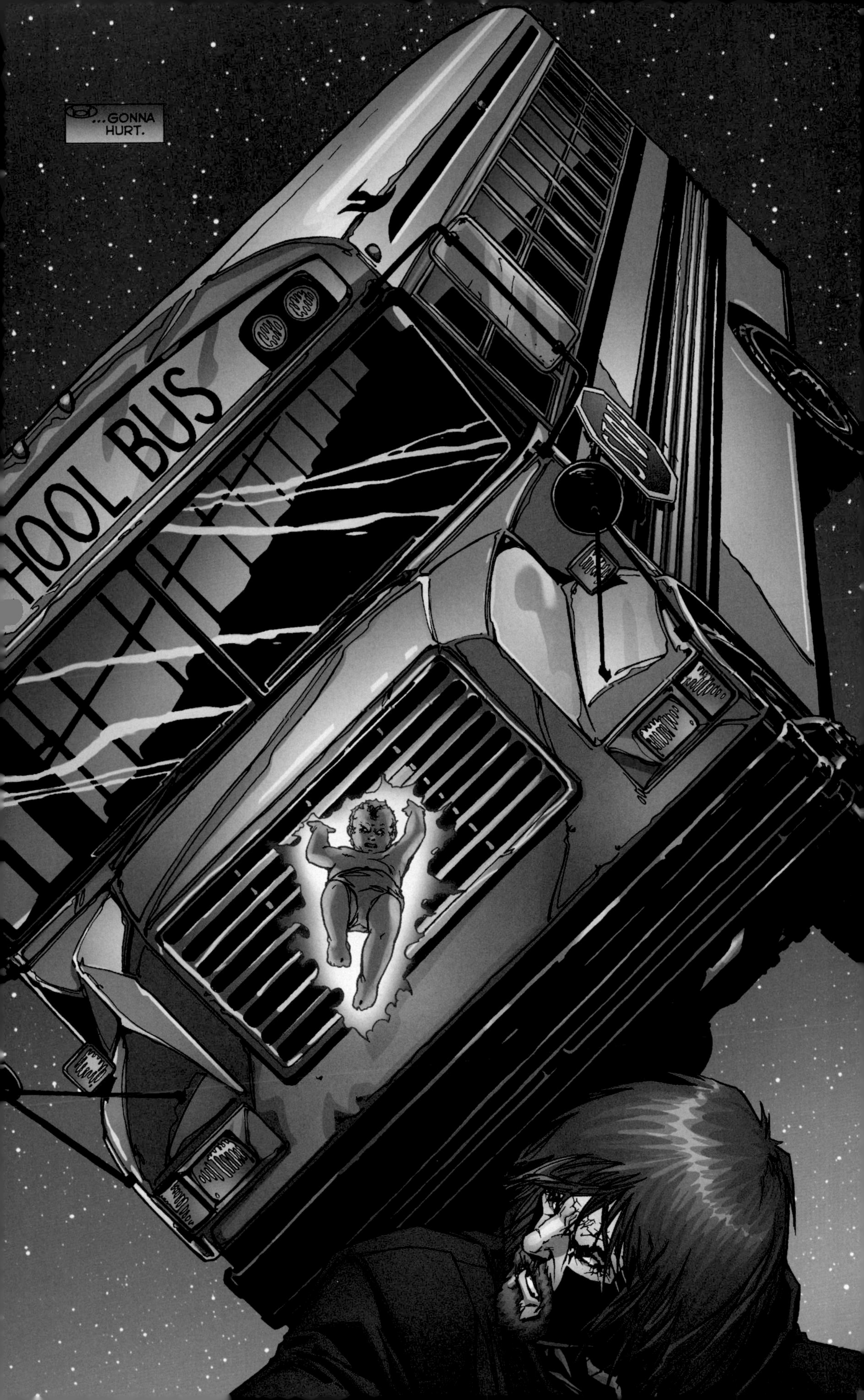
...GONNA HURT.
HOOL BUS

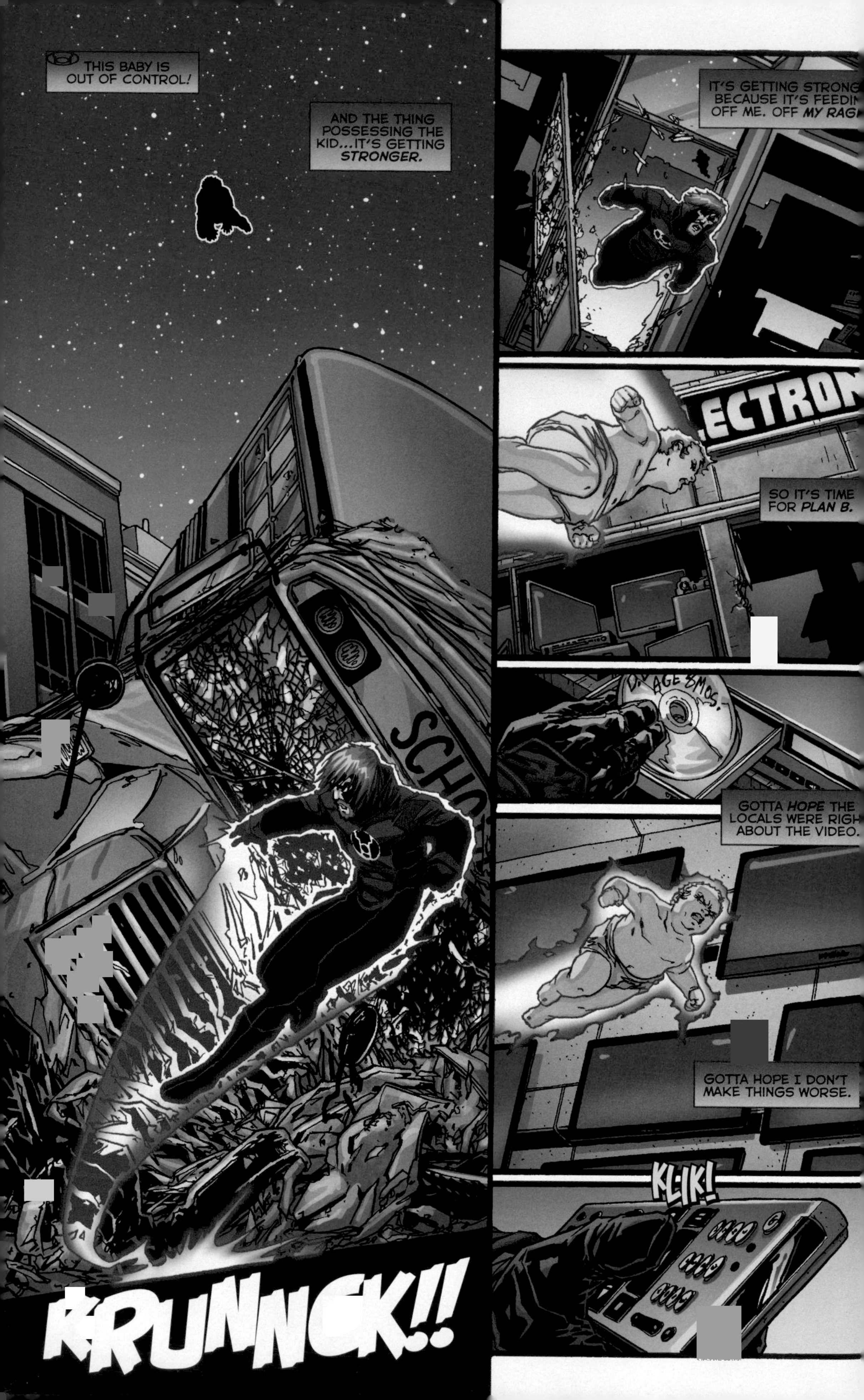
THIS BABY IS OUT OF CONTROL!
AND THE THING POSSESSING THE KID...IT'S GETTING STRONGER.
SCHO
KRUNNCK!!
IT'S GETTING STRONG BECAUSE IT'S FEEDI OFF ME. OFF MY RAG
ECTRON
SO IT'S TIME FOR PLAN B.
AGE 8MOS.
GOTTA HOPE THE LOCALS WERE RIGH ABOUT THE VIDEO.
GOTTA HOPE I DON'T MAKE THINGS WORSE.
KLIK!

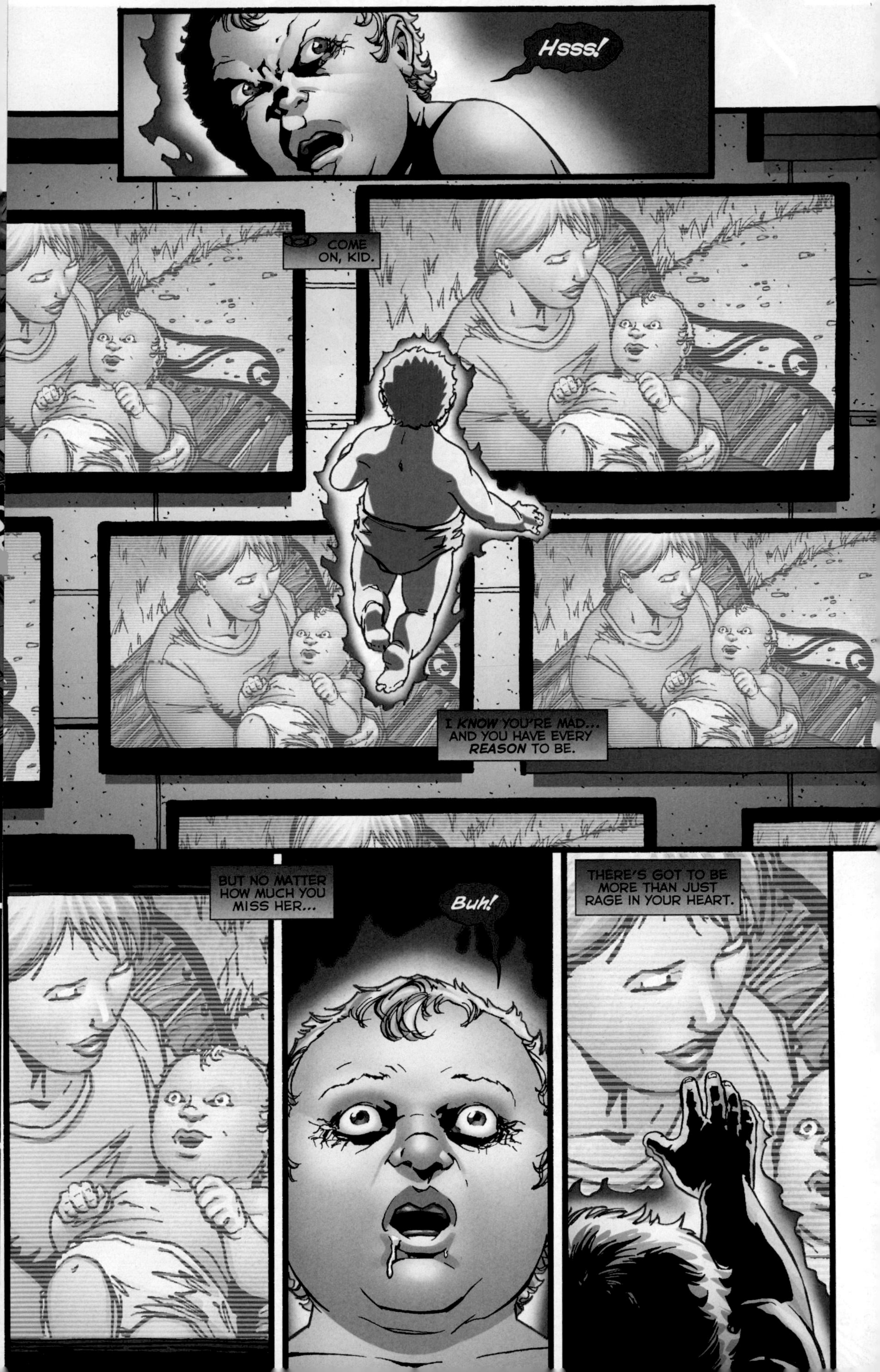
Hsss!
COME ON, KID.
I KNOW YOU'RE MAD... AND YOU HAVE EVERY REASON TO BE.
BUT NO MATTER HOW MUCH YOU MISS HER...
Buh!
THERE'S GOT TO BE MORE THAN JUST RAGE IN YOUR HEART.

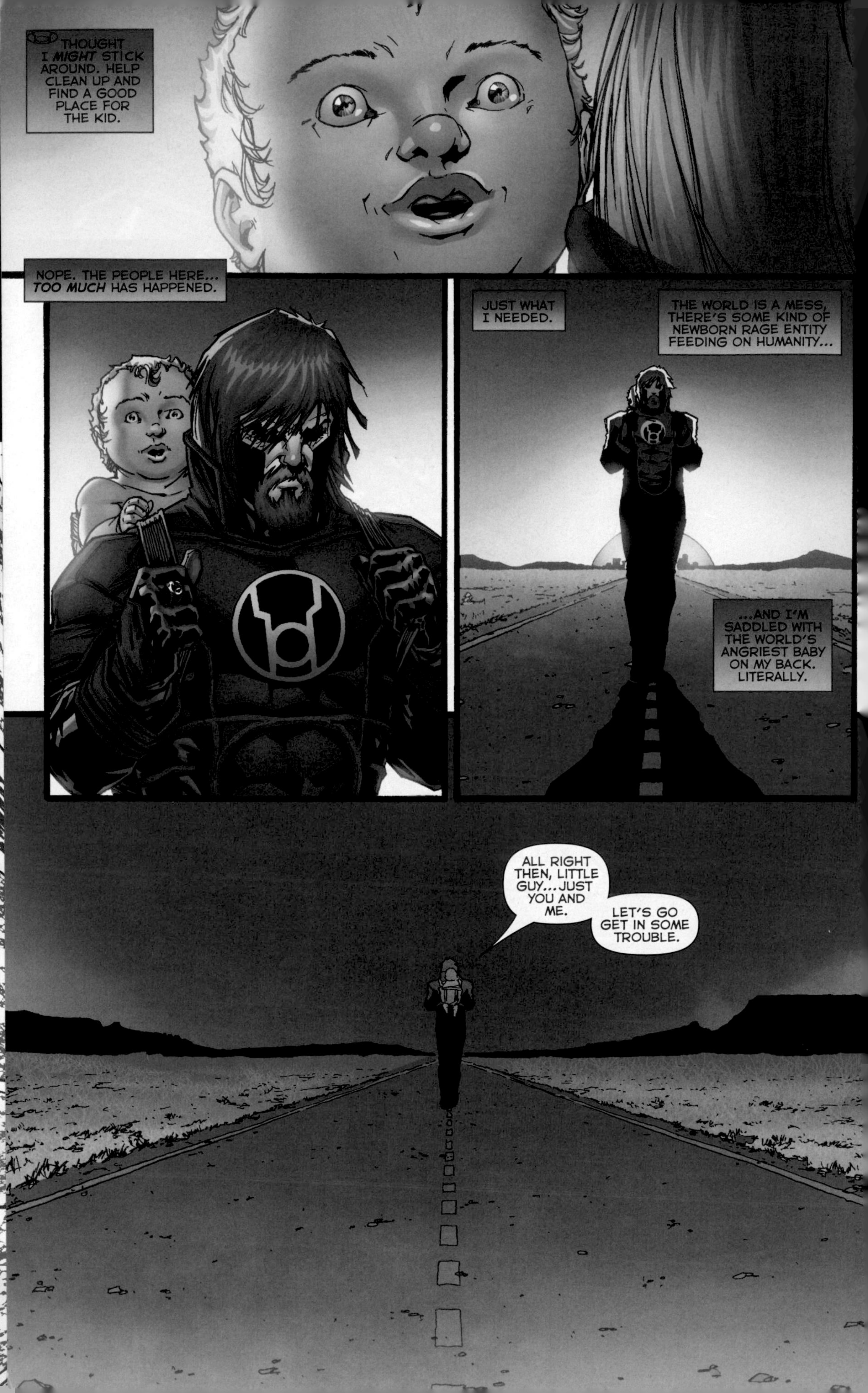
THOUGHT I MIGHT STICK AROUND. HELP CLEAN UP AND FIND A GOOD PLACE FOR THE KID.
NOPE. THE PEOPLE HERE... TOO MUCH HAS HAPPENED.
JUST WHAT I NEEDED.
THE WORLD IS A MESS, THERE'S SOME KIND OF NEWBORN RAGE ENTITY FEEDING ON HUMANITY...
...AND I'M SADDLED WITH THE WORLD'S ANGRIEST BABY ON MY BACK. LITERALLY.
ALL RIGHT THEN, LITTLE GUY... JUST YOU AND ME.
LET'S GO GET IN SOME TROUBLE.

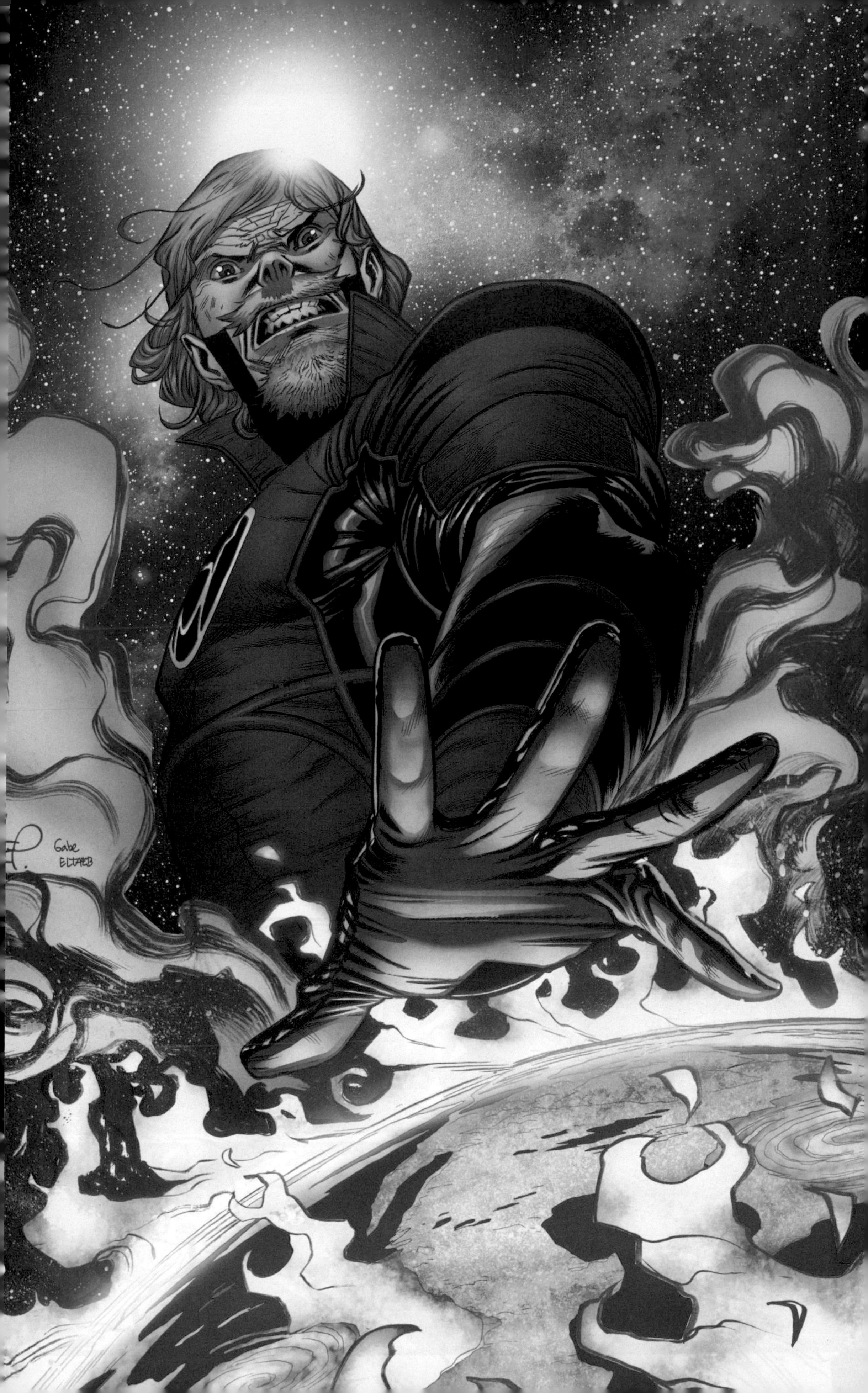
Gabe
ELTAEB

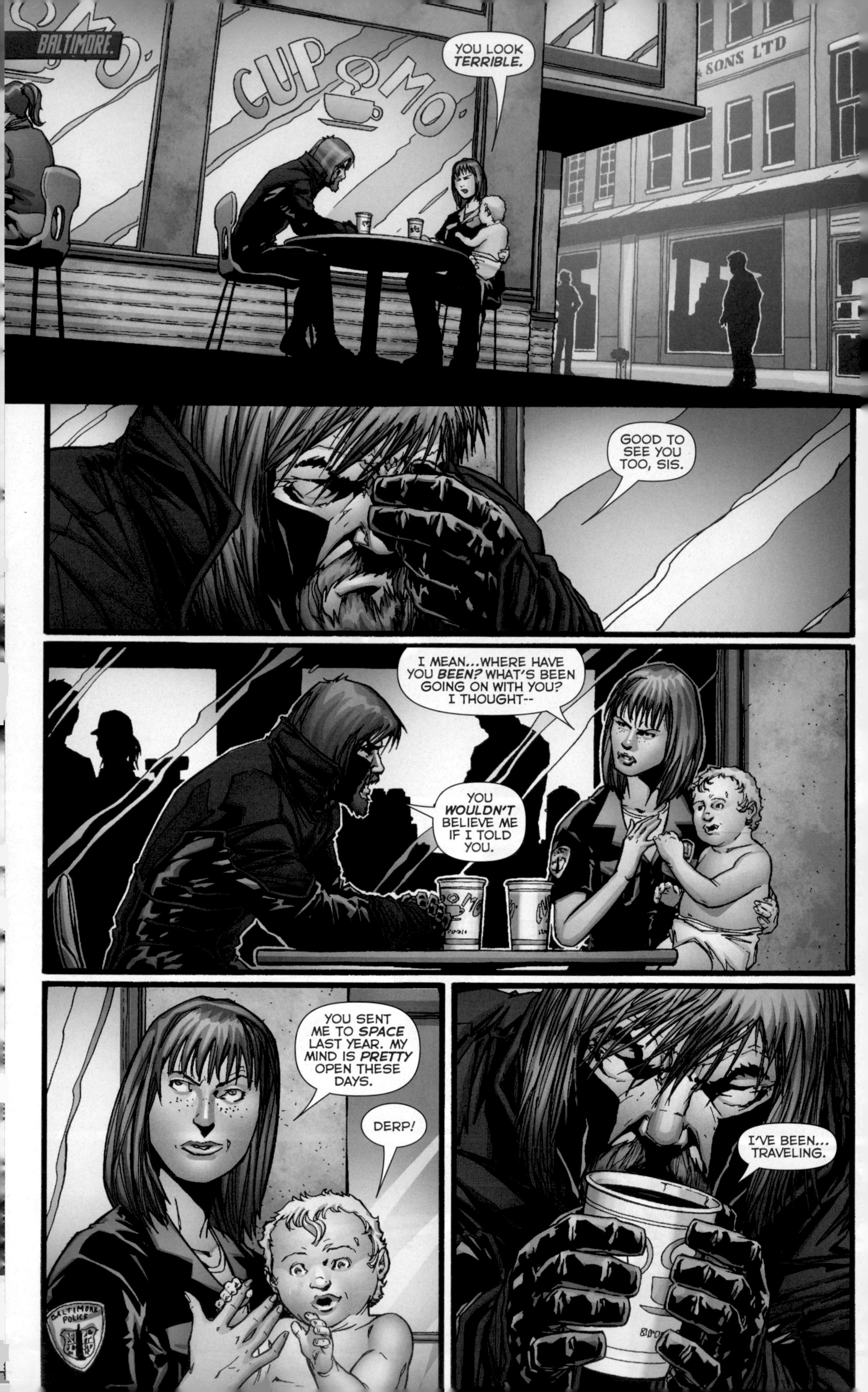
BALTIMORE.
CUP O MO
& SONS LTD
YOU LOOK TERRIBLE.
GOOD TO SEE YOU TOO, SIS.
I MEAN...WHERE HAVE YOU BEEN? WHAT'S BEEN GOING ON WITH YOU? I THOUGHT--
YOU WOULDN'T BELIEVE ME IF I TOLD YOU.
YOU SENT ME TO SPACE LAST YEAR. MY MIND IS PRETTY OPEN THESE DAYS.
DERP!
BALTIMORE POLICE
I'VE BEEN... TRAVELING.

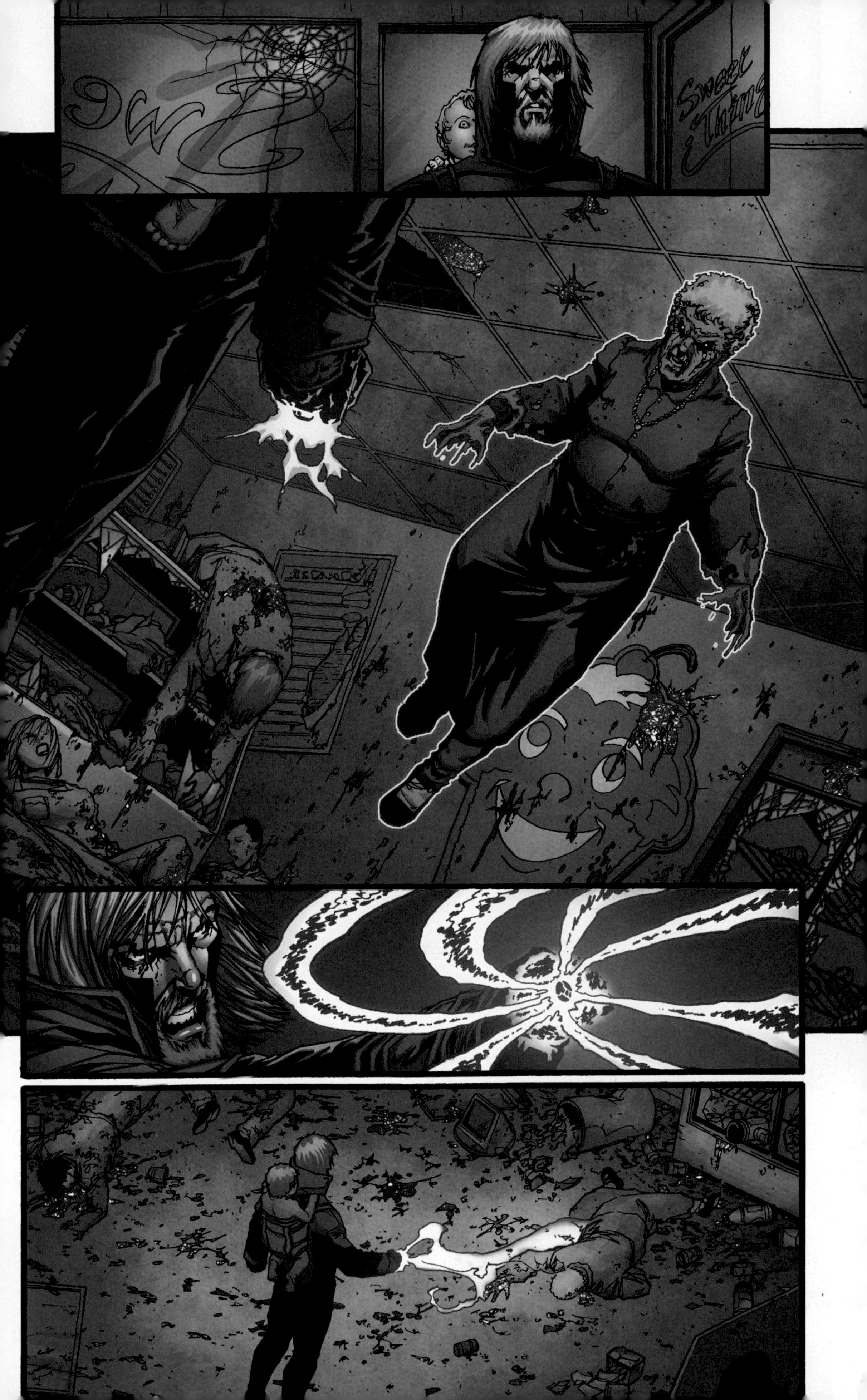
Sweet Thing

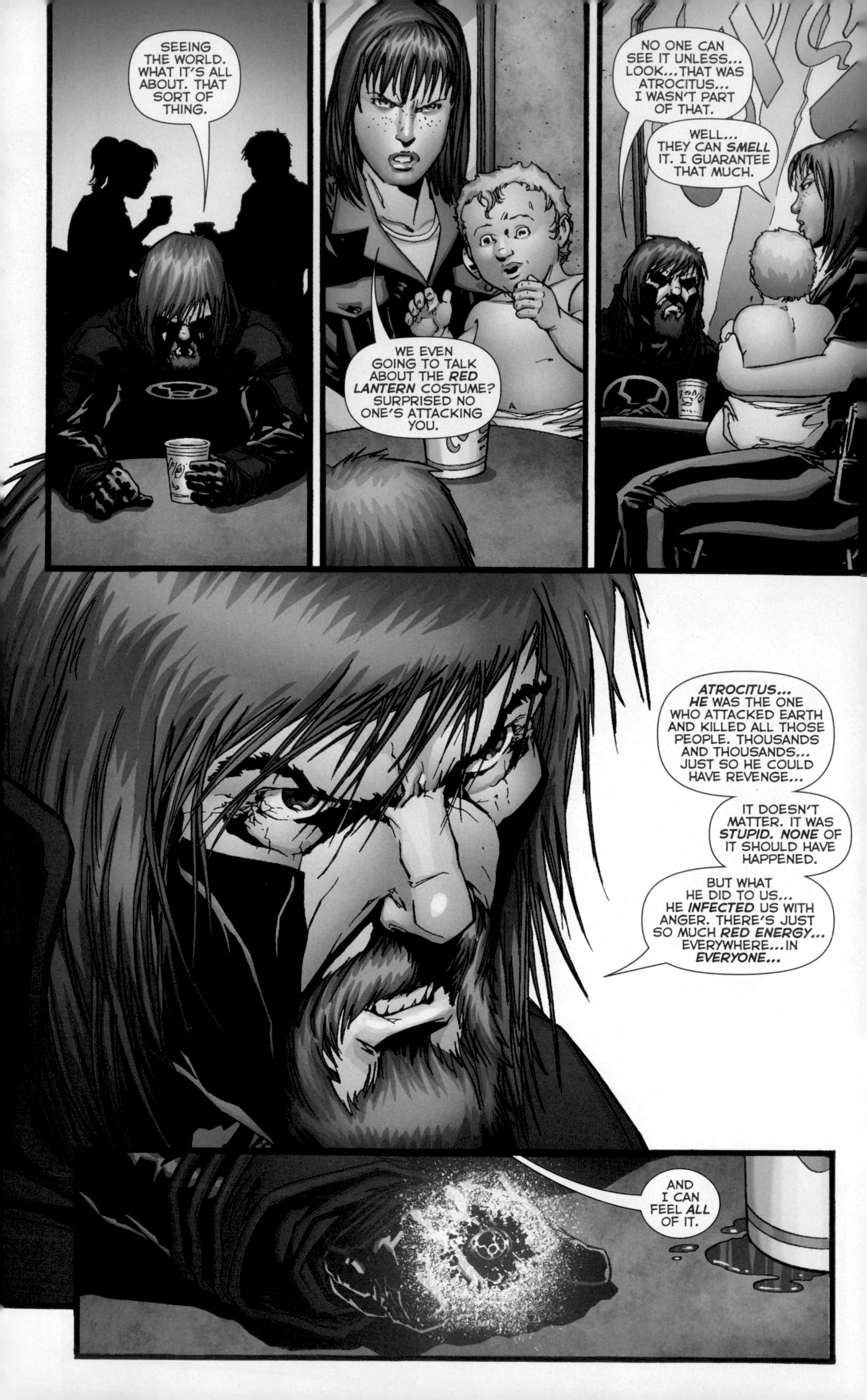
SEEING THE WORLD. WHAT IT'S ALL ABOUT. THAT SORT OF THING.
WE EVEN GOING TO TALK ABOUT THE *RED LANTERN* COSTUME? SURPRISED NO ONE'S ATTACKING YOU.
NO ONE CAN SEE IT UNLESS... LOOK...THAT WAS ATROCITUS... I WASN'T PART OF THAT.
WELL... THEY CAN *SMELL* IT. I GUARANTEE THAT MUCH.
ATROCITUS... HE WAS THE ONE WHO ATTACKED EARTH AND KILLED ALL THOSE PEOPLE. THOUSANDS AND THOUSANDS... JUST SO HE COULD HAVE REVENGE...
IT DOESN'T MATTER. IT WAS *STUPID. NONE* OF IT SHOULD HAVE HAPPENED.
BUT WHAT HE DID TO US... HE *INFECTED* US WITH ANGER. THERE'S JUST SO MUCH *RED ENERGY...* EVERYWHERE...IN *EVERYONE...*
AND I CAN FEEL *ALL* OF IT.

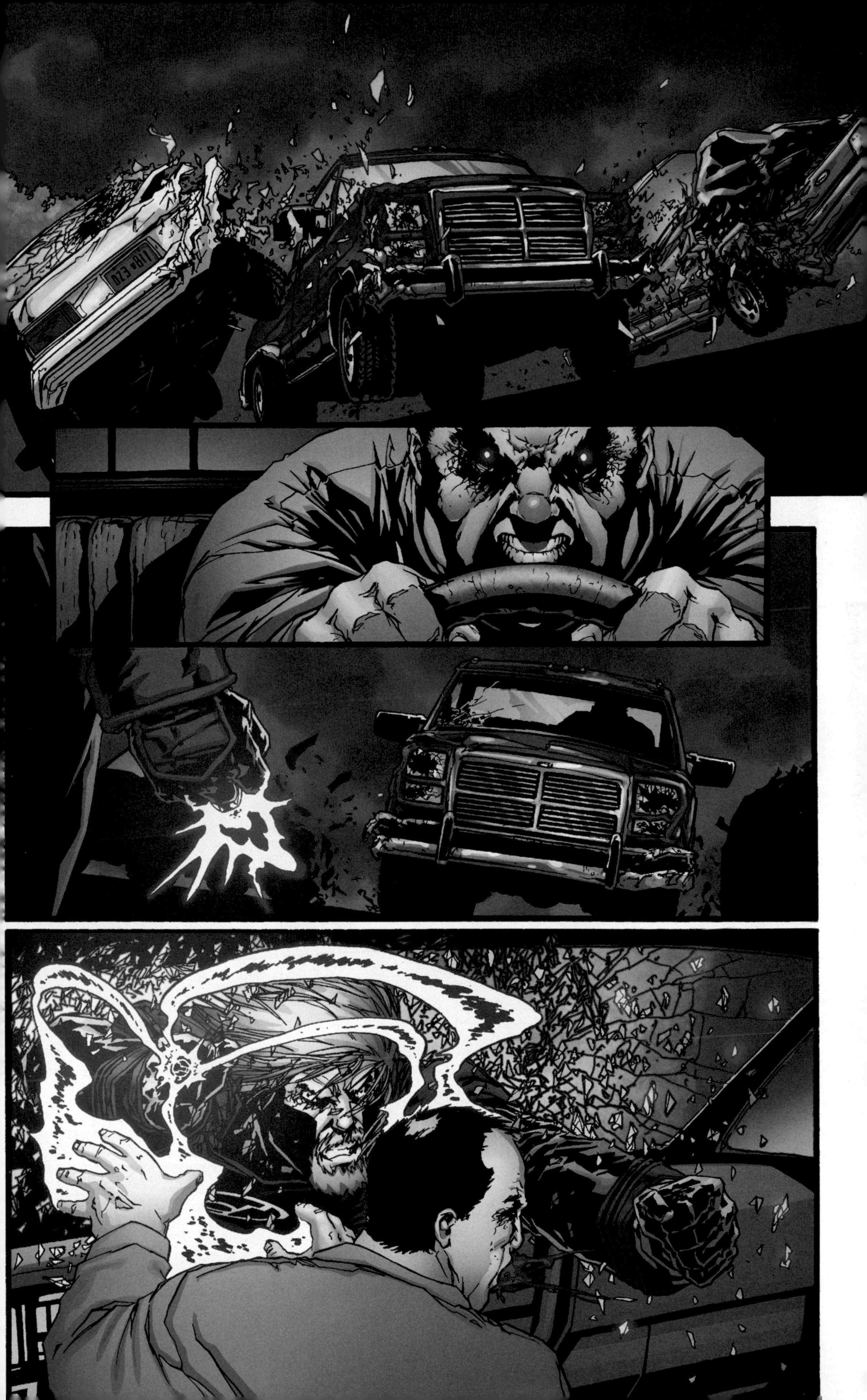

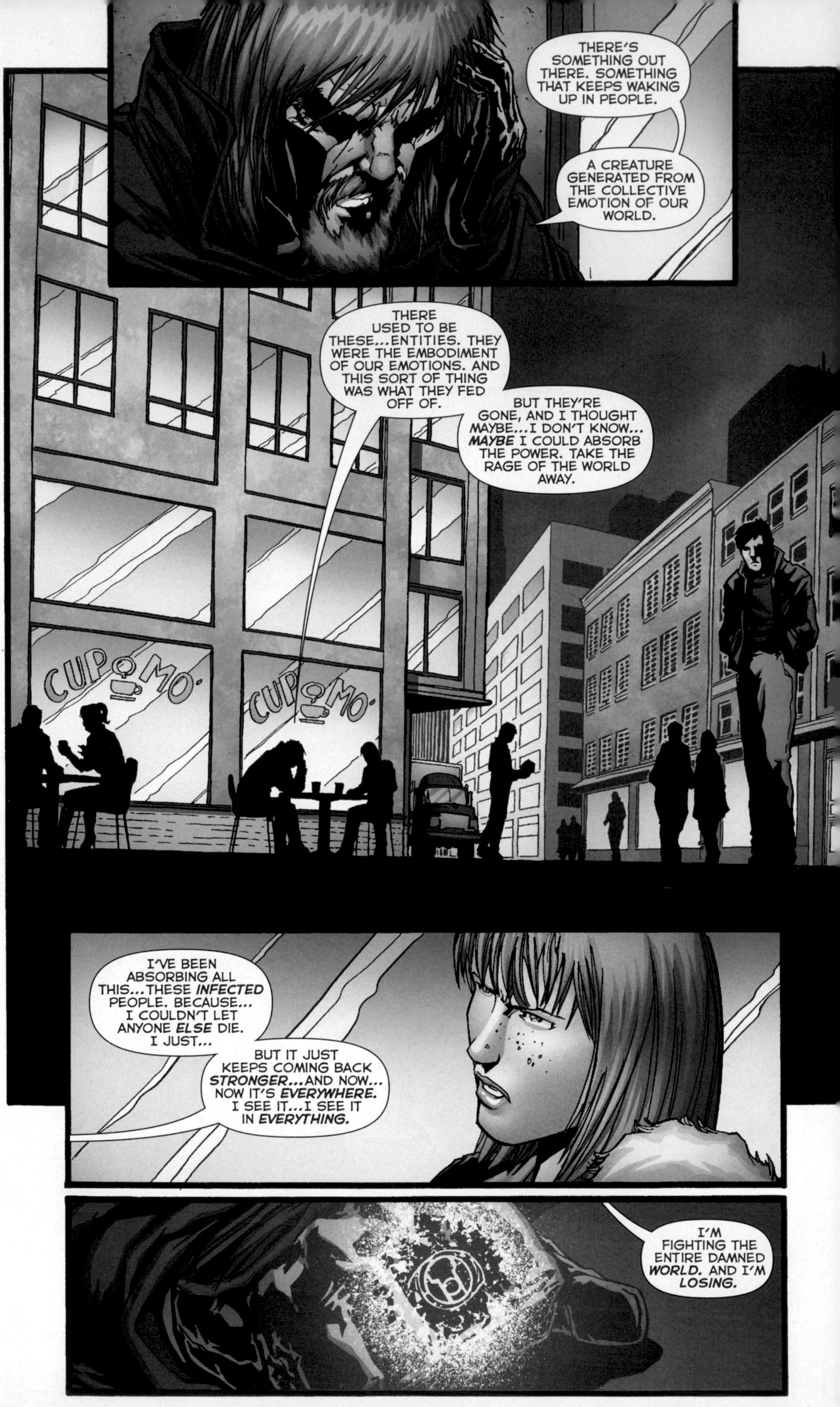
THERE'S SOMETHING OUT THERE. SOMETHING THAT KEEPS WAKING UP IN PEOPLE.
A CREATURE GENERATED FROM THE COLLECTIVE EMOTION OF OUR WORLD.
THERE USED TO BE THESE...ENTITIES. THEY WERE THE EMBODIMENT OF OUR EMOTIONS. AND THIS SORT OF THING WAS WHAT THEY FED OFF OF.
BUT THEY'RE GONE, AND I THOUGHT MAYBE...I DON'T KNOW... *MAYBE* I COULD ABSORB THE POWER. TAKE THE RAGE OF THE WORLD AWAY.
CUP O MO
CUP O MO
I'VE BEEN ABSORBING ALL THIS...THESE *INFECTED* PEOPLE. BECAUSE... I COULDN'T LET ANYONE *ELSE* DIE. I JUST...
BUT IT JUST KEEPS COMING BACK *STRONGER*...AND NOW... NOW IT'S *EVERYWHERE.* I SEE IT...I SEE IT IN *EVERYTHING.*
I'M FIGHTING THE ENTIRE DAMNED *WORLD.* AND I'M *LOSING.*

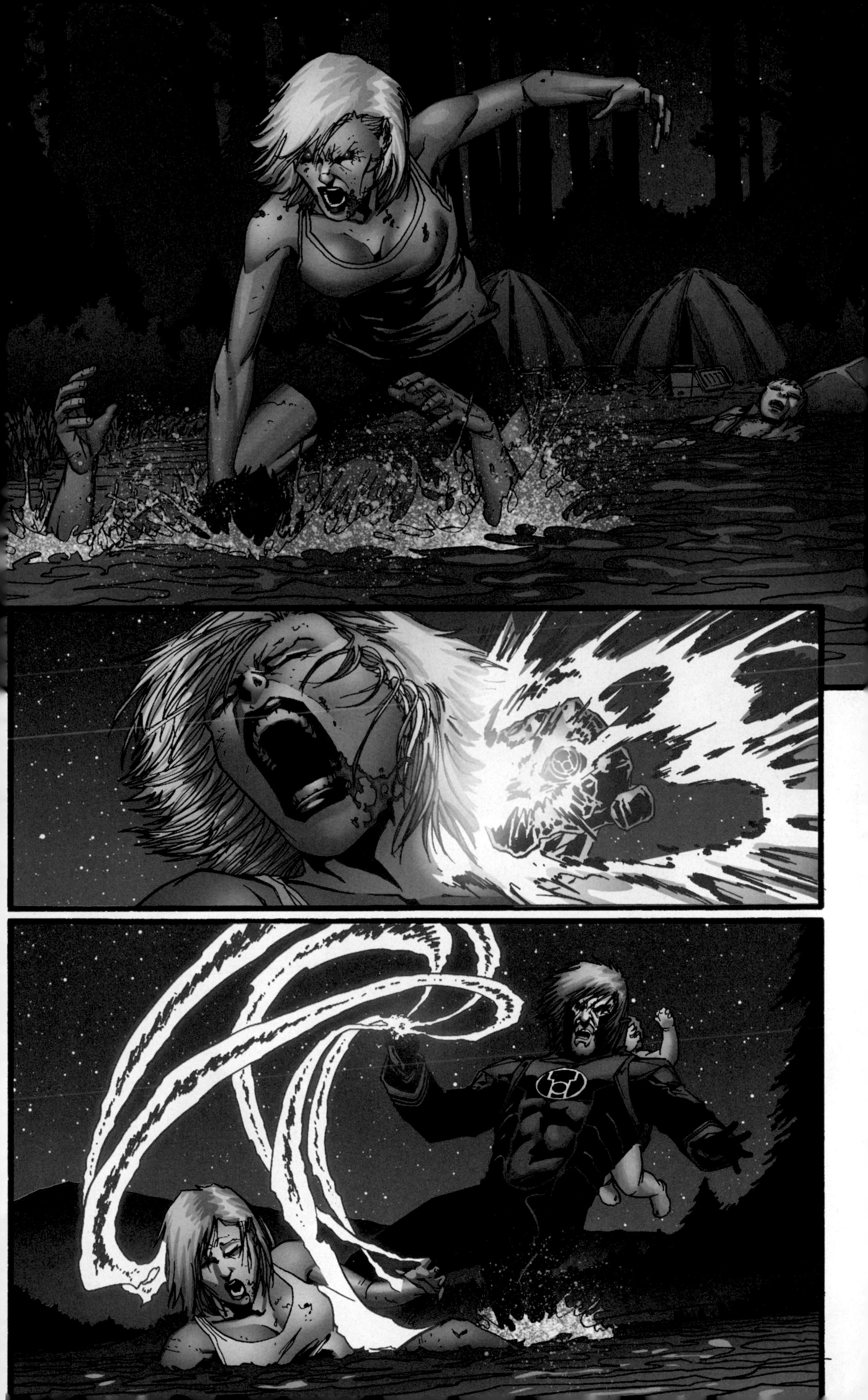

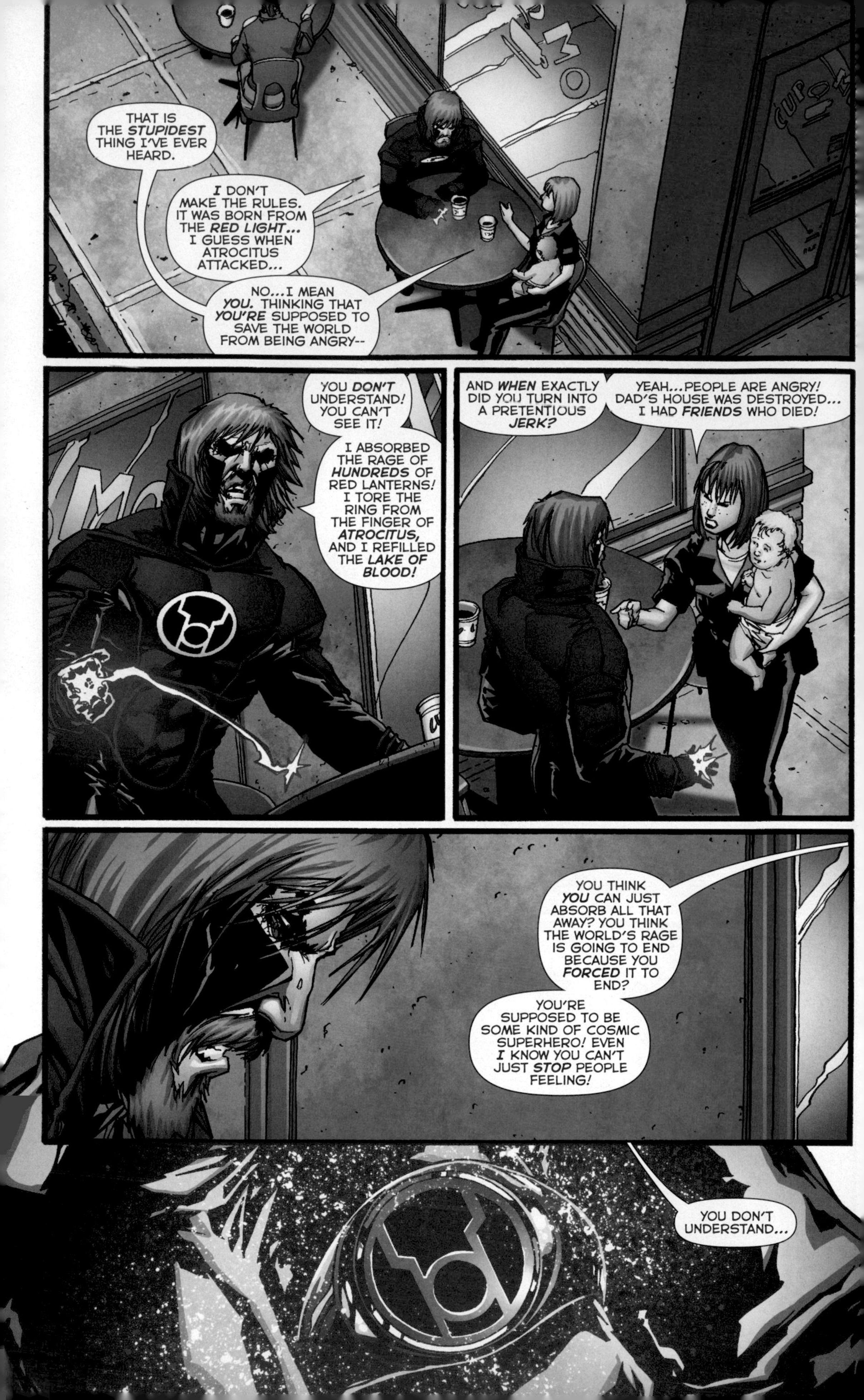
THAT IS THE STUPIDEST THING I'VE EVER HEARD.
I DON'T MAKE THE RULES. IT WAS BORN FROM THE RED LIGHT... I GUESS WHEN ATROCITUS ATTACKED...
NO...I MEAN YOU. THINKING THAT YOU'RE SUPPOSED TO SAVE THE WORLD FROM BEING ANGRY--
YOU DON'T UNDERSTAND! YOU CAN'T SEE IT!
I ABSORBED THE RAGE OF HUNDREDS OF RED LANTERNS! I TORE THE RING FROM THE FINGER OF ATROCITUS, AND I REFILLED THE LAKE OF BLOOD!
AND WHEN EXACTLY DID YOU TURN INTO A PRETENTIOUS JERK?
YEAH...PEOPLE ARE ANGRY! DAD'S HOUSE WAS DESTROYED... I HAD FRIENDS WHO DIED!
YOU THINK YOU CAN JUST ABSORB ALL THAT AWAY? YOU THINK THE WORLD'S RAGE IS GOING TO END BECAUSE YOU FORCED IT TO END?
YOU'RE SUPPOSED TO BE SOME KIND OF COSMIC SUPERHERO! EVEN I KNOW YOU CAN'T JUST STOP PEOPLE FEELING!
YOU DON'T UNDERSTAND...

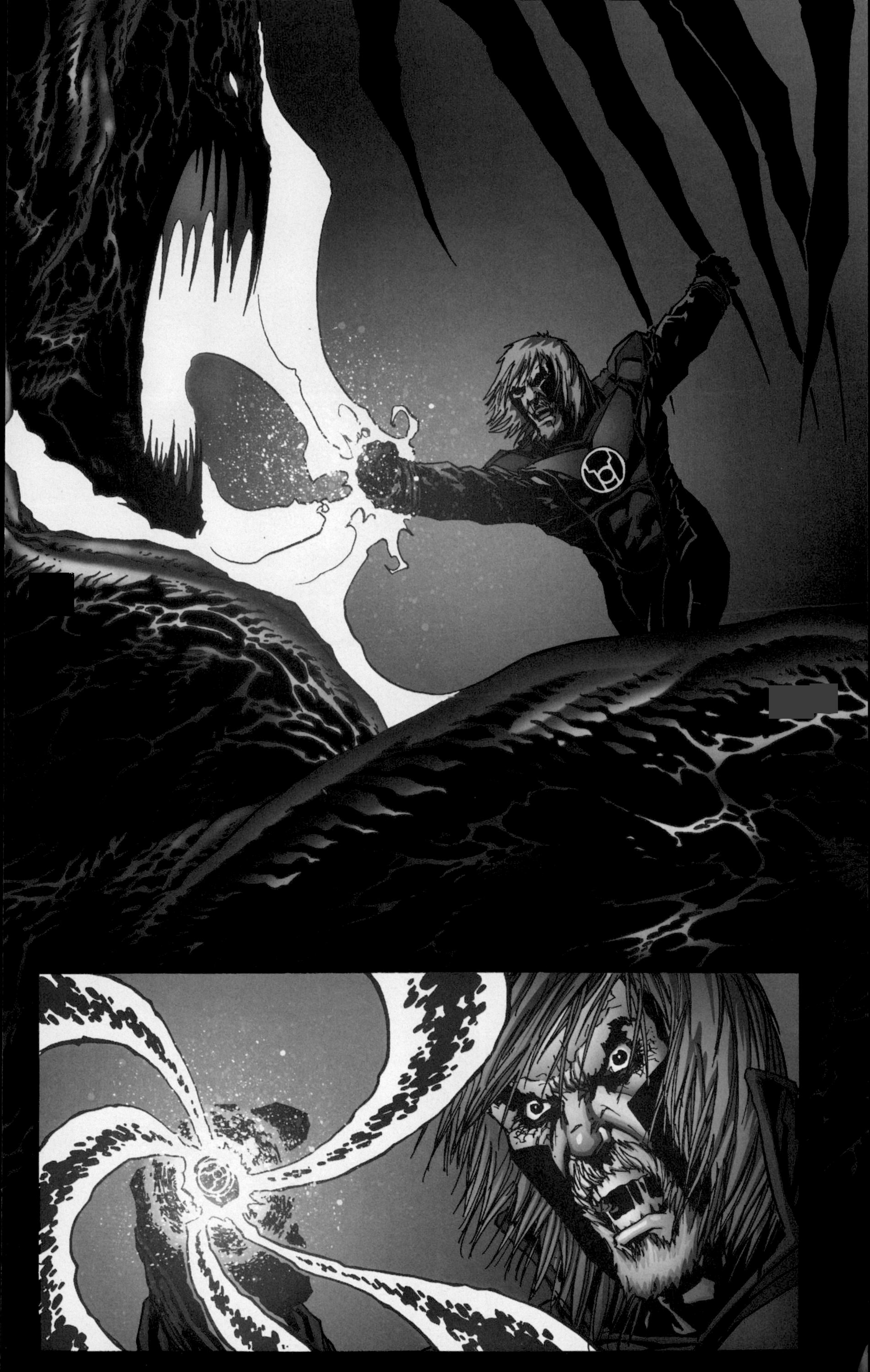

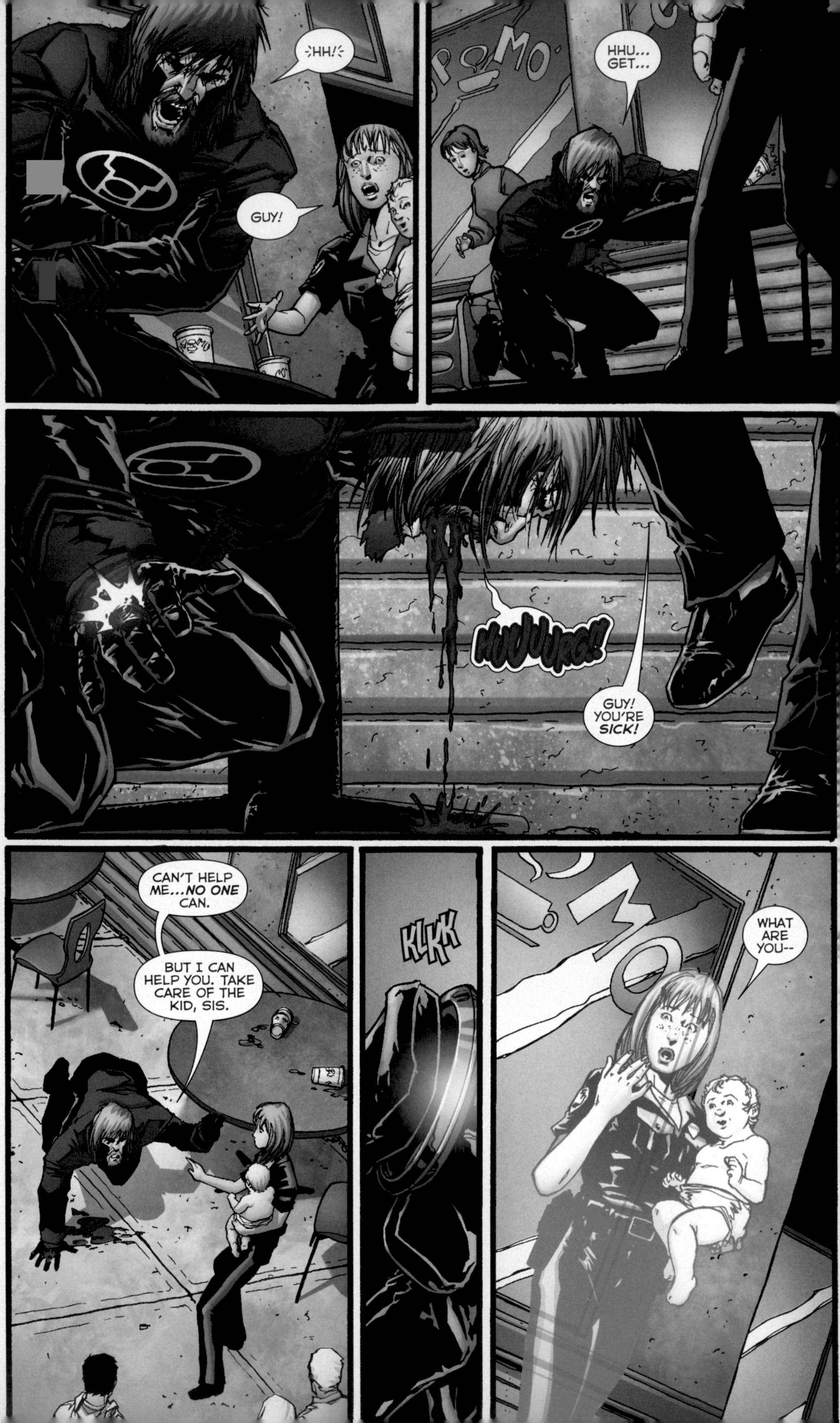
HH!
GUY!
HHU... GET...
HUUUURG!!
GUY! YOU'RE SICK!
CAN'T HELP ME...NO ONE CAN.
BUT I CAN HELP YOU. TAKE CARE OF THE KID, SIS.
KLKK
WHAT ARE YOU--

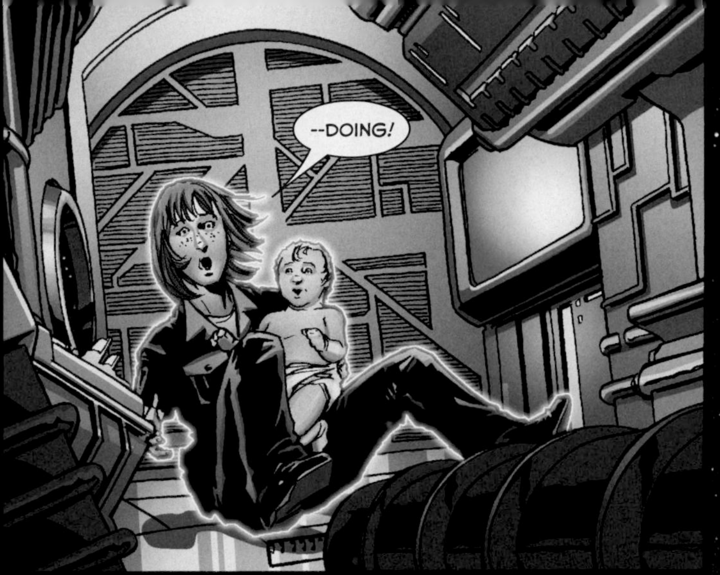
--DOING!

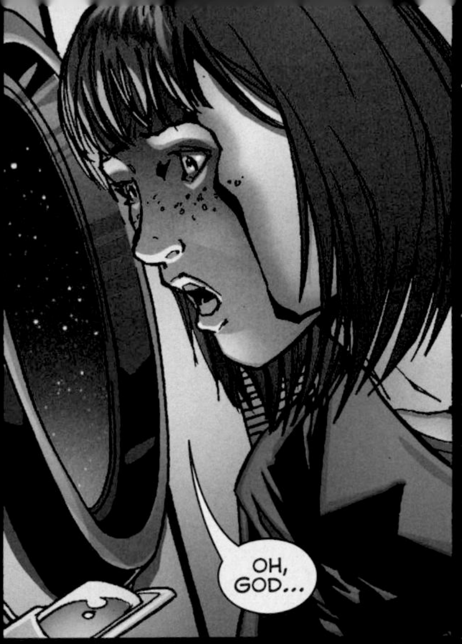
OH, GOD...

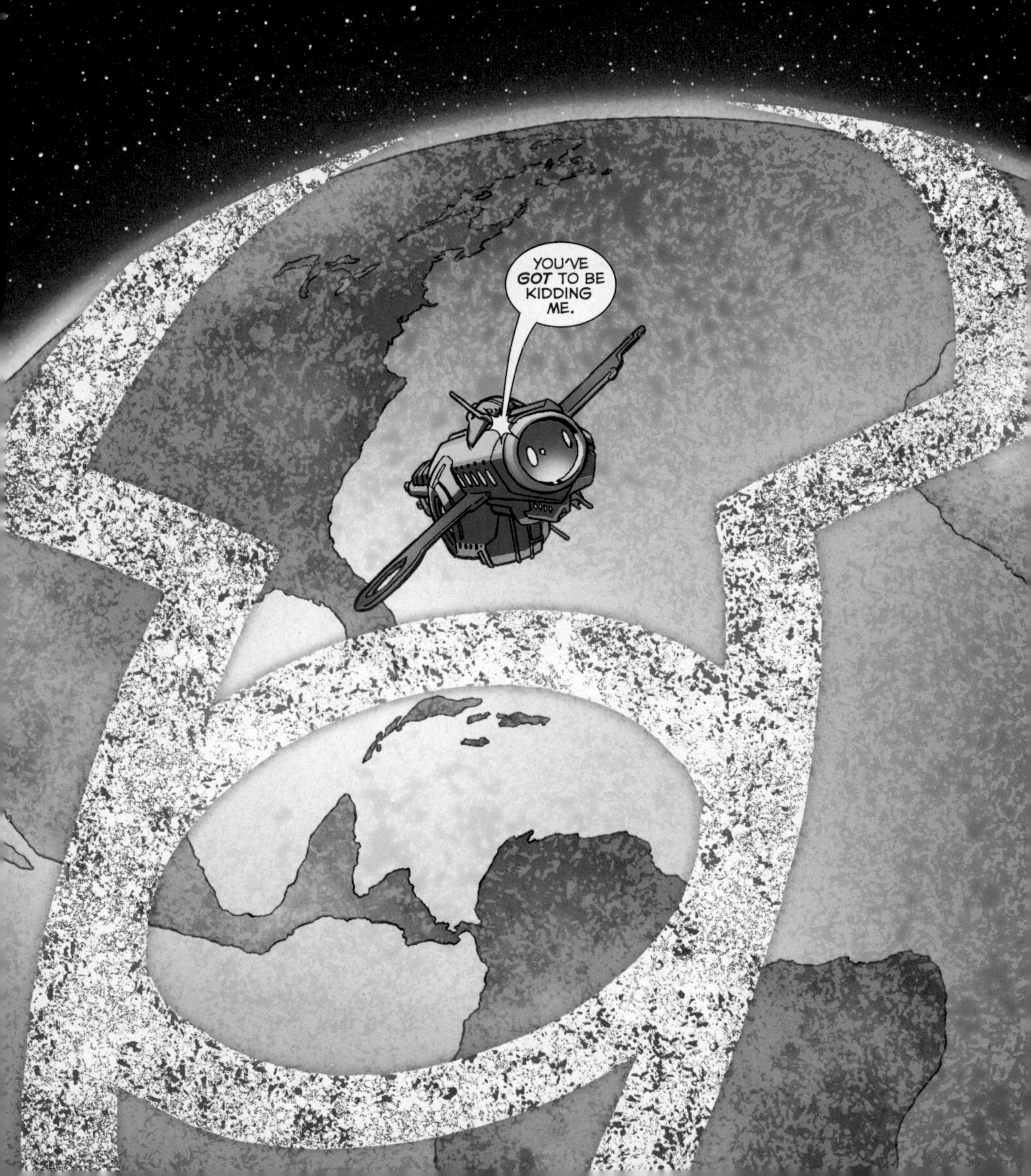
YOU'VE GOT TO BE KIDDING ME.

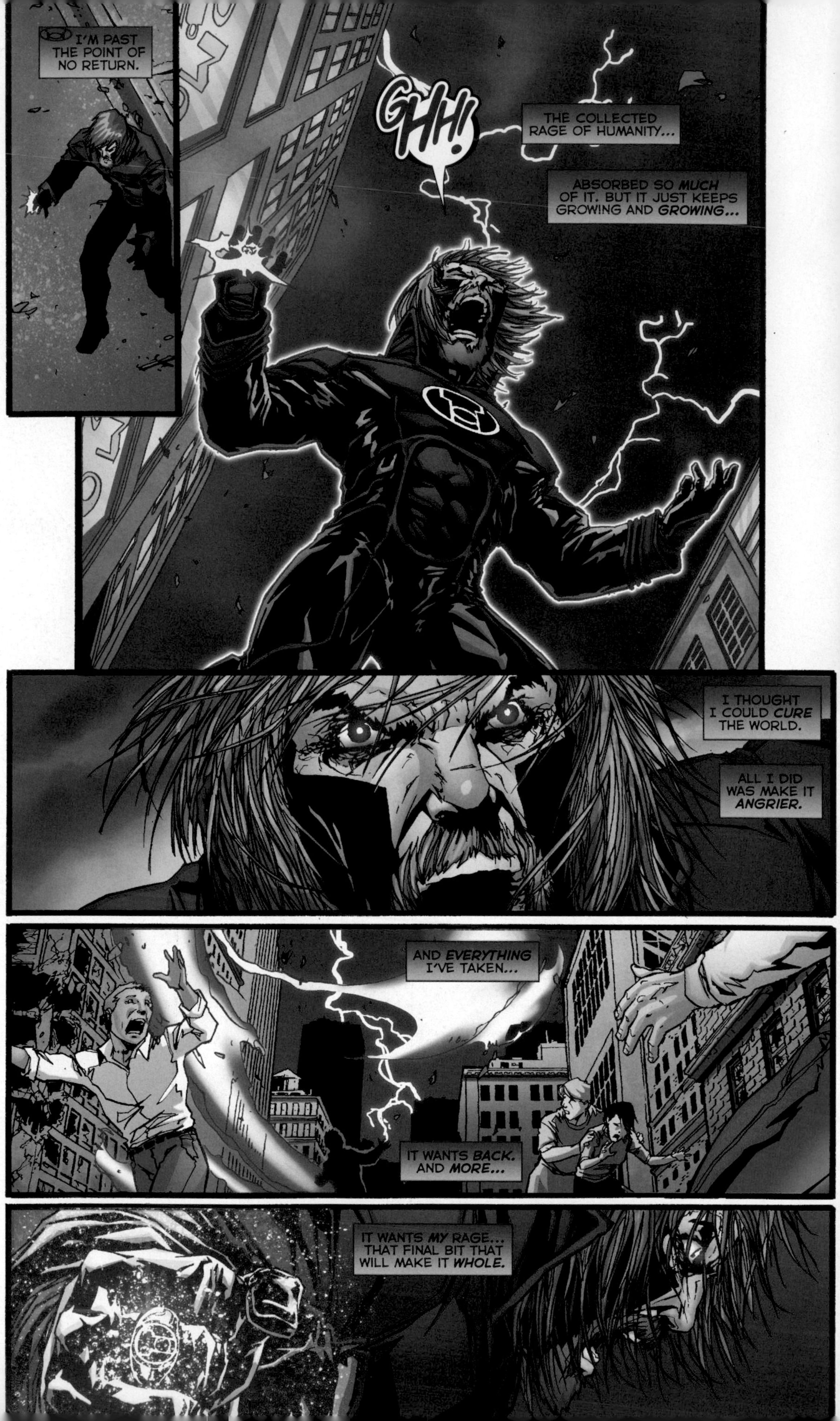
I'M PAST THE POINT OF NO RETURN.
GHH!
THE COLLECTED RAGE OF HUMANITY...
ABSORBED SO MUCH OF IT. BUT IT JUST KEEPS GROWING AND GROWING...
I THOUGHT I COULD CURE THE WORLD.
ALL I DID WAS MAKE IT ANGRIER.
AND EVERYTHING I'VE TAKEN...
IT WANTS BACK. AND MORE...
IT WANTS MY RAGE... THAT FINAL BIT THAT WILL MAKE IT WHOLE.

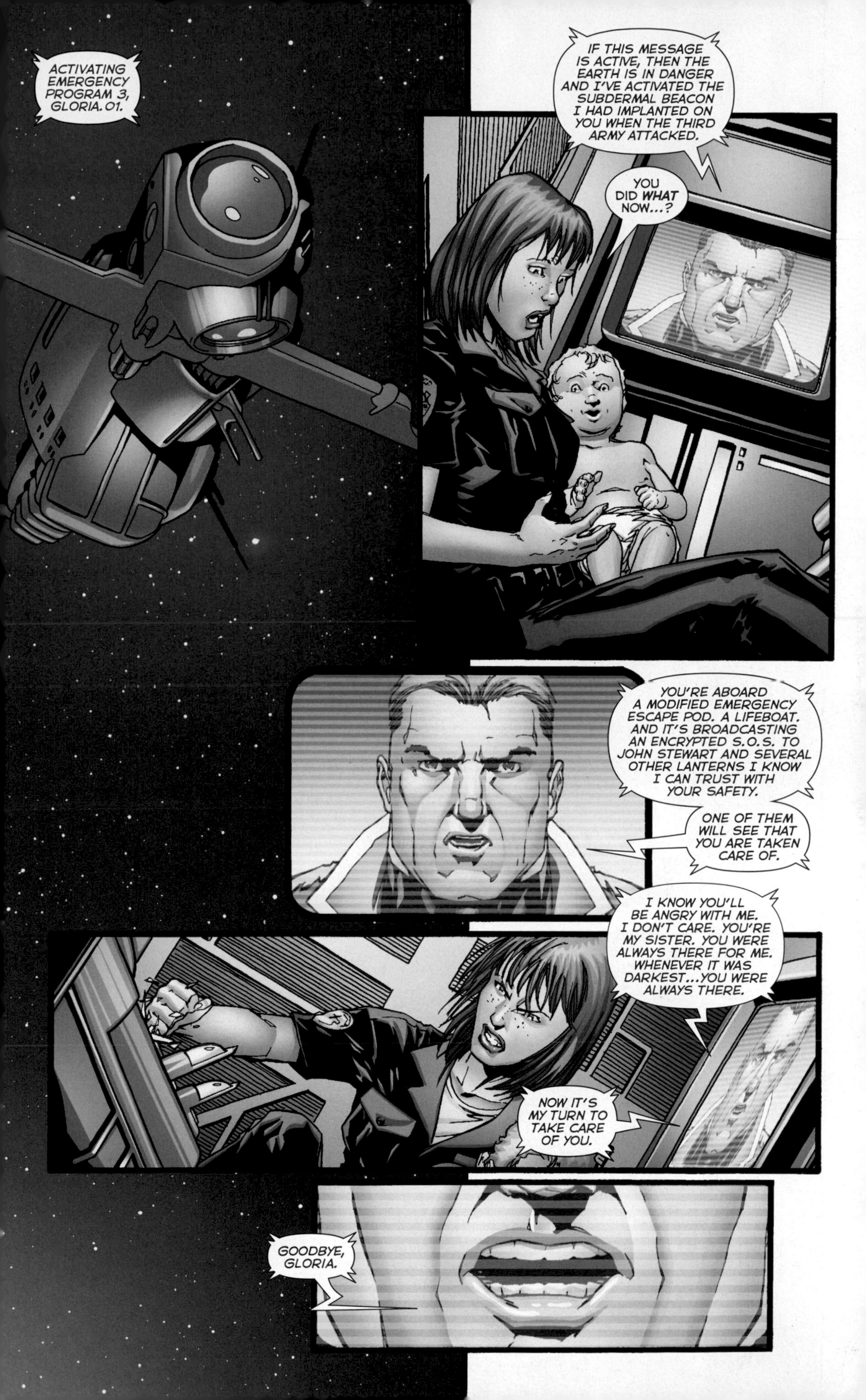
ACTIVATING EMERGENCY PROGRAM 3, GLORIA. 01.
IF THIS MESSAGE IS ACTIVE, THEN THE EARTH IS IN DANGER AND I'VE ACTIVATED THE SUBDERMAL BEACON I HAD IMPLANTED ON YOU WHEN THE THIRD ARMY ATTACKED.
YOU DID *WHAT* NOW...?
YOU'RE ABOARD A MODIFIED EMERGENCY ESCAPE POD. A LIFEBOAT. AND IT'S BROADCASTING AN ENCRYPTED S.O.S. TO JOHN STEWART AND SEVERAL OTHER LANTERNS I KNOW I CAN TRUST WITH YOUR SAFETY.
ONE OF THEM WILL SEE THAT YOU ARE TAKEN CARE OF.
I KNOW YOU'LL BE ANGRY WITH ME. I DON'T CARE. YOU'RE MY SISTER. YOU WERE ALWAYS THERE FOR ME. WHENEVER IT WAS DARKEST...YOU WERE ALWAYS THERE.
NOW IT'S MY TURN TO TAKE CARE OF YOU.
GOODBYE, GLORIA.

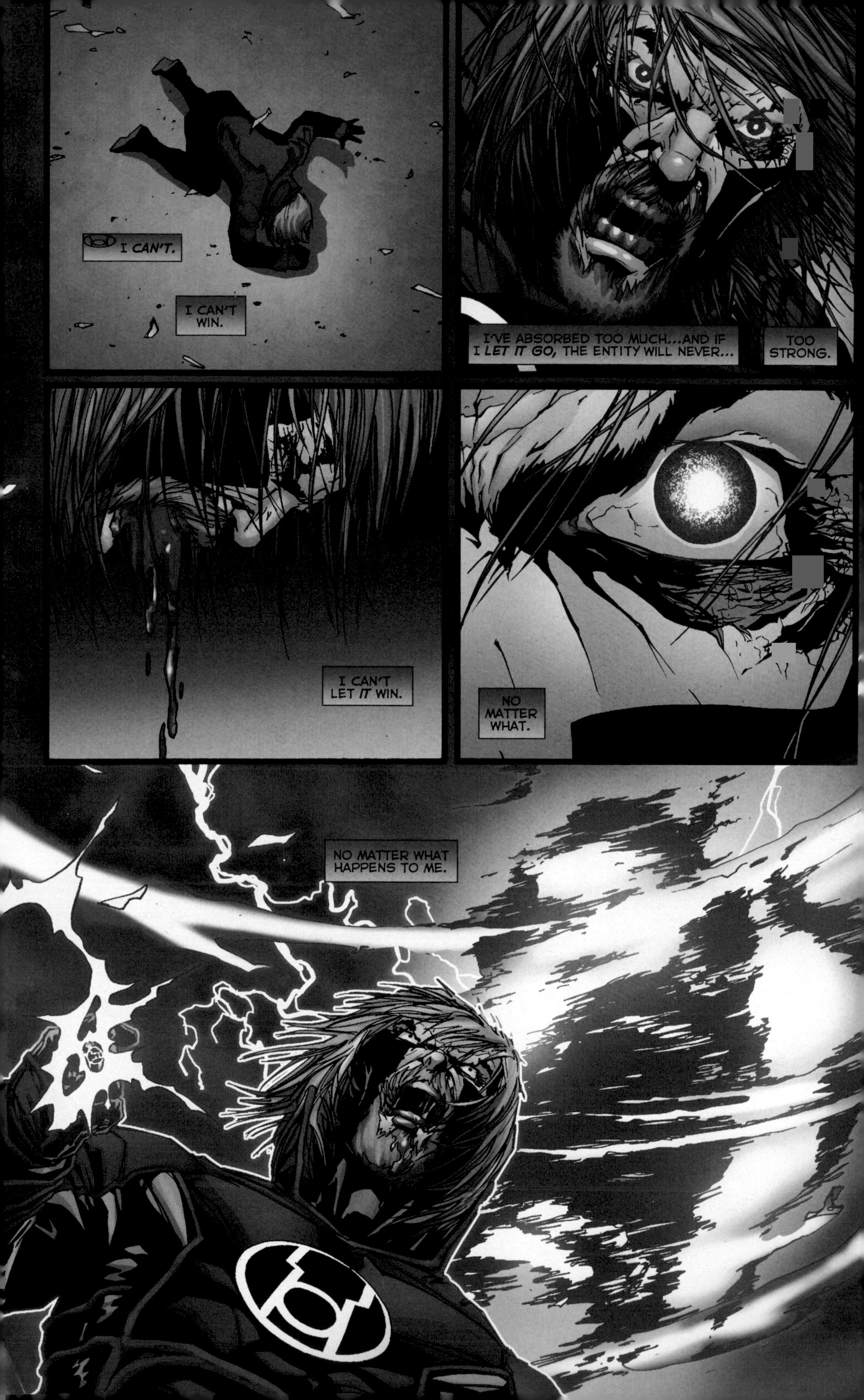
I CAN'T.
I CAN'T WIN.
I'VE ABSORBED TOO MUCH...AND IF I LET IT GO, THE ENTITY WILL NEVER...
TOO STRONG.
I CAN'T LET IT WIN.
NO MATTER WHAT.
NO MATTER WHAT HAPPENS TO ME.

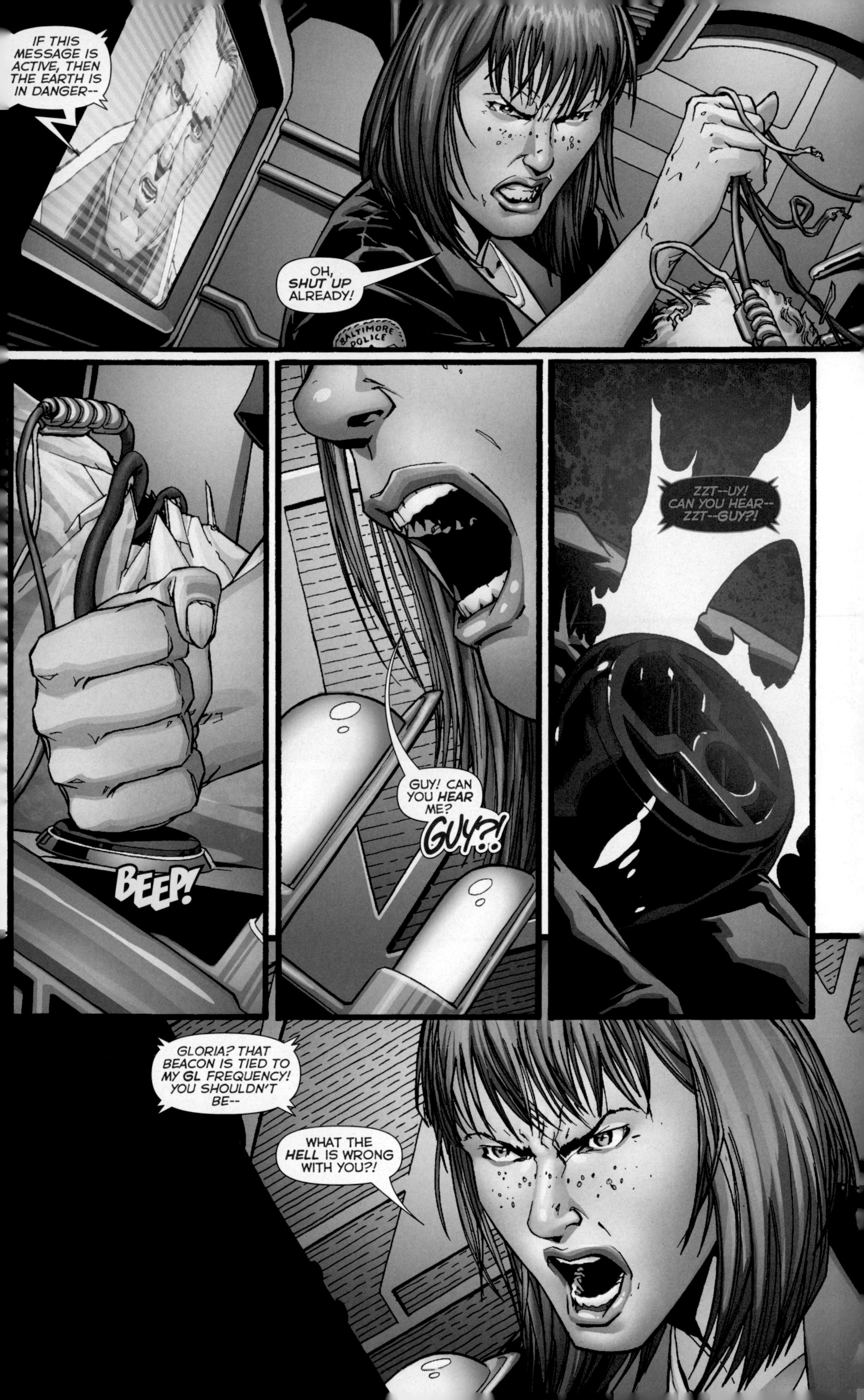
IF THIS MESSAGE IS ACTIVE, THEN THE EARTH IS IN DANGER--
OH, SHUT UP ALREADY!
BALTIMORE POLICE
BEEP!
GUY! CAN YOU HEAR ME? GUY?!
ZZT--UY! CAN YOU HEAR-- ZZT--GUY?!
GLORIA? THAT BEACON IS TIED TO MY GL FREQUENCY! YOU SHOULDN'T BE--
WHAT THE HELL IS WRONG WITH YOU?!

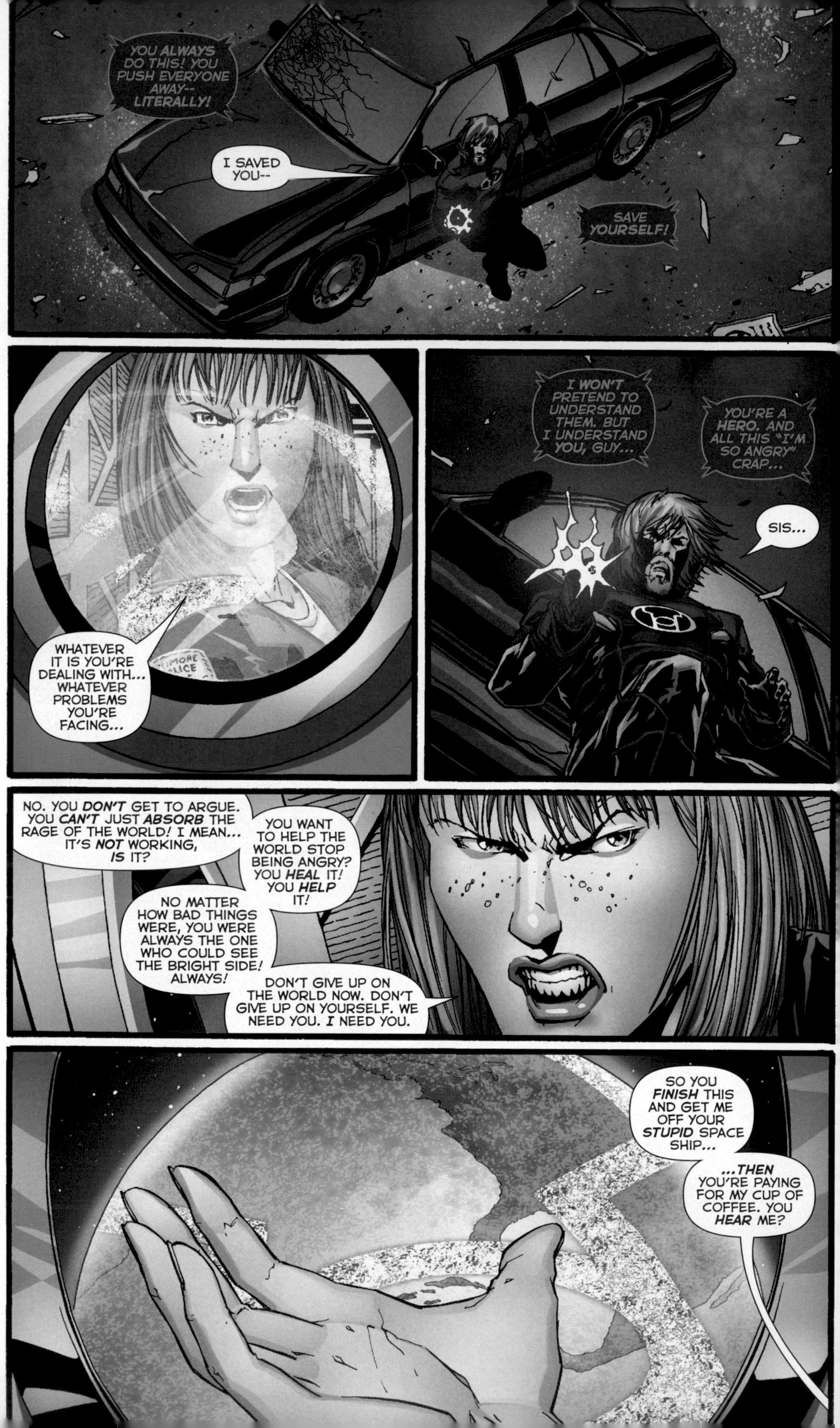
YOU ALWAYS DO THIS! YOU PUSH EVERYONE AWAY-- LITERALLY!
I SAVED YOU--
SAVE YOURSELF!
WHATEVER IT IS YOU'RE DEALING WITH... WHATEVER PROBLEMS YOU'RE FACING...
I WON'T PRETEND TO UNDERSTAND THEM. BUT I UNDERSTAND YOU, GUY...
YOU'RE A HERO. AND ALL THIS "I'M SO ANGRY" CRAP...
SIS...
NO. YOU DON'T GET TO ARGUE. YOU CAN'T JUST ABSORB THE RAGE OF THE WORLD! I MEAN... IT'S NOT WORKING, IS IT?
YOU WANT TO HELP THE WORLD STOP BEING ANGRY? YOU HEAL IT! YOU HELP IT!
NO MATTER HOW BAD THINGS WERE, YOU WERE ALWAYS THE ONE WHO COULD SEE THE BRIGHT SIDE! ALWAYS!
DON'T GIVE UP ON THE WORLD NOW. DON'T GIVE UP ON YOURSELF. WE NEED YOU. I NEED YOU.
SO YOU FINISH THIS AND GET ME OFF YOUR STUPID SPACE SHIP...
...THEN YOU'RE PAYING FOR MY CUP OF COFFEE. YOU HEAR ME?

RIGHT.

THE WORLD IS AN ANGRY PLACE.

NO ONE KNOWS THAT BETTER THAN *ME.*

I'M THE *RED LANTERN* OF EARTH. *ANGER* IS MY SUPER POWER. AND I'M FIGHTING THE LIVING *INCARNATION* OF EARTH'S RAGE.

AND I *CAN'T* WIN. I CAN NEVER WIN THIS FIGHT.

YOU WANT THIS...YOU WANT THIS POWER?

YOU CAN *HAVE* IT.

BUT MY SISTER DOESN'T BELIEVE THAT. THE PEOPLE IN THIS CITY. IN *EVERY* CITY...EVERY TIME SOME TERRIBLE ENEMY THREATENS THEM...

THEY DON'T *JUST* HAVE ANGER OR FEAR.

THEY HAVE *FAITH.* AND TRUST.

AND THEY HAVE *HOPE.*

TAKE IT.

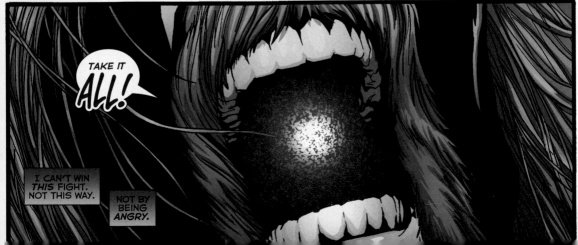

TAKE IT ALL!

I CAN'T WIN *THIS* FIGHT. NOT THIS WAY.

NOT BY BEING *ANGRY.*

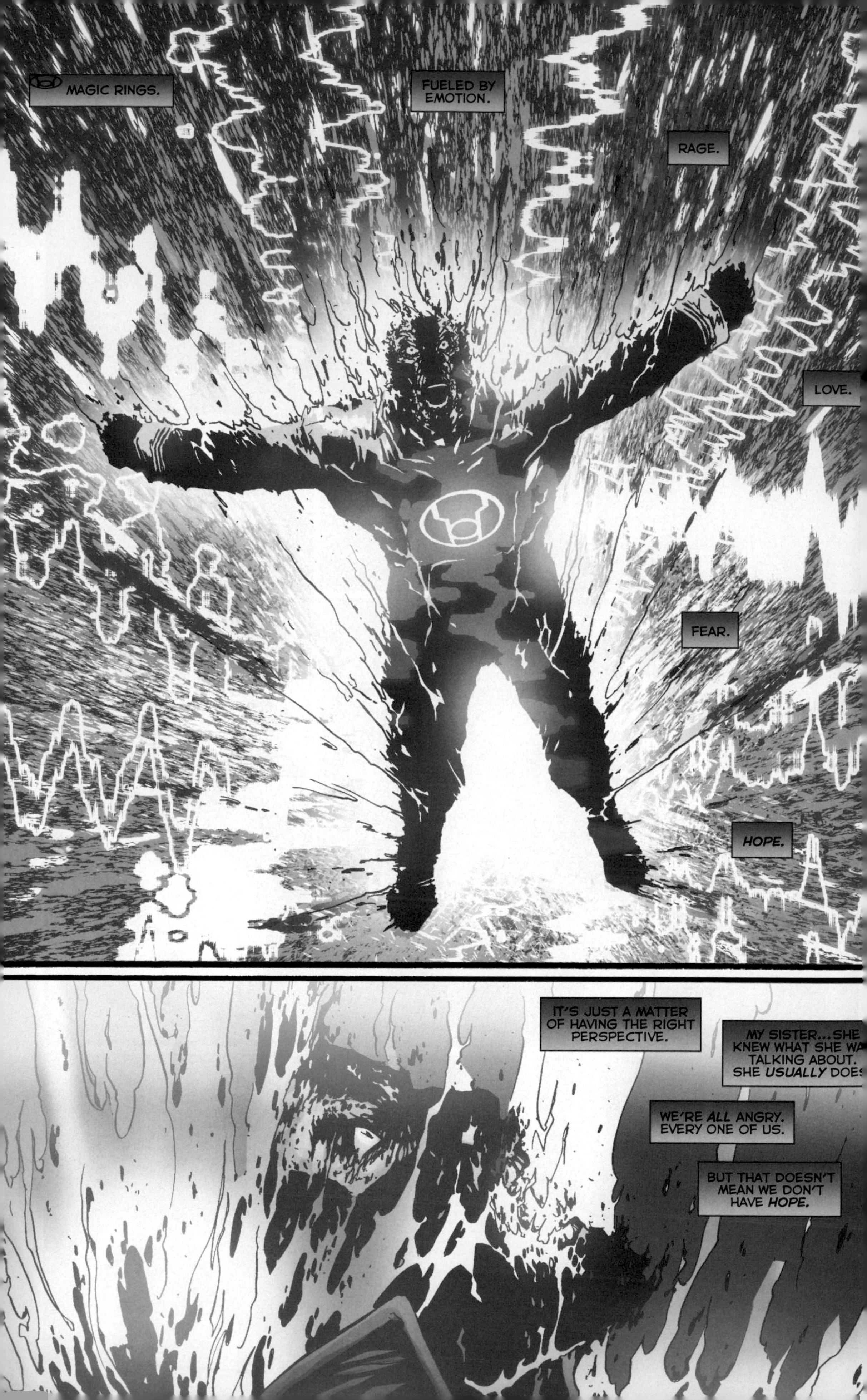
MAGIC RINGS.
FUELED BY EMOTION.
RAGE.
LOVE.
FEAR.
HOPE.
IT'S JUST A MATTER OF HAVING THE RIGHT PERSPECTIVE.
MY SISTER...SHE KNEW WHAT SHE WA TALKING ABOUT. SHE *USUALLY* DOES
WE'RE *ALL* ANGRY. EVERY ONE OF US.
BUT THAT DOESN'T MEAN WE DON'T HAVE *HOPE.*

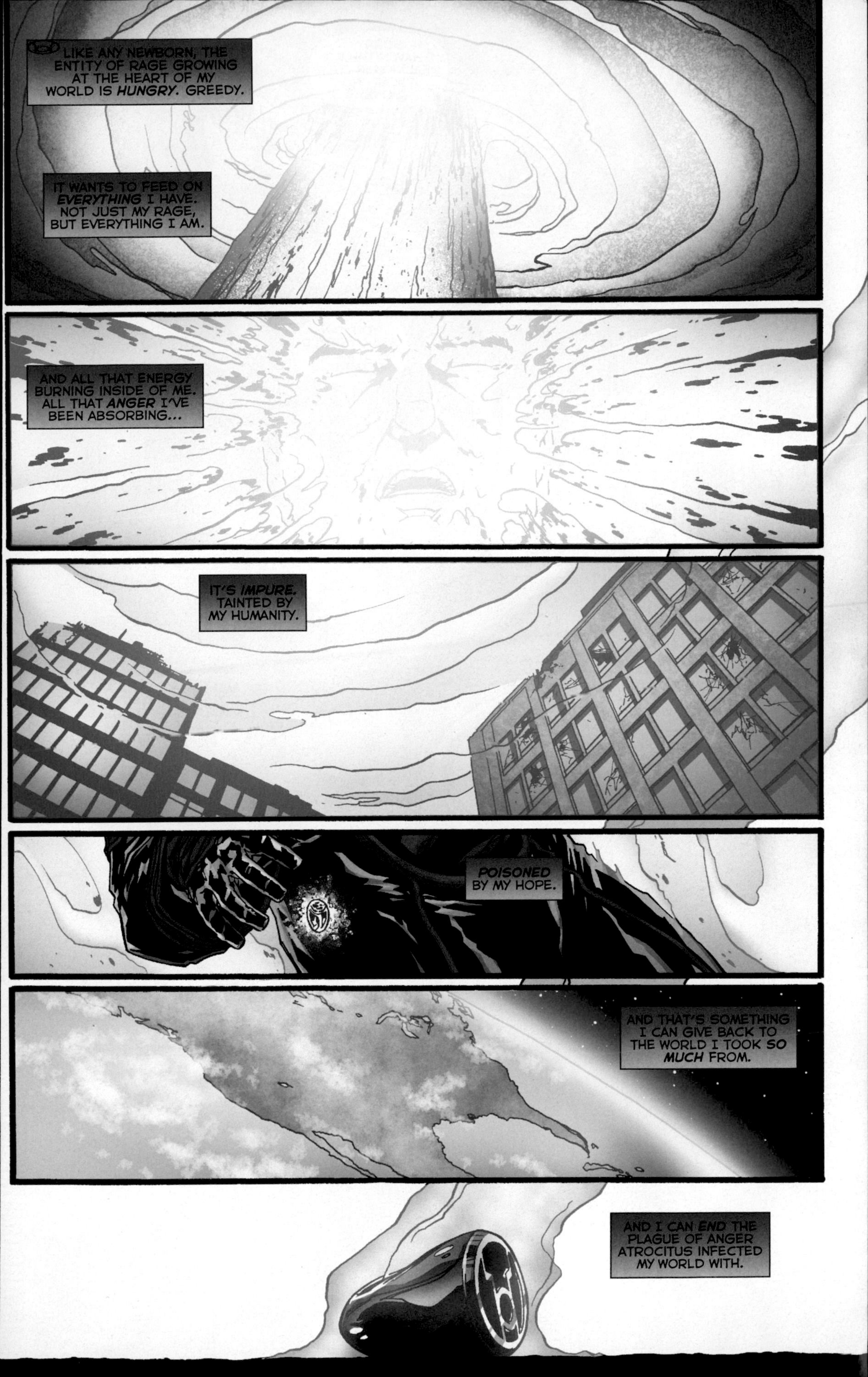
LIKE ANY NEWBORN, THE ENTITY OF RAGE GROWING AT THE HEART OF MY WORLD IS *HUNGRY*. GREEDY.
IT WANTS TO FEED ON *EVERYTHING* I HAVE. NOT JUST MY RAGE, BUT EVERYTHING I AM.
AND ALL THAT ENERGY BURNING INSIDE OF ME. ALL THAT *ANGER* I'VE BEEN ABSORBING...
IT'S *IMPURE.* TAINTED BY MY HUMANITY.
POISONED BY MY HOPE.
AND THAT'S SOMETHING I CAN GIVE BACK TO THE WORLD I TOOK *SO MUCH* FROM.
AND I CAN *END* THE PLAGUE OF ANGER ATROCITUS INFECTED MY WORLD WITH.

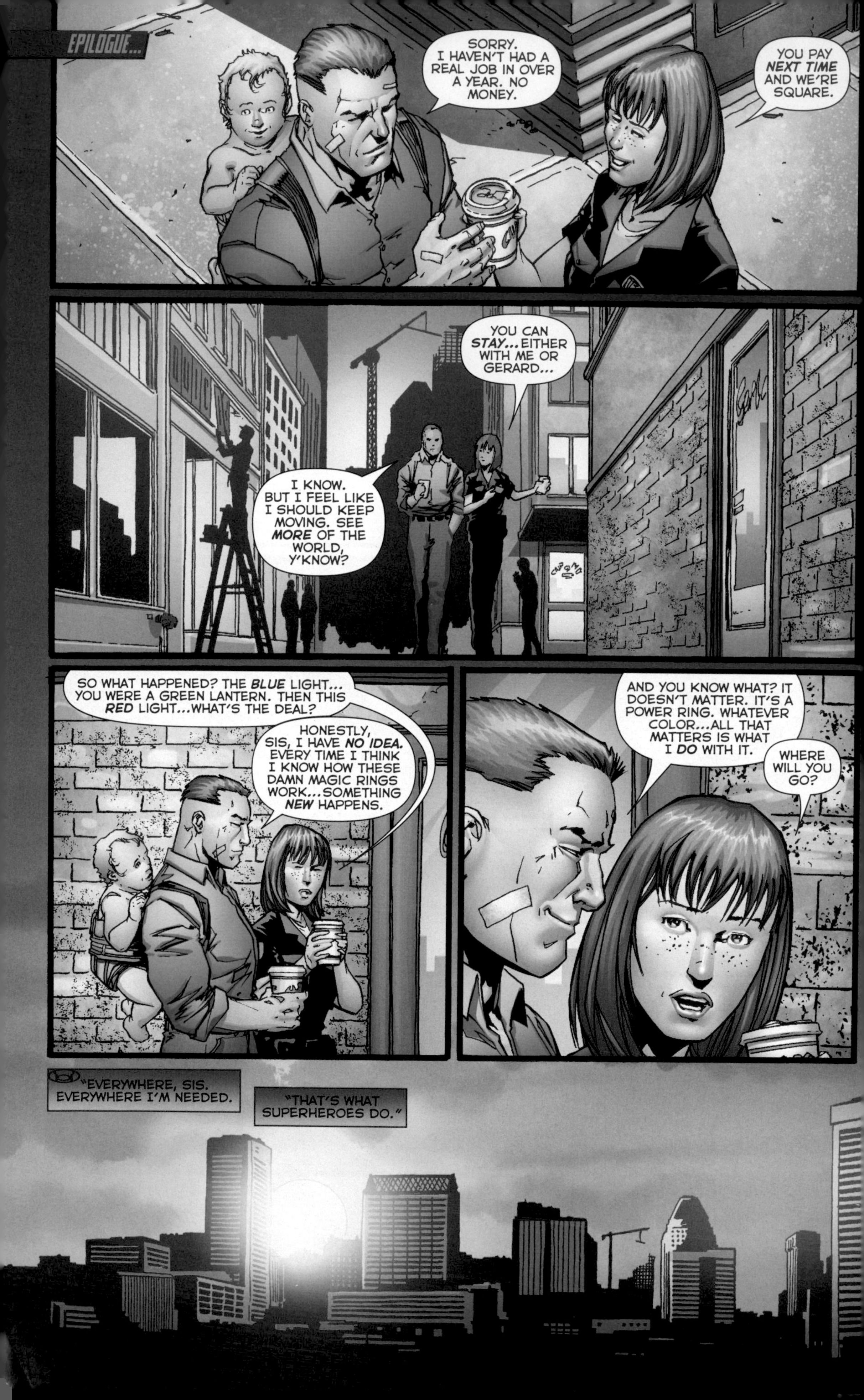
EPILOGUE...
SORRY. I HAVEN'T HAD A REAL JOB IN OVER A YEAR. NO MONEY.
YOU PAY NEXT TIME AND WE'RE SQUARE.
YOU CAN STAY... EITHER WITH ME OR GERARD...
I KNOW. BUT I FEEL LIKE I SHOULD KEEP MOVING. SEE MORE OF THE WORLD, Y'KNOW?
SO WHAT HAPPENED? THE BLUE LIGHT... YOU WERE A GREEN LANTERN. THEN THIS RED LIGHT...WHAT'S THE DEAL?
HONESTLY, SIS, I HAVE NO IDEA. EVERY TIME I THINK I KNOW HOW THESE DAMN MAGIC RINGS WORK...SOMETHING NEW HAPPENS.
AND YOU KNOW WHAT? IT DOESN'T MATTER. IT'S A POWER RING. WHATEVER COLOR...ALL THAT MATTERS IS WHAT I DO WITH IT.
WHERE WILL YOU GO?
"EVERYWHERE, SIS. EVERYWHERE I'M NEEDED.
"THAT'S WHAT SUPERHEROES DO."

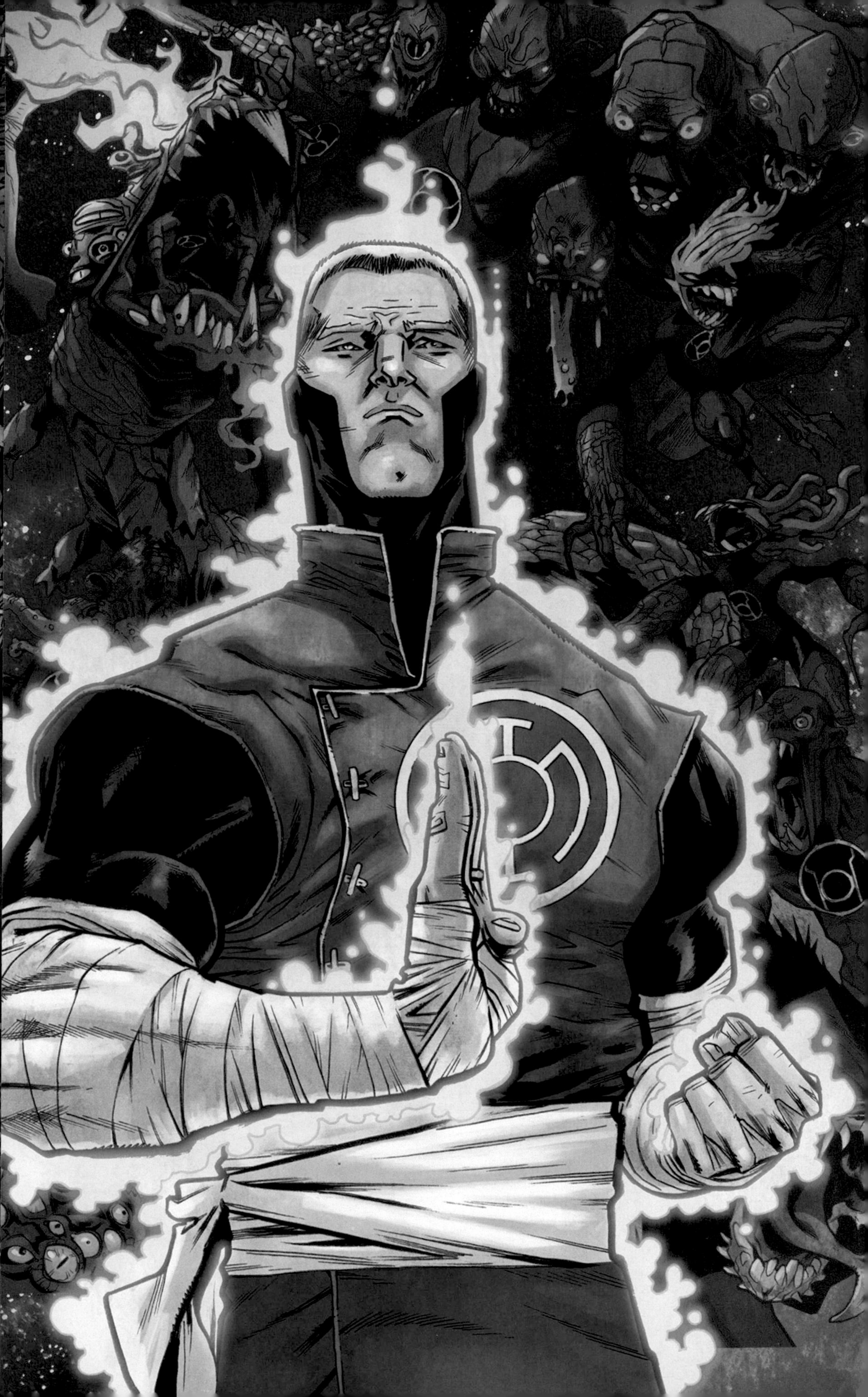

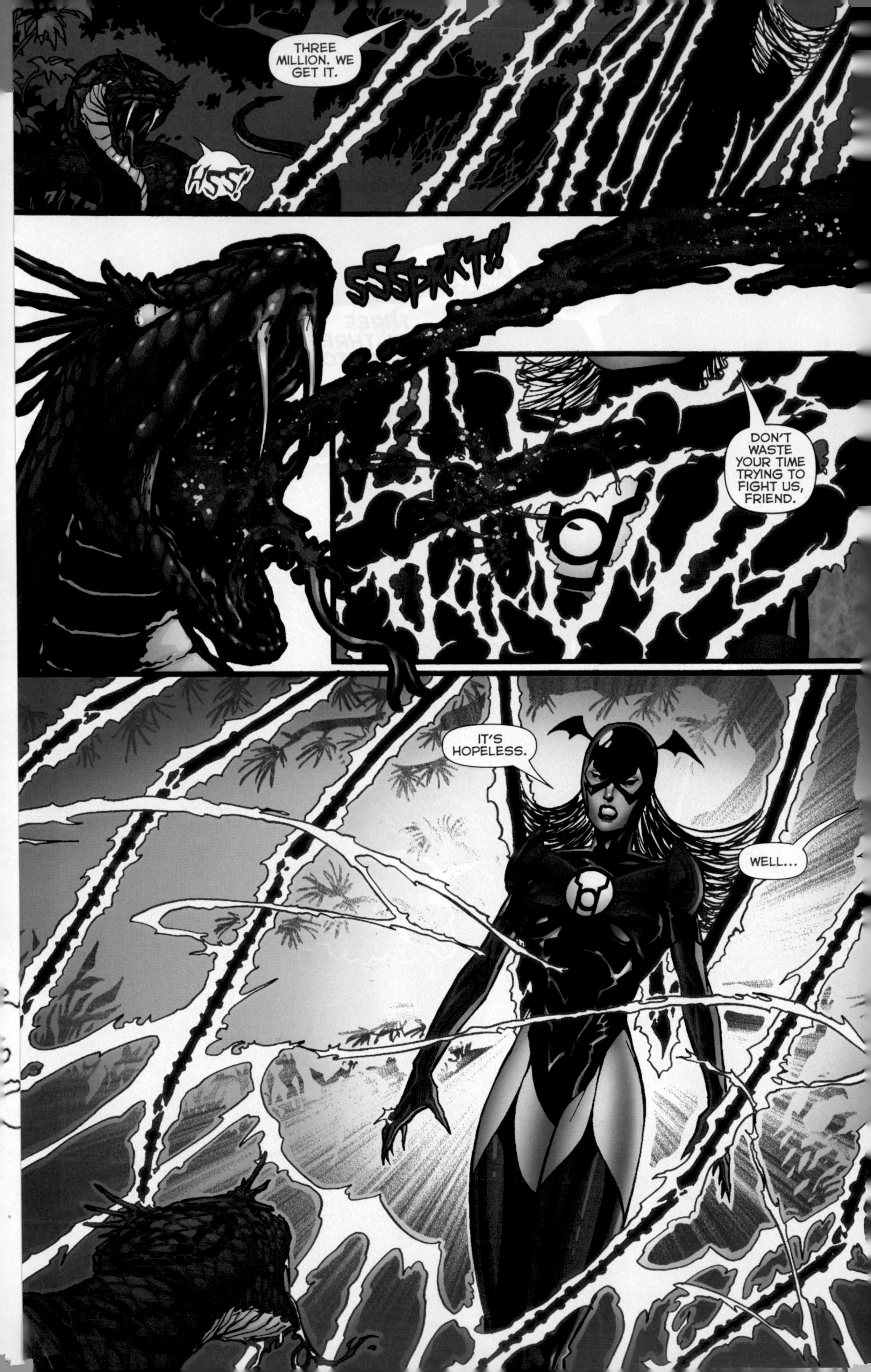
THREE MILLION. WE GET IT.
HSS!
SSSPRKT!!
DON'T WASTE YOUR TIME TRYING TO FIGHT US, FRIEND.
IT'S HOPELESS.
WELL...

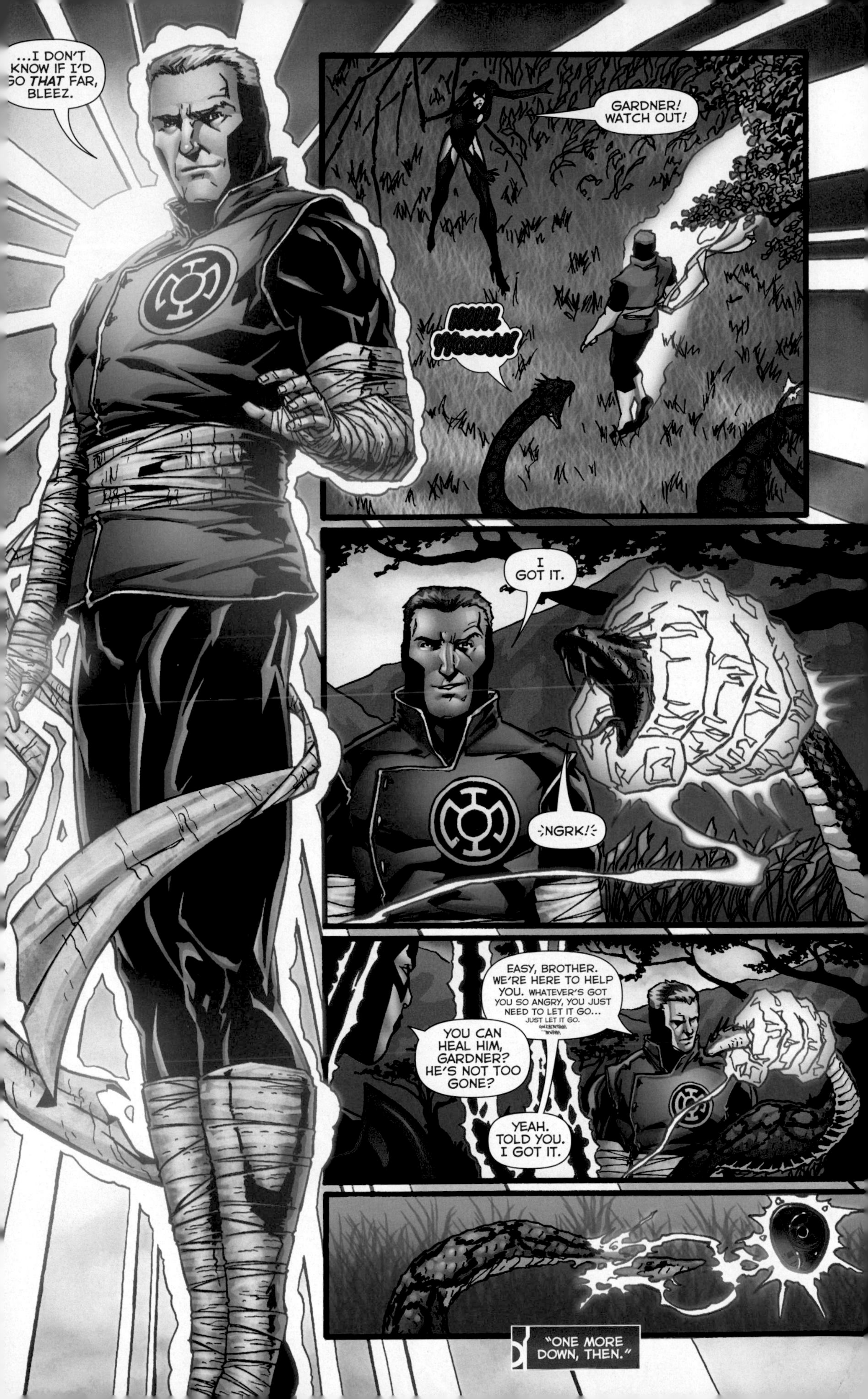

...I DON'T KNOW IF I'D GO *THAT* FAR, BLEEZ.
GARDNER! WATCH OUT!
I GOT IT.
NGRK!
EASY, BROTHER. WE'RE HERE TO HELP YOU. WHATEVER'S GOT YOU SO ANGRY, YOU JUST NEED TO LET IT GO... JUST LET IT GO.
YOU CAN HEAL HIM, GARDNER? HE'S NOT TOO GONE?
YEAH. TOLD YOU. I GOT IT.
"ONE MORE DOWN, THEN."

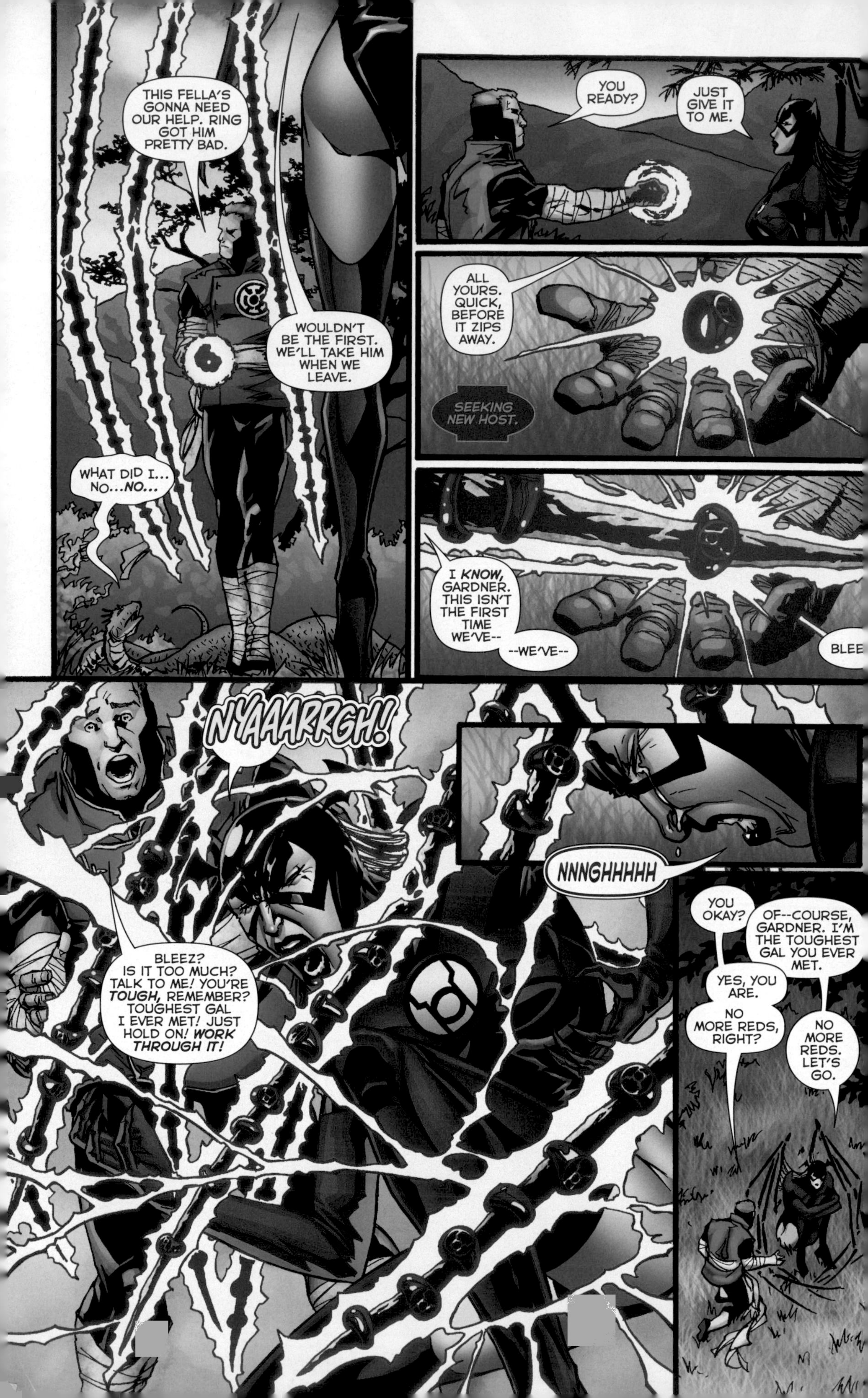
THIS FELLA'S GONNA NEED OUR HELP. RING GOT HIM PRETTY BAD.
WOULDN'T BE THE FIRST. WE'LL TAKE HIM WHEN WE LEAVE.
WHAT DID I... NO...NO...
YOU READY?
JUST GIVE IT TO ME.
ALL YOURS. QUICK, BEFORE IT ZIPS AWAY.
SEEKING NEW HOST.
I KNOW, GARDNER. THIS ISN'T THE FIRST TIME WE'VE--
--WE'VE--
BLEE
NYAAARRGH!
BLEEZ? IS IT TOO MUCH? TALK TO ME! YOU'RE TOUGH, REMEMBER? TOUGHEST GAL I EVER MET! JUST HOLD ON! WORK THROUGH IT!
NNNGHHHHH
YOU OKAY?
OF--COURSE, GARDNER. I'M THE TOUGHEST GAL YOU EVER MET.
YES, YOU ARE.
NO MORE REDS, RIGHT?
NO MORE REDS. LET'S GO.

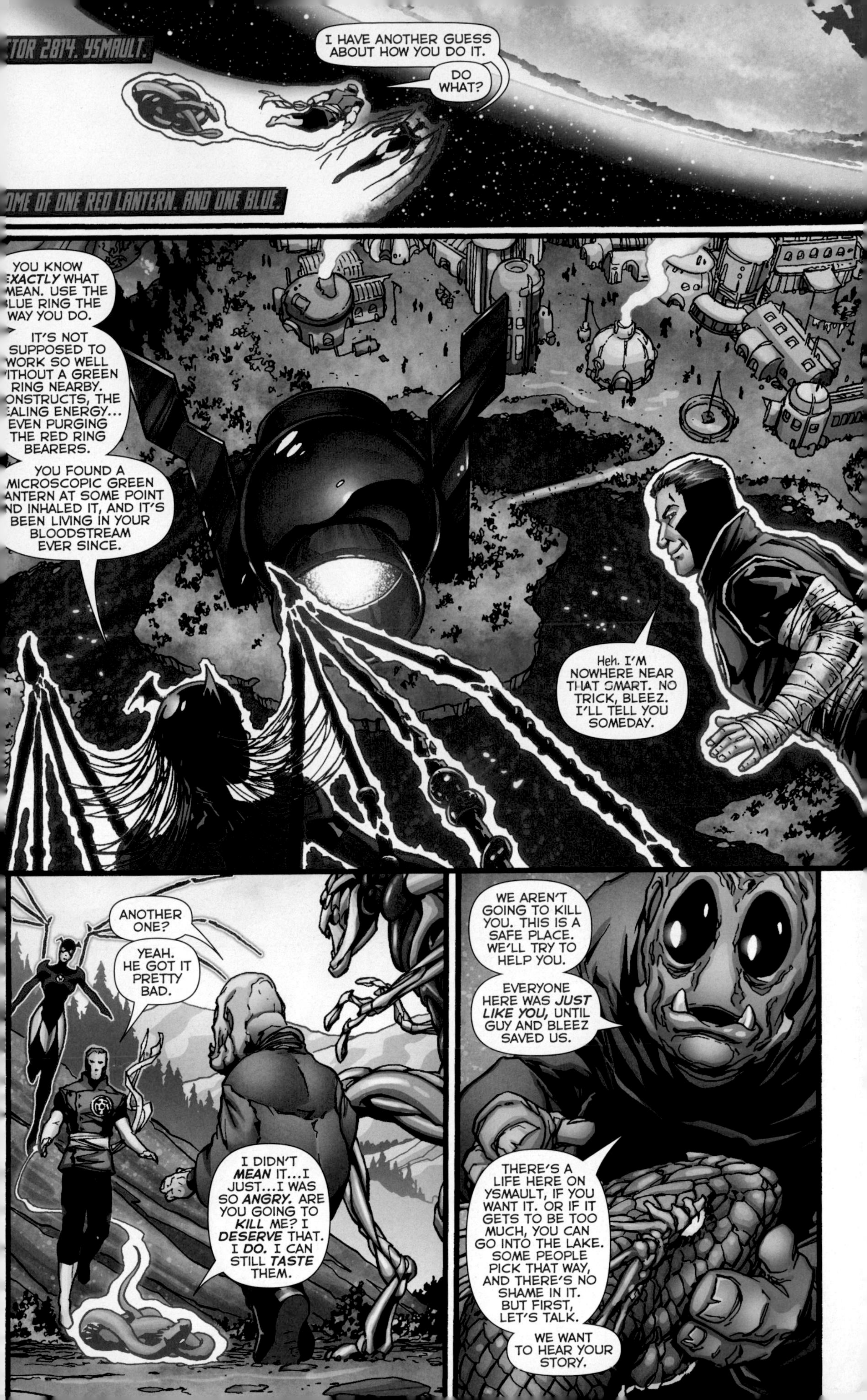

TOR 2814. YSMAULT.
I HAVE ANOTHER GUESS ABOUT HOW YOU DO IT.
DO WHAT?
OME OF ONE RED LANTERN. AND ONE BLUE.
YOU KNOW EXACTLY WHAT MEAN. USE THE BLUE RING THE WAY YOU DO.
IT'S NOT SUPPOSED TO WORK SO WELL ITHOUT A GREEN RING NEARBY. ONSTRUCTS, THE EALING ENERGY... EVEN PURGING THE RED RING BEARERS.
YOU FOUND A MICROSCOPIC GREEN ANTERN AT SOME POINT ND INHALED IT, AND IT'S BEEN LIVING IN YOUR BLOODSTREAM EVER SINCE.
Heh. I'M NOWHERE NEAR THAT SMART. NO TRICK, BLEEZ. I'LL TELL YOU SOMEDAY.
ANOTHER ONE?
YEAH. HE GOT IT PRETTY BAD.
I DIDN'T MEAN IT...I JUST...I WAS SO ANGRY. ARE YOU GOING TO KILL ME? I DESERVE THAT. I DO. I CAN STILL TASTE THEM.
WE AREN'T GOING TO KILL YOU. THIS IS A SAFE PLACE. WE'LL TRY TO HELP YOU.
EVERYONE HERE WAS JUST LIKE YOU, UNTIL GUY AND BLEEZ SAVED US.
THERE'S A LIFE HERE ON YSMAULT, IF YOU WANT IT. OR IF IT GETS TO BE TOO MUCH, YOU CAN GO INTO THE LAKE. SOME PEOPLE PICK THAT WAY, AND THERE'S NO SHAME IN IT. BUT FIRST, LET'S TALK.
WE WANT TO HEAR YOUR STORY.

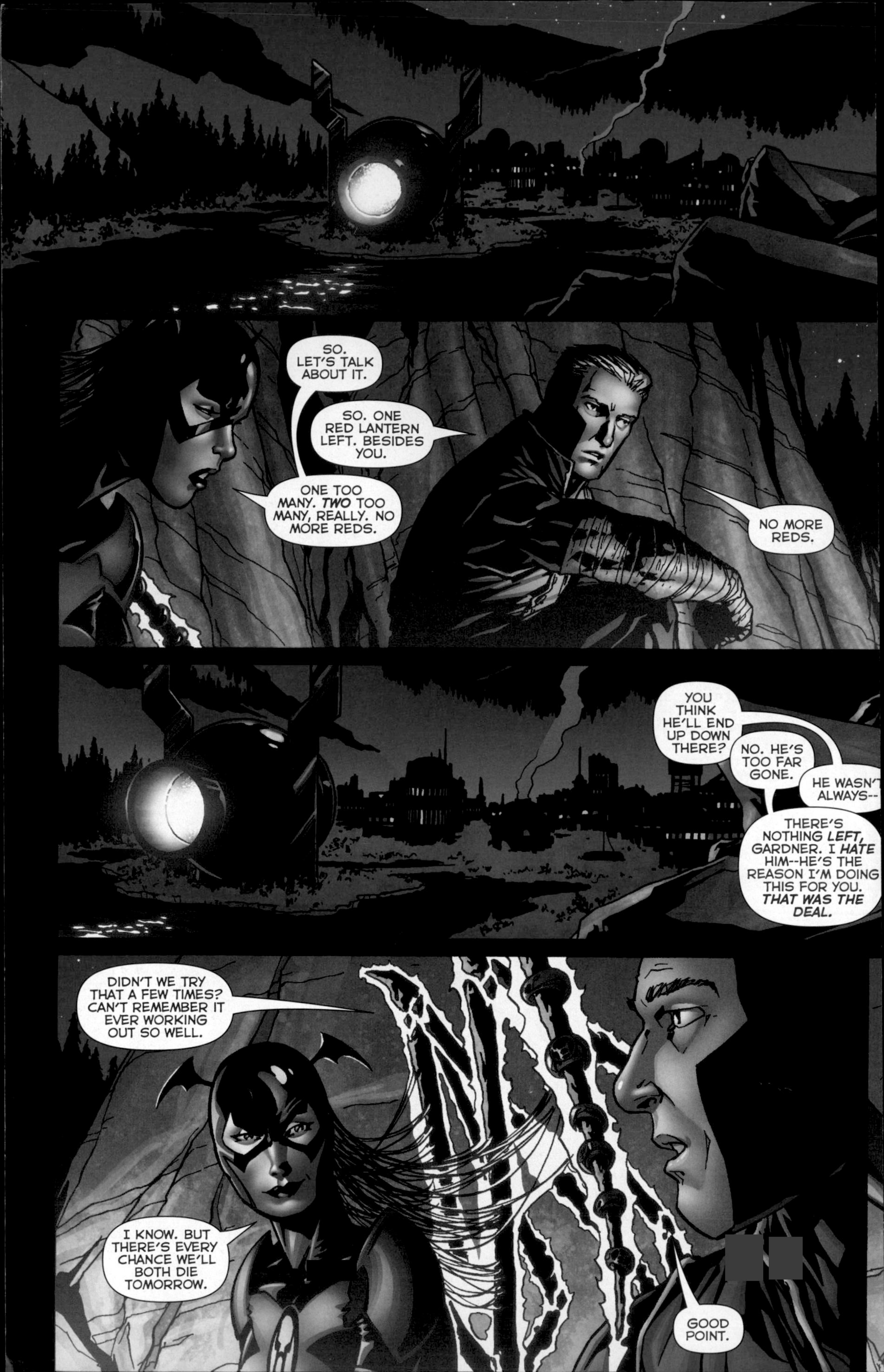
SO. LET'S TALK ABOUT IT.
SO. ONE RED LANTERN LEFT. BESIDES YOU.
ONE TOO MANY. TWO TOO MANY, REALLY. NO MORE REDS.
NO MORE REDS.
YOU THINK HE'LL END UP DOWN THERE?
NO. HE'S TOO FAR GONE.
HE WASN'T ALWAYS--
THERE'S NOTHING LEFT, GARDNER. I HATE HIM--HE'S THE REASON I'M DOING THIS FOR YOU. THAT WAS THE DEAL.
DIDN'T WE TRY THAT A FEW TIMES? CAN'T REMEMBER IT EVER WORKING OUT SO WELL.
I KNOW. BUT THERE'S EVERY CHANCE WE'LL BOTH DIE TOMORROW.
GOOD POINT.

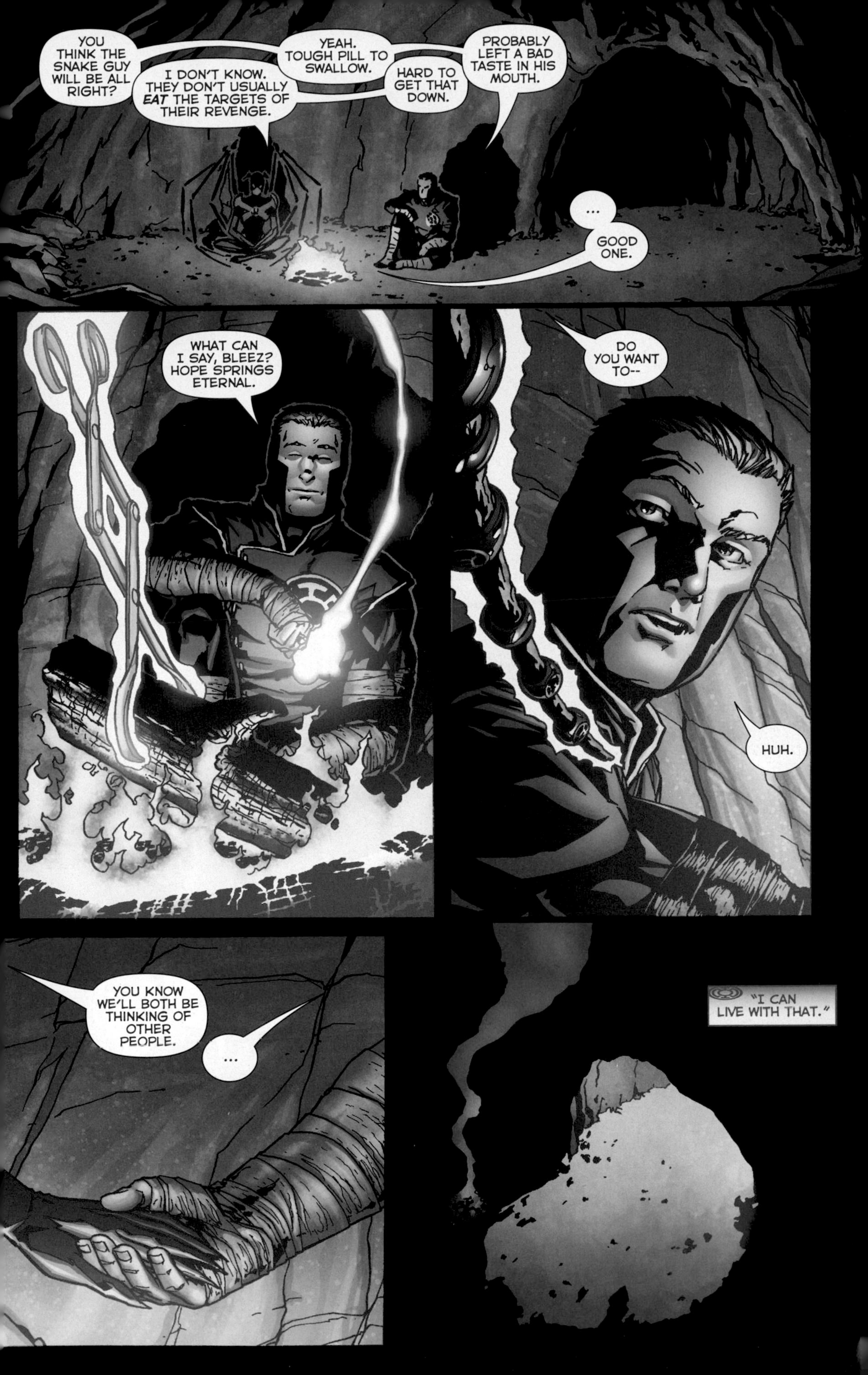

YOU THINK THE SNAKE GUY WILL BE ALL RIGHT?
I DON'T KNOW. THEY DON'T USUALLY EAT THE TARGETS OF THEIR REVENGE.
YEAH. TOUGH PILL TO SWALLOW.
HARD TO GET THAT DOWN.
PROBABLY LEFT A BAD TASTE IN HIS MOUTH.
...
GOOD ONE.
WHAT CAN I SAY, BLEEZ? HOPE SPRINGS ETERNAL.
DO YOU WANT TO--
HUH.
YOU KNOW WE'LL BOTH BE THINKING OF OTHER PEOPLE.
...
"I CAN LIVE WITH THAT."

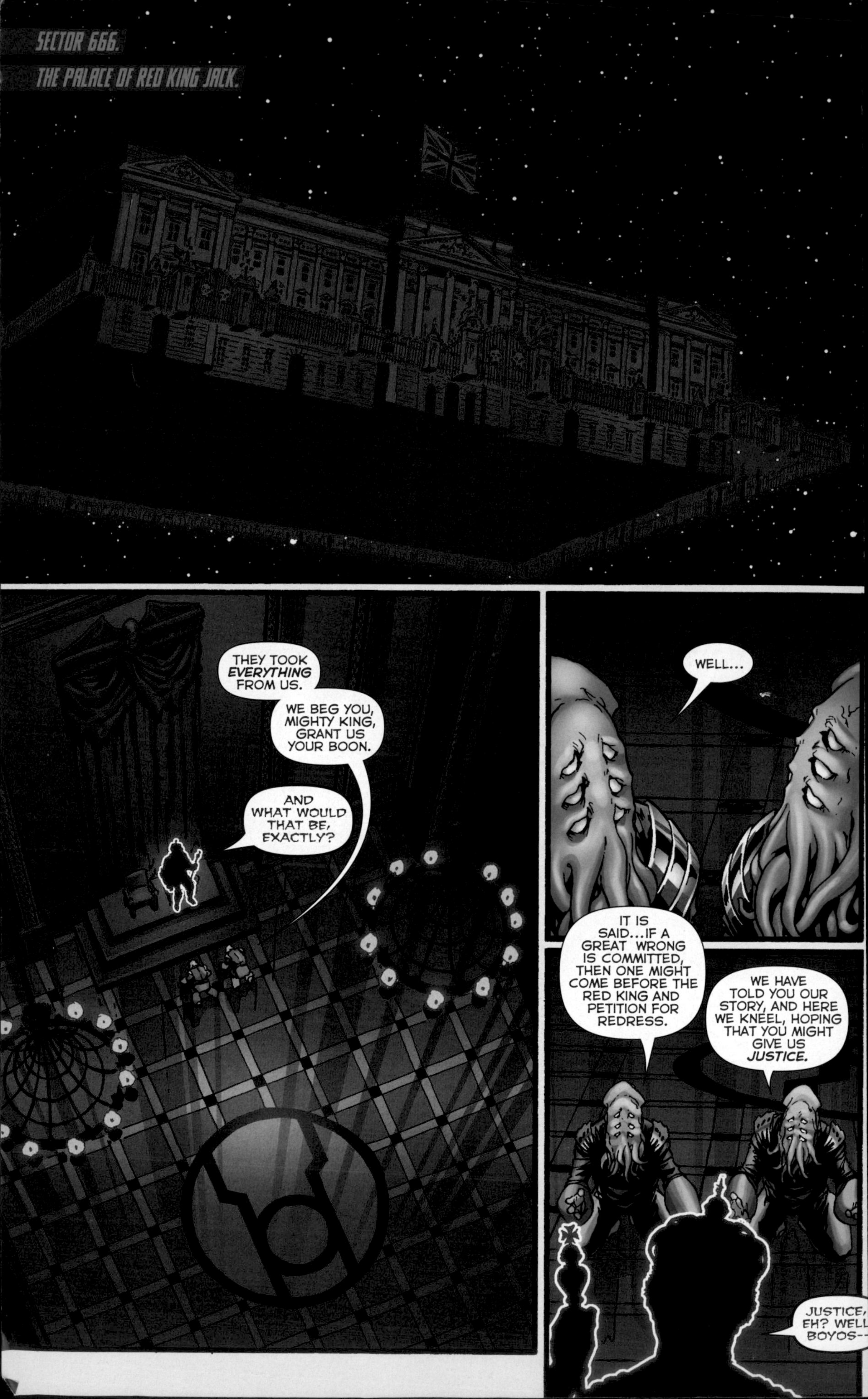
SECTOR 666.
THE PALACE OF RED KING JACK.
THEY TOOK EVERYTHING FROM US.
WE BEG YOU, MIGHTY KING, GRANT US YOUR BOON.
AND WHAT WOULD THAT BE, EXACTLY?
WELL...
IT IS SAID...IF A GREAT WRONG IS COMMITTED, THEN ONE MIGHT COME BEFORE THE RED KING AND PETITION FOR REDRESS.
WE HAVE TOLD YOU OUR STORY, AND HERE WE KNEEL, HOPING THAT YOU MIGHT GIVE US JUSTICE.
JUSTICE, EH? WELL BOYOS--

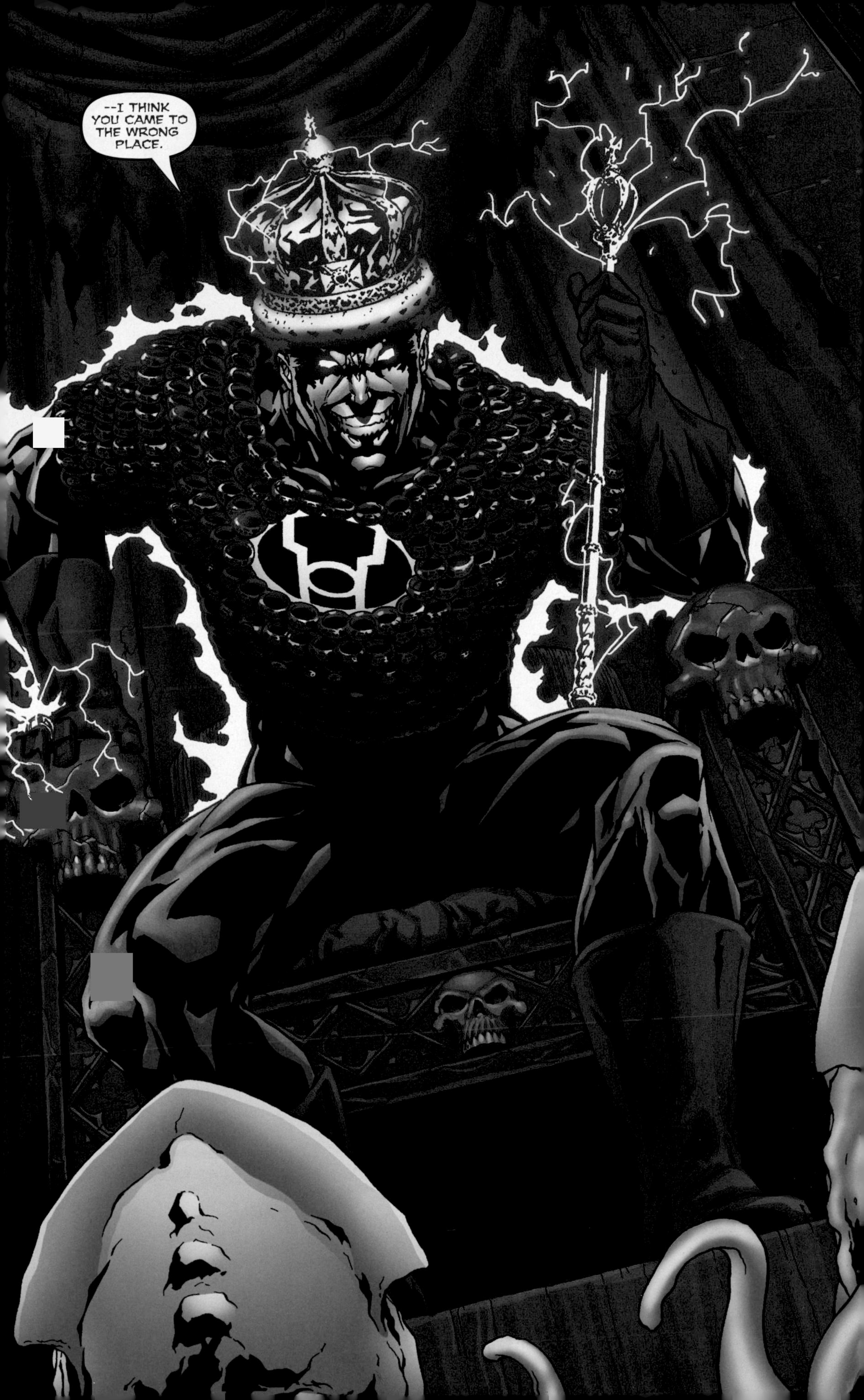
--I THINK YOU CAME TO THE WRONG PLACE.

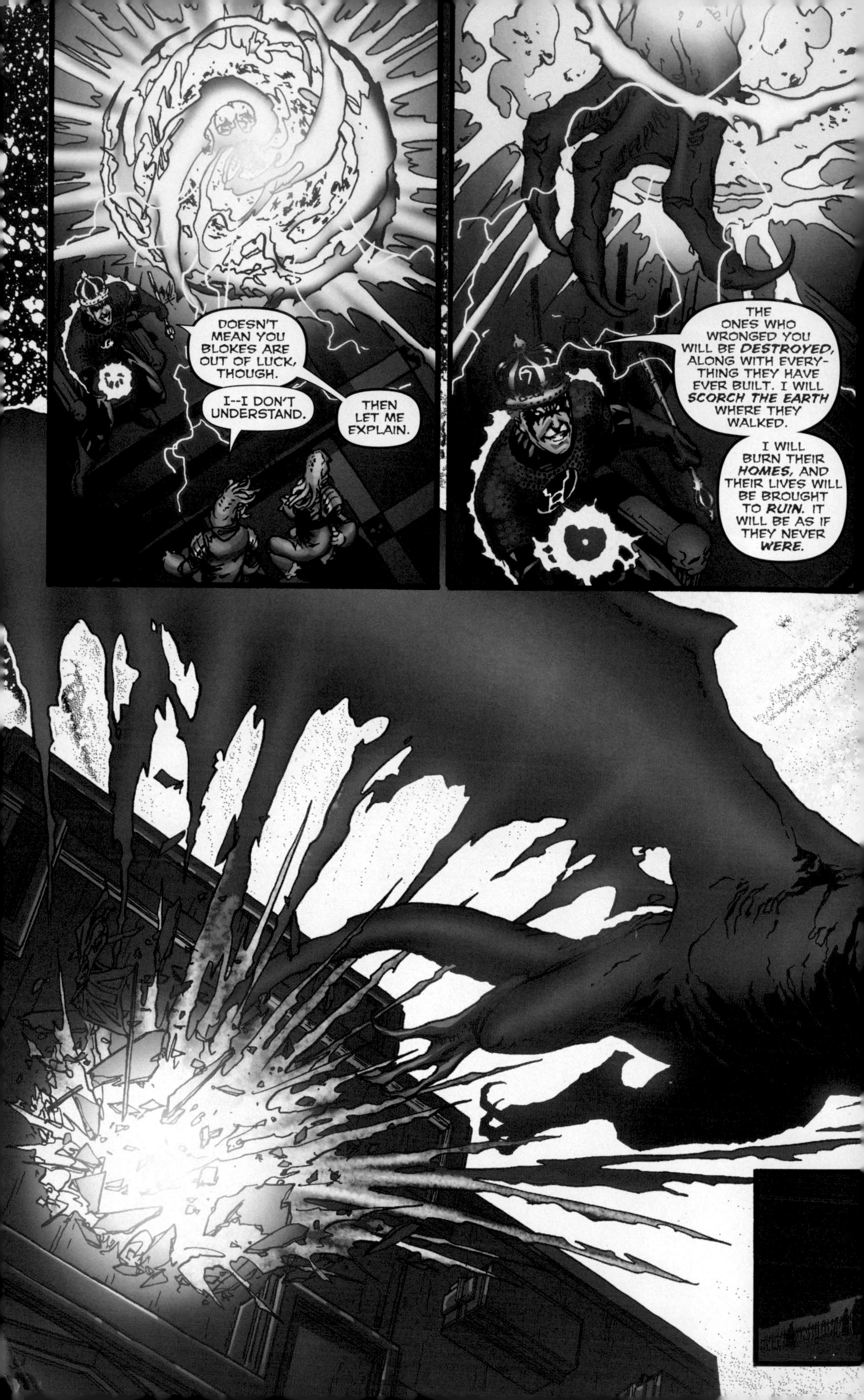
DOESN'T MEAN YOU BLOKES ARE OUT OF LUCK, THOUGH.
I--I DON'T UNDERSTAND.
THEN LET ME EXPLAIN.
THE ONES WHO WRONGED YOU WILL BE DESTROYED, ALONG WITH EVERYTHING THEY HAVE EVER BUILT. I WILL SCORCH THE EARTH WHERE THEY WALKED.
I WILL BURN THEIR HOMES, AND THEIR LIVES WILL BE BROUGHT TO RUIN. IT WILL BE AS IF THEY NEVER WERE.

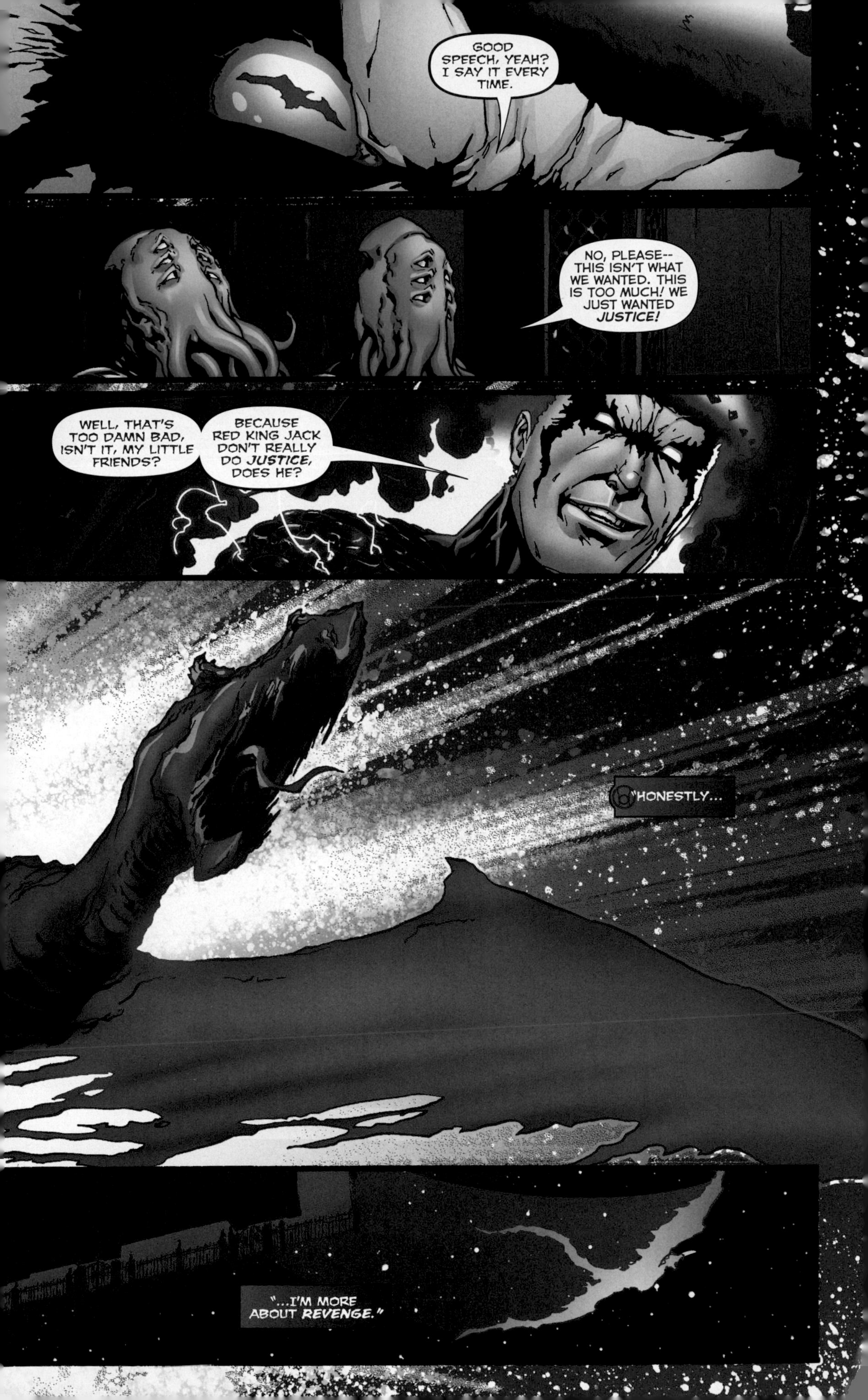
GOOD SPEECH, YEAH? I SAY IT EVERY TIME.
NO, PLEASE--THIS ISN'T WHAT WE WANTED. THIS IS TOO MUCH! WE JUST WANTED JUSTICE!
WELL, THAT'S TOO DAMN BAD, ISN'T IT, MY LITTLE FRIENDS?
BECAUSE RED KING JACK DON'T REALLY DO JUSTICE, DOES HE?
"HONESTLY...
"...I'M MORE ABOUT REVENGE."

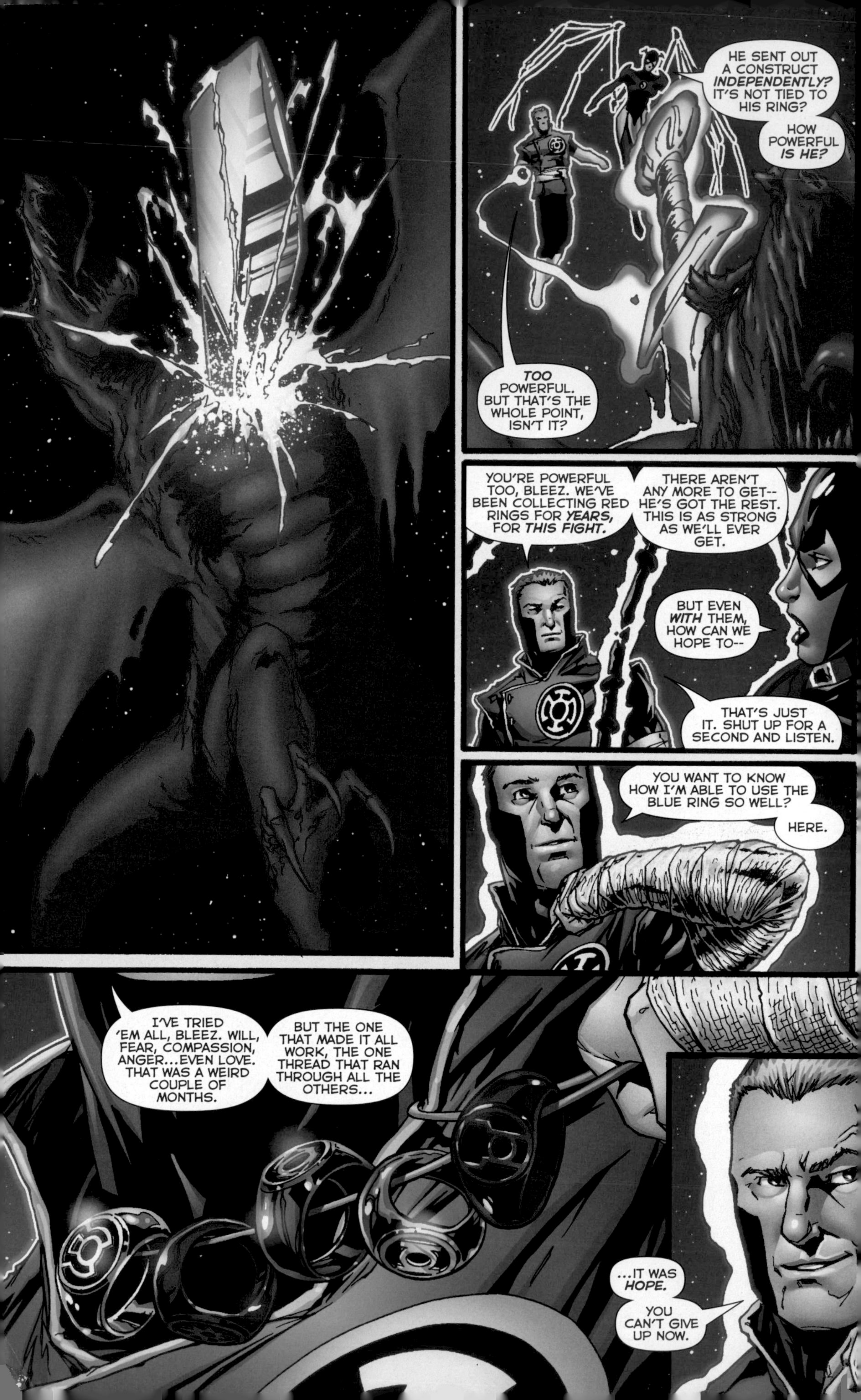
HE SENT OUT A CONSTRUCT INDEPENDENTLY? IT'S NOT TIED TO HIS RING?
HOW POWERFUL IS HE?
TOO POWERFUL. BUT THAT'S THE WHOLE POINT, ISN'T IT?
YOU'RE POWERFUL TOO, BLEEZ. WE'VE BEEN COLLECTING RED RINGS FOR YEARS, FOR THIS FIGHT.
THERE AREN'T ANY MORE TO GET-- HE'S GOT THE REST. THIS IS AS STRONG AS WE'LL EVER GET.
BUT EVEN WITH THEM, HOW CAN WE HOPE TO--
THAT'S JUST IT. SHUT UP FOR A SECOND AND LISTEN.
YOU WANT TO KNOW HOW I'M ABLE TO USE THE BLUE RING SO WELL?
HERE.
I'VE TRIED 'EM ALL, BLEEZ. WILL, FEAR, COMPASSION, ANGER...EVEN LOVE. THAT WAS A WEIRD COUPLE OF MONTHS.
BUT THE ONE THAT MADE IT ALL WORK, THE ONE THREAD THAT RAN THROUGH ALL THE OTHERS...
...IT WAS HOPE.
YOU CAN'T GIVE UP NOW.

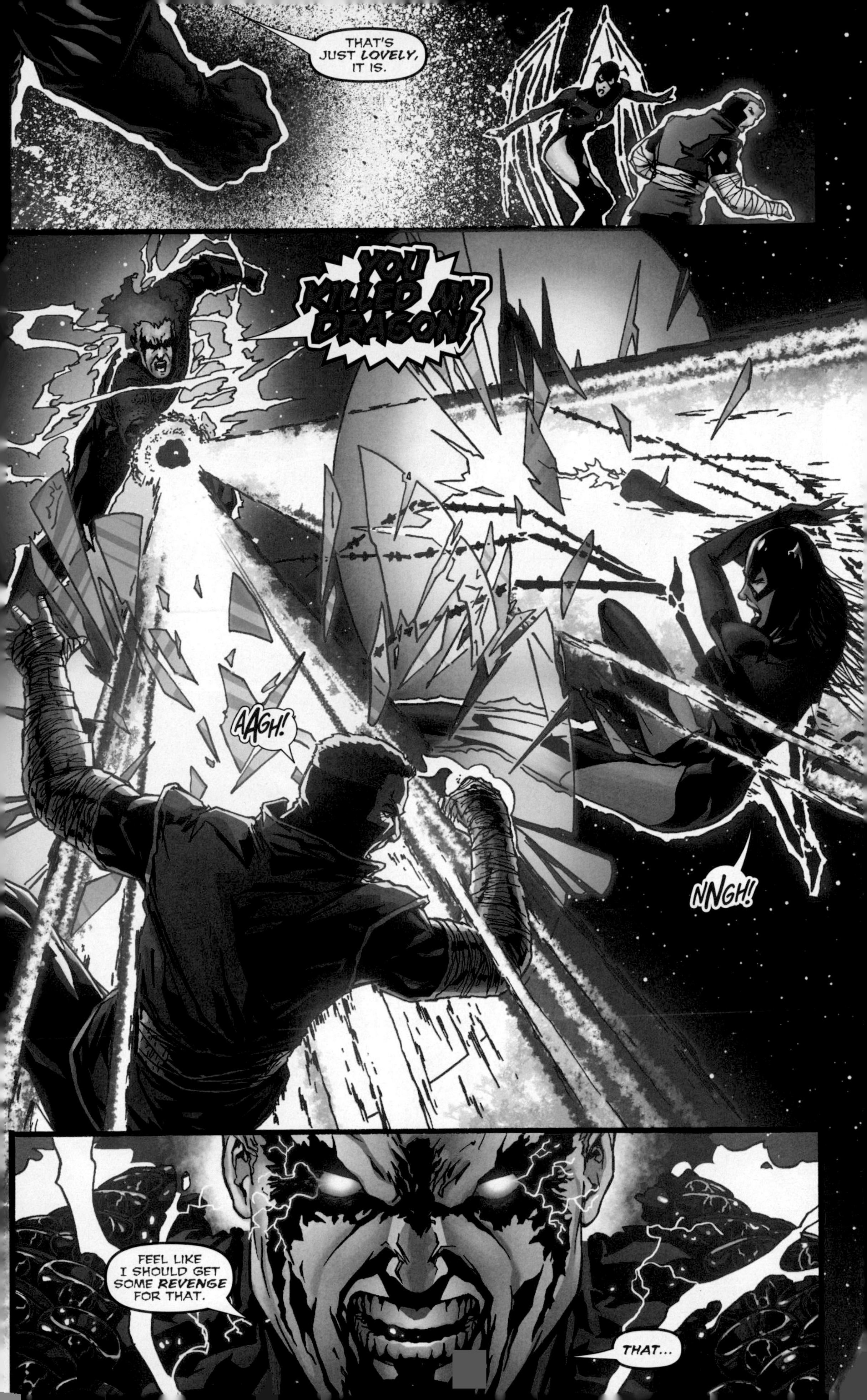
THAT'S JUST LOVELY, IT IS.
YOU KILLED MY DRAGON!
AAGH!
NNGH!
FEEL LIKE I SHOULD GET SOME REVENGE FOR THAT.
THAT...

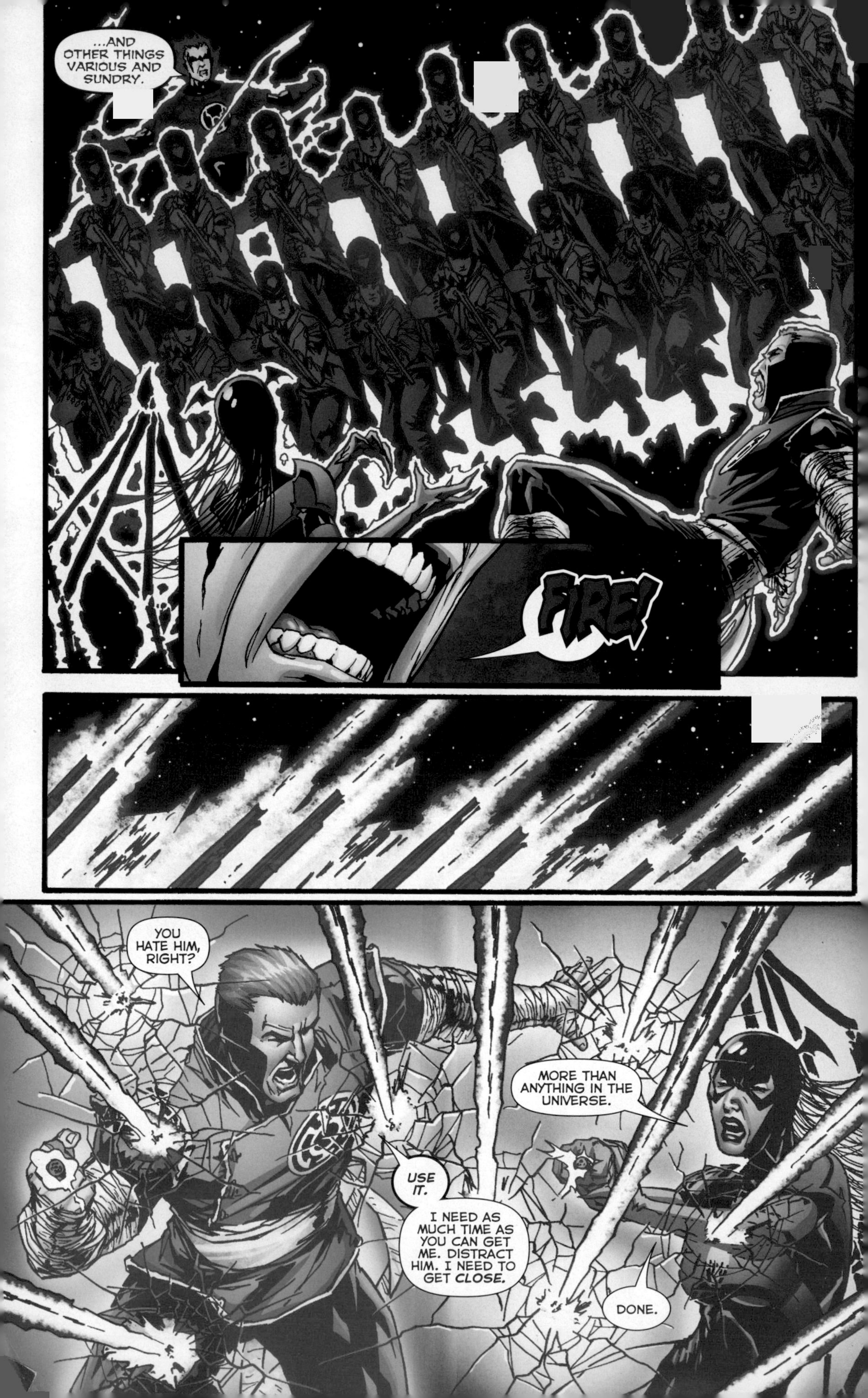
...AND OTHER THINGS VARIOUS AND SUNDRY.
FIRE!
YOU HATE HIM, RIGHT?
MORE THAN ANYTHING IN THE UNIVERSE.
USE IT.
I NEED AS MUCH TIME AS YOU CAN GET ME. DISTRACT HIM. I NEED TO GET *CLOSE.*
DONE.

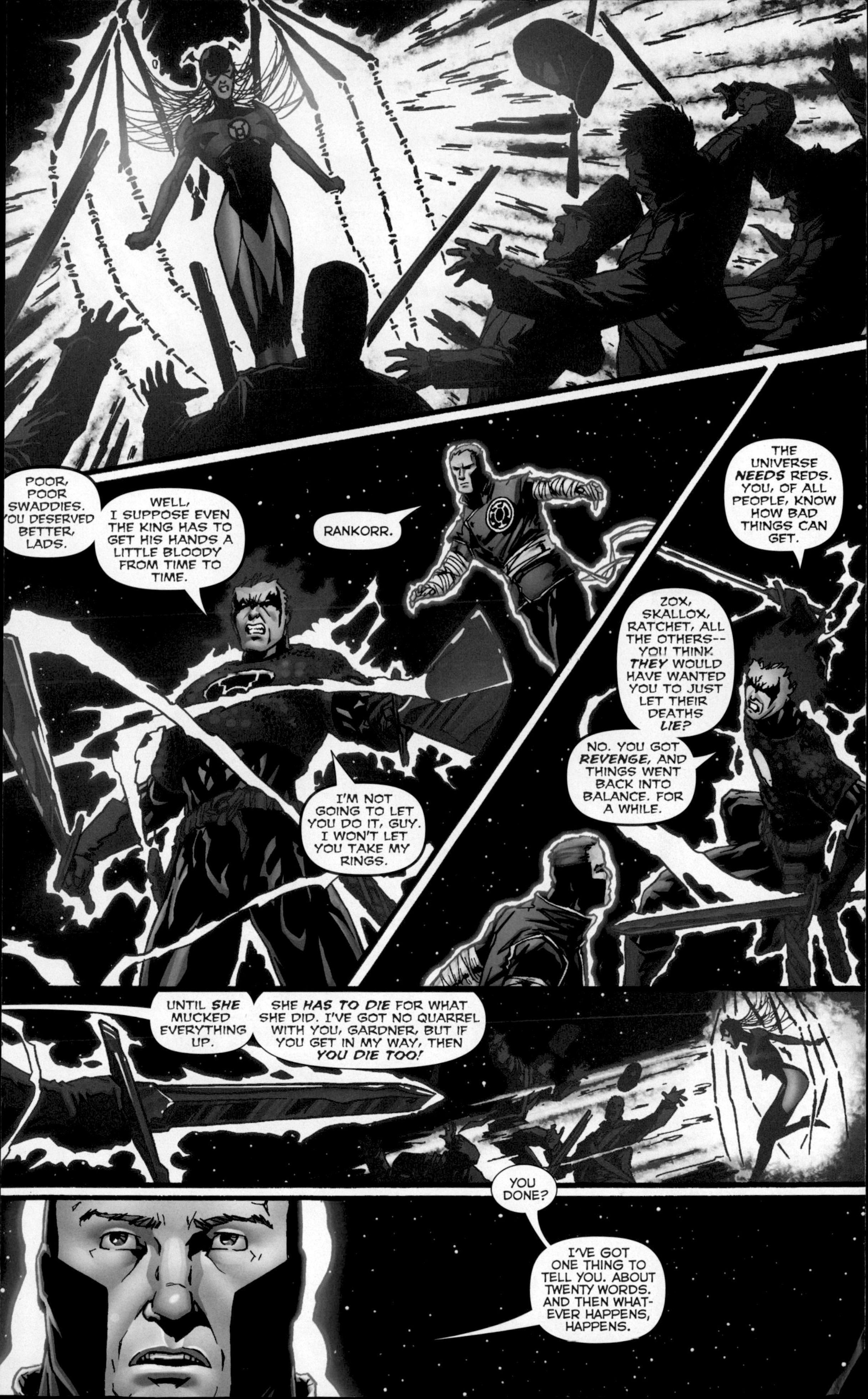
POOR, POOR SWADDIES. YOU DESERVED BETTER, LADS.
WELL, I SUPPOSE EVEN THE KING HAS TO GET HIS HANDS A LITTLE BLOODY FROM TIME TO TIME.
RANKORR.
I'M NOT GOING TO LET YOU DO IT, GUY. I WON'T LET YOU TAKE MY RINGS.
THE UNIVERSE NEEDS REDS. YOU, OF ALL PEOPLE, KNOW HOW BAD THINGS CAN GET.
ZOX, SKALLOX, RATCHET, ALL THE OTHERS-- YOU THINK THEY WOULD HAVE WANTED YOU TO JUST LET THEIR DEATHS LIE?
NO. YOU GOT REVENGE, AND THINGS WENT BACK INTO BALANCE. FOR A WHILE.
UNTIL SHE MUCKED EVERYTHING UP.
SHE HAS TO DIE FOR WHAT SHE DID. I'VE GOT NO QUARREL WITH YOU, GARDNER, BUT IF YOU GET IN MY WAY, THEN YOU DIE TOO!
YOU DONE?
I'VE GOT ONE THING TO TELL YOU. ABOUT TWENTY WORDS. AND THEN WHAT-EVER HAPPENS, HAPPENS.

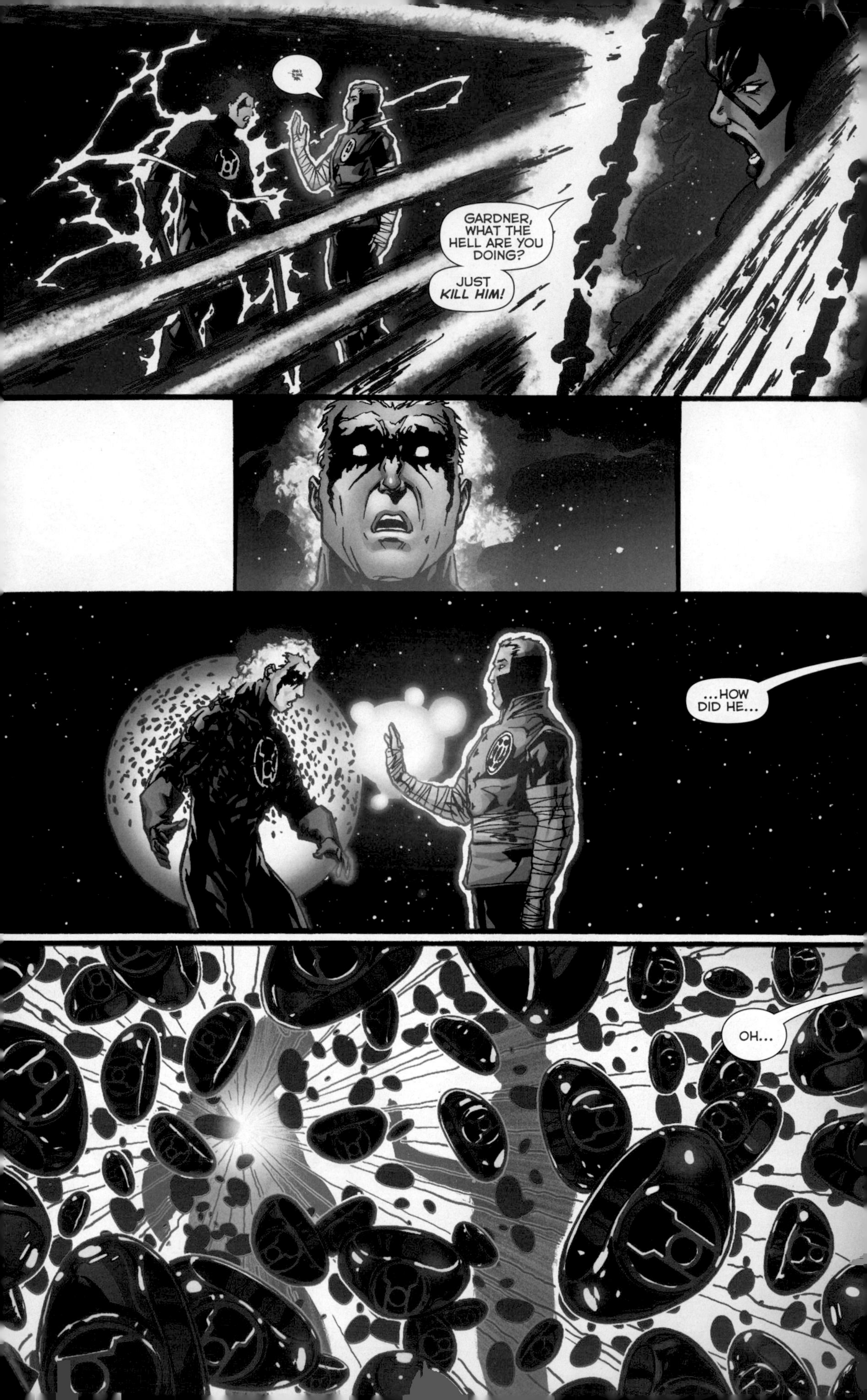
GARDNER, WHAT THE HELL ARE YOU DOING?
JUST KILL HIM!
...HOW DID HE...
OH...

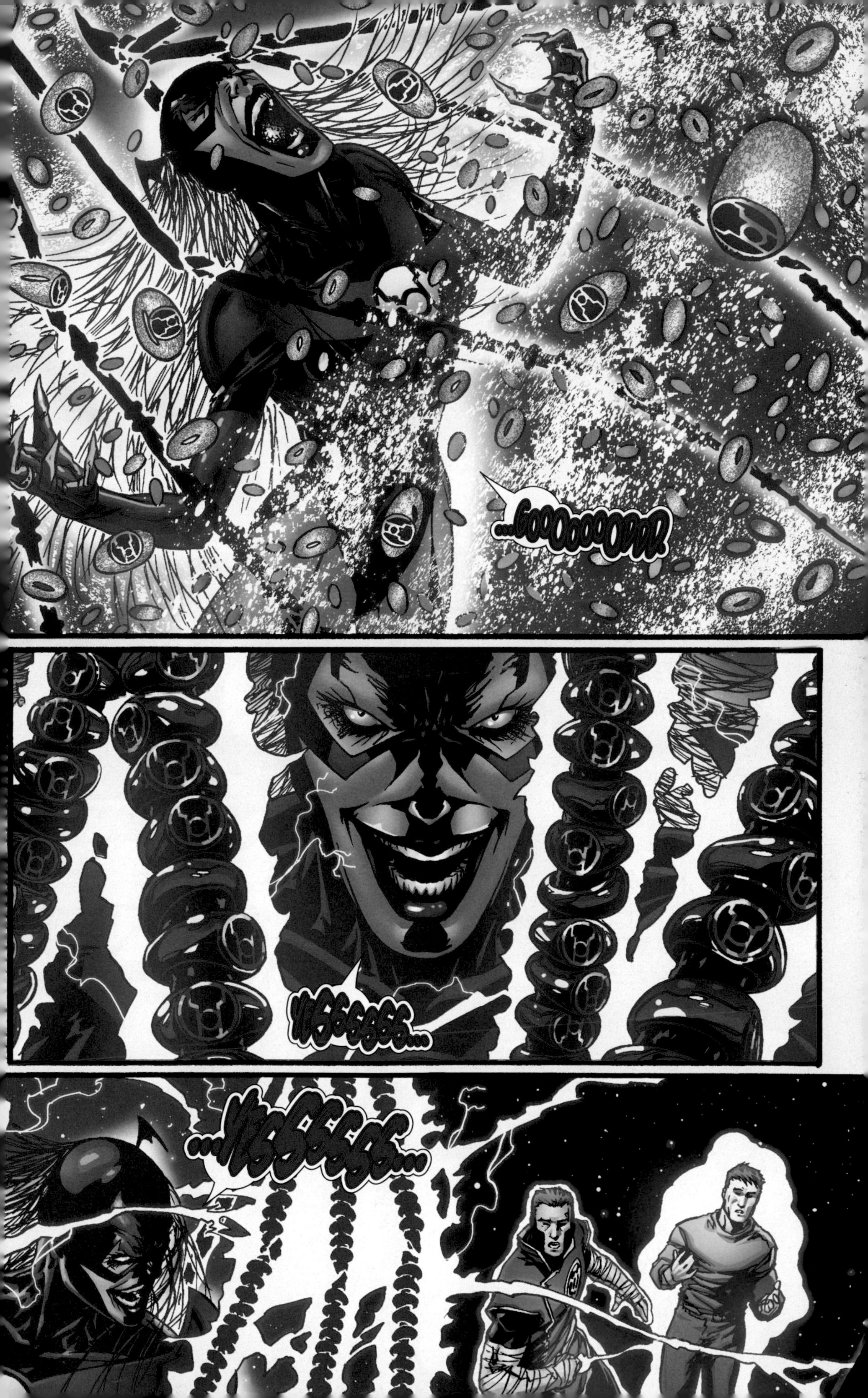

...GOOOOOOOD!
YESSSSSS...
...YESSSSSS...

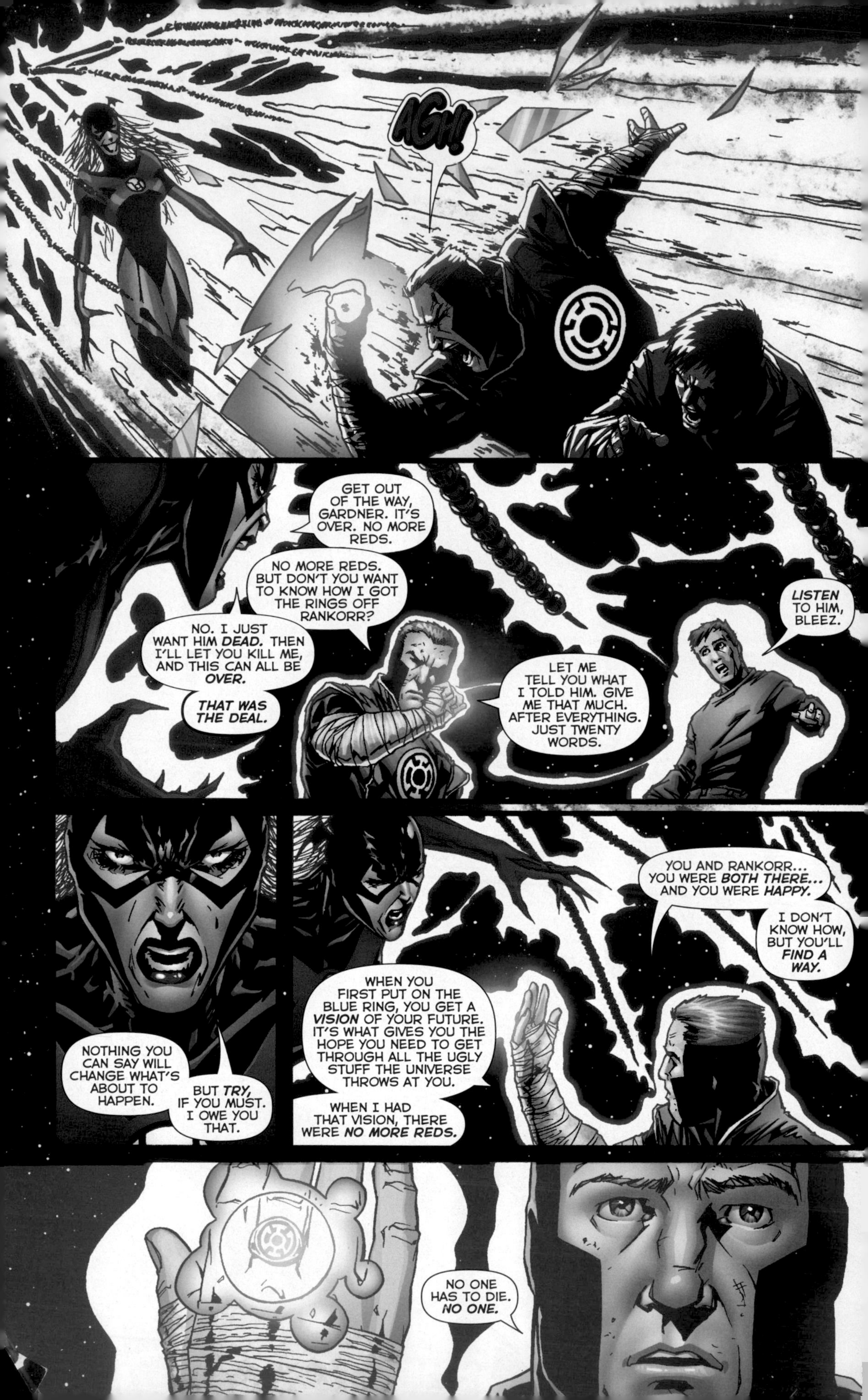
AGH!
GET OUT OF THE WAY, GARDNER. IT'S OVER. NO MORE REDS.
NO MORE REDS. BUT DON'T YOU WANT TO KNOW HOW I GOT THE RINGS OFF RANKORR?
NO. I JUST WANT HIM *DEAD.* THEN I'LL LET YOU KILL ME, AND THIS CAN ALL BE *OVER.*
THAT WAS THE DEAL.
LET ME TELL YOU WHAT I TOLD HIM. GIVE ME THAT MUCH. AFTER EVERYTHING. JUST TWENTY WORDS.
LISTEN TO HIM, BLEEZ.
NOTHING YOU CAN SAY WILL CHANGE WHAT'S ABOUT TO HAPPEN.
BUT *TRY,* IF YOU MUST. I OWE YOU THAT.
WHEN YOU FIRST PUT ON THE BLUE RING, YOU GET A *VISION* OF YOUR FUTURE. IT'S WHAT GIVES YOU THE HOPE YOU NEED TO GET THROUGH ALL THE UGLY STUFF THE UNIVERSE THROWS AT YOU.
WHEN I HAD THAT VISION, THERE WERE *NO MORE REDS.*
YOU AND RANKORR... YOU WERE *BOTH THERE...* AND YOU WERE *HAPPY.*
I DON'T KNOW HOW, BUT YOU'LL *FIND A WAY.*
NO ONE HAS TO DIE. *NO ONE.*

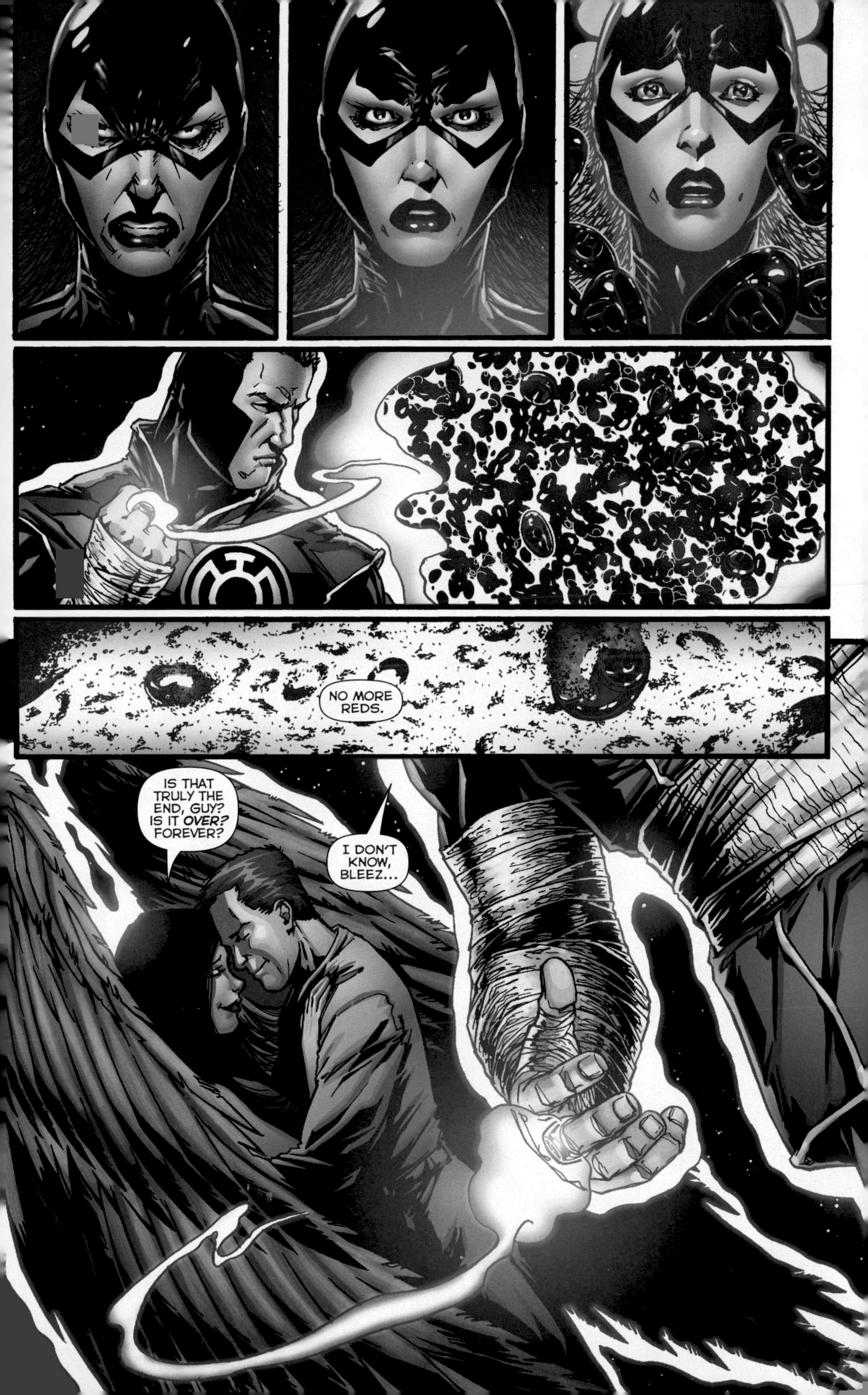
NO MORE REDS.
IS THAT TRULY THE END, GUY? IS IT *OVER?* FOREVER?
I DON'T KNOW, BLEEZ...

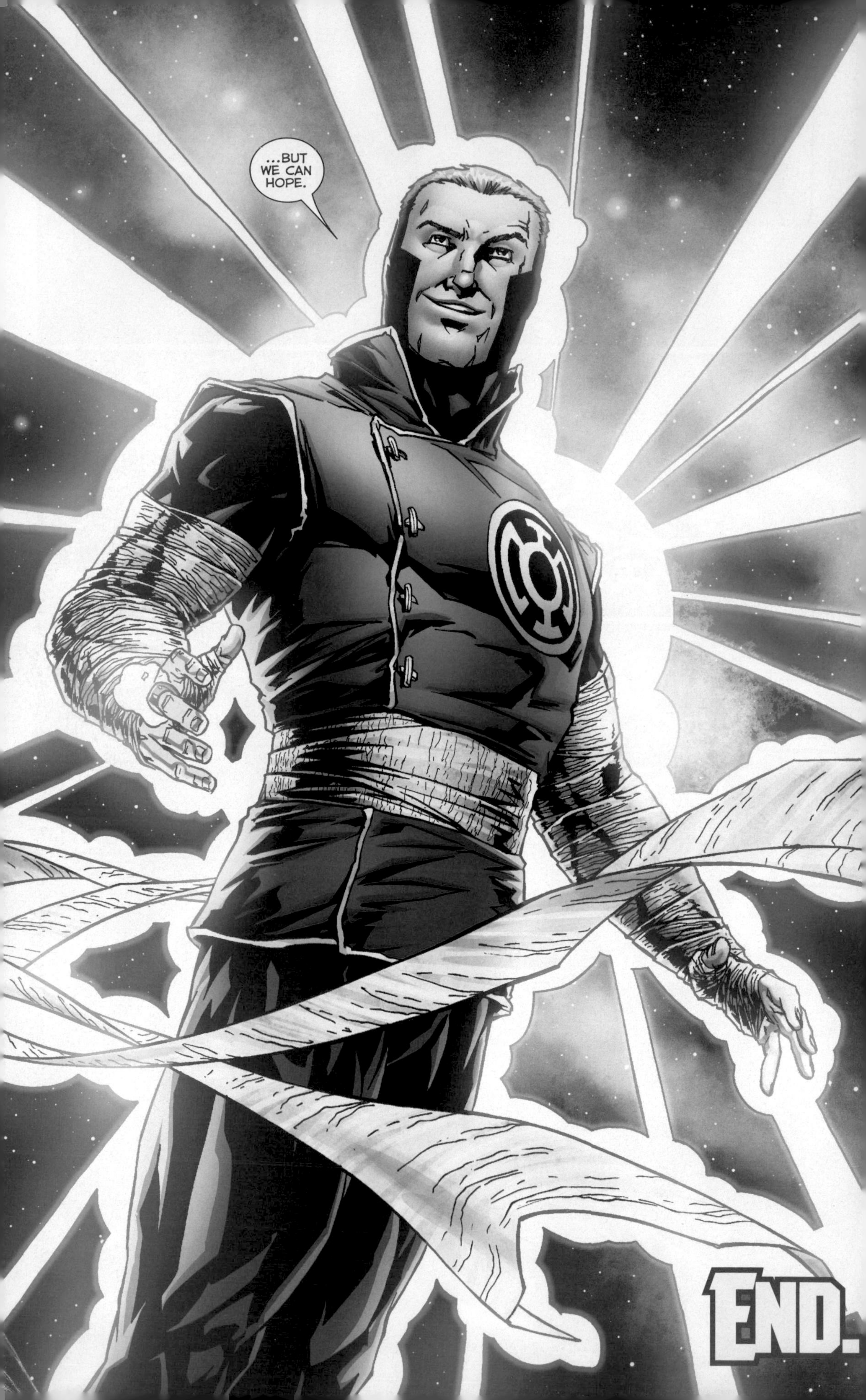
...BUT WE CAN HOPE.
END.

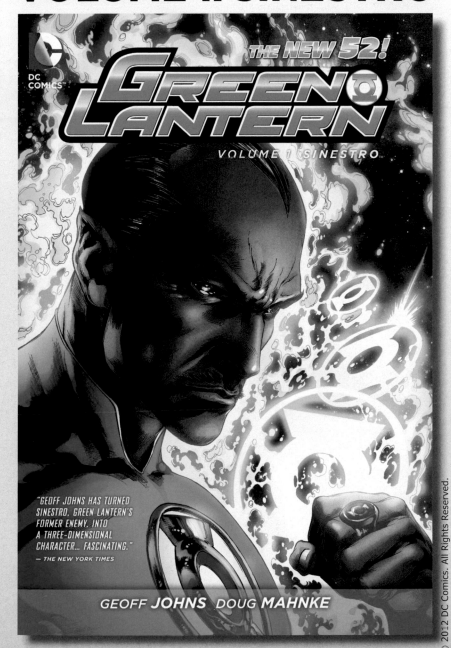

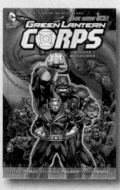

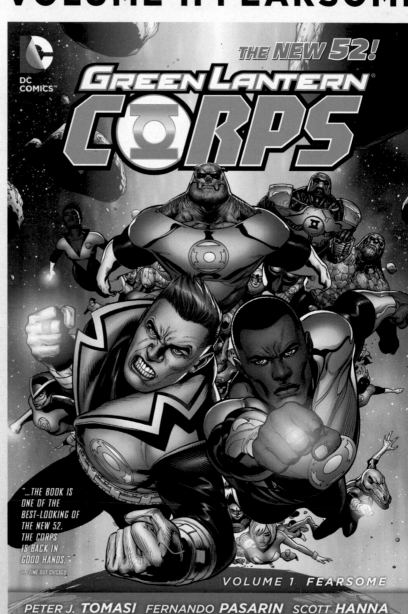